A CELEBRATION
OF DEMONS

A CELEBRATION OF DEMONS

Exorcism and the Aesthetics of Healing in Sri Lanka

BRUCE KAPFERER

Indiana University Press

Bloomington

First Midland Book Edition 1983

Copyright c 1983 by Bruce Kapferer

Manufactured in the United States of America

Library of Congress Cataloging in Publications Data

Kapferer, Bruce.
    A celebration of demons.

    Bibliography: p.
    Includes Index.
    1. Exorcism--Sri Lanka. 2. Demonology--Sri Lanka.
I. Title
BF1559.K36 1983   133.4'2'095493   81-48677
ISBN 0-253-31326-0
ISBN 0-253-20304-X(pbk.)
1 2 3 4 5 87 86 85 84 83

FOR

Chandra Jayawardena (1929 - 1981)

Teacher and Friend

Contents

Foreword by Victor Turner   ix

Preface   xiii

1. Introduction   1

2. Exorcism, Class, and Change in Urban Sri Lanka   12

3. Exorcists   37

4. Demonic Illness: Diagnosis and Social Context   49

5. Exorcisms and the Symbolic Identity of Women   92

6. The Demonic Illusion: Demons and the Cosmic Hierarchy   111

7. The Exorcism of the Great Cemetery Demon:
   Event and Structure in Major Exorcisms   129

8. Music, Dance, and Trance   178

9. The Comedy of Gods and Demons   207

10. Epilogue: A Celebration of Demons   232

Notes   239

Bibliography   264

Glossary   277

Subject Index   284

Author Index   291

Illustrations

Map: Sri Lanka and Research Area   xx

Figures

1. Main exorcists from whom Nandoris learnt
   and with whom he performs   44
2. Principal participants in Asoka's illness (Case 1)   65
3. Principal participants in Sunil's illness (Case 2)   77
4. Principal participants in Indranie's illness (Case 3)   82
5. The setting of exorcism performance   132
6. Demon palace and demon baskets   141
7. Main phases and media in construction
   and destruction of demonic   182

Tables

1. Major Exorcism Patients: sex, age, and occupation   54
2. Major Exorcism Patients: sex, exorcism type,
   and other treatment   56
3. Patient symptoms   58
4. Proportion of patients receiving minor to major
   exorcism treatment   99
5. Major events of the **Mahasona**   138

Plates

1. Major Demons: Suniyam, Kalu Kumara,
   Mahasona and Riri Yaka   119
2. A photographic description of the
   Great Cemetery demon exorcism   Between pages
3. Some events in the **Rata Yakuma, Sanni Yakuma,**
   and **Suniyama**   177 and 178

Foreword

Sri Lanka has recently become a major focus of international anthropological attention, due to the research and writings of a number of extremely gifted anthropologists, both native and foreign. Earlier important studies (Leach 1962; Yalman 1962, 1964) had discussed Sinhalese religion and ritual in terms of Gallo-structuralism and British empiricism. H. L. Seneviratne's **Rituals of the Kandyan State** (1978) has recently provided us with a lapidary description and analysis of the Kandyan Sinhalese theory of society as a balanced hierarchy embracing social and natural orders and made annually visible in the complex and colorful **Asala** festival, "perhaps one of the largest ever held in the Buddhist world" (p. 70). Other Sri Lankan and British and American scholars, such as Pieris, Tambiah, Obeyesekere, Gombrich, and Ames, have made rich ethnographic and elucidative contributions on which Bruce Kapferer, the author of this volume, was fortunate to have been able to draw.

Kapferer's book is a pioneering study in the emerging field of performance studies — represented, to my knowledge, by but a single university department in the United States, the Department of Performance Studies at New York University, which aims to bring the social sciences and arts together to shape theory and methods and is cross-cultural and interdisciplinary in perspective. Kapferer's approach is, however, less eclectic and cleaves more closely to traditional anthropological concerns, combining structuralist, semiotic, and processual concepts and procedures into an original and powerful mode of analysis which takes aesthetic features of ritual into full theoretical account. For him, aesthetics involves the study of the processes of producing and experiencing ritual performances. He views the demon exorcism ceremonies of the Sinhalese working class and peasantry as a set of intersecting "scores" orchestrating a range of performative genres — drumming, dance movements, gesturing, singing of sacred texts, the manipulation of ritual paraphernalia (masks, costumes, offering-baskets, coconut palm leaves), food preparation, feasting, improvised "low comedy," and the like, which themselves pass irreversibly through major phases. For each phase certain genres are

dominant and critical: for example, chanting, singing, dance, and music
prevail in the "midday to midnight period," reaching a climax at midnight,
when "the terrible sense of the demonic builds in the quickening rhythm and
tempo of the music and the movement of the dance . . . and often
culminates in the demonic possession of the patient."   Contrastingly, a
sequence of dramatic acts begins after midnight in the important **Mahasona**
(Great Cemetery Demon) exorcism, which amount to a comedic, indeed
"profane," "obscene," Rabelaisian "put down" of the hitherto menacing and
darkly numinous mood of demonic possession.   There begins a comedic
dialogue between dancers and drummers, full of "puns, spoonerisms,
profanities, sexual innuendo . . . " These shifts in genre, mood, and tempo
are in no way arbitrary.   They are responsive to cosmological beliefs,
paramount among which is the idea of a hierarchy of all living beings, which
places deities above humans, and humans above animals.   The health and
welfare of human society and individual, the smooth functioning of the
natural and cultural orders, the purity of society's places and times, a right
relationship between and among all classes of living beings depend upon the
recognition of and willing acquiescence in this cosmic arrangement of
beings, persons, and things arranged in order of rank, grade, and class. For
Sinhalese (not only the lower classes, but the middle and upper classes too),
reality is mapped by this determinate, asymmetrical ordering of invisible
and visible entities, at whose obscure summit is the Buddha (though, in a
sense, he is outside all "chains of being" whatsoever in a locus of Absolute
Nothingness —— as the Kyoto School of Buddhist philosophy might define
nirvanic emptiness).   The "real" is hierarchical, in Kapferer's reading of
Sinhalese thought. He argues that demons are masters of "illusion." They
cause illness (both what Westerners might call "mental" and "physical"
illness) by deluding human beings that they (the demons) occupy a higher
place in the unalterable hierarchy of beings than they do, are in fact not
demons but deities (who also possess the power of generating illusions, but
only for some ultimately edifying purpose). Subversion of hierarchy is to
substitute chaos for cosmos, illness for health, disorder for order, falsity for
truth, pollution for purity, delusion for plain sensory evidence, vainglory for
humility, solipsism for awareness of others, negation for affirmation of
social interaction, and so on.

Kapferer contends that there is a deep link between cosmology and
aesthetics. For example, the nature of the music and dancing during the
midnight watch produces the almost Kierkegaardian obsession with the
demonic, the condition in which the self is aware of nothing but its own
experiences and states, and hence, since men and women are defined in
Sinhalese terms as "relational" beings, is in alienated terror.   This is
explained as the hallucinatory power conceded in the scheme of things to
demons, who can make things appear not only other than they are but also
twist reality itself by subverting human behavior. Yet within the frame of
exorcizing ritual, the "show" of demonic behavior itself becomes a means
directed towards the ultimate therapeutic intention of such ritual. For it
makes manifest to the "real" senses of the patient and onlookers the "real"
intention of demons, which then becomes accessible to the remedial action
of the ritual process. To disclose, as Western depth psychologists well know,
is to expose to therapeutic action. The unknown is the dangerous: while
demons can clothe their deception in glamorous numinosity, they have
power.   When they are manifested —— as Mahasona is revealed
(paradoxically) in his masked representations —— they can be humiliated,
which is a crucial part of the patient's "treatment." Demons seek to hide
themselves from "reality," that is, from exposure of their "true" place in the
cosmic hierarchy. Once they are "caught out," they have nowhere to go,

except into ridiculous disgrace. In parallel fashion, the patient is brought out of her/his demonic obsession/possession and restored to the world of social relationships and recognition of "others." Thus the comic is the performative genre through which the "normal" hierarchical order is restored as the model for "reality." When demons are mocked into their proper place in the scheme of things, they cease to be awesome and become ridiculous.

In the course of his scrutiny of the rites, Kapferer discusses Sinhalese interpretations of key symbols and concepts, and relates rites to myths which explain them to the participants' satisfaction. His critical examination and investigation of the processual normative and aesthetic structures of the **Mahasona** exorcist rites are, to my knowledge, the best work anywhere available on the performative sequencing of an institutionalized ritual ensemble. His discussion of the peculiar affinity of such aesthetic modes as music and dance with the cultural construction of the "demonic" is unsurpassed, and recalls Kierkegaard's descripton of the "dumbness" of demonical possession (**Journals:** New York, Harper and Row, 1959:136): "Christ cast out a devil and it was dumb . . . have you never been so indescribably distressed, that the power of sorrow over your whole being was almost like the powers of nature: then you have experienced what it means to be dumb, experienced the feeling of being unable, even though your life were at stake, to express the agony that rocked deeply within you, and selfish of itself made you dumb —— in order that you might not rid yourself of it. For that is how infinite sorrow is egotistical; it makes a man dumb in order to keep him in its power." Yet music, in Sinhalese exorcism also has its redressive and restorative modes.

Music and dance are clearly basic codes controlling the therapeutic process. Yet Kapferer is not content with "emic" explanation of exorcism, one making use of indigenous categories of organization and explanation. Instead he draws on the "etic" explanations (aspiring to universal, comparative efficacy) of George Herbert Mead (1863-1931), the distinguished Professor of Philosophy at the University of Chicago, a leading figure in the Deweyan tradition of pragmatist instrumentalism. Mead argued that voluntary conduct is constructed in a sequence of adjustments in which a person responds to himself as well as to what else he perceives. He discriminates between the Me, the object one forms of oneself from the formal or accepted standards of society mediated through significant "others," and the I, the response of the unique indvidual to his perception of the concrete historical situation in which he finds himself. The Me is multiple, consisting of the sum-total of the role-statuses, the self is conditioned by others to occupy or interiorize. The succession of I's responding to Me "images" forms the basis of individuality. The self constantly refers to the standpoint of the salient group in which he/she occupies status-roles. Kapferer argues that demonic possession occurs when, for some reason, the I is radically detached from the Me and is solipsistic, aware of nothing but its own experiences and states. Initial possession, to the contrary, according to Kapferer, is characterized by absorption of the I in the Me, or in Durkheimian terms, the substitution of collective representations for individual representations. Here the transcendental displaces the individual self. But in demonic possession, the multiple social "selves" are nullified and the patient is encysted in her/his I, a condition reminiscent of the Western concept "schizophrenia," in which there is held to be a separation between thought process and emotions and the generation of delusions and hallucinations.

Kapferer sees the processual structure of exorcist rites in Sri Lanka as directed to the "resocialization" of the patient, who "becomes as a little child," a social **tabula rasa,** who must be reinscribed with the multiple **personae** representing the Me, the cluster of social "selves." He recognizes that there are many cultural "kinds" of demons —— and hence many modes of withdrawal from participation in the social fields and networks of Sri Lankan cultural existence. But he postulates that a pan-human process underlies all specific Sinhalese modes of ritual redressal through exorcism myths, rituals, and symbols. In all societies individual human beings construe their pathways through life, he would argue, in terms of adjusting to a series of bodily conditions, perceptions of objects, enculturated images, and learned behavior **vis-a-vis** subjectively important others, beginning with members of one's own family. Pressures to self-control are present from the beginning; it soon becomes subjectively advantageous to anticipate the social structure of the situation in which the I will be involved, and thus to cooperate and oppose successfully. Feedback is therefore an important attribute of self-control, and feedback depends in social life on the help of social conventions, society's crude means of securing predictability. In Meadian terms, the fact that all participants in a given sociocultural system control themselves from the same perspective —— which he describes as "the Generalized Other" —— makes the intercalibration of social action possible. Kapferer presents a substantial sample of case studies of exorcism rites. His concern is with the social construction of illness and its definition in context, and the process of this as it is mediated culturally.

This magnificent book reveals clearly how the very "weakness" of demons "in structure," and the manifestation of "their extreme disordering power when they are freed from a subordination in the structure of hierarchy" are linked to the marvellous aesthetic efficacy of the rites. For demons are master of "illusion" and hence masters of art, particularly art in performance. The fascination for Sinhalese (particularly those of the lower classes) of these rituals, with their sumptuous costumes, terrifying masks, transvestite episodes, masterful drum rhythms, swirling and tumbling dances, thematic code-switchings, trancings and possessions, transitions from fear and trembling to slapstick laughter, consists not solely in the high religious meanings conveyed through symbolic action but also in that possibly more mysterious domain, play and entertainment. To entertain is, etymologically, "to hold between," that is, to place in a "liminal" condition, on a threshold between mundane spaces and times. Normative structures of everyday are pushed aside, except in so far as they are "symbolically" and "ludically" represented, as in the comedic episodes, where they form an intrinsic part of the demonic scenario. Demons, then, are supreme entertainers; they allow workers to enter into a "subjunctive" realm where all is magical possibility, where gods and demons mingle (often literally, through possessions) with mortals, and fantasies both standardized and personal may be enacted in thought, word, and deed. Kapferer wonderfully captures for us the mood, the life, smack and color of exorcist rituals, while revealing the great design, the cosmological schema, which forms the solemn ground for the ludic figure and which vouchsafes and allows the latter its lustrous, illusory moment of therapeutic chaos.

Preface

    This is a study of major Sinhalese demon ceremonies or exorcisms performed in and around the town of Galle in southern Sri Lanka. These rites richly display many of the ideas by which Sinhalese Buddhists, and urban working class and peasants especially, comprehend their world. I explore through exorcism aspects of the social and political life of Sinhalese, the nature of the Sinhalese Buddhist religious system and most specifically the logic of exorcism cure. I describe one rite in particular, the ceremony of the Great Cemetery Demon, and extend from this into a discussion of the way exorcism ritual effects key transitions and transformations in identity, experience, meaning and action. The analysis develops an approach to ritual which stresses the critical importance of considering performance and especially the role of the aesthetic. Music, dance and comic drama are key aesthetic forms in the splendid performances of demon ceremonies and I examine their role in the organization of ritual experience and the communication of its vital import.

    Exorcisms are not to be understood by confining them within the interpretational or theoretical scheme of a particular sub-discipline in anthropology. They are healing rites, but to restrict their understanding to the types of problems which conventionally arise within the field of medical anthropology, for example, is to risk overlooking many significant aspects of them which are of relevance to other fields of enquiry within and outside anthropology. Within the limits of my own training as an anthropologist, I have tried to adopt a perspective which examines the phenomenon of the demonic and exorcism in its own terms and which reveals them as being of multiple interest not only for the understanding of Sinhalese culture, but also for understanding dimensions of human action and experience more generally, whether in Sri Lanka or elsewhere.

    One of the great benefits of engaging in ethnographic research in Sri Lanka is the high quality of available ethnographies and the many excellent articles and books published by local and overseas scholars about what is a highly complex cultural scene. Without the work of such scholars as M. B. Ariyapala, Ralph Peiris, Edmund Leach, Michael Ames, S. J. Tambiah, Gananath Obeyesekere, Kitsiri Malalgoda, H. L. Seneviratne, Nur Yalman,

Richard Gombrich, to name but a few, even the limited scope of the study I have attempted would have been a far more difficult exercise than it has been. The advantage to readers of this book is that they can evaluate some of the analytical statements I make, some of which are likely to appear controversial, against the independent cultural evidence collected by other scholars.

The research for this book was carried out between 1970 and 1976, and supported by several small grants. A three-month study of Galle town in 1970 was made possible by a Nuffield Foundation Small Grant and a longer twelve-month study in the same locale, between August 1971 and September 1972, was supported by the British Social Science Research Council. I am grateful to both these foundations for their financial assistance and to the Universities of Manchester and Adelaide, who granted small amounts of money, as well as research equipment, for shorter stays in Galle of between four and six weeks in 1973, 1974, 1975, 1976 and 1977.

Many people in Sri Lanka afforded me their companionship, hospitality, and intellectual stimulation, and without their help my various stays on the island would have been far less enjoyable and considerably less the personal learning experience I regard them to have been. My warmest thanks go to Mr. Dharnapala Hewa and his delightful family who, almost as soon as I set foot in Sri Lanka, gave me a room in which to sleep and introduced me to the warmth and many kindnesses of their household. I treasure the discussions I had late into the night with Mr. Hewa on the complex ideas underlying Sinhalese Buddhism. The games of Carrom with his children, who consistently thrashed me, provided me with much-needed relaxation. I am similarly grateful to Mr. A. Navaratnam and his family for their friendship and hospitality. Mr. L. Kuruppu, then A. G. A. Galle, was most helpful and he and Mrs. Kuruppu were always interesting and welcoming company. Dr. Lalith Dias and Mrs. Malsiri Dias also gave freely of their assistance in the early stages of fieldwork. Mrs. Dias, who was then Lecturer in the Department of Sociology at Colombo University and now is working with the United Nations in Sri Lanka, gave me many insights into Sinhalese society, as did Professor Laksiri Jayasuriya, then also of the Department of Sociology at Colombo University and now Professor of Social Work at the University of Western Australia.

I owe a considerable intellectual debt to many other scholars, colleagues, and friends both in and outside of Sri Lanka. Mr. Sunimal Fernando, an anthropologist then at the Department of Sociology, Peradeniya Campus, University of Sri Lanka, gave me the enormous benefit of his extensive cultural knowledge and anthropological skills. His friendship and intellectual stimulation will always be highly valued by me. Mr. I. V. Edirisinghe, at the Department of Sociology, University of Colombo, was always willing to discuss with me aspects of my work and regularly helped in my research. Daya Dissanayake and Lakdasa Dissanayake were regular companions, and their sense of humor and general compassion towards others was always engaging and helpful. Finally, I benefited greatly from the friendship and criticism of Mr. Mahen Vaithianathan whose knowledge of Hindu and Buddhist cultures I found both penetrating and invaluable.

Mr. Chandra Vitarana, my research assistant and confidant, took my research as his own. He has a firm commitment to, and fascination with, his own culture, which is continually productive of valuable insights. Those ideas which readers might discern of interest in this book are often ones which Chandra suggested in his urgency to understand his own culture. My knowledge of Sinhala is very imperfect and I cannot claim a marvelous facility with the language, although exorcists listened and responded with patience to my fumblings. Chandra's knowledge of colloquial Sinhala was invaluable, and, especially, his sense for the subtle nuances of working-class and peasant speech which in my view only someone like Chandra could have. Chandra is deeply part of the working-class and peasant world. Time and again his knowledge proved more accurate and sensitive than that of others whose formal education and other socially generated advantages far exceeded his.

Much of my interest in Sinhalese culture was generated by Professor Nur Yalman. When I first arrived in Sri Lanka, I went on a short trip with Professor Yalman around the island, and he opened up many interesting facets of the island's culture. The discussions I had with him then must have appeared strange (I was fresh from an urban study in Zambia), and I suspect he will be amused at the "about face" which this book represents. I will always appreciate his generosity to a neophyte in the study of Sinhalese culture.

Of the scholars outside the context of Sri Lanka who have contributed extensively to the argument in this book, I must single out Don Handelman of the Department of Sociology, The Hebrew University, Jerusalem; Victor Turner of the Department of Anthropology, University of Virginia; and Terence Turner of the Department of Anthropology at the University of Chicago. It has been during the course of a long friendship and intellectual association with Don Handelman that the analytical framework for this study developed. In many places it is difficult to separate his ideas from my own. Although he bears no responsibility for the errors and failure in logic readers might detect, he certainly must have responsibility for much of the analytical worth in this study. Terence Turner took the trouble to make a detailed critique of a draft of this book. His extremely stimulating ideas provoked me into rethinking major parts of the analysis and drew to my attention many aspects of my own ethnography which I had not seen. This book in certain respects is the result of a dialogue with him, and one which I hope will continue. I was drawn to my interest in ritual through the work of Victor Turner, whose influence on the kinds of questions I raise goes back to the days of my first research in Zambia and my later experience while teaching in the Department of Anthropology, University of Manchester. He has been a constant source of encouragement and stimulation while I was grappling with demons and struggling to understand the complexity and magnificence of the rites to ward off their attack. I continually learn from his ideas. His wife Edie, an anthropologist in her own right, also gave freely of her ideas and encouragement.

My colleagues at the Universities of Manchester and later Adelaide have listened patiently to my material. In particular, I thank Wes Sharrock, Martin Southwold, Richard P. Werbner, John Comaroff, Roy Fitzhenry, Kingsley Garbett, and John Gray. Michael Roberts has been extremely helpful. While I was in the field and later back in Adelaide he continually offered useful criticism and pointed me in new directions. His knowledge of the cultural and sociopolitical history of Sri Lanka has been invaluable. Tom Ernst, also in the Anthropology Department at Adelaide University, has discussed with me most of the arguments in this book. His disagreement and questioning have forced me to clarify and sharpen many of my ideas. Jeff Collmann, Michael Muetzelfeldt, Jadran Mimica, and Andrew Lattas, all of the Adelaide Department, contributed extensively through their enthusiastic discussions and clarification of some of the ideas I present in the following pages. Sylvia Sharpe, also assisted greatly. Her interest in comedy, drama, and the performing arts, in general, was a constant source of stimulation while I was preparing a first draft.

Georges and Marie-Claude Papigny took the photographs which are included in this book. The photographs are a vital adjunct to my description and, therefore, any acknowledgement to their work displayed on these pages cannot be great enough. They have generously allowed their work to contribute to my own. They worked closely with me for a period of six weeks and made many excellent observations, which I have added to my own. We are preparing for future publication a full photographic record of exorcism ritual.

Numerous others have contributed at various stages of my writing. These include Jonathan Friedman, Roger Keesing, Hilda Kuper, Jane Fajans, Ivan Karp, Lew Langness, John MacAloon, Roberto da Matta, Mervyn Meggitt, Sally Falk Moore, Barbara Myerhoff, Shelley Rosaldo, Marshall Sahlins, H. L. Seneviratne, Tony Stephens and Anselm Strauss.

This book was completed in early 1979 but since then has been considerably revised. I wish I could continue to improve it.

The final version of the book was written while I was a Fellow at the Center for Advanced Study in the Behavioral Sciences, Stanford, California, in 1980-81. My Fellowship was supported by a National Science Foundation Grant BNS78-24671. The relaxed atmosphere of the Center was ideal for writing, and I thank all the staff, especially the Director, Gardner Lindzey, and the Librarian, Margaret Amara, whose encouragement and willingness to search out references is much appreciated. The greatest benefit of the Center, however, were the stimulating criticisms and ideas of Charles Altieri, Toby Gross, Louis Harlan, Luc de Heusch, Adam Kuper, Barbara Laslett, Paul Reissman, and Renato Rosaldo. None of them complained about the many interruptions I must have caused to their work while they contributed to my own.

The editorial staff at Indiana University Press have been especially helpful. I am grateful to Greta Swenson, who has made numerous and valuable editorial suggestions, to Robert Cook, and especially to Natalie Wrubel, who has pushed the book through its final stages. In Adelaide, Gail Applin, Teresa Ashton, Ursula Cornish, Velma Ernst and Marian Thompson have given their undivided attention, and have shown amazing patience in circumstances of great provocation, during the final stages of manuscript preparation.

The influence of my teachers, particularly Clyde Mitchell and the late Max Gluckman, is evident in this study. I have dedicated the book to the late Professor Chandra Jayawardena, Foundation Professor of Anthropology at Macquarie University, whose recent and untimely death means the loss of a great teacher and a close personal friend. It was Chandra who developed my interest in anthropology, who encouraged me to pursue fieldwork in Central Africa and later in his home country of Sri Lanka. Chandra always coupled considerable enthnographic skill with major theoretical insights, and his work was a model to other anthropologists in his country of adoption, Australia. But one of his most attractive qualities, and a source of much inspiration to others, was his healthy and often creative disrespect for orthodoxies and conventional wisdom. I trust that some of this quality has found its way into this volume.

My wife, Judith, has lived with exorcisms for nearly ten years now, and with me appreciated their artistry. I have been most fortunate to have her as a constant discussant and to have the advantage of her own sociological training and expertise. Ultimately, however, my greatest debt must be to the many berava exorcists who gave freely of their knowledge and their considerable practical sociological insight into the culture of their own society. In my view they are deserving of the highest respect. I hope they will forgive the errors in this book and will continue to assist other scholars through the labyrinthine path of their art.

For technical and economic reasons diacritical marks have been omitted from the transliteration of Sinhala and Sanskrit words appearing in the text. The glossary of transliterated words at the end of this book gives the appropriate diacritical marks.

Adelaide
May, 1982   Bruce Kapferer

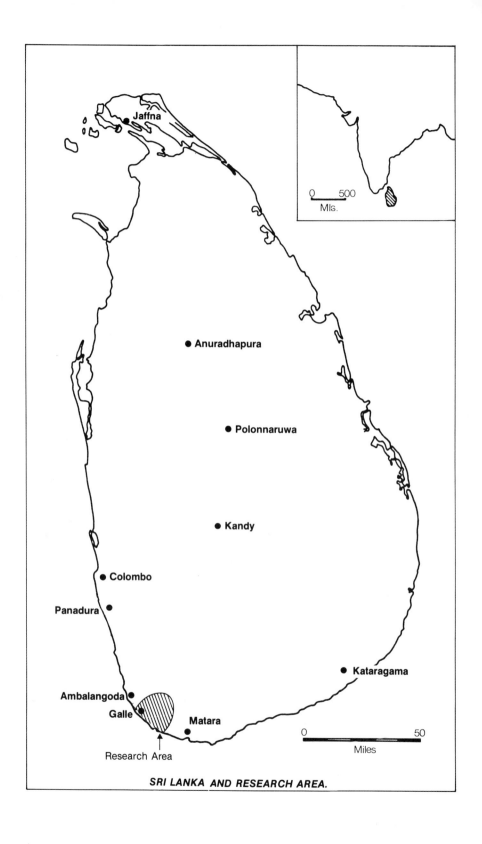

SRI LANKA AND RESEARCH AREA.

1. Introduction

If evil is coextensive with the origin of things,
as primeval chaos and theogonic strife, then the
elimination of evil and of the wicked must
belong to the creative act as such.

Paul Ricoeur, **The Symbolism of Evil, 1967**

When demons intrude upon the social world of the Sinhalese, they disturb its ordering. They manifest their presence and their disorienting and disruptive powers in the illness of individual Sinhalese and threaten to overturn and reorder the world encompassing victims of demonic attack. Demons introduce an abnormal ordering of the world, confounding reality as it should, in a normal view, be comprehended and experienced. Demons order disorder.

This book is about the culturally constituted modalities of the normal and the abnormal as these are constructed by Sinhalese Buddhists through reference to demons and the nature of the demonic. In the conception of Sinhalese, suffering, misfortune, disease, and illness can find their own particular ordering, their meaning and experience, within a world commanded and structured by malign demonic forces. Most significantly, the demonic, that morbid possibility of being, is emergent within those processes which define the ideas and actions of the healthy and unafflicted. The abnormal, that which is strange and threatening, rests and can become active in the midst of the normal. Life and death for Sinhalese Buddhists are joined in a single dialectical process, each negating the other, but founded upon essential contradictions underlying a greater cosmic unity. Demons, creatures of disorder and harbingers of death, take root and achieve their own particular vitality in some of the cultural ideas and principles through which the world of human beings and its incorporation within an encompassing cosmic whole finds its normal ordering.

I am here concerned with demons and the demonic as they become manifest in the everyday social action and experience of Sinhalese and with the specific definition of reality which the idea of the demonic imposes and describes. My ultimate analytical focus is upon the major ceremonies which Sinhalese arrange to exorcise demons, to restore individuals to a sense of well-being, and to return to normality the order of a world threatened by demonic intrusion. Demon exorcisms are one practical means whereby Sinhalese can act directly upon their world of meaning and experience and can alleviate some of its inherent possibilities for suffering and illness. These ceremonies are also occasions during which Sinhalese Buddhists can explore for themselves and in public the realms of the abnormal and the normal, and the ideas, actions, and experiences appropriate to what are culturally conceived of as different accents upon reality.

I essay ethnographically an approach to ritual which attends to its social and political context, to the logic of ideas which are incorporated and organized within ritual performance, and to ritual performance as the **modus operandi** of these ideas and of their transformation. Central to my analysis is the importance of the role of the aesthetic in exorcism ritual, for example, of music, song, dance, and drama. It is through the aesthetic of exorcism that a "world" of experience and meaning takes form and is potentially transformed. Altogether, through a focus on exorcism ritual I explore aspects of the complex relation of ideas to action, both the circumstances in which specific ideas come to govern and direct action in the world, and the transformational dynamic of ideas and action and the identities and relationships formed through them.

The early chapters of the book discuss the situation of demon exorcisms within Sinhalese society, and those broad social categories for whom the idea of the demonic appears to have greatest force. I examine the circumstances which may lead to the apprehension and comprehension by Sinhalese of their personal experience and of a social and political world in terms of a demonic idea. In everyday life the cultural ideas relevant in the ordinary worlds of routine social interaction are continually being shaped in the course of social interaction as they are shaping of this interaction. Moreover, in most everyday activities key cultural ideas which might relate to social action are not always at the forefront of conscious reflective awareness. They are taken-for-granted and unexamined aspects of everyday life. But in a social process which engages a demonic conception of personal and social experience, the cultural idea of the demonic moves into a dominant and determinant relation to action. Major demon ceremonies, the inner dynamic of which I examine in the later chapters of the book, are performed under conditions where the ordinary and routine practices and characterizations of everyday life are created as problematic, and where many dimensions of a "prereflective," taken-for-granted world, are thrown open to examination. In exorcism, action and experience are constituted within and, initially at least, controlled and determined by the idea of the demonic. My discussion of the ritual process of exorcism examines some of the ways in which a demonic idea can gain its terrible force and illusory power in experience and in action. It is precisely because of the particular relation of ideas to action in ritual, exorcism being one dramatic example of this, that the analysis of the ritual process is of wider anthropological and sociological significance.

The definition of cultural phenomena is always a hazardous activity. In the case of ritual, it is unlikely that such a rich, complex and varied cultural form could fit neatly into the Procrustean bed of anthropological definition. I think the following definition does relatively little violence to the phenomenon as it might be widely observed. I define ritual as a multi-modal symbolic form, the practice of which is marked off (usually spatially and temporally) from, or within, the routine of everyday life, and which has specified, in advance of its enactment, a particular sequential ordering of acts, utterances, and events, which are essential to the recognition of the ritual by cultural members as being representative of a specific cultural type.

There are doubtless many other features of ritual which could be included in a general definition. But I consider that any further elaboration of a definition of ritual could obscure, rather than clarify, key aspects of what ritual is about. Too often anthropologists become enmeshed in their definitions, so much so that a particular definition can take on a life of its own and become what it seeks to comprehend. Rappaport (1979) discovers the "liturgical order" of ritual, its formality and invariance, to be its principal and "obvious" characteristic. It is in the liturgical order of ritual that Rappaport extends an understanding of other obvious aspects of ritual (the communicative, expressive, informational, performative, sacred or "holy" aspects of ritual, and so on). His approach is undeniably productive of insight into the ritual process, but with his "over-definitional" orientation to cultural phenomena, Rappaport seems to me to have neglected what is perhaps **the** most obvious aspect of ritual.[1]

Regardless of how one defines the cultural phenomenon of ritual, ritual is a social practice where ideas are produced in a determinant and dominant relation to action, and it is a practice where action is continually structured to the idea. The various definitional characteristics of ritual isolated and shared by anthropologists of different analytical persuasion implicitly contain the notion of ritual as a form in which ideas dominate. Tambiah (1981:119) lists the commonly recognized features of ritual as "formality (conventionality), stereotypy (rigidity), condensation (fusion), and redundance (repetition)" and these, with Rappaport's related concept of invariance, might generally be understood as devices for the organization of the idea as dominant and determinant of action.[2]

Ritual practice is typically described as occurring in those contexts in which human beings commune and establish relationships with the supernatural. Supernaturals are in themselves and in the cosmic relations they form with each other, embodiments and objectifications of ideas. Religious rites are obviously occasions when the supernatural, or that constitutive of the "sacred", dominates and structures the relations of the human actors in its presence. But the supernatural is only one mode of the objectification of an idea. There are social practices outside the domain of religion, the sacred, or the supernatural, which involve the objectification and reification of ideas and which form action to these ideas. The list of such practices could be quite extensive and might include birthday parties, reunions, the organization of formal meals, the order of action in a court of law, and so on. Such contexts are likely to be described by outside observers and cultural members alike as being ritual or as having ritualistic qualities (see Moore and Myerhoff 1977).

I stress that in ritual, ideas, and not necessarily those framed or formed by the supernatural, are objectified and reified so much that they are made controlling and determining of action. Insofar as this is so, **action in ritual is made continually symbolic of the idea.** The ideas in ritual are abstractions from those relevant to, or implicit within, the action of the everyday world and are established apart from it while they might simultaneously reflect upon a routine ordinary world. It is the apartness and abstraction of ideas from their embeddedness in the action of everyday life which creates them as symbolic in a heightened and reified sense, and greatly empowers ideas to structure action to their terms. These aspects are vital in the formation of ritual as a particular "bracketing off" from the everyday world and as an organization of action in which the symbolic qualities of action are intensified.

Ritual, as a systematic organization of ideas in a dominant relation to action, can be regarded as both a model **of** and a model **for** action in the world (Geertz 1965). Thus it has been repeatedly described as a powerful agent in the reproduction, regeneration, and even transformation of the world order as this is culturally defined. Ritual in its organization draws from that ensemble of ideas, beliefs, concepts, and constructs which compose what anthropologists broadly refer to as culture, or that complex of social practices in which actions and ideas form an overall, if loose, unity. Ritual is one kind of social practice in which ideas (as a part of a relatively loosely textured cultural fabric which shrouds and can hide from human beings the objective terms of their existence) become systematically ordered. In ritual, ideas realize their full force, and can transform the world of experience and action in accordance with their illusory and mystifying potential.

I do not consider ritual to be simply expressive or reflective of major cultural ideas or of the social and political circumstances in which such ideas are embedded. Neither ideas nor the rituals in which ideas find their most abstract and explicit composition sit or rest upon the real objective conditions of human existence. An objective reality cannot so easily be separated from the ideas, principles, and relations within which such an objective reality is embedded. It might be possible, for example, to isolate the "material" from the "non-material" terms of existence, the base from the superstructure, but the direction of analysis here views them as intertwined in a mutual and dialectical process of determinations. Rituals and the ideas they incorporate are active in the world, intimately engaged in structuring and restructuring the relations, actions, and experiences of human beings. They are the products of the consciousness of human beings and of the fundamental conditions of their existence, but in turn, and as products of consciousness, they are vital in the reproduction of the conditions of existence in which a certain consciousness becomes possible.

I have referred to ritual as the production of ideas which are illusory and mystifying of the objective conditions of human existence. Ritual can be illusory in a general sense. This is so insofar as it makes statements about the world or achieves resolutions and transformations in terms of ideas which disguise the real and objective conditions of existence from its participants and/or is integral in the reproduction of those conditions the effects of which the practice of ritual is directed to alleviate or overcome. Sinhalese exorcisms can be seen as illusory and mystifying because they ultimately discover the source of individual and social disturbance in the demonic and seek to restore order by expelling demons from the world of human beings. Anthropologists or observers whose own conditions of existence are not those of the people whom they study may be able to discover such illusory and mystifying processes in the cultures they examine. However, the analyst should not overlook the capacity of people within a particular cultural context to uncover those aspects of their cultural world whereby they delude and mystify themselves. For Sinhalese who recognize the possibility of the demonic, exorcism ritual is demystifying and dis-illusioning. To be subject to the demonic is to be deluded in a world of illusion. Exorcisms aspire to efficacy through their ability to dispel illusions and to restore individuals to a "real" sense of the world as it should normally be defined in the terms of Sinhalese Buddhist culture. This does not deny, from a standpoint outside of Sinhalese culture, that in the process of demystifying the world, Sinhalese exorcisms are also engaged in reproducing those conditions in which the illusory and mystifying nature of the demonic is an ever-present possibility.

The argument of the book builds towards a consideration of ritual **as performance.** I contend that any examination of ritual divorced from an attention to ritual performance is likely to be severely impoverished, regardless of the particular analytical problem which a student of ritual chooses to explore. In this I am in agreement with Mikel Dufrenne in his approach to aesthetic form or the Work. For him, the Work "is irreducible to its performances and yet only graspable through them or, rather, in them" (1973:27).

An understanding of the importance I attach to performance, and my specific use of the term, in the analysis of ritual can be developed by contrasting two major approaches to cultural form and practice applied in anthropology. These are, on the one hand, the particular structuralist and semiotic methods represented by the work of Lévi-Strauss and Roland Barthes (approaches which have not been applied to ritual as much as they might have been), and on the other hand, the approach elaborated in the rich ethnographic studies of ritual by Victor Turner. These latter studies are often labelled as examples of "symbolic anthropology." "Symbolic anthropology" strikes me as an unsatisfactory descriptive label. So many different theoretical orientations are embraced by the term, including structuralist and semiotic approaches, as to make it virtually useless. It is far less discriminatory than the terms "structuralism" and "semiotics." These terms, however, also include a variety of brands which stress widely different methodological commitments to the analysis of culture. Generally, there is to borrow from Geertz (1980), a "blurring of genres" and relatively clear unambiguous theoretical contrasts **appear** to be disappearing. This is more apparent than real, however, for fundamental contradictions in theoretical assumptions are being obscured in the blurring.[3] The approaches of Victor Turner and, for example, of Lévi-Strauss represent distinct methodological perspectives on the analysis of culture (see Sperber 1975).[4] My own approach in some ways steers a course between them, and for this reason alone it is important to be aware of their opposition. But a broad account of this opposition also enables me to throw into sharper focus my own position regarding the analysis of performance and the related problem of meaning.

Broadly, the structuralist and semiotic perspectives to which I refer take their direction from Saussurian linguistics.[5] Culture, and the variety of forms in which it is manifested, is analyzed as a "text" independent of its situated production in practice. Form or "text" is regarded as relatively fixed, though attention is directed to the transformational and variational possibilities of the "text" as a property of the rules governing its underlying structure and the logic of its guiding principles. The meaning of the "text" is a function of the systematic interrelation of signs within the structure of the "text." This meaning is independent of any particular interpretation by cultural actors. The specific bracketing imposed by many structuralists is undoubtedly responsible for the achievement and advance which this method has yielded to cultural analysis. However, they are open to the kind of criticism expressed by Ricoeur, who regards them as having sacrificed "the message for the sake of the code, the event for the sake of the system, the intention for the sake of the structure, and the arbitrariness of the act for the systemacity of combinations within synchronic systems" (1976:6).

Turner, in contrast to the structuralist and semiotic approaches to which I refer, stresses performance. Accordingly, he is directed to the examination of meaning in the context of action and experience and extends this to a consideration of such aspects as reflexivity, the communication of meaning, and meaning as emergent through the concrete articulation of symbols in practice (see also Firth 1973; A. Cohen 1974; Moore and Myerhoff 1977). Parallels can be drawn between his approach and divers other schools of thought on the problem of meaning. Thus there are similarities between Turner and the philosophical tradition of phenomenology and hermeneutics, a tradition from within which Ricoeur bases his critique of structuralism and semiotics. This is a tradition to which Lévi-Strauss has expressed his opposition (Lévi-Strauss 1964, 1966, 1981; see also Kultgen 1975).[6] Turner's orientation to meaning might also be likened to the approach of the later Wittgenstein, who regards language, for example, as a "form of life" and meaning as emergent in use.

I emphasize these differences because my own approach to meaning is broadly in agreement with that of Turner, although it is more consciously shaped within the phenomenological paradigm of Husserl (1952) and its extension in the social phenomenology of Schutz (1963, 1967; Natanson 1974). Thus I view meaning as defined in a context of action and experience in which both subjective "intentional" (noetic) and objective (noematic) components of meaning are joined. For cultural actors ". . . **meaning is a certain way of directing one's gaze at an item of one's own experience"** (Schutz 1967:42). Meaning arises from a process whereby actors project their own action in relation to themselves and others in such a way as to intend further acts, and it is framed in accordance with typifications or ideal conceptions shared by cultural members as to how typical actors within a culture think or act in typical situations.

There are other major differences between Turner and some structuralist and semiotic approaches which bear upon both Turner's stress on performance and his broader orientation to meaning. The structuralist searches beneath the surface of actors' cultural practices and interpretations for the deeper structural code which systematically produces, through various transformations occasioned in the combinations of the coded elements, those variations manifest at the surface level of cultural practice. The actors themselves recede from analytical view, as do the historicity of the system and the positional location of actors within it. Conversely, Turner casts his analyses at the surface level of the actors' cultural interpretations and their practical social relations. Such "deeper" meanings as Turner discovers are found, for example, in the capacity of the practical articulation of symbols to resonate with individual emotional and experiential significance and simultaneously to connect actors with wider culturally and socially shared meanings and understandings in which individual emotions and experiences are shaped. Turner's analyses of ritual concentrate on its dramaturgical properties and revolve around such key terms as dynamics, flow, and process. Cultural actors are always prominent in his descriptions, as is their position in a set of social relations and their historicity in a world of continual becoming which shapes and is shaped by the actions of cultural members. While for Turner the symbolic action of the ritual process is systematizing, it is also transforming, in the sense of changing the world order in which individuals are engaged, as well as changing their positions and standpoints within it. Turner focuses on the creative moments within ritual and explores them as generative of new ways of interpreting reality. It could be added, as a broad characterization, that Lévi-Straussian structuralists mainly attend to the skeleton of cultural form, whereas Turner is concerned with the flesh and blood, with the spirit and vitality of cultural practices.

Regardless of where one's analytical sympathies may lie, the two general perspectives outlined have a very restricted view of performance: a view which is remarkably similar despite otherwise important theoretical differences. Both are wedded to the notion of performance as enactment or "execution" as Bourdieu (1977:24) says of those Saussurian orientations which neglect the study of practices. Performance as enactment presupposes some concept of a "text." The structuralist or semiologist understands the surface variation of performance to be based upon, as it is productive of, a "text" which either written or unwritten, exists independent of its practice as a relatively coherent sequence of events together with the rules for the production of these events. In this view culture is a "text" which awaits its practice, the meaning of this practice being reducible to the structure of the "text" abstracted from its practice. Put another way, performance is nothing other than the possibility of the "text," a practice of structure. The other side of the equation —— performance as a structure in its own right, a structure of practice —— is ignored. Turner in contrast, has a view of enactment which has some similarity with what I mean by a structure of practice in his usage of Van Gennep's triadic schema, but ultimately this schema reduces to a kind of universal "text" for all ritual. Enactment, in Turner's descriptions, is the fleshing out of this schema and gains its meaning and significance as the expressive moment of the "text" in its structural or "anti-structural" process (e.g., in his well-known accounts of ritual "liminality," 1967, 1969, 1974).

Performance, in my usage, is never mere enactment reducible to terms independent of its formation as a structure of practice. The interrelation of the elements of a "text", their **contextualization** and the organization of the field of perception of cultural actors (who are made part of, and made "interior" to, the "text") upon them, is emergent in a structure of practice, through performance. In this sense, a "text" takes its form and shape through performance and is inseparable from it.

To analyze a "text," therefore, independently of its performance structure is to risk a serious violation of cultural form. A "text" abstracted from performance creates an object devoid of key dimensions of its structure, a structure through which it achieves its meaning for cultural members.[7] As Derrida says, performance is the "structuring of structure." It is in the structuring of performance **qua** performance that the gaze of cultural participants finds direction, and a meaning in and of experience is formed. Ritual performance, as a structure of practice, is not simply the vehicle of a "text", or a means for the expression of cultural and social meaning, or a way of communicating information which somehow lies outside it. I stress that ritual performance is itself constitutive of that which it intends, expresses, or communicates.[8] Ritual as performance, therefore, is integral to any understanding of the ritual process and not just in the restricted senses of enactment or as the situated production of a "text," but as a structure of practice.

In the later chapters of this book I concentrate my analysis on the media of ritual performance (e.g., music, song, dance, and comic drama) and discuss them as distinct structures of practice. Their ordering through performance is central to the understanding of the ritual process of exorcism: how in exorcism transformations in the experience and meaning of experience are effected for ritual participants as, too, are changes and transformations in the organization of ideas and their relation to action.[9] I attend to the structuring properties of the media of performance in a way which aims to avoid the Scylla of the over-abstraction of form from practice, the creation of lived form into the dead artifact of the "text," and the Charybdis of a subjectivism, which reduces to the individual experiencing, feeling, and interpreting subject without examining the context through which such subjectivity is constituted. Here again I follow Dufrenne in his approach to the work of art. The mode of performance as a structure of practice has the initiative in understanding the experiential reality for those individuals introduced into its realm, and "forbids any subjectivism. Far from the Work's existing in us we exist in the Work . . . The ideas it suggests, the feelings it awakens, the concrete images —— Ansichten, as Ingarden calls them —— which nourish its meanings vary with each spectator. But they vary like perspectives which converge at the same point, like intentions which aim at the same object. All these views only display or exfoliate its possibilities . . . " (Dufrenne 1973:59-60).

The major Sinhalese demon ceremonies compose a great variety of performance modes: a range of the pictorial and plastic arts; incantational, and poetic verbal forms, often cast in esoteric language, as well as the speech of everyday discourse; music, song, dance, and drama. All these modes vitalize the process of exorcism, but are variously articulated and accentuated at specific moments in the ritual progression. This I show to be directly relevant to the project of the rite, to the transformational purpose of exorcism. Exorcism, I posit, reveals the power of the aesthetic formed through practice: the distinctive opening and limiting of experiential possibility in different aesthetic forms, and the varying capacity of aesthetic modes (dependent on the ordering of participants to the realities couched and formed in the aesthetic) to constitute experience and to enable reflection upon experience.

My analysis of the performance modes of exorcism concentrates on their aesthetic structure in practice, and as a unity of form and content. I incline in the argument I develop towards a phenomenological perspective, but I also acknowledge the influence of some structuralist and semiotic approaches, while remaining uncomfortable with their frequent insistence on the methods and metaphors of linguistics. In my view, such approaches make all form conform to their method and thus are an example of the tyranny of method. Their analyses frequently involve the fragmentation of form and the structural rearrangement of the internal elements of form in a way which gives primacy to a method over and above the integrity of form as revealed in practice. The method creates the form and all form is reduced to a dull repetition of all other form.[10] My own approach seeks to analyse the significance of the aesthetic of exorcism in a way which attempts not to reduce it to terms independent of its structural features as these are revealed in performance. This is important for the thesis which I develop, which argues that the distinct qualities of, for example, music, dance, and comic drama, are integral to an understanding of the transitional and transformational efficacy of exorcism.[11]

My concern with performance modes and the aesthetic of Sinhalese exorcism is part of a broader interest which has implications beyond the specific cultural context or the particular practical purpose of the rituals I examine. Sinhalese exorcisms, and rituals elsewhere in the world which similarly engage a complexity of performance modes, **combine in the one context of action** many of the ways through which human beings generally communicate and realize their experience. Exorcisms place major aesthetic forms **into relation** and locate them at points when particular transformations and transitions in meaning and experience are understood by exorcists to be occurring or are to be effected. Demon ceremonies are then occasions where the communicational, meaningful, and experiential possibilities of specific aesthetic forms within a particular culture can be subjected to examination. Ritual is a "laboratory" of the aesthetic and exorcism is one cultural practice through which a broader understanding of the powers of the aesthetic might be comprehended.

The ethnography I present is based on fieldwork done in Galle town and its immediate rural surroundings. Galle is the capital of Sri Lanka's Southern Province and, at the time of my major fieldwork in 1971 and 1972, had a population of over 70,000. Most of its inhabitants are Sinhalese Buddhists, but there is a significant minority of Muslims. Smaller populations of Hindu Tamils and Sinhalese Christians are also present. All these populations tend to be congregated in particular municipal urban wards, and Sinhalese Buddhists, especially, are further divided into neighborhoods numerically and socially dominated by particular castes. The various national and local government administration and service departments, and the commercial and entrepreneurial activity upon which the urban economy is largely based, form the major areas of employment in Galle. The town is a center for the gem and jewelry trade, and there has been some industrial development with the building of a plywood factory and a cement factory, both of which are located just outside the urban municipal limits. Galle was once a thriving port, but the smallness of the harbor and its regular silting have rendered the town almost defunct as a port of call. These factors combined with the growth and economic dominance of Colombo, some seventy miles to the north, have contributed to an overall decline in the town's economy. Galle, in some ways, is a relatively distant urban satellite of Colombo, and many in its adult population journey daily or each week, by rail or bus, to their places of employment in the capital city.

The chapters which follow cover different aspects of exorcism practice and are organized to provide a progressive understanding of the cultural and social world of the Sinhalese as it relates to exorcism. But at the same time, each chapter is oriented to a particular problem.

Chapter 2 presents some general background to exorcism and focuses on economic, political, and ideological forces which have shaped the social and cultural world of Sinhalese, particularly along the urbanized south western coastline of the island. I describe the broad range of traditional and other practices available to Sinhalese for the treatment of illness and the alleviation of misfortune. I also describe some of the Sinhalese Buddhist cultural ideas relevant to these practices and particularly to exorcism. The central argument of the chapter turns on the question of why major exorcisms are chiefly performed for members of the urban working class and rural peasantry.

Chapter 3 specifically discusses the specialist practitioners who perform major exorcisms, and who are involved in diagnosing illness caused by demons and ghosts. I focus attention on the berava caste from which are drawn most of the exorcists among whom I worked. I examine the position of berava exorcists in Sinhalese society and the way they learn their art. Exorcism is a cultural specialism which embraces a great variety of skills and involves a profound knowledge of the numerous facets of Sinhalese culture. However, exorcists are socially subordinate within the wider cultural and social order in which they live and work. Victor Turner has described ritual as a storehouse of cultural knowledge (1968:2). In Sri Lanka, it also would be true to say that it is the communities of berava exorcists which are a major storehouse of Sinhalese cultural knowledge and are among its chief custodians.

Chapter 4 examines the diagnosis and social definition of demonic illness, and the selection and legitimation of an appropriate method of ritual treatment. The description begins with an account of the diagnostic system of exorcists and then, through the examination of extended-case material, explores the way exorcist knowledge is articulated into practice.[12]

Overall the chapter examines the definition of illness as developing in a discourse involving exorcists and their clients. I outline exorcist and lay Sinhalese understandings about the demonic and how the patient, as a demonic victim, comes to symbolize problems in a wider social context. The understanding by Sinhalese of an event of demonic attack often transcends the patient, and in the identification and legitimation of the patient's demonic malaise the patient's illness comes to incorporate the problems of others. The wider social import which a particular case of demonic malevolence can assume is integral to the logic of exorcist diagnosis and to the way exorcist clients validate a suspicion of demonic invasion.

I do not examine the demonic as merely a cultural idiom, as simply a vehicle for the expression of physical, mental, and social disorders. An expressivist or reflectionist approach to cultural forms risks viewing them as passive rather than active elements of the social worlds of their engagement. The demonic is a particular construction of reality in which, for example, the signs of physical, mental, and social disorder are as much metaphors of the demonic as they might be the real or objective motivation behind a demonic conception of reality. Moreover, to conceive of reality demonically is also actively to form a reality to the terms of the demonic. Here is one key to the potential efficacy of exorcism, which is an issue I raise in this chapter and explore further in later ones. Exorcisms, through expelling and destroying the demonic, in effect also restructure and transform a context which has been formed to the shape of the demonic. The demonic and the particular ordering of context it actively constitutes and symbolizes, is the illness.

The analysis I present is complementary to other approaches. In Sri Lanka demonic attack, and similar cultural forms elsewhere (e.g. Spiro

1967), have been interpreted largely through some application of psychoanalytic theory and an attention to psycho-dynamic processes (see Obeyesekere 1970b, 1975b, 1977b, 1981). My description of the definition of demonic attack and the efficacy of exorcism treatment does not reject the importance or relevance of such perspectives. Psychoanalytic and psychodynamic orientations lie outside my areas of competence. While some anthropologists might see this as a severe limitation for the analysis of the cultural practice I have chosen to examine, nonetheless, I essay an approach which aims to account for aspects of demonic attack and its treatment without reducing them to individual psychological explanation, and without depending on possibly unwarranted assumptions about human personality in a cultural situation which is not my own.

Chapter 5 addresses the question of why women are most often the victims of demonic attack. I discuss the cultural construction of Sinhalese female identity, and the principles which underlie this cultural construction. These are explored as the bases for common-sense action which systematically leads to the identification of women as demonic victims and to their frequent treatment by exorcism. The argument, which assumes the ethnography and analysis of the preceding chapter, begins by evaluating some general anthropological theories concerning the motivation of women to particpate in rites of healing and possession. I develop an analysis which accounts for women **and men** as patients in Sinhalese exorcism. This is important, for while women outnumber men as patients in major exorcisms, the latter are, nonetheless, numerically significant.

Chapter 6 extends the consideration, begun in Chapter 5, of the logic of Sinhalese cultural ideas about themselves and about the supernatural. Here I focus on some of the central principles underlying the hierarchical order of the Sinhalese Buddhist cosmos. These principles are critical for understanding the performance of exorcism and its transformational process. The abnormality of demonic attack is tantamount to a subversion of the cosmic hierarchy, but this subversion inheres in principles which underlie the cosmic order. Exorcisms work by rebuilding the hierarchy as it should ideally be conceived, and it is the experiential and reflective engagement of the patient in this process which can be instrumental in restoring a patient to health. I discuss the notion of demonic power as founded in the demons as masters of illusion and the trick. It is through illusory powers that demons can fool human beings and even the gods. The power of the demons is broken, as one of the principal objectives of exorcism ritual, through the dispelling of the demonic illusion and the ensnaring of demons as victims of their own cruel artifice.

The stage is now set for a closer examination of the major Sinhalese demon ceremonies. Chapter 7 is an extended description of the ritual events of exorcisms and their sequencing. One exorcism, the **Mahasona,** or the ceremony for the Great Cemetery Demon, is described in detail. This is the demon ritual which is most frequently performed in the area in which I worked. While I concentrate upon it, I also deal with other major exorcisms and their key distinguishing ritual events in order to demonstrate that they are essentially similar in structure to the **Mahasona.** The ethnographic description in this chapter is vital in the reading of the succeeding Chapters 8 and 9, and constitutes, at least in part, a demonstration of the argument of these later chapters. It is in these chapters that I attend specifically to the aesthetic of exorcism performance, its structure of practice.

Chapter 8 deals with the media of music, song, and dance through which the demonic as a finite province of meaning, a reality apart from the everyday world, is progressively established around the patient. The cultural typifications of patient subjectivity are potentially made a property of patient experience (and of the experience of others) through the specific media employed, as these media also are involved in establishing the conditions for the objectification or outward realization of patient experience. In Chapter 9 I discuss the comic drama of exorcism, which becomes the dominant medium of the later phases of exorcism and which can occupy almost half the performance time of the ritual. It is in the comedy that a demonic reality is shattered and the erstwhile domination of demons revealed in its full absurdity. Through the comedy the patient is returned to a reality as this should ideally be grasped by the healthy and the unafflicted.

Both Chapters 8 and 9 concentrate on the properties of specific performance media as integral to the ritual context and to particular possibilities of meaning and experience. But I also relate a discussion of them to the changing roles of patients, exorcists, and other participants as a regular feature of exorcism performance. I raise the problem of the audience in ritual. The argument is directed to showing that the processes whereby members of a ritual gathering are systematically, but differentially, structured to the central events is critical to an understanding of the parameters of their experience and their reflection upon and interpretation of experience. I also examine how exorcisms establish a complex and changing field of communicational domains. Bateson (1973) has argued that one communicational event can contain contradictory or conflicting messages, and that what is communicated operates at a number of different levels of abstraction and removal from the concrete situation of experience. My treatment of performance modes in conjunction with the ways members of a ritual gathering are ordered to their context explores dimensions of this argument.

The book as a whole essays a multifaceted approach which examines exorcism ritual both in its cultural and social milieu and in terms of the structural process of its performance. I aim to present some of the complexity of Sinhalese ideas concerning health and illness and some sense of the artistry and splendor displayed in the ceremonies performed by Sinhalese exorcists. But I am also concerned to elaborate an approach to ritual which, while it builds on the work of others, extends our knowledge of the ritual process and the dynamics of its transformations.

2. Exorcism, Class, and Change
in Urban Sri Lanka

Sri Lanka's remarkable recorded history covers a period of over two thousand years, more than four hundred years of which were under Western colonial domination. The Sinhalese are enormously conscious of their history; subject to constantly changing interpretation, it is the stuff not just of myth and legend, but of modern political debate and of ordinary daily discourse. Religion is a major element in this history, and its current elaboration reflects the diverse historical influences from other parts of Asia and from the West that have been integral to its development. Throughout the island's history, religious ideas and practices have always been changing, dynamic phenomena, important in the politics of kings, and in forging national and social identity.

Exorcism no less than other Sinhalese cultural practices is subject to the movement, change and dynamic, in history. My observations on demon ceremonies are simply a record of their form and practice at one historical moment. Demon exorcisms are not static and unchanging but are continually being forged anew on the anvil of everyday life. But exorcisms retain elements of their past even while they are re-created or re-formed in the present. A history is sedimented in their symbolic order. Indeed, the details of the symbolic organization of exorcism reflect a Sinhalese historical consciousness and the diverse influences which have acted upon the forming of this consciousness. Sinhalese who participate and are engaged in the experience of exorcism performance are brought into vital contact with a specific cultural conception of their history, though the experience of exorcism, as I will explore in later chapters, is much more than this. Multiple realities constituted in the prism of culture are moulded to the service of the practical aims of exorcism. Demon exorcisms refract the mythical, legendary, historical, and current realities of their participants and, most importantly, bring these realities into conjunction or into relation within the experience of participants. Here is a critical dimension of exorcism ritual, and perhaps of ritual more generally, which awaits exploration.

My interest in this chapter is with setting the broad context of exorcism. The description begins by outlining the wide field of cultural practices available to Sinhalese for the alleviation of illness, misfortune, and suffering. Many of the cultural practices I describe constitute different accents or perspectives upon the particular illness or misfortune encountered by individual Sinhalese. These different accents partly explain, as I will elaborate, the pattern of individuals to explore a number of practical alternatives in the instance of a single illness or misfortune.

However, there are certain alternatives which individuals systematically do not take. This is not simply a matter of personal whim or a function of the socially defined nature of the illness but often relates to the class or status position of the person concerned. The appeal to treatment by a major exorcism is a case in point. Large public and relatively costly demon exorcisms are mainly performed at the houses of Sinhalese working class or peasants, and usually not at middle-class houses. My discussion of this problem places exorcism practice within its social context and raises questions concerning religious and cultural change. The factors which relate to the social structuring of appeal to exorcism reveal major ideological and class-based forces engaged in the historical process of Sri Lanka which are critical to an understanding of cultural changes in Sinhalese society, changes reflected and refracted in exorcism practice itself.

Practices for the Alleviation of Suffering

Demon exorcisms are a regular part of everyday life in the villages and towns of the western and southern coastal areas of Sri Lanka. Scholars and travelers have long been fascinated by them, as much for the insight they provide into the occult supernatural worlds that influence the lives of Sinhalese, as for the magnificent costumes and decorations, the marvelous masks, the exciting rhythms, dance and drama that accompany many of the performances. These rituals are directed to the removal and destruction of malign and illness-causing demons and ghosts. Of course demons and ghosts are not the only cause of illness and misfortune and there are many other cultural possibilities for the interpretation and alleviation of suffering.

The specialists to whom Sinhalese can appeal at times of crisis include physicians trained in Western medicine, hypnotherapists (largely influenced by Western psychology and psychoanalysis), traditional practitioners (**vedarala**) who work within the Indian **ayurvedic** medical tradition, holy men (**sami**), Buddhist monks (**bhikkhu**), astrologers (**sastra karayo**), operators of oracles (**pena**), priests (**kapurala**) at the local shrines to the deities, and exorcists (**adura**). Depending on the mode of explanation and the method of alleviation or remedy controlled by a specific specialist, an individual might attend a hospital or medical clinic; receive herbal decoctions and/or be advised to regulate his or her diet by a **vederala**, learn from an astrologer who reads a personal horoscope that he or she is in a dangerous planetary period (**apale**), and perhaps have a protective **yantra** (magical design) drawn up; or receive from an oracle the information that he or she is the subject of sorcery and be advised of necessary protective and precautionary measures. Buddhist monks on occasion are appealed to for astrological advice, but more often will be asked to officiate at purificatory and curative rites (**pirit**) in Sinhalese households. A **kapurala** will mediate between a deity and a patient, intercede on the patient's behalf, organize the giving of offerings, and intone the appropriate chants. An exorcist has an array of possible ritual measures at his disposal. These range from the application of curative and protective oil, the performance of a short thread-tying ceremony, and the giving of small propitiatory offerings to specific ghosts and demons **(pideni)**, to the organization of elaborate lime-cutting ceremonies **(dehi kapima)**, large-scale rites to exorcise demonic influence **(yak tovil)**, and intricate ceremonies to placate planetary deities and demons **(bali tovil)** (see Chapter 7; also Wirz 1954).

This list does not exhaust the possibilities, for there are many other rituals of a prophylactic and alleviative nature. There are complex rituals for the deities (e.g., **gam maduva, devol maduva)**, which also have demonic reference, that are performed in the neighborhood (and not on temple grounds). These protect the community from misfortune as well as from a variety of communicable diseases such as measles, chicken pox, and smallpox. Illness and misfortune that strike a particular house or cluster of households might be prevented or alleviated by the performance of a **kiriamma** or "milk mother" rite (see Gombrich 1971b; Winslow 1980).

Most of these practices share fundamental ideas and principles, and, excluding Western medical practice and hypnotherapy, are rooted in Sinhalese cultural beliefs. Exorcism is one of the eight branches of traditional **ayurvedic** medicine (Wirz 1954:6-11; see also Obeyesekere 1970c, 1976, 1977b). Exorcists and **vedaralas** subscribe to a humoral theory of physical illness and recognize the importance of dietary factors. Both consider that illness is produced by an imbalance of the three body humors, wind **(vata)**, blood/bile **(pitta)** and phlegm **(sema)**. A humoral imbalance can be caused by such improper habits as bathing at the wrong time of day or by a dietary irregularity. Sinhalese distinguish between heating **(giniam ahara)** and cooling **(sitala ahara)** foods and their unbalanced consumption can lead to illness. The major difference between **vedaralas** and **adura**, however, is in the way such ideas enter into their diagnosis and treatment. Thus the **vedarala** approaches the physical nature of the illness directly, for example, by prescribing a more controlled diet and by administering herbal decoctions. The exorcist regards the various symptoms of humoral imbalance as indicative of demonic malevolence and seeks to restore mental and physical equilibrium by uttering magical words **(mantra)**, performing an exorcism, or both, in order to break the demonic hold over a patient. But some **vedarala** will also intone **mantra** over their decoctions, just as exorcists will administer herbal treatments. Exorcists and **vedaralas** also refer to the horoscopes of their clients, thus incorporating the work of the professional astrologer.

I cannot overstress that the various specialisms and practices to which Sinhalese refer are constituted in the one culture, and that the ideas which are influential in leading Sinhalese to one kind of practitioner are also likely to be influential in leading them to another. Similarly, different traditional specialists will often urge clients to seek other professional advice, outside their own particular expertise, yet linked to it. Thus, priests at the deity shrines often refer their clients to astrologers and exorcists and, in turn, receive referrals from them.

In the treatment of physical ailments, the practice of Sinhalese doctors trained in Western medicine would appear, on the surface at least, to be outside the traditional range of practices. Their scientific rationality opposes them to the supernatural treatment of physical illness, and especially to the practice of exorcists. But rarely are they openly antagonistic to traditional **ayurvedic** medicine upon which **vedaralas** base their practice. The chemical agents of some traditional herbal decoctions are known to have curative properties acknowledged by Western medicine. Sinhalese Western medical practitioners recognize an auxiliary function for **ayurvedic** physicians in treating common, everyday complaints. Furthermore, **ayurvedic** physicians are supported by the State, and there is an **ayurvedic** training college in Colombo and government authorized **ayurvedic** hospitals and dispensaries. These functions, and the fact that **ayurveda** is a traditional Sinhalese specialism and contains principles and ideas relevant to other traditional practices, give the other Sinhalese practices - including exorcism - some of their legitimacy among ordinary Sinhalese.

Sinhalese frequently appeal to a variety of specialists in diverse areas of practice for a single event of illness. Thus, someone who is ill may seek the services of both a Western-trained medical doctor and an **ayurvedic** physician, visit an astrologer, attend a deity shrine, and have an exorcism performed. These specialists are not seen as mutually exclusive. In the view of Sinhalese they can all combine to alleviate illness and misfortune and contribute towards understanding and managing the problem. This attitude is reinforced by the readiness with which one traditional specialist will often refer clients to the services of another. But Sinhalese are additionally motivated to appeal to several practitioners, because each elaborates one or more possibilities of the Sinhalese Buddhist world view as this engages individual action and experience.

The appeal to a variety of specialists, and especially those who mediate supernaturals, is connected with the Sinhalese concern to explain the particularity of illness and misfortune, to establish why it is that one individual and not another should be exposed to suffering. Illness is not viewed as an accidental, discrete event, unrelated to other misfortunes that may befall an individual or family. A specific illness is frequently regarded as but part of a general syndrome which may include other calamities and misfortunes, such as the loss of a job, failure in business, accidents, or a quarrel with a friend or neighbor. Western medical explanations of sickness, and to some extent the explanations and treatments of **vedaralas**, relate to a specific instance and do not address its particularity in the manifold dimensions which many Sinhalese consider important. Those areas of practice more concretely concerned with mystical beliefs and the intervention of supramundane agents in the personal life of an individual place the individual in a broader context of everyday experience and action. They situate the patient and the illness in a way which attends to the particularity of the illness as it relates to the social location of the patient and others, and in a manner which is comprehensible in terms of everyday, common-sense understandings (see Chapter 4).

The Buddhist concept of **karma** (coll. Sinh. **karuma**) embodies and reflects many of the ideas which motivate much of the Sinhalese attitude to illness and misfortune, and is implicit in many aspects of everyday Sinhalese understanding. According to the doctrine of **karma**, individual experience and action is the result of previous volitional acts in this and former lives (Gombrich 1971b:145; Rahula 1974:32; Ling 1973). **Karma** is the single most powerful system of causation affecting the affairs of human beings and the activities of supernaturals (Gombrich 1971b:68). Accumulated **karma** affects the astrological sign under which a person is born and, therefore, exposure to bad or good planetary influence. Rebirth, transmigration **(samsara)**, the continuity and manner of rebirth, and the station in life to which a person is born, are all affected by **karma**, the result of voluntary good and bad actions. Gender, caste, and occupation are seen as the result of **karma**. Behavior in this life can be related to **karma**, at least indirectly. A thief, as Gombrich (1971b:146) explains, will not claim that he steals because of his **karma**, but that it is **karma** which accounts for the manner of his rebirth, which in turn leads him to steal in order to keep alive.

Theoretically, individuals do not know the nature of their previous existence or actions or the manner of their future rebirth. This does not mean that individuals, and particularly members of the middle class, are not interested in finding out. Astrologers are sometimes asked for information on future births. Some aspects of the predominantly middle-class interest in hypnotism and hypnotherapy derive from a concern to discover the nature of previous lives. Of broader interest, however, is the widespread belief among all social classes that action in this life can also have its results in this life. A Galle fisherman went so far as to specify that one-seventh of the good and bad actions performed in this existence will have their effect in this life. Most important is the popular belief that **karma** attaching to individuals which has its results in this life can affect others with whom they are closely associated. This is evident in the custom of matching the individual horoscopes, cast at birth, of prospective marriage partners. An astrologer's interpretation of the two horoscopes determines whether the two are sufficiently compatible in temperament, in thrift or generosity, in the correspondence of life fortunes, and even in their sexual life, as indicated by the astral nature of their sex organs (Yalman 1967:163; Kemper 1980).

The concept of **karma** is implicit in Sinhalese beliefs about ghosts **(preta)** and their malign effects on the living. Human beings doomed to become ghosts are those who, through wrong action or extreme attachment, craving, and desire for worldly things (wealth, power, property), have failed to proceed to one of the Buddhist heavens or to be reborn in another existence. They remain in limbo, haunting their living kinsfolk or the residents of the house they once inhabited. The Sinhalese category of house ghosts **(gevala preta),** in the urban milieu in which I worked, were sometimes considered to be the spirits of the landlord's dead kin. Ghosts of whatever type can cause all kinds of misfortune, disease, and sickness for the living. Through ghosts, therefore, living kin or house residents can be afflicted by the results of actions, of **karma** in effect, that accrued to another in his or her life.

Many other concepts relating to **karma** doctrine are important to everyday Sinhalese life. Critical for the present argument is the association of misery and suffering with **karma.** This connection and the way out of an endless cycle of rebirth and misery were expressed by the Buddha in the Four Noble Truths. These are: (1) unhappiness, (2) the arising of unhappiness, (3) the destruction of unhappiness, and (4) the path leading to the destruction of unhappiness (see Gombrich 1971b:69). The Sinhalese term for unhappiness, **duka** can be translated in a variety of other ways as "suffering," "unsatisfactoriness," "pain," "sorrow," and "misery" (see Gombrich 1971b:69; Rahula 1974:17), all of which impart some of its essential meaning. **Duka,** as Rahula notes, is, among other things "association with unpleasant persons and conditions, separation from beloved ones and pleasant conditions, not getting what one desires, grief, lamentation, distress - all such forms of physical and mental suffering, which are universally accepted as suffering or pain" (1974:19). **Duka** is produced by attachment to worldly things, by the desire, among other things, for sensual pleasure, wealth, and power. Release from suffering, pain, and unhappiness, and from the cycle of rebirth can only be achieved by abandoning desire, ending individuality, nonattachment to worldly things, and by adhering to the Buddha's Middle Path.

This brief summary of major Sinhalese Buddhist concepts has combined statements from textual sources with those made by lay Sinhalese. Sinhalese at all social levels espouse, though with differing emphases and sophistication, ideas which relate to major concepts appearing in the texts. As Weber would have said, these ideas contain "the spirit," the essence, of much that might be recognized as pertinent to **karma** doctrine. Myths and legends tell of the trials and tribulations wrought upon deities, demons, and ancient Sinhalese heroes, as the result of their previous good and bad actions. Demons and ghosts, in their lowly, filthy, and uncivilized state, are presented as being consumed by this-worldly attachment, of unchecked craving and desire, of uncontrolled emotion and passion.

For Sinhalese Buddhists the nature of both individual existence and experience are formed within a play of cosmic forces which are brought into conjunction through action. Suffering, its manifestation in illness, in grief, in despair, in hardship, and in loss, results from the conditions of existence and the attachment to existence. The particular personal experience of suffering can be a consequence of a specific interplay of cosmic forces; the specificity of this conjunction also being influenced by past and present action in a mundane world. Concepts like **duka** and **karma** encapsulate these notions, which are inscribed in an ordinary, common-sense, and taken-for-granted Sinhalese cultural consciousness and mediate understandings about experience in an everyday social order. Furthermore, the ideas relating to such concepts as **karma** and **duka** underlie, and are frequently explicit in, the various instituted cultural practices which Sinhalese employ both to comprehend experience and to alleviate suffering.

Gombrich (1971a:150) states that Sinhalese will pass from one type of practice to another as each fails to alleviate suffering. This is undoubtedly so in many cases, but a general pattern for Sinhalese to engage a multiplicity of practices is also much more than a response to failure (or a safe-guard against possible failure). Sinhalese cultural ideas are integral in motivating Sinhalese to explore the meaning of illness in its widest cultural significances, and to connect the deep emotional and physical resonances which may be part of the personal experience of illness with the social and cosmic realities in which Sinhalese are engaged. Many of the specialist practices which Sinhalese have available to them accent different dimensions of the multiple realities which can join in an instance of individual suffering. The appeal to several specialist practices is consistent with a cultural view which understands them as addressing different facets of an illness. This cultural view, of course, is also supported by the particular conceptual and technical emphasis of the several specialist practices available. It is in the serial or simultaneous combination of practices that Sinhalese can deal with illness in the fullness of its potential significances as these may be conceived of, and inter-related, through cultural ideas. Much of the strong appeal of major demon ceremonies to many Sinhalese is because these rites combine in performance the multifarious personal, social and cosmic aspects of illness.

Some medical anthropologists would describe the variety of practices, traditional and introduced, as typical of a pluralistic medical system (Leslie 1976), in which there is a wide range of choice. Implicit in this view is that the various practices, within the terms of the culture concerned, are functionally alternative, and that they appear to cultural members as equivalent and freely available choices. I have already argued that from a perspective within Sinhalese Buddhist culture many of the practices, rather than being alternatives, are potentially complementary in the treatment of the illness as a whole. In the situation of Sri Lanka, therefore, the range of choice is more apparent than real. My own argument also opposes a notion that members of a culture are simply making "medical" choices, and that they can choose freely among a number of available opportunities. This latter assumption is often conducive to an individual reductionist orientation of a psychological or sociological kind which focuses on the mechanisms of individual choice to the neglect of wider social and political processes which form and structure individual perspective and action.

The various practices available to Sinhalese have a cultural and social meaning over and above that which is directly related to their "technical" function. They are not simply healing practices. Moreover, the meaning of these practices, and the choices which Sinhalese may make among several practices, is founded upon, and formulated within, a structure of social and political relations. Put another way, the various practices theoretically available to Sinhalese have a differential cultural meaning, and consequent appeal, as a product of their articulation within a social and political order. Demon exorcisms are mainly a working-class and peasant practice, and are devalued by the middle class often because of their class associations and connotations.

I broadly define the categories of "peasant," "working class," and "middle class" in terms of their relation within the complex socioeconomic and political formation of Sri Lanka as a whole, and, in terms of the degree to which the members of these categories have control over their own means of economic and social production and reproduction.[1] This is a relatively objective definition of class categories and should be kept distinct from the way Sinhalese themselves may objectify class. These two dimensions of class, the way I define class and the way Sinhalese may define class membership, are, or course, interconnected in the routine of everyday life. Thus exorcism is both a particular class practice as I define class, and is an objectification, a typification of class membership, as class is culturally defined by Sinhalese. It is important to my argument that the power and symbolic import of Sinhalese class objectifications derive in large part from their basis in the "real" structure of class relations as I define them. For the present, my usage of the term class is in accordance with my definition and not in terms of the various Sinhalese conceptualizations of class.

Members of the Sinhalese middle class, especially its dominant fractions (e.g., such individuals as big businessmen, major landowners, senior government officials, wealthy lawyers and doctors), openly state that demon ceremonies are contrary and inappropriate to Buddhism. Generally, middle class seek the services of a traditional exorcist as a last resort, and consider exorcism to be socially demeaning.

Middle-class attitudes to exorcism and the fact that exorcism is mainly a working-class and peasant practice are recent phenomena. Prior to colonial rule, exorcism was probably common among all ranks and classes of Sinhalese and this receives some support in the historical record (Geiger 1960:164-79; Ariyapala 1968). Further support for this proposition is contained in the internal symbolic order of exorcisms themselves, if the assumption can be accepted that all cultural forms incorporate dimensions of the historical context of their development, and include aspects of the social identities of those for whom they were performed. Exorcisms are filled with reference to the social and political hierarchy of ancient and medieval Sri Lanka. Exorcists tell of the origin of the rites in the royal courts of India and Sri Lanka. The costumes worn by exorcists are the resplendant finery of kings and queens, as well as of the gods. Against the usual Sinhalese middle-class view, exorcisms find much of their logic in many of the central ideas and principles of Sinhalese Buddhism. They also give expression to anti-Hindu and anti-Tamil aspects of earlier Sinhalese Buddhist nationalisms, aspects which are alive with political relevance in the present-day situation of ethnic tension and violence. This is so in the myths and legends of Tamil and Sinhalese conflict recounted during exorcisms, and in the dramatic enactments of certain ceremonies where Brahmin priests and demons characterized as Tamils are lampooned and subjected to the biting satire of exorcism comedy. My information suggests that exorcism was a more frequent event than it is now among the Sinhalese middle class well into the colonial period. Middle-class adults in Galle, whose family wealth and position go back several generations, recall from their early childhood, some 40 to 50 years ago, large public exorcisms being performed at their houses. It is these same people who will remark that demon ceremonies are a survival of the past, usually performed today by the poor and uneducated.

The class differences in both the attitudes towards and practice of exorcism, especially regarding the major rites, are a product of an historical process involving many other beliefs, ideas, and practices of Sinhalese Buddhist culture. This historical process was and is one in which that culture became moulded within the developing structural relations of class. The class structure of modern Sri Lanka began to take shape in the context of a developing capitalist economy which was established in Sri Lanka under the conditions of colonial rule. The engagement of Sinhalese cultural ideas and practices with the formation of an emergent class structure is a fact which is vital to an understanding of the social and political significance and symbolic import of much contemporary Sinhalese Buddhist practice, including exorcism.

The terms "ideology" and "culture" are integral to the development of this argument, and they demand some definition. By culture I refer to an ensemble of beliefs, ideas, and instituted practices which constitute the common-sense, taken-for-granted and, usually, not consciously reflected upon aspects of routine daily action. Ideology, by way of contrast is a creation of reflective consciousness and is typically manifested in the problematic and non-routine dimensions of social life. People do not proselytize their culture, but they do proselytize ideology. In the overt and observable ideological process, ideas are held consciously and openly before action, guiding but not determining the organization of action. Thus religion is often taken as the clearest example of ideology, and ceremony and ritual provide illustrations of ideological practice (e.g. Geertz 1973). It is in ritual that action is systematically formed to ideas and where ideas are made overt objects of reflective consciousness. In ritual, the ideological aspects of culture are revealed, as is the cultural basis of ideology.

Ideology is a particular organized selection of ideas and practices **within** a cultural ensemble or wider cultural terrain (Gramsci 1971; Poulantzas 1978:203), which is made a matter of conscious reflection. This selection takes shape in a social and political process and incorporates the structured interests of the ideological producers and their audience. Such a selection and its force in a larger cultural, social and political transformation is apparent at major historical moments of ideological formation. These moments are important to examine for not only do they indicate some of the transformational properties of ideology, they also point to that which is ideological but now submerged in the taken-for-grantedness of cultural ideas and practices. Ideology gains much of its force in its "naturalness" in its unquestioned aspect as "custom." Thus it can be a factor in the reproduction of social and political inequalities by its mode of appearance to social actors as routine, normal, and expected practice. As a result individuals may engage in practices which are integral to the legitimation of a particular social and political order; indeed, through their action, they may contribute to the continued legitimation of an order in which they are socially and politically subordinated and disadvantaged.

The history of many cultures may be described as a continual movement into and out of formative ideological phase. A movement into ideological phase is exemplified, as Max Weber so brilliantly described, by those great moments in history when the contradictions, conflicts, and struggles in a social and political world engender **the formation** of overtly proselytized ideologies. A movement into ideological phase is frequently a time of major, often cataclysmic, cultural, social and political transformation. In these circumstances, transformational processes are given shape in ideology which then acts back upon the world from which it springs, perhaps empowering further the radical changes and re-orderings which are taking place. By way of contrast, a movement out of ideological phase is a process of the normalization and routinization of ideology. In this, ideology does not necessarily lose its overtly consciously reflected aspect, but, as a result of its implication in a social transformation or radical re-ordering of society, becomes a new orthodoxy. There is another aspect to the routinization of ideology which I stress. Ideology becomes robed in the cloth of culture and is no longer a dimension of the radical transformation of a social order, but it is rather intricately engaged in the reproduction of social and political inequalities. When I state this, I do not, of course, mean that a cultural and political world is not undergoing continual change when it has moved out of ideological phase. Change is a function of social reproduction, and ideology and culture continue to develop and elaborate within the dynamics of reproduction, but as they do so they are forces in recreating a structure of social and political inequality.

In the following discussion I examine briefly a period of major ideological formation in Sri Lanka, known broadly as the Buddhist revival. I then extend this into a description of the historical context of an urban community in Galle town, illustrating that what was a national process also was deeply involved in the development of social and political relations in local communities.

More specifically, I argue that the developing class structure of Sri Lanka gave rise to a distinct middle-class ideology, framed in terms of Buddhism. This ideology in itself constituted a particular selection and organization of the beliefs, ideas, and practices of Sinhalese Buddhist culture, and, through the position of its adherents in the class structure as a whole was to have major influence on changes and developments in Sinhalese culture generally. A further significance of middle-class religious ideology was that it turned many Sinhalese against certain traditional practices, exorcism among them, in effect contributing to the making of such practices into cultural typifications of class or status inferiority and subordination. To extend upon this last point, Sinhalese Buddhist practices began symbolically to incorporate meanings (potency, weakness, domination, and subordination) derived from their articulation within a class structure, and signed as well as symbolized the power and weakness of the main adherents of specific practices within the relations of class.

The Buddhist Reformation and the Historical Development of the Culture of Class[2]

The arrival of the Portuguese in Sri Lanka in 1505 heralded a long colonial presence, which included a period of Dutch rule, followed by one of British control which formally ended with Sri Lanka's independence in 1948. The colonial domination was at first uneasy and uncertain. This was a consequence of rivalry among the colonial powers and strong Sinhalese resistance, based mainly in the central mountainous regions of the island around Kandy. The Portuguese, for example, were never militarily strong on the island and, as well as fighting the Sinhalese almost constantly, from the middle of the seventeenth century had to contend with the presence of the Dutch (see Winius 1971). Portuguese and Dutch control was limited to the littoral, and it was only with the arrival of the British and their capture of the Sinhalese capital of Kandy in 1815 and the subjugation of the Kandyan rebellion of 1817-1818, that colonial rule over the entire island was securely established. By 1834 the British had consolidated their dominion with the setting up of a unified administration over the whole island. The early colonial experience of Sri Lanka records a complex web of political intrigues in which the agents of colonial power were enmeshed in the internal social order of the Sinhalese population they sought to control. The fall of Kandy is at least partly attributable to the intrigues of Sir John D'Oyly (who was appointed Chief Translator to the British colonial authorities and placed in charge of negotiations with the Kandyans), who spied upon and exploited the political divisions within the Kandyan kingdom to the advantage of the British (Codrington 1917).

The secure establishment of British colonial rule and the conquest of Kandy meant that Buddhism lost the support of the Sinhalese state. Ames (1963) argues that this resulted in increased schismatic tendencies in the Buddhist order of monks manifested in the virtual unchecked proliferation of Buddhist monastic fraternities (Malalgoda 1976; Roberts 1982). Also, with British rule, a Sinhalese laity was freed from monastic authority and was able to take a more active part in forming the meaning of their social and political situation through the reorientation of religious values. The new Buddhist orders and various dissident monks became the focus of an active laity, forming in concert novel interpretations of the Buddha's teachings and developing new modes of worship. The ideological innovations in Buddhism, the hallmark of the Buddhist revival, were also fueled by the spread of schooling under the British, which removed control over education from the monks and led to the emergence "for the first time in 2,300 years, of a new status group of non-monastic educated intellectual elite" (Ames 1963:47). The interpretations of Buddhism made by this intellectual elite took new turnings as a function of its independence of "orthodox" Buddhist institutions.   The intellectual elite was largely educated in Christian schools, at least before the foundation of Buddhist schools in the course of the movement of Buddhist revitalization, and this, according to Ames, sharpened the interest of the elite in their Buddhist heritage.

Notwithstanding, I cannot overstress that the Buddhist revival gained its impetus and took its ideological form within the dynamic of class relations and in the attendant social and political struggles among Sinhalese themselves **and** between Sinhalese and their colonial rulers. From the moment the Portuguese arrived off the coast of Sri Lanka, Sinhalese were engaged with a developing capitalist world economic system. New social and political relations emerged, especially among coastal Sinhalese, as a consequence of their participation in a world monetary and trading economy. But these relations were contradicted by those formed in a traditional culture based in what may be described as a "feudal" social and political order, an order still potent in the manifest continuity of the Kandyan state. With the Portuguese and Dutch presence, the power of a feudal order along the coast was weakened, but its ideological arm and apparatus, a Kandyan controlled Buddhist monastic order, still continued. It must have been a vital resource in the Kandyan subversion of colonial power and perhaps this was a reason for the attacks, sometimes violent, which the colonial rulers made upon Buddhist institutions. Regardless of whether the monastic fraternities were agencies in the subversion of colonial rule, that they were controlled by a Kandyan ecclesiastical establishment meant they must have undermined, in ideological terms at least, the claims to social and political superiority of a rising Sinhalese entrepreneurial and trading class. Members of this class who remained Buddhist (and many had converted to Christianity and especially Roman Catholicism, see Roberts 1982) may have been expected to support schism in the monastic orders away from Kandyan control, and to take an active part in the development of new doctrines and practices. There is evidence of this occurring under the Dutch (Malalgoda 1976; Roberts 1982).

The flowering of the Buddhist revival in the British colonial period was an extension of processes begun in Portuguese and Dutch times. The stability of British colonial rule, and the fact that Sri Lanka (through the British who were then dominant in the world economic system) was articulated more strongly into a developing capitalist economy, constituted the further growth of a Sinhalese middle class which provided the main intellectuals and active proponents of the Buddhist revival.[3] The British period, however, was more than a culmination or elaboration of processes already begun in a previous colonial experience. No other colonial power had established absolute dominion over the Sinhalese and thus had not forced, as a function of complete domination, a restructuring of the total fabric of Sinhalese society. British domination involved a re-ordering, effected in the elaboration of the governing apparatuses of the colonial state, of Sinhalese social and political relationships within the totality of a single colonial system and in the terms of the overpowering ideological and symbolic order of the colonial state.

The Buddhist revival, its expression in the proliferation of monastic fraternities, the spread of lay associations for the furtherance and protection of the Buddha doctrine, and its ideological reinterpretation of the Buddha's teaching, gained an intensity under the British directly proportional to the radical restructuring of Sinhalese society within the overarching framework of the colonial state.[4] The imposition of British rule opened the way for Sinhalese to define or to redefine their social and political relationships among themselves and is likely to have increased a struggle between dominant fractions of Sinhalese society whose power was variously founded in "traditional" or pre-capitalist or developing capitalist modes of production. British rule empowered members of a Sinhalese capitalist class to assert their social and political dominance over other Sinhalese and a claim to prominence in the new order. This was so if for no other reason than that the power of a Sinhalese capitalist class was inscribed in the structure of the colonial order, an order in which a capitalist mode of production was in a dominant position within the overall social and political formation of Sri Lanka. The apparatuses, the institutions and organizations of the Buddhist revival —— the new monastic fraternities, the lay associations, the establishment of Buddhist schools —— were and are mainly controlled and supported by the middle class.

A Sinhalese middle class empowered within a British imposed political and economic colonial structure may have been expected to develop ideas and practices in terms which also defined the relations of social and political power within the hierarchy of the British colonial order as a whole. This is well exemplified in the broad ideological characteristics of Buddhist reformism as these began to develop under the British and continue today. Broadly, the new Buddhism of the revival stressed a this-worldly asceticism rather than a doctrine of world renunciation, that action in a material and practical world could lead to salvation as long as this action was guided by the Buddhist virtues. Commentators on the Buddhist revitalization refer to the "protestantism," "enthusiastic pietism," and "Victorian moralism" of the participants in the Buddhist revival.

A major feature of the Buddhist revival was and is its scientific rationalism (Ames 1963:273; Obeyesekere 1970a:62). In this the teachings of the Buddha are seen to have a scientific validity preceding the discoveries of Western science. This rationalism is perhaps one of the clearest examples of the adoption by a Sinhalese middle class of the ideology of domination of their British rulers and it is a rationalism maintained today in Sri Lanka's continuing subordination to a Western economy and technology. The British claim of a "natural" right to rule was founded in their belief in the advanced stage of their civilization, its basis in a rationality validated in their expansion of scientific knowledge and technological progress. The power of the British appeared to rest in their "rational knowledge." This view was likely to be incorporated into a Buddhism which was being actively developed by a growing Sinhalese capitalist class whose own power and position, both in relation to the British and to other Sinhalese, was founded in the capitalist order of colonial society. A scientific rationality as an ideological component of the new Buddhism was also likely given the traditional cultural emphasis within Sinhalese Buddhism upon knowledge, mind, and the dangers of illusion.

The particular synthesis of the Buddhist revival not only involved an incorporation of the colonial political ideology of domination but also took form in a fundamentalist concern to sweep away the impurities of ideas and practices which were understood to have crept into Buddhism. A feature of the purification of Buddhism was a renewed emphasis upon and a reinterpretation of the Buddhist texts and an "attack" on a variety of Sinhalese Buddhist cultural practices and their declaration as not Buddhist. The movement of Buddhist revitalization was partly responsible for the distinction which many Sinhalese middle class now draw between "Buddhism" and "folk religion." Demon ceremonies, in accordance with this distinction, are labeled as "folk religion." I will return to a discussion of the "Buddhist" and "folk religion" contrast later in this chapter. What I stress here, however, is that the re-empowering of Buddhism was to some extent initiated in, and received its impetus from, the symbolic significance of British domination.

Effectively, British power (its apotheosis being the British conquest of Kandy) re-signed the value of Sinhalese Buddhist cultural tradition. It exposed Sinhalese Buddhist culture as "weak" in relation to the power of the colonial order, and made "tradition" indicative of Sinhalese political subordination —— especially where the British engaged what they defined as the traditional order of Sinhalese society in the governance of Sinhalese.

The colonially suborned and "weakened" condition of Sinhalese Buddhist culture extends an understanding of the incorporation of ruling colonial ideas and practices into an ideology of Buddhist reform, their remaking into Buddhist ideas and practices, and their role in the revitalization and strengthening of Buddhism. What the Buddhist reformists did was to appropriate what appeared to them, from their class position within the structure of the colonial order, to be the symbols of power of their colonial rulers. Buddhism, in other words, was vested, and renewed, with the symbolic power of that order which had successfully subordinated Sinhalese, their culture and their religion.

The symbolic impact of British rule also explains some aspects of the simultaneous concern to "purify" Buddhism, to redefine Buddhism and to remove those "non-Buddhist" ideas and practices counter to a redefinition of Buddhism. The declaration of such cultural practices as exorcism to be not Buddhist was nothing less than an attack on those practices which, especially in the rational order of colonial rule, symbolized the subordination and "weakness" of Sinhalese Buddhist culture in relation to colonial power. Moreover, the attack on "tradition" by Sinhalese middle class reformists placed them in a similar distanced and dominant relation to their own Sinhalese Buddhist cultural ensemble as were the British colonial rulers. In this sense, the attack on tradition was a metaphor of Sinhalese middle class power **vis à vis** other Sinhalese in the colonial formation of Sri Lanka.

The strong association of the Buddhist revival with Sinhalese nationalism further shaped and intensified the ideological direction of Buddhist reformism, both in its incorporation and development of the ideas and practices symbolic of dominance and power in the cultural terrain of colonial and post-colonial society, **and** in the revival's formation as an ideology of a dominant class functional in the reproduction of class power. This latter aspect was particularly noticeable after 1931 with the granting of universal suffrage, whereby a politically powerful Sinhalese middle class, hitherto largely dependent on the support of the colonial state was made reliant on a mass popular vote.[5]

Some scholars have seen the Buddhist revival as a continuation of earlier Sinhalese resistance to foreign rule (De Silva 1979:144-47). This fails to recognize sufficiently that the revival and Sinhalese nationalism were of a piece born of a social and political process within **the structure of British rule**. The force behind Sinhalese nationalism was a class force committed to the capitalist principles of colonial society yet opposed to British domination. The Buddhist revival married to nationalism received additional symbolic import and was further created as a powerful ideology of class and as an instrument of class control.[6]

Obeyesekere (1970a:46) stresses the nationalist purpose of the revival and notes that despite the revival's modelling of some of its ideas and organization on Christianity,[7] the new Buddhism was "from the contemporary point of view, . . . a protest **against** Christianity and its associated Western political dominance prior to independence." Buddhist reformists claimed Buddhism as an ethical system **superior** to Christianity, a system which included many of the virtues of Christianity but none of the vices of Western Christian civilization (Ames 1963:53).

One of the chief architects of the Buddhist revival was the Anagarika Dharmapala, and his social background, career, and voluminous writing encapsulated the many themes, often contradictory, of the revival (see Guruge 1965:xvii-lxxxiv; Obeyesekere 1970a, 1979).[8] He was born in 1864, the son of a wealthy furniture dealer of the numerically dominant goyigama caste. He assumed the title of Anagarika (lit. homeless) after coming under the influence of the theosophists, Colonel Olcott and Madame Blavatsky, who were themselves important to the Buddhist revival. Colonel Olcott first observed the eight Buddhist precepts at a temple in the center of Galle town. The Anagarika Dharmapala was one of the founders of the Mahabodhi Society, an institution which disseminates Buddhist literature throughout the world, and established an influential Sinhala newspaper.[9] Obeyesekere states that in Sri Lanka, Anagarika Dharmapala's

> avowed goal was to rehabilitate Buddhism and the Sinhalese race which had become denationalized, dereligious, and degenerated owing to Western conquest and Western influence. A hard hitting, vitriolic polemicist he was fluent in both English and Sinhalese. He ridiculed mercilessly Sinhalese "upper classes" who had become "Westernized" and idealized the glories of the Sinhalese past. His goals, idealism, polemicism, and nationalism are part of the current ideology of modern Buddhism (Obeyesekere 1970a:53).

The Anagarika's writings exemplify the many dilemmas of a rising capitalist class and its internal oppositions and struggles. He attacked the traditional institution of caste (a social and political barrier to some individuals coming into wealth and prominence) and claimed that caste was antagonistic to the Buddha's teaching (e.g. Anagarika Dharmapala 1965:20, 143, 571, 577, 582). The metaphors of the Anagarika's discourse reveal his appeal to the educated, and a scientific rationalism.   In one article explaining Buddhism, he likens the growth of the Buddha doctrine to "the gradual evolutionary development as we find in the biological evolution of the human germ cell" (Anagarika Dharmapala 1965:79). In another article, the virtues of a purified Buddhism are extolled in contrast to the vulgar sciences of "Astrology, occultism, ghostology, palmistry . . . that require no investigation," and he expresses antagonism to Western materialism and religious corruption stating, "We shall not enter into a polemical discussion as to which religion is best but in these days of competition, when religions are advertised like 'Pears Soap', 'Dewar's Whiskey', 'Beecham's Pills', 'Zambuk', 'Sanatogen', and 'Eno's Fruit Salts'; we know how easily people are led to accept error on the strength of a book" (Anagarika Dharmapala 1965:217).

Perhaps the best demonstration of the Buddhist revival as an ideology of class and of class domination is to be found in the Anagarika's setting out of a systematic code for lay ethical behaviour - over 200 rules under twenty-two headings (see Obeyesekere 1970a:56-57; Anagarika Dharmapala 1963:31-46). He advocated hard work, saving, and thrift. His pamphlet on lay conduct deplores the peasantry's "bad" eating, dress, and lavatory habits, indiscriminate betel chewing, and use of impolite forms of address. At one point the Anagarika set out the rules for the correct use of a fork and spoon.

The Anagarika, and the Buddhist revitalization movement generally, was influential in the popularization among the middle class of practices which signified pious devotion to the Buddha and his teaching: the worship before small Buddha shrines **(buduge)** inside the house, the observance of the eight precepts **(ata sil)** on holy days, and meditation. These are modes of worship mainly practiced by the middle class and as such are cultural markers of class membership and status.

The Buddhism of the revival is no less Buddhist because it was synthesized out of an historical process in which the modern social and political structure of Sri Lanka took shape. To suggest anything else would be nonsense. Many of the teachings and practices of the revival are now regarded as religious orthodoxy; but this is not because of the veracity of the reformists' religious interpretations or because of the authenticity and purity of the revival's practices. To insist upon this would deny history and is tantamount to accepting one of the principal ways by which the legitimacy of an ideology can be asserted. Buddhist reformist orthodoxy derives from its role in the formation of the Sri Lankan state, the apparatuses of which are controlled by a Sinhalese middle class and its dominant fractions. (The teachings of the revival are disseminated in schools and through government publication.) This middle class produced the interpretations and practices which simultaneously form Buddhist orthodoxy and create it as legitimating of the hierarchy of modern Sri Lanka's social and political order based on the relations of class.

Class, Community, and the Control of the Temples

The general processes underlying the Buddhist revitalization as an ideology of class are well-evidenced at the level of local urban communities where it is the middle class who have gained control over the central institutions of Buddhist practice and ideological production: the Buddhist temples. Throughout Galle town it is the middle class who control the lay Buddhist temple associations, who are involved in the appointment of new monks, and who are concerned with the morality of monks, with the organization of temple donations, with improvements and additions to temple structures, and with the organization of major Buddhist calendrical events centering on the temple. The temples have become a largely middle class preserve.

The effective social and political boundaries of local urban communities, and occasionally major social divisions within them, are defined in the relation of their members to particular temples. This receives overt expression in the organization of temple processions **(perahara)** which typically take a route which describes community social and political boundaries. Such processions in some areas of Galle town can occur as frequently as once a month, and sometime more often. The internal social and political differentiation of urban communities also finds symbolic expression in the degree to which individuals take an active and controlling role in the organization of temple worship and ritual practice. This can be illustrated by an account of some of the historically rooted circumstances which brought members of the middle class in one urban community I studied — a community in which I observed numerous exorcisms — into a controlling relation to the Buddhist temple. An understanding of such a process is important for it is through the command of central Buddhist institutions like the temple that Sinhalese Buddhist religion and culture became, and continues to be, both structured to the relations of class and ideologically reformed as a culture of class.

I describe a community dominated by the karava caste and take it as an example of general social and political processes which have shaped the class structure of many urban communities within Sri Lanka. This is not to suggest that the community I discuss, as any other urban caste community, is in any way "typical." The history of local urban communities varies according to the way their members were positioned within processes established under the conditions of colonial rule and according to the way such factors as caste rank, the principal economic activity of caste members, and ethnic religious allegiances affected the degree of control which their members could exercise over the basic circumstances of economic and social reproduction.[10] Karava families in Galle and throughout the island have contributed markedly to the formation of a national elite and are a significant component of the urban middle class. Most towns have karava businessmen and shopkeepers. Expanding out of the coastal villages and towns, they assumed great importance as arrack rentiers, and owners of copra, rubber, and tea estates. They are also heavily represented in the professions and among intellectuals. Historically this has much to do with their traditional caste occupation of fishing and their fortuitous proximity to colonial centres of commerce and trade (see Roberts 1969, 1982).

The particular Galle karava community I describe numbers approximately 6,000 members, located on both sides of the main Galle-Colombo road near the eastern boundary of Galle Municipality. On either side of the roads cutting across the neighborhood one can see the often magnificent residences of the wealthy — houses with richly carved wooden eaves and gables (attesting to the architectural influence of the Portuguese and Dutch), often surrounded by large well-kept gardens. Alongside them are other houses, somewhat more modern in style, occupied by doctors, lawyers, bank managers, high officials in government corporations and in the government bureaucracy, and large shop owners in the town center. A few once impressive houses have fallen into disrepair, indicating the present economic decline of the community. Some of the wealthy have moved to Colombo, leaving their houses in the care of an aged widow or servants.

Other karava have fallen on hard times due to government reforms which stripped them of much of their landed wealth. Scattered among these dwellings are, now and then, the poor houses of laborers or fishermen. But in most cases the meaner houses of working-class karava, with their cadjan leaf rooves and walls of mud or wood, are huddled together out of sight along muddy paths behind the more imposing dwellings of the middle class.

The economic success of this karava community with its internal social divisions is inextricably interwoven with the history of Galle, and the once heavy involvement of the karava in fishing. Until the 1880s, when Colombo was made the island's principal port, Galle was a major port of call for foreign vessels. Its harbor was relatively sheltered, and it had an abundant supply of fresh, clean water. Sailing ships would stop there **en route** farther east or west to replenish food and water supplies or to load up with copra. However, the harbor was difficult to navigate, and with the changeover in world shipping from wooden-hulled to iron-hulled ships, it became hazardous. This change together with the greater accessibility of Colombo, particularly to the great tea estates in the highlands, led the major shipping line, the P & O, to abandon Galle in 1882 as a port of call and to transfer to Colombo.

During the period when Galle was a major port of call, some karava were launched on the road to economic prosperity. As fishermen who owned and controlled small fishing craft, they began to engage in petty trade with visiting ships. Foreign visitors were interested in curios, and the karava became the entrepreneurs for such objects as tortoiseshell combs, wooden carvings, and gemstones. There was great demand for the celebrated "Galle lace," which karava women had learned to make as servants in Dutch households. Indeed, there is still a small factory, which trains young girls in the craft, in the neighborhood. Operators of large fishing craft **(maha oru)** assisted with off-loading, loading, and revictualing of the trading vessels. My evidence suggests that it was these large boat operators, who also controlled considerable bodies of men from their own community, who began to broaden the community's economic horizons. Through their contacts with ships' captains and shipping authorities, they secured passage for themselves and their kin to open up trading establishments in other colonial ports overseas. Small shops selling curios and gems were established in Mombasa, Zanzibar, and Dar-es-Salaam in East Africa; Penang, Kuala Lumpur, and Singapore in Malaya; in Shanghai and Hong Kong; and even in Australia, Argentina, Chile, and the Canary Islands. Well after Galle ceased to be an important port, karava men used their links with kin and connections into the shipping companies to seek their fortunes overseas.

Undoubtedly many other factors aided their enterprise. There are instances of individual karava using their connections with British colonial officials and Christian missionaries to secure contacts for overseas trade and assistance with passage. They were also aided by the very breadth of the British Empire, within which travel was relatively unimpaired, and the ease of international travel generally, which lasted until the Second World War. After the War, the crossing of international borders became subject to greater control, and the necessary travel documentation harder to obtain. The collapse of the British Empire and the emergence of independent nation states hostile to foreign nationals, together with a clamp-down on exit visas from Sri Lanka, virtually ended the karava overseas adventure.[11] The period of great prosperity for the community is largely over. But there are still karava from the community who maintain large jewelry and curio shops overseas, and they will occasionally visit the community and find employment for their relatives in their businesses. Even now there remain a few bumboat operators **(dubash)** of the kind who initiated the karava economic expansion.

The karava who prospered overseas reinvested much of their profits in land and businesses at home. Their families intermarried and kept control of their wealth. They and their close relatives, who also prospered, emerged as the social and economic elite of the community. Of course they had deep emotional ties to their place of birth, but there was a more practical reason to maintain and extend control over social life in Galle: business depended on it. Success in a competitive market required a continuous supply of cheap gems and curios from home, of trustworthy relatives to assist in running their shops, as well as access to craftsmen, usually drawn from the artisan or navandanna caste, to make jewelry and curios. Indeed, the first karava from the community to establish an overseas business did not himself travel abroad, but managed it from his home in Galle. Many of the overseas entrepreneurs left their wives at home, not so much because of the hazards and uncertainties of foreign travel, but to organize the Galle end of their trade. Thus, a major consequence of the development of overseas trade was the emergence of a class which did not separate itself from less fortunate members of the community, but rather sought actively to control and dominate them.[12]

The leading business families became the social, political, and moral leaders of their community. Religion was an important element in their domination. The great period of karava expansion into overseas trade, from the 1880s, coincided with the Buddhist national revival. The new Buddhist ethic was harnessed to their community interests, and, with its emphasis on thrift, saving, and hard work, it legitimated their enterprise —— indeed they were living examples of its verity. But more than this, attached as the Buddhist revival was to the expression of Sinhalese identity and nationalist feelings, it provided an ideological framework within which traders who were overseas for long periods of time could maintain their leadership role and communicate an identity with those at home.

It was the traders who promoted and sponsored the establishment of two temples within the community specifically for the karava. The first, Gangarama, was largely built with money provided by the first men in the community to embark on overseas trade. The successful early trading ventures were mainly in East Africa, and it was the families who had connections in this area of business who supported this temple. At the time of my fieldwork, the head **dayaka** (temple donor or association member) of the temple was a descendant of an East African trader and was to become Sri Lanka's ambassador to Nairobi. A later wave of trading activity was directed into Southeast Asia and the Far East, and it was these karava entrepreneurs who built Suddhammarama temple in a different area within the karava dominated neighborhood. The Far Eastern trade was the more profitable, as a relic room inside the temple testifies; it is packed with Buddha statues sent home from all parts of Asia by the successful traders. After the Second World War, trading in East Africa came to an end, and today none of the Gangarama temple **dayakas** engage in foreign trade, although some owe their present social positions to forebears who did. The families who supported Suddhammarama temple reestablished trade in Asia after the war, and Asia continued to be a major source of income for the community until the late 1950s. Indeed, there are a few traders from the neighborhood who still run shops in various parts of Asia.

The establishment of Suddhammarama temple marked a major social and political division among economically dominant families in the karava community. This division remains significant and continues to find symbolic expression both in the social relations focused upon the temples and in the organization of Buddhist worship at them. The most influential families in the respective temple associations are descendants of those who founded the temples. During religious festivals and other temple events, supporters of the two temples often express rivalry, and the two temple associations argue over which temple is the most "true" to the Buddha's teaching. This rivalry has both local and national political relevance and has implications for the articulation of the karava community into the wider national political scene. The members of the two temple associations tend to support opposing national political parties. It is in their control of the temples and the nature of their temple practice that economically and politically powerful families present their claims to high social standing among all karava in the local area. Regular worship appropriate to a Buddhist orthodoxy, as defined by the temple's controlling families, is one basis upon which the families, and others associated with them, rest their claim to local social and political leadership. The support of the karava community **as a whole** to the organization of temple festivals gives public expression to social and economic affiliations and to internal social and political differentiation within the karava community.

I have discussed an historical process for one community where relatively wealthy traders converted their accumulated economic capital into the "symbolic capital" (Bourdieu 1977:171-83) of the temples. In doing so, they gained control over the major local centers of ideological production, the temples, where religious ideas are formed, expressed, and translated into practice, and which are also the places of residence of specialist ideological producers, the monks, whose selection is influenced by the controlling karava families. Through their control of the temples, therefore, dominant fractions of the karava middle class, not only expressed their social, economic, and political domination, but also, by ensuring that temple practice accorded with their interpretation of Buddhism, to some extent determined the ideological basis of their own superiority. In this same process, the temple was created the symbolic locus of middle-class social relations and of middle-class domination.

To summarize the implications of my argument so far: in the general historical course I have outlined an essentially middle-class Buddhist ideology, illustrated by the Buddhist revitalization, was formed in the colonial and post-colonial circumstances of a developing capitalist economy. Buddhist reformism was part of a broader transformation in which the ideas and practices of Sinhalese Buddhism were redefined and achieved new meanings in the structure of class relations. Thus exorcism flouted the rationalism of a Buddhism defined by a rising capitalist class, and embodied all the trappings of "tradition," a tradition of the subordinate and the weak, a meaning established in the symbolic order of colonial rule. This is also a meaning reproduced in a structure of class relations. Buddhist orthodoxy, defined by a middle class, both signs and is a metaphor of middle class power. Exorcism as unorthodox or defined as inappropriate to Buddhist practice, is made significant and metaphoric of social and political inferiority.

Sinhalese Buddhist cultural ideas and practices have become part of a culture of class whereby they constitute objectifications and typifications of relationships in a social and political hierarchy. Put another way, they are the modes of appearance of an underlying and dynamic structure of class relations formed around a dominant capitalist economy. Religious and ritual practices assume a fetishistic quality.[13] In this, individuals who are members of powerful groups or who lay claim or aspire to such membership, are likely to constrain their action to certain ritual practices because such practices are seen **in themselves** to constitute social and political position. Such constraint is all the stronger because particular modes of religious and ritual practice do coincide with what may be determined as the objective foundations of social, economic and political power in modern Sri Lanka. Thus middle-class orthodoxy is supported by the state, and in local communities it is the economically and politically powerful groups which have control over Buddhist temples and influence their practice.

The following discussion extends on the notion of religious and ritual practice as part of the symbolic language of class and status. I focus especially on the issue of religious and ritual change as this is continually produced in a social discourse based on the contradictions and oppositions of class.

Class, Change, and the Structure of Religious and Ritual Practice

One debate in the sociology of Sri Lanka has concerned the structure of Sinhalese Buddhist religion and the direction of its change. Ames treats the traditional religion as two distinct but related systems. One, the system of Buddhist worship, is concerned with sin, rebirth, and the fate of the soul. The other, which Ames terms "magical animism," or the system which relates to the worship and placation of deities, demons, and ghosts, is directed to the handling of everyday misfortunes and frustrations (1963:46). According to Ames, the two systems of belief and practice coexist because the Sinhalese Buddhist "concept of salvation is so systematized, abstract, and other-worldly that there is need for something like healing rituals that are more specific, concrete, and mundane, much more part of the mundane world, to serve as a bridge between man and his ultimate concerns" (1964a:80). Ames is, of course, applying a version of the well-known anthropological dichotomy of the Great Tradition of the texts and the Little Tradition of "folk" religious practices (Redfield 1956; Marriott 1955). Tambiah (1970:367-77) has strongly criticized this distinction. It is static and ahistorical, for it fails to recognize the fact that the texts themselves were written at different social and political periods and have been subject to various and changing interpretations.

In the context of Sri Lanka the distinction is demonstrably false, for as Gombrich (1971a; also Marasinghe 1974) records, the texts themselves make frequent reference to the supernaturals. Obeysekere states, correctly in my view, that Ames depends too greatly on the ideological system as laid down in the texts, at the expense of examining the practice of Buddhism. For Obeyesekere, Sinhalese Buddhism is a single system, and not two. The Buddhist pantheon "is neither a Theravada Buddhist nor a specifically 'animist' one, but a Sinhalese Buddhist pantheon. The Buddha, gods, demons, and an array of lesser supernatural beings constitute a single system, which displays a wholly consistent structure" (1963a:148). Theoretically the Buddha, having attained Enlightenment, is in a state of nonexistence **(nirvana).** He cannot be approached for help. But in practice individuals direct rituals and offerings to him in the expectation that this show of devotion and piety will bring rewards. At times of personal crisis, individuals will appeal to him for assistance. The Buddha has presidential status in all rituals which address supernatural beings, as the organization of gesture and offerings in rituals shows. The Buddha is worshipped with hands on the head or forehead, deities are approached with hands clasped at the chest or further down, while the demons are shown no respectful obeisance at all. Offerings given to the Buddha are white or yellow flowers, rice, and sometimes fruit juices; the deities receive flowers of vivid hues and whole fruit; while demons receive torn flowers and a variety of impure cooked vegetables and meats.

The disagreement between Ames and Obeyesekere extends to the direction of religious change in Sri Lanka. Ames suggests that the ideas and practices of "magical-animism," those centering on the deities and demons, will be displaced, particularly in the industrializing and urbanizing areas of Sri Lanka, by a new "enthusiastic pietism and ethical asceticism" (1963:53). Obeyesekere's disagreement with Ames is on factual grounds. Contrary to Ames, he records, among the urban middle class, an increase in the popularity of worshipping at the shrines to the deities (Obeyesekere 1970a, 1977a) and in the practice of sorcery (Obeyesekere 1975a). It is the Sinhalese urban middle class which largely swells the crowds at the great festival to God Kataragama every July in the Eastern Province of the island (Obeyesekere 1977a). At other times throughout the year, too, they will visit Kataragama's shrine to solicit his aid and protection before traveling overseas, in business, at times of personal or family misfortune, or before taking an examination (Obeyesekere 1970a:59). The change in Sinhalese Buddhism to which Obeyesekere points, **contra** Ames, is expressed by the middle class with its increasing emphasis on the deities. However, Ames and Obeyesekere disagree only about the quality of the change, with both maintaining that it has a unidirectional or linear character. Nor do they differ fundamentally in their explanations for the practices they observe. Both stress ideological factors, specifically **karma** and the middle-class interest in purifying Buddhism. Obeyesekere, however, gives greater consideration to the social and psychological context of Buddhism, arguing that middle-class anxiety, frustration, and tension in their daily lives motivates members to the worship of deities.

My own approach, while it builds on the work of the forementioned scholars, also differs from theirs. I agree with the general and specific criticisms of the Great Tradition/Little Tradition dichotomy as it has been used in scholarly work. Nonetheless, the distinction is alive in everyday discussions among Sinhalese about their religious ideas and practices. Middle-class Sinhalese repeatedly refer to their own worship and ritual practice as consistent with the teachings of the Buddha. They will distinguish among themselves as to the extent to which their practices and those of others conform to Buddhist ideals, as laid down in their reading of the texts or otherwise received by them, at school, in discussion with monks, and so forth. Middle-class Sinhalese consider the practices which they observe among the working class and peasantry (e.g., traditional community rituals to the deities such as the **an keliya, gam maduva, devol maduva,** and demon exorcisms, see Wirz 1954) to be "folk" practices that are not to be confused with "true" Buddhism. In other words, the Great Tradition/Little Tradition dichotomy is a typification of everyday life and is largely a construction of the middle class. It is this which scholars as critics or proponents of the distinction have failed to emphasize. The distinction is an integral part of a symbolic language of class and status, constituted and taking its form in a continuing historical process of the structuring of class relations, and active in the definition of class membership and status position. It is part of a cultural language of domination and, as such, incorporates to it conflicts and oppositions founded upon the social, economic and political processes in which class and status find their particular structuring.

The Buddhist temple —— the sacred **bo** tree, the **dagaba,** the Buddha statue, the monks —— is the central symbol of Buddhism for all Sinhalese Buddhists regardless of class or status. But in the historical processes I have outlined, it is the middle class who have appropriated it and appointed themselves as its principal custodians. They have defined themselves as the guardians of Buddhism and of the Buddha's doctrine and thus, have control over and play a determining role in directing their own religious practice, while denying such control to others. Insofar as the members of the

Sinhalese working class worship at the temple, they do so in a context dominated by the middle class and are made continually conscious of their subordination in the wider social order.

Within the karava community I have described and in Galle town generally, it is the middle class who organize and participate in temple processions **(perahara)** marking important days in the Buddhist calendar. Working-class Sinhalese will be enjoined by their middle-class patrons to collect money for temple festivals or assist in the preparation of ceremonial events, but they are not accorded a prominent place in the proceedings. It is the middle class who predominate in such overt acts of Buddhist piety as pilgrimages to the sacred centers of Sinhalese Buddhist history, who regularly observe **ata sil** (the eight Buddhist precepts) at the temple, who most frequently engage in the relatively expensive merit-making rituals **(pinkama),** and who give **dana** to the temple monks on their own behalf or for deceased relatives.

Middle-class Sinhalese point to the frequent participation in "true" Buddhist practices as evidence of their piety and in justification of their claim to social esteem and community leadership. These claims are not undisputed. Some working-class Sinhalese criticize middle-class religious behavior as more concerned with the display of wealth and social standing than with devotion to the Buddha. There is a small branch of the Vinaya Vardhana Samitiya (Society for Rejuvenating the Discipline) in the karava community, which continues much of the "fundamentalist" spirit of the Buddhist revival. Its few members are of lower status (small traders and shopkeepers, office clerks) in the middle class. Their criticism of the more powerful members of their community is similar to that sometimes made by working-class Sinhalese but focuses as well upon matters of doctrinal purity, which they believe are violated by the monks and their middle-class patrons.

The worship of the major Sinhalese deities is a feature of the religious and ritual practice of all Sinhalese regardless of class. Their worship is integrated with that of the Buddha both at the temple and at ritual occasions outside the temple grounds in the neighborhood. Deities are conceived of as following the Buddha's Path and are ultimately oriented to achieving the Buddhist ideal of **nirvana.** They advance along this way by helping human beings and receiving merit **(pin)** from Sinhalese through the latter's acts of Buddhist devotion. Some middle-class Sinhalese regard the worship of the deities to be counter to "true" Buddhist practice, and this is probably the influence of the teachings of the Buddhist revival and a middle class concern with doctrinal purity. Socially and politically prominent individuals within the karava community, for example, sometimes say that worship of the deities is outside true Buddhism. These same individuals (major landowners, professionals, and businessmen) through their influence on the lay associations of the two karava temples have not allowed **kapuralas** to operate the deity shrines. **Kapuralas** are essential to a fully functioning shrine, and most of the middle-class karava frequent other temple shrines in the general area. The individuals who have opposed the presence of deity priests, nonetheless, will make pilgrimage to the shrine of God Kataragama, which they note is also the site where the ancient Sinhalese Buddhists began their resurgence against Hindu Tamil domination.

Despite the disapproval of deity worship among certain fractions of the middle class, appeal to the deities is more **apparent** as a middle-class practice than it is as a working-class or peasant practice. Such an appearance is partly a function of the fact that religious and ritual practice is most observable at the temples which are largely a middle-class preserve. But this should not ignore the active role which middle class play in **making** the temples major centers for the worship of the deities. It is the middle class who contribute funds for the refurbishing of deity shrines and who are influential for the building of new ones. The middle class are actively oriented to the worship of deities and on temple grounds, for in a temple context their appeal to the deities is made to appear all the more Buddhist (and is likely to be experienced as such given the context). The symbolic significance of this is clear in a situation where there is debate among a middle class about the place of deities in Buddhism.

There is considerable evidence for an increase in the Sinhalese middle class worship of the deities (Obeyesekere 1977a;1978). This increase as a statistically demonstrable fact is part of the same process which underlies the middle-class appropriation of the central institutions of Buddhism. That is, the increasingly evident close relation of the middle class to the deities is nothing other than the appropriation to middle-class control of major symbolic forms of domination and power in the Sinhalese Buddhist cosmic order. Deities and a close relation to them constitute a metaphor of class power. Sinhalese sometimes describe the hierarchy of their supernatural universe in practical social and political terms —— the everyday social world is a metaphor for a supernatural order as this order is a metaphor for a mundane reality (see Gombrich 1971a:181-82; Obeyesekere 1966). I once asked a Sinhalese laborer to clarify for me a distinction between two Sinhalese categories of spirit. I was told that one category **(kumbhanda)** were the spirits of the wealthy, who frequent temples, whereas the other category **(preta)** were usually the ghosts of the poor.[14]

The close ritual relation which a Sinhalese middle class has formed with the deities has a fetishistic character about it, somewhat similar to a concern with Buddhist orthodoxy referred to earlier. This fetishism is formed in conditions where ritual practice surrounding the deities has come to sign social, economic, and political position and, as a function of its signing, has become vested with an apparent capacity to control and create what it signs. The seeming increase in ritual practice directed to the deities among a middle class is, perhaps, the struggle of an economically and politically threatened middle class (threatened by the principles of the development of a capitalist system which gave rise to a middle class and which are all the more intensified in the current beleaguered situation of the Sri Lankan economy) to control the circumstances of its existence at the level of its appearances as these are mediated ideologically and culturally in experience.[15]

Increasing middle-class worship of the deities is also associated with various and distinct class-related modes of deity worship. There is a tendency for middle class to focus on the Buddha and the deities to the exclusion of the lower reaches of the Sinhalese Buddhist pantheon. In contrast, the ritual practices of working-class and peasant Sinhalese address the pantheon in its hierarchical totality. The selectivity of a middle class is most evident in its ritual innovations. This is one of the more obvious features of middle-class religious practice, as is the production by the middle class of its own ritual specialists who have little or no connection with traditional experts in ritual work.[16] Both these aspects of religious action are most apparent among lower-status middle class who do not have control over the temples which, as I have said, are largely in the hands of dominant fractions of the middle class.

An example of a middle-class ritual innovation I witnessed was that of a **gam maduva**, a major rite for the goddess Pattini, which was performed at the house of a small shopkeeper. Customarily this rite is organized by a number of households in a village or neighborhood as a protection against illness or misfortune which may befall the community. Traditionally it is a village co-operative occasion but in this instance it was organized by one household and principally for the benefit of its members. One of the more remarkable features of the ritual performance was that the shopkeeper's wife assumed a central role **as** the goddess Pattini. This was not only a departure from customary practice but an illustration of the identity which middle-class individuals will establish with deities. In the karava community I have described, a primary school teacher assumed an important role as a ritual specialist and frequently organized a fire-walking ceremony, which included other modes of mortification of the flesh, in a clearing in front of his house. The model for this ceremony were the rituals which surround the annual festival for Kataragama in Sri Lanka's Eastern Province, but the details of the schoolmaster's ritual activities, and of others who joined with him, were decidedly his own.

If middle class are positively oriented to the worship of deities and have fashioned their ritual practice as a culture of class, they are negatively oriented to demon exorcism. This negative orientation is a product of an historical process as I have argued, and is reproduced in the tautology of a cultural logic of a class discourse which has been instrumental in further creating exorcism as a working-class and peasant practice. In the social discourse of class and status, middle class who have exorcisms, and especially the major ceremonies, will sometimes be ridiculed by their peers for practice inappropriate to Buddhism and for submitting to superstitions inconsistent with their social standing and education. I have heard tell of a prominent Colombo Buddhist intellectual who, to hide his own treatment by exorcism, traveled to the other side of the island for his ritual performance. A canard no doubt, but significant nonetheless. One wealthy karava woman in the community where I lived, indeed a benefactor of one of the temples, was a constant source of amusement to fellow middle class for her engagement in exorcism. On one occasion, during a vow-making procession to a temple deity shrine, to seek the help of Vishnu for the successful outcome of a lung operation for a temple monk (the woman's son, the procession being organized by the Young Man's Buddhist Association and the Young Women's Buddhist Association), the woman presented Vishnu with areca-nut flowers, a common offering at exorcisms. The secretary of the Young Women's Buddhist Association exclaimed, "What's that for —— a **tovile** (exorcism)?" The comment brought much laughter.

Middle-class Sinhalese, or those who define themselves as such, may be expected to refrain overtly from exorcism especially in the context of a social discourse where exorcism practice signs a social inferiority and constitutes a contradiction of the ideologically established premises of power and social position. Typically, middle class restrict themselves to minor exorcisms held within the privacy of their houses, and not outdoors in full public view as the major ceremonies are typically performed. Should a larger-scale exorcism be held at a middle-class house, not only will it likely be performed indoors but also it will be very much abbreviated. Thus central dance episodes and the concluding drama of exorcism, which respectively elaborate the power of the demonic and the debased and polluting absurdity of demons, are often excluded with the emphasis being placed on curative mantra and song. Many middle class complain about the coarse crudity of the comic humor which characterizes the closing drama of exorcism and exorcists conscious of middle-class sensitivity will sometimes censor their dialogues if individuals present at a performance demonstrate unease.

Interestingly, given the middle-class relation to the deities, the major demon ceremony most often performed at middle-class houses is the **Suniyama**. This rite is specifically designed to alleviate the effects of sorcery, and of the supernatural being to whom it is addressed (and after whom the rite is named and who may take the form of either deity or demon). Shrines to Suniyam as deity are found in some Buddhist temples. The **Suniyama** exorcism is regarded by exorcists as bordering on that of a traditional deity rite. It is distinct from other large-scale exorcisms, and in fact bears many structural similarities in performance to major traditional rites for the deities (see Chapter 7, 135).

Major demon ceremonies, much middle-class opinion notwithstanding, are not an embarrassing cultural residue of a rapidly disappearing past. While they display a clear continuity with historical tradition, the label "traditional" is inaccurate. The label obscures the fact that exorcism of the kind I am concerned with in this book, and especially the large-scale rites, is a modern working-class and peasant practice, which achieves a significance in the dynamics of Sri Lanka's class structure, and also is a practice to which a working class and peasantry are actively and positively oriented.[17] Demon exorcisms are not a specific class practice by default. Furthermore, they are continually being shaped and reformed to the demands of their audience.

The continuing vitality of exorcism among the working class and peasantry, along with certain other "traditional" rites, is influenced by the fact that it is in these practices that working-class and peasant households can retain a degree of control over their own religious and ritual action. Conducted, as these rituals are, independently of the temple, working-class Sinhalese are enabled to participate in a context organized by them and outside a setting which is dominated by those who exercise political, economic, and social superiority over them. Those processes, therefore, which have led the middle class to appropriate and to become the custodians of the central symbols of Sinhalese Buddhist life, and which deny to the working class the same active controlling relation to such symbols, are integral to the continuing emphasis which the working class place on "traditional" practices —— practices in which they can play a more vital individual and collective determining role.

In addition to their curative aims, major demon ceremonies are a public entertainment of the working class. The specialists who perform the major exorcisms, though generally from a caste subordinate to their clients', occupy a similar social and economic position. The comic drama of exorcisms comments upon the social and political order which members of the working class daily experience. The dramatic dialogue pokes obscene fun at national and local dignitaries and offers a critical discourse on everyday frustrations and hardships. The drama of exorcism engages the audience in an awareness of its social condition and often derives its humor from contrasts between working-class life and the lives of those wielding authority and influence in the wider social world. In 1971 there was a major political insurgency against the government. The movement had a considerable following among the urban working class, although the rural peasantry took the most direct action (Halliday 1971; Obeyesekere 1974). While I entered the field after the main events of the insurgency, criticisms of government response to the insurgency, which cost the lives of many rural youth, were frequent themes in exorcism drama. The violence of the insurgency was itself seen as a manifestation of the demonic.

Demons when they attack are fearsome beings of domination who isolate their victims in a horrifying reality and determine their every action. In many ways, therefore, demonic attack symbolizes the subordination of a Sinhalese working class and peasantry who are caught in an obdurate world, weakened in its structure, and who are socially and politically fragmented by economic and political forces beyond their control. Demons are the terrors which prowl at the base of hierarchy. But also, like their working class and peasant victims, demons are the contradiction of an order in which they are normally subjugated and are a hidden power waiting to break free. Historical forces in the shaping of modern Sri Lanka and in the transformation of Sinhalese Buddhist culture have made demon ceremonies a specific class practice and the demonic as metacommunicative of the dynamics of class.

3. Exorcists

Exorcism, or "the science of spirits" (**yaksabhuta vidyava**), is a complex art. Its practice rests in a wide and deep cultural knowledge, and its practitioners command the numerous artistic skills for which Sri Lanka is famous. In the Galle area, most exorcists belong to the berava caste, as is generally the case throughout the island. It is berava who command, and reproduce in ritual practice, much of the traditional knowledge which plays so considerable a part in the everyday lives of Sinhalese. Ryan states that "Except for navandanna, the berava is the only numerically important caste preserving an artistic tradition in Ceylon" (Ryan 1953:124).[1] Their caste name indicates that the berava are drummers. But they engage in a great many artistic activities besides music, for which, in Sri Lanka, the drum is the main instrument. Members of the berava caste provide many of the artists, who paint the colorful scenes from religious myth and history to be found in temples throughout Sri Lanka, and who make the images of the Buddha and the gods. Berava frequently are the architects and builders of the numerous temples and shrines. Many of the most skilled performers of traditional dance and drama are berava, and some have achieved fame internationally as exponents of exorcism dance and drama. Within the berava caste, apart from excorcists, are to be found such important figures in daily life as astrologers (**sastra karayo)** and marriage matchmakers **(kapua),** though as with exorcism, these activities are by no means exclusive to the berava.

Traditionally the berava is viewed by others as principally a service caste, providing a variety of ritual services. Its members are the drummers at temple ceremonies, at curing rites **(pirit)** presided over by Buddhist monks, at weddings, at funerals, and at official functions. They are hired to drum and dance in religious processions to mark events in the Buddhist calendar. Berava are prominent in the organization of various rites of community protection, held to honor the deities. However, the fact should not be ignored that berava are engaged in diverse occupations, apart from those directly associated with their traditional roles. The berava have become internally differentiated, in accordance with their participation in a

modern society. Some berava control construction businesses, some are
building contractors, or carpenters; others are employed in the curio
business, which is growing along with Sri Lanka's tourist industry. Some are
also tailors.[2] These are major occupations among members of the caste, and
often involve skills developed on the basis of traditional caste knowledge. A
few of the berava are employed as civil servants in the vast government
bureaucracy. But those berava who are not engaged in ritual
practice —— still the main occupational role of caste members and usually a
full-time job —— are mainly employed as laborers and servants.

Life histories I have collected from a number of individual berava
indicate that they have been regularly drawn back to ritual work and
associated activity as a result of periodic unemployment. The cultural and
ritual knowledge held in the various berava communities, because of its
importance in the daily lives of Sinhalese, gives potential access to a
regular, though usually small, income. The principal male income earners of
berava households I interviewed earned little more than 150-250 rupees a
month, roughly equivalent to the regular wage earned by other members of
Sri Lanka's large urban working class at the time of fieldwork. The only
large berava community (67 houses) in the Galle area is situated on a small
stretch of land on the outskirts of the town.[3] The houses are, in general,
small and contain relatively few material possessions, and this is true also
for the small clusters of two or three berava owned houses, usually
belonging to exorcists, one finds scattered among other urban neighborhoods
dominated by members of other castes.

The berava are among the most numerous of the low-ranking Sinhalese
castes, but they are a small fraction of the caste-identified populations in
the southern part of the island (Ryan 1953:291).[4] In terms of cultural ideas
relating to caste rank in both urban and rural Sri Lanka, the berava are close
to the bottom of the caste order, at least in the view of members of other
castes. Their low rank is directly related to the nature of their ritual
duties, and to their traditional position as a caste serving most of the other
castes. For example, their identification with exorcism and the malign
supernatural contributes to their low caste rank.[5] Moreover, there are no
other castes who perform, or who theoretically could perform, caste
services for the berava. For instance, members of the rada caste perform
ritual services for higher-ranked castes, such as the goyigama and the
karava, washing and preparing clothes for funerals, washing girls at their
puberty ceremony, and so on. The rada do not perform such service for the
berava, who must provide these services within their own community. I
might add, however, that the berava community in Galle recognizes a close
relationship with members of the rada caste. This contrasts with a certain
degree of tension and hostility between the berava and members of the
similarly ranked neighboring oli community. Much of this antagonism can be
attributed to a series of continuing land disputes between families belonging
to the separate communities, but also, I suspect, to the fact that many oli
are engaged in similar ritual work, as astrologers and exorcists, and,
therefore, are in a relation of competition.

That the berava are among the poorer elements of the population also
contributes to the low esteem accorded to them. I draw attention here to
the interrelation between caste and class, whereby each is engaged in the
reproduction of the other, such a process giving to caste and to class their
cultural form both in their appearance to Sinhalese consciousness and in
their manifestation in social practice. Thus caste (the identity, social
relations, access to and control over the means of a livelihood, constituted
as a function of caste membership) is an important factor involved in the
unequal distribution of life chances in the capitalist dominated social

formation of Sri Lanka. As such, caste is engaged in the structuring of class relations, even though, as many scholars have commented, it is fractionalizing of class and can militate against a wider class unity. Caste, especially in such large urban centers as Colombo and Galle, in numerous respects takes its form, and continues as a vital element of Sinhalese everyday life, in the contradictions of class processes. In this sense, caste is an institution of class domination **and** of class survival. So too, caste ideology (which stresses social inequalities on the basis of an idealized traditional order) becomes shaped and re-shaped in modern economic and political conditions, thereby achieving its force in the structuring of class and assuming importance as a "language" of social and political struggle mounted upon the relations of class. An examination of the foregoing thesis is beyond the scope of this book but the experience of the berava lends some support to the argument (as does the description of the karava community in Chapter 2 and the case material presented in Chapter 4).

The berava are an example of a caste which have not had direct control over their own material conditions of social and economic livelihood, depending for their social and economic reproduction on the possession of immaterial ritual skills. Being largely a service caste, having little command over the material circumstances of existence, the berava (and other relatively unlanded and low-ranked, subordinated castes within a caste system e.g. oli, rada, panikki), therefore, were placed in a disadvantageous position within the historical context of a developing capitalist economy. A comparison of the berava, and other castes similarly situated, with the karava discussed earlier, highlights the general point. The karava, as fishermen owning or having shares in boats and nets, had more direct control over their means of economic production, and were better placed in the developing structure of social, economic, and political relations that began under colonial rule.

Broadly, the caste situation of the berava was and is a factor which systematically creates its members as part of an expanding working class and landless and powerless peasantry. This process is exacerbated by the force of discriminating caste ideology which has operated to exclude berava from educational institutions and which has denied to them certain economic and political roles in a modern society.

The berava are one of a few caste minorities who have been subject to what can only be termed overt caste discrimination until relatively recent times. Members of the caste were forbidden by the higher caste Sinhalese to wear short-sleeved vests. Ryan (1953:292-94) writes of disputes that came to a head in the late 1940s over the wearing of vests by the berava, especially disputes between the berava and the politically dominant and numerically strong goyigama. Berava refer continually to fights with goyigama and other castes over this issue. I have recorded instances in which incidents dating back to the turn of the century are still recalled with an intense hostility. Many of my informants referred to the issue of schooling, claiming that it was because of antagonism from other castes that they left school earlier than they otherwise would have.[6] Ryan (1953:293) cites an example from the Tangalle area, south of Galle, where in 1949 a group of fifty berava school children had their vests torn from their backs. My data indicate that similar incidents occurred well into the 1950s.

It seems likely that the poverty of the berava has been the more important factor in their early termination of schooling. But what I would emphasize is that the caste antagonism which they encountered was likely to make them not only conscious of their inferiority in relation to others, but also aware of caste as a factor restricting their entry into various urban opportunity structures —— the more so given the dominance of these structures by the higher castes. This, together with other forementioned factors, influences, I suggest, a continuing dependence on traditional skills, which in turn maintains their traditional caste image and role.

The berava have an acute consciousness of social injustice in their caste position, which is underlined even in their own ritual practice. At an exorcism ritual, for example, unless wearing apparel dictated by the rite itself, they ideally should perform without wearing vests. They are not given chairs and are expected to take food and refreshments seated on the ground, at the level at which ghosts and demons receive their offerings. For much of my field study I lived in the annex of a house owned by a high-caste Sinhalese. For quite some time, exorcist friends felt wary of entering any further than the front gate.

Names often identify a person's caste, and I encountered among the berava a considerable amount of name changing, which can be interpreted as a response to the difficulties berava confront in their everyday lives as members of their caste. Even so, berava who are exorcists or ply other traditional skills, take an enormous pride in these skills and in the cultural knowledge which, as a caste, they control.

Not all exorcists are berava. Most other castes, including the highest ranked, have individuals who practice the art of healing through exorcism. But in the Galle area, at least, most of the exorcists I encountered were berava. In nearly all cases, members of other castes who practiced exorcism had learnt the art from berava or from a relative who had done so. Some of the regularly performing berava exorcist groups around Galle had one member from another caste who was in the process of learning the art. Although berava exorcists vary widely in the skills they bring to the several arts of exorcism, the most adept practitioners are all berava. Exorcists from other castes nearly always hire berava for the ritual performances which they are responsible for organizing. In addition, they will often consult berava exorcists regarding the appropriate charms to be used in treating minor illnesses.

The relationship of berava exorcists to their clients is potentially problematic, particularly when the clients are of a higher-ranking caste. The difficulty stems from the disjunction between the exorcists' low-caste rank, and the authority and control which they command over their clients in the organization of exorcism ritual. I do not wish to overstress this point, for the generally accepted low-caste rank itself of berava exorcists, and the public communication of their low-caste rank at ritual performances, are enough to offset much of the surface disjunction. Moreover, low-caste rank and the authority and power of exorcists are related. Exorcists have power over demons, and their power over them and over human beings is greatest when the demons are exercising control. Exorcists are accorded the greatest respect by members of a household when the the householders are subject to demonic malevolence, when the social and cosmic order has been disrupted by demonic intrusion (see Chapters 4, 5, and 6). The ritual authority of exorcists, therefore, is consistent with the subversion of hierarchy as this is culturally constituted in the normal everyday world, a subversion wrought by demonic attack.

While the low-caste rank of berava exorcists and their authority in the ritual context is not irreconcilable given the cultural logic of the demonic circumstances, members of higher-ranked castes nonetheless recognize a conflict between their social position and the ritual authority vested in exorcists. The problem arises because Sinhalese Buddhist culture not only places a premium on knowledge, and social and spiritual advancement through the acquisition of knowledge, but also tends to equate knowledge, particularly cultural knowledge, with positions of dominance and power.

Some non-berava exorcists have risen to prominence within their own communities by exploiting the disjunction between the ritual authority of an exorcist and his low-caste rank. This was so among the karava described in the previous chapter, a community that views itself as highly-ranked in the caste hierarchy of the island. During my stay, a retired fisherman assumed a full-time exorcist's role, gathering fellow members of his caste as drummers, actors, and dancers for ritual performances.[7] He explicitly argued that people in his neighborhood should hire members of their own caste rather than a certain berava exorcist who had for a long time served the neighborhood. The new exorcist claimed that as a result of fishing expeditions to the Maldive Islands, he had acquired powerful curative mantra. This new exorcist, who to my knowledge had no social connections with berava, developed his own variants along the general lines of berava ritual exorcisms. His exorcisms differed markedly in detail and in the explanatory logic underlying the various events organized into ritual performance. For the period of my stay, the new exorcist had some success in gathering clients from his own community. This instance demonstrates both an awareness of the potential disjunction between ritual authority and low caste rank, and the exploitation of this disjunction. It also indicates processes that, especially in an urban context, can lead to changes and variations in Sinhalese ritual practice.

Insofar as the coupling of low-caste rank with ritual authority presents a problem for clients, it is often partly overcome through the mediation of an exorcist who belongs to the same caste as the patient. This exorcist takes an important role in the initial diagnosis of demonic illness and in the organization of treatment. He is responsible for hiring a group of exorcists and assumes a "master of ceremonies" role in the ritual performance.

Berava exorcists guard aspects of their knowledge of the healing art, particularly mantra and songs (**kavi**) in their possession. They regard the mantra and songs as central to treatment, and consider possession of them essential to their reputation as healers. Berava exorcists share this knowledge with relatives and members of their own community. I have encountered a number of angry disputes over the sharing of this knowledge with exorcists from a different caste. However, sharing more general knowledge of the art of exorcism with other castes is not frowned upon, provided the outsider has had a long association with individual berava and has apprenticed himself to a berava exorcist. There are a few high-caste exorcists in Galle who have close, long-standing contacts with the berava community. Berava exorcists recognize the importance of establishing relationships with exorcists of other castes, who can refer clients to them. In return, provided the relationship has been developed over time, berava will share some of their exorcism knowledge.

Berava exorcists differentiate among themselves in terms of level of skill and knowledge, and in terms of that aspect of the exorcist art they mainly practice. Some general principles which underlie Sinhalese culture as a whole, as might be expected, influence the relative status of different exorcists. Thus, those exorcists who engage in work which is regarded as highly polluting, or as a service to other castes requiring little skill or knowledge, are generally considered low in status.

For example, those berava whose main work is performing the service to other castes of drumming at funerals, are low in status. This work is understood as requiring little skill and as being highly polluting and in the course of personal disputes scornful references may be made to employment of this kind. Some exorcists regularly act as the ritual servant (**madu puraya**) at demon exorcisms, preparing the food for offerings and otherwise attending to the ritual requirements of the performing exorcists (see

Chapter 7). This, too, is regarded as polluting, lowly work. Occasionally, a member of a patient's household is asked to perform these tasks. I witnessed one occasion when a relative in the patient's household —— a karava and a prominent lay member of his local Buddhist temple, who had been tactless enough to adopt a bullying attitude towards the berava exorcists —— was given some of the duties of the **madu puraya** as an "honor."

Berava often distinguish among themselves in terms of the class of ritual work in which they primarily engage. Those exorcists who mainly perform rituals **(yak tovil)** associated with the lower demons in the Sinhalese cosmology (see Chapter 6) are widely viewed as lower in status than those who regularly perform rituals **(bali tovil)** for the higher planetary demons. Exorcists who command their own practice and regularly organize other performers under them tend to be high in status. Individually, however, exorcists can achieve high status and wide repute through their excellence in one or more of the arts of exorcism, for example, in drumming, dancing, or acting. The government occasionally organizes cultural competitions, in which individual exorcists can display their artistry. The certificates awarded the winners of these competitions are highly prized and prominently displayed.

High standing among berava exorcists is generally achieved through the long-term accumulation of the skills and knowledge entailed in the exorcist's art. No one exorcist controls anything approaching the entire body of relevant knowledge, which involves knowledge of astrology, the principles of traditional **ayurvedic** medicine, religious history, and tradition. This is quite apart from the other practical skills and knowledge that performing exorcists must master: knowledge of the numerous mantra and songs appropriate to particular exorcisms and the events enacted within them; of the art of decorating and building ritual structures and of making the various other ritual objects used in performance; of the art and gesture of dance; of drumming, of the ordering of ritual events in specific exorcisms; and so on. Individual practitioners are acknowledged by other exorcists as masters or teachers **(guru)** in a particular field such as mantra work, drumming, dancing, or dramatic acting. Even within these fields, however, some exorcists are regarded as more knowledgeable in particular areas of exorcist practice; for example, one exorcist might be highly regarded for knowing the mantra and verse forms relevant to planetary **(bali)** rituals, and another for knowledge of the mantra and songs appropriate to demon exorcisms **(yak tovil)**.

Recognized exponents of the art of exorcism attract students. All the exorcists I interviewed named a number of teachers from whom they had learned the various aspects of their art. Berava exorcists usually begin their apprenticeship at a young age, often as early as six or seven. Most frequently they join the exorcist group **(kattiya, iyalle)** of their father or another close male relative. Instruction usually begins with the dance, novices participating in exorcism dance, during which they learn the five basic poses **(matra)** of the dance and the thirty-two rhythmic movements **(tala)** and gestures **(angika)** that accompany the drum (Wirz 1954:18-20). Dance and music are closely integrated. Exorcists have a verbal "notational" system. This consists of a set of vocables (having no meaning outside their structural relation in the dance and music), which in their organization into utterances specify both the ordered sequence of dance steps and body gesture and the appropriate organization of drum beats. In learning dance, therefore, young exorcists also progressively learn the structure of the related drum music. When a young novice is performing with a group, the skilled dancers take him through the basic dance steps, vocalizing them and matching them to specific drum rhythms. From the dance, the young exorcist proceeds to learn aspects of the art of drumming and also the necessary mantra and songs specific to the exorcism rituals in which he performs. Wirz (1954:20) comments that novices learn the mantra and songs by listening to them in performance and not through direct instruction. Most of the exorcists whom I interviewed had learned the mantra and songs in this way, but a few had memorized mantra recorded on **ola** palm leaves given them by their father or teacher. The whole process of gaining the knowledge and skills of an exorcist takes many years. Young exorcists generally do not become independent of their teachers or develop their own practices until they are well into their twenties.

Aspiring exorcists learn their art by joining an exorcism group, usually one controlled by a relative who is the **gurunanse** or acknowledged leader of it. Exorcist groups comprise, at the least, one exorcist, generally the **gurunanse,** who is skilled in the uttering of mantra and songs, two or three drummers, and as many dancers, one of whom acts in the comic dramatic episodes of large-scale demon ceremonies. As a rule, those who form these groups are close relatives. It should be added that these groups are highly labile, in part because it is usual for apprentice exorcists to change groups frequently so they can learn different skills from exorcists with different specialties. Many exorcists normally work alone; when the occasion demands a large-scale exorcism, they will search among their relatives for the necessary performers.

Certain aspects of the above description can be illustrated by brief case histories of the learning careers of two exorcists.

Jothipala **Gurunanse**

Jothipala is a highly respected **adura** in the Galle area, well regarded for his knowledge of mantra. He tends to rely on this knowledge and values it above other aspects of the art of exorcism. Jothipala considers mantra the center of exorcist practice, for without such spells the malevolent demons and ghosts could not be controlled. He frequently is hired by other exorcists to present the necessary mantra at major demon ceremonies. While Jothipala occasionally organizes a large-scale exorcism, he prefers to work on his own and, like many other **adura,** depends for his income on short curing rites (see Chapter 4) which can be managed by a single exorcist.

Jothipala is now fifty-three and was born in Galle town, not far from his present home. He has learned his art from numerous exorcists, all of whom are relatives, on both his mother's and his father's sides. While he has been effectively practicing exorcism for most of his life, it has only been in the last twenty years that Jothipala has worked on his own or has been an independent organizer of major demon ceremonies.

Jothipala can remember attending exorcisms with his father from about the age of four. He was not directly instructed by him, but would listen to his father's performances at countless exorcism occasions and copy his actions. Indeed, from the age of seven he began to accompany his father in the chanting of mantra and in the songs and verses of exorcism. At approximately the same time, he was taken under the wing of a well-respected **adura,** Somapala, to whom he was related through his elder sister's marriage. It is to Somapala, as well as to his father, that Jothipala feels he owes much of his present knowledge of mantra and the organization of exorcisms.

When Jothipala was ten he left home and school and journeyed to Ambalangoda (a coastal town north of Galle) with his mother's sister. There he came into contact with relatives of his sister's husband who were

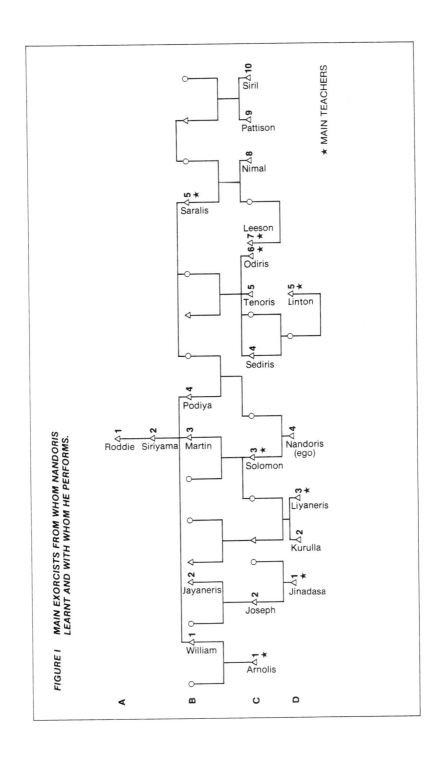

FIGURE I   MAIN EXORCISTS FROM WHOM NANDORIS LEARNT AND WITH WHOM HE PERFORMS.

★ MAIN TEACHERS

Key to Figure 1

A 1	Roddie	Well-known drummer and **adura** to whom Liyaneris (D3) and Solomon (C3) trace their knowledge of drumming and exorcism in general
A 2	Siriyama	Drummer
B 1	William	Drummer and expert in **bali** ritual
B 2	Jayaneris	Drummer and dancer
B 3	Martin	Drummer and well-known dancer trained Liyaneris (D3) in dancing and taught Solomon (C3) the art of drumming
B 4	Podiya	Sculptor and artist
B 5	Saralis	Drummer and dramatic actor in exorcism; taught Nandoris some of the dramatic arts of exorcism
C 1	Arnolis	Drummer in **bali** ritual, also artist and sculptor, taught Nandoris the drum rhythms of **bali** ritual and also how to mould clay images of demons
C 2	Joseph	Well-known dancer and dramatic actor, the main teacher of Jinadasa (D1)
C 3	Solomon	Father of Nandoris and his main teacher of drumming, and mantra, and songs
C 4	Sediris	Drummer in all forms of exorcism ritual
C 5	Tenoris	Drummer and actor
C 6	Odiris	Well-known exorcist dramatic actor, a major influence on Nandoris' own acting style.
C 7	Leeson	Exorcist for **bali** ritual; has taught Nandoris drumming and mantra for these rituals
C 8	Nimal	Dancer who works regularly with Nandoris
C 9	Pattison	Dancer and drummer who works regularly with Nandoris
C10	Siril	Dramatic actor and drummer who works regularly with Nandoris
D 1	Jinadasa	Well-known dramatic actor, specializing in Mahasona, and has taught Nandoris much of his art
D 2	Kurulla	Exorcist with whom Nandoris works regularly in the Matara area
D 3	Liyaneris	Well-known dancer and early teacher of dance to Nandoris
D 5	Linton	Drummer and dancer who taught Nandoris

primarily engaged in puppetry (see Sarachchandra 1966:121-24). He learned some aspects of this art and joined in some performances. But Jothipala claims that he was uninterested in this work. After five years in Ambalangoda, Jothipala returned home to Galle, where he participated in the exorcisms of his relatives, especially those organized by his mother's brothers. One brother, Odiris, was an astrologer who also was a ceremonial drummer at funerals and other occasions. Jothipala assisted Odiris in this work, but also was engaged as an expert in mantra by his father's sister's husband Hin, a well-known exorcist who had developed a large practice in the area. From Odiris, Jothipala extended his knowledge of astrology, the drawing of magical designs, and to some extent, drumming. Jothipala stated that the art of drumming is complex and requires a stout physique, which he does not possess. He felt he was ill-suited to the drum, but considered the knowledge useful in his general mastery of the exorcist arts. From Hin, Jothipala built up his knowledge of dance, and especially the organizational form of such exorcisms as the **Suniyama** (the exorcism for the demon of sorcery).

Jothipala maintains close relationships with members of the berava community. However, he is now not on friendly terms with Hin. He left Hin's group in 1960 after performing regularly with it for seventeen years, during which time he acquired a considerable reputation as a maker of spells and charms **(mantra karayo).** When he left he established his own practice in the same neighborhood where Hin works. Hin feels that Jothipala has drawn much of his business away.

Jothipala currently lives in a small thatched wooden house in a clearing owned by a member of the karava caste, and close to a cemetery reserved for the karava caste. His wife's brother (a mask maker) and his family occupy a neighboring house. There are two other houses in the area, and these are occupied by low-caste rada families. The main neighborhoods in which Jothipala practices are dominated by families belonging to the salagama[8] and karava castes.

Nandoris **Gurunanse**

Nandoris is one of the most respected drummers in southern Sri Lanka, and to my untrained ear he is certainly deserving of the fine reputation he has achieved. He is also in much demand as the "straight man" in the comic drama which concludes major exorcism performances.

Nandoris is forty-nine. He left school at the age of twelve, but by seven he was participating regularly in exorcisms organized by his father. There is an extremely close bond between the two men, and Nandoris' father, Solomon, speaks with great pride of his son's achievements. Nandoris' father recounts that when his son was only seven, people would marvel at his drumming. Solomon, however, as well as Solomon's father, wanted Nandoris to become a dancer. Solomon had been crippled in one leg when he was small, which caused some disappointment to his father, a highly reputed dancer, skilled in the ceremonial dances for the demons and for the gods. Solomon was encouraged to become a skilled drummer instead, and family pressure developed for Nandoris to become a dancer.

When he left school, Nandoris left home and journeyed from a small berava village some twenty-five miles outside Galle to the large berava neighborhood in Galle town. His father's elder sister's son, Liyaneris (D,3), had married into this neighborhood, and he and one of his affines, Linton (D,5), became responsible for Nandoris' education as an exorcist. Linton was at the time a well-known dancer and also highly regarded as a comic actor in exorcism drama. Nandoris served his apprenticeship as a dancer for five years, but during this time came into contact with a number of other experts in the various fields of exorcism (see Figure 1). In particular he learned mantra, dance, and the art of comic drama from Pattison (C,9), who is the elder brother of a young but now extremely popular comic actor with whom Nandoris frequently performs, and developed his expertise as a drummer from Arnolis (C,1). Arnolis is an expert in the drum rhythms for bali ceremonies and the large community rituals performed to honor the gods.

By seventeen Nandoris had decided to develop his drumming skills. He was extremely stout and did not feel that he had the dancer's requisite grace. Besides, Nandoris claimed, he found himself exhausted after only an hour or so of dancing. His true skills lay, he decided, in drumming and in comic acting.

Nandoris then joined, for short periods, a number of exorcist groups and gradually enlarged on his skill at drumming and his knowledge of songs. He does not regret his early training as a dancer, believing that it contributed greatly to his excellence as a drummer. Nandoris has now returned to his natal village, where he lives with his wife. To his regret they have no children, but he cares for the children of his deceased brother, who was killed in an accident. He practices as an **adura** in his local area, providing curative and protective charms and, like Jothipala, performs short curing rites. His main income, however, is derived from drumming at major exorcisms organized by other exorcists. With his excellent reputation, Nandoris is in considerable demand among exorcist groups from Galle to Matara, to the south. He has even performed in exorcisms held in Colombo, and once in Jaffna at the northern tip of the island. For all this, his monthly income is relatively meager, and he has few material possessions. His reputation has been enhanced by his winning of a number of drumming competitions in festivals of folk art organized by the government. Nandoris' acknowledged skill as a drummer has attracted around him a small number of apprentice drummers who are learning his art.

The above cases are much like other exorcist histories I have collected. One feature they all stress, to which I have already referred, is that the skills and knowledge important in exorcism practice are seldom commanded by any one man. They are the property of the berava as a community. This fact and the nature of exorcism practice itself creates a high degree of interdependence among exorcists. Of course they compete for clients, but competition is offset by their reliance upon one another to provide the skills required for a particular exorcism performance. Even those exorcists who are in direct competition for clients will hire one another for the ritual performances they organize. Moreover, even though exorcists may work in specific local areas, they are constantly moving from one area to another, to assist in the performances organized by other exorcists, usually relatives. Any one exorcist has an extremely wide range of relationships, which extend along the coast from Galle and into the hinterland. These ties tend to draw berava together despite their regional dispersal, and this intensifies their consciousness and pride in their identity as berava. In addition, the wide-ranging network of relationships between exorcists and their participation in one another's ritual performances assures a degree of continuity in the traditional art they practice. These ties also encourage the rapid dissemination and incorporation of new styles of ritual performance and the relatively quick acceptance of these as legitimate practices. I was often struck, for example, by the similarity in comic dialogue in ritual performances held in areas separated by considerable distance and engaging different actors. The material was often highly topical, reflecting local political and social events which had gone unreported in the press. Exorcists recognize innovations in the style and content of their ritual practice and attribute them to particular exorcists.

As indicated by the two summary individual histories, exorcists undergo their training within a set of closely related kindred. It is these kin with whom they continue to work after they have acquired most of their skill and knowledge. Furthermore these kin, though they may be dispersed, are usually concentrated within one general regional area and have been so for as long as most can remember, despite their frequent individual movements through the island. For example, most of the kin who were important to both Jothipala's and Nandoris' training live between Galle and Matara, towns which are separated by some thirty miles. Jothipala had some connection in the Ambalangoda area, but he maintains that his experience there was relatively unimportant to his current practice. The foregoing observations help explain regional variation in exorcism practice along the western and southern coastline of the island.

Exorcists note that the styles of ritual performance and the episodes included in the major demon ceremonies vary up and down the coast. My own observations confirm their reports. Thus, the exorcisms I observed, for instance, in the area to the north of Galle, towards Ambalangoda, differed in certain important ways. The design of some of the offering baskets and ritual structures built for an exorcism ceremony were distinct. Specific episodes that were not part of the the Galle ceremonies were included in the Ambalangoda versions, and **vice versa**. In addition, certain exorcisms seemed to be more regularly performed in one area than in others. For example, I have the impression that the **Sanni Yakuma** exorcism is performed more often in the area between Galle and Ambalangoda than in the area between Galle and Matara, where to my knowlege the **Mahasona** exorcism is the most frequently enacted. Exorcists with whom I discussed this distribution confirmed regional differences of this sort; they stated that the Matara-Galle practice of exorcism differs from that around Ambalangoda, and that there are further differences in exorcism practice to the north of Ambalangoda, towards Colombo. While the particulars of this require further research, it seems clear to me that the concentration of learning and practice within a particular region, and the tendency to continue practice in association with those among whom an exorcist learned his art, encourages the development and maintenance of slightly different artistic and exorcism traditions. This would also explain variations in the form of exorcism ritual, and to some extent, knowledge within the particular regions.[9]

What the nature of exorcist knowledge and practice precisely is requires further description and analysis, as does the character of the several arts which exorcists bring to the often marvelous occasions of their ritual performances. This is the primary concern of the following chapters.

4. Demonic Illness:
Diagnosis and Social Context

The diagnosis and social definition of demonic illness is a discourse which engages the expert knowledge of exorcists and the lay understandings of exorcists' clients and others. This discourse is both structured in a context, and as it develops, structures or frames a particular conception of the context in which demonic illness is recognized and eventually treated by appropriate ritual action. The knowledge of exorcists, while formed within the Sinhalese Buddhist culture of clients, constitutes a relatively abstract framework of ideas against which lay Sinhalese can legitimate their more common-sense understandings and interpret the world of their everyday experience. Exorcist knowledge, articulated into practice, gives meaning to the personal disturbances of mind and body and links these to the disorders and disruptions of a social world in which individuals daily participate. Moreover, the situated elaboration of exorcist knowledge can gather into it the many different and often conflicting interpretations which lay Sinhalese place upon their experience. It can contain and resolve them in a coherent but abnormal order commanded by demons.

The discussion begins with an outline of the main ideas engaged in exorcist diagnostic practice and the range of ritual treatments which exorcists can apply to end demonic attack. I discuss how demonic illness is generally conceptualized and some of the factors which may account for the efficacy of exorcism in the treatment of demonic illness. The description leads into a discussion of the process of diagnosis and social definition of demonic illness which surrounds the eventual performance of one of the major rites. I do this through an extended analysis of three instances of demonic attack.

Exorcist Theory and Diagnostic Practice

Exorcists' practice is concerned with that individual illness, in both its physical and mental manifestations, which results from the attack of malign demons (yakku) and ghosts (preta). Exorcist diagnosis discovers the specific malevolent supernatural agents involved in illness and uncovers those events in the experience of the patient and of others which have exposed the patient to demonic attack, or else are indicative of demonic maleficence. Exorcists then organize appropriate ritual treatments.

Exorcists typically trace the onset of demonic attack to a patient's experience of sudden fear or fright, and will inquire after the time and place of unusual frightening or unsettling experiences in dreams and in the course of a patient's everyday activity. Patients report disturbing dreams or nightmares in which they see the shapes of animals (indicative of demons), or are visited by frightening monsters with which they sometimes (in the case of women) copulate. Dreams apart, patients describe a vast range of unsettling experiences which lead them, as well as exorcists, to suspect demonic malevolence. Among the most common are: seeing dark mysterious figures moving in the stillness of the night; unexpectedly smelling a foul stench; being startled, inexplicably, by rocks and stones falling on their roof; being surprised by a snake crossing their path, or being attacked by a dog. If the patient experiences a sudden jolt when encountering such an event, this is taken to mean that the patient is in the grip, mentally and physically, of a demon. Typically, demons are understood, by exorcists and their clients, to take their victims suddenly and by surprise, and to attack from a world (**yaksa loka**) outside that of normal human experience. Demons intrude into the experiential world of their victims and are conceptualized as capturing them in their malign eyesight or gaze (**yaksa disti**). So caught, demonic victims experience emotional, mental, and humoral imbalance.

Extreme emotional states of, for example, fear, anger, attachment to deceased kin, acute sexual longing either overt or repressed, envy, and jealousy, are evidence of mental imbalance and are symptomatic of demonic illness. Such emotional states can be a precondition of demonic illness, attractive of demonic attention, as well as a condition of demonic attack. Fear is the one emotional state which most commonly signs the onset of demonic illness. Unbalanced emotional states reflect a weakness in mental attitude, and this renders individuals vulnerable to the malevolence of malign supernaturals. Women as a category are regarded by exorcists and Sinhalese men as mentally weak. This, together with other cultural attitudes (for example, that women are more impure than men, that they come into greater contact with impurity, and that they evince a greater attachment to matters of the everyday world), is sometimes given as reason for the propensity of women to suffer demonic illness (see Chapter 5). While it remains unchecked, emotional disturbance, and particularly fear, once it is connected with malign demons or spirits, is likely to increase mental and/or physical distress. Exorcists understand this to relate to a growing attitude in the patient whereby the patient dwells abnormally and increasingly upon the bloodthirsty and malicious world of demons. Such an overriding concern with the world of demons has the effect of deepening the demonic hold over the mental and physical experience of the patient.

Individuals are likely to be attacked by demons when they are psychologically and/or physically alone. Aloneness (**tanikama**) is conceptualized in this dual sense by Sinhalese (see Obeyesekere 1969:176; Kapferer 1979c:112). Essentially it is a state of isolation, of existential solitude in the world, and is a precondition of demonic attack as well as connoting the experience of the demonically afflicted. The term **tanikam dosa** (alone illness) is often used as a synonym for illness caused by demons (**yaksa dosa**). The demonic condition referred to in the concepts of **tanikama** and **tanikam dosa** is in some ways similar to Goethe's understanding of the demonic, but from within a European world view, as everything which is individual and separates one from others (Jaspers 1971). Exorcists and Sinhalese laity view demonic victims as confined within their own subjective experience, controlled and dominated by the terrible thought of demons. Demonic victims, caught in their isolation by demons and further separated from others through the agency of the demonic, are culturally conceived as adopting an individually unique position upon the world of their experience and the nature of its encompassment in a wider cosmic ordering. The view of a patient is understood to be one which sees demons as dominating and powerful figures superior to human beings and free from the constraint of a cosmic order commanded by the Buddha and the deities, in which demons and ghosts are ideally the most inferior of beings (see Chapter 6). The subjective standpoint of demonic victims is in effect solipsistic and is opposed to reality as it should be conceived by healthy others who are outside demonic control.

Patients and exorcists commonly associate the first experience of demonic attack with occasions when patients were by themselves or away from areas of human habitation. Victims regularly reported being frightened while alone at night or walking on a lonely path. Demons and ghosts, although they hover around and intrude into the communities and dwellings of human beings, are outside, are apart from the cultural and social order in which human beings live. This order provides support and protection from demonic attack. When individuals are removed from the companionship of others, either physically or through their mental withdrawal, they become vulnerable to demonic malevolence.

Central to exorcist practice is a humoral theory of disease and illness. Exorcists regard a healthy person as having a balance in the three body humors of wind **(vata)**, blood/bile **(pitta)** and phlegm **(sema)**. An excess in any one of these humors (known collectively as the **tri** or **tun dosa**, the three illnesses) results in a generalized humoral imbalance. An accentuation or concentration of specific mental and physical symptoms in a patient indicates which humor is primarily responsible for an overall humoral imbalance. Symptoms indicative of an imbalance in the humor of blood/bile are a rapid pulse, a high fever, bloodshot eyes, blood in the faeces, urine or vomit, and headache. This humor mainly affects the head, but like the other humors it can also have its effect in other parts of the body. Disorder of the reproductive organs, for example, often will be connected with blood/bile, as will some stomach ailments. The humor of blood/bile is most likely to be thrown out of balance if patients are frightened at midday or in the early evening, and if they eat any of the foods in the heating **(giniam ahara)** category (which includes fish with red flesh, animal meat, breadfruit, mango, and papaya).

The humor of phlegm indicates its excess in symptoms such as body chills, head colds and bronchial congestion, mucous in the faeces, and white pustulent boils. An imbalance of phlegm is most likely to occur in the early hours of the morning and can follow upon the eating of various foods in the cooling category **(sitala ahara)**, such as cow and buffalo curds, potatoes, ash plantains, ash pumpkin, melons, cucumber, and jackfruit. Phlegm mainly affects the head and chest.

Individuals are most likely to get the symptoms of an excess in wind over the midnight period. It is indicated by vomiting, stomach cramps, dysentery, and aches and pains of the limbs. Patients might have an excess in this humor after eating certain fruits and vegetables, such as jackfruit, breadfruit, and cassava. Wind is particularly affected by eating foods prepared by an admixture of oil **(tel kama)** or by frying **(badun)**. The humor of wind especially affects the limbs. Exorcists, however, stress that the humor of wind has a pervasive quality in that it can affect most parts of the body. They also argue that there is a close connection between wind and the humor of blood/bile, and that they frequently appear together in the particular symptoms of the patient.

The examination of the symptoms of humoral imbalance and of the factors attendant on this imbalance provides an important indication of the demonic agent(s) primarily responsible for the illness. Specific demons affect certain humors. Of the five main illness-causing demons, Mahasona affects the humor of wind, Riri Yaka principally the humor of bile/blood, and Kola Sanniya, the chief of the **sanni** (disease-spreading) demons, the humor of phlegm. However, these three demons also have certain forms that affect the other humors as well. Thus Riri Yaka has nine forms and each of these causes an excess in one or another of the three humors.[2] Three of the eighteen **sanni** demons (Vata, Slesma and Pitta Sanni) take their names from, and directly affect the humors after which they are named, but all the **sanni** demons are grouped into one or the other of the three humoral categories. The two other major demons which inflict illness and misfortune, Suniyam (or Huniyam, the Sorcery demon) and Kalu Yaka (or Kalu Kumara, the Black Prince who primarily attacks women and causes illness in their nursing or young children) affect the humors generally.

In their diagnosis exorcists also examine the social context of the patient and the patient's household for indications of malign demonic attention. Quarrels at work or in the neighborhood, conflict over land, and intercaste rivalry are among some of the factors which can precipitate demonic attack. There is a widespread belief in sorcery among Sinhalese, and this enters into exorcist diagnostic practice. Suniyam can have his malign attention involved through black magic **(kodivina)**. Sinhalese have a cultural belief in eye, mouth, and thought evil **(as vaha, kata vaha,** and **ho vaha)**. Evil or poisonous thought held by others towards a patient can cause mental upset and madness. Poisonous or malicious talk, which, like evil thoughts, mainly activates Suniyam, can cause marital and general family discord, failure in business, and loss of property and wealth. Evil eye involves the malign attention of Riri Yaka as well as Suniyam and can result in irritating rashes, skin boils, and open sores.

Demons and ghosts are understood to act capriciously and without warning. Individuals are attacked while they go about their normal everyday lives, as a result of eating ordinary foods, while bathing at particular times, because they have entered a bad planetary period, in the course of fulfilling everyday social obligations such as attending a funeral or a girl's puberty ceremony, and so on. For exorcists and Sinhalese generally, patients have only a limited responsibility for illness (Waxler 1972:2). There is a tendency in the course of exorcist diagnosis, supported by patients and others, to place the responsibility for the illness not just upon demons and ghosts who are the cause of particular symptoms of illness, but also upon other human beings who act in the immediate environment of the patient.

Most of what Sinhalese experience and identify as symptomatic of illness can be dealt with in the diagnostic and treatment framework of exorcists. The diagnosis of demonic illness stresses malign supernatural intervention in the causation of illness and assembles and codifies many of the ideas and attitudes by which Sinhalese interpret, understand and order their daily lives. The diagnosis of demonic attack will, of course, vary in its details in the hands of particular exorcists, but the principles which underlie it are essentially the same. The principles employed by the exorcist in his diagnosis articulate the mental, emotional, and physical symptoms of illness, situated as they are in the patient's body, with the wider cosmological, cultural, and social realities in which the patient lives and acts.

Exorcist Treatment

Exorcists may be called in by a household at any time during the development of an illness. Usually it is the exorcist who comes to the house to visit the patient; this contrasts with other traditional practice. For example, when Sinhalese consult **vedaralas** or astrologers in cases of personal illness or misfortune, the common pattern is for the person concerned to visit the house or establishment of the **vedarala** or astrologer. Frequently, an exorcist is appealed to after other methods have been tried, after treatment by a medical doctor or a **vedarala**. Patients and others may resort to an exorcist because in their view these other treatments have failed to alleviate aspects of the illness or because they were in some way dissatisfied with the treatment they had received. However, nothing prevents patients' being treated by an exorcist while other methods of alleviation are in progress.

The rituals which treat malign demonic and ghostly attack can be ordered along a scale of increasing complexity and understood efficacy. These range from relatively small rites, generally referred to as **pideni**, to the most complex major ceremonies for demons **(yak tovil)**. The small rites are short in duration and typically are performed by a single exorcist. They are performed before a restricted audience comprising the patient and household members, although often the household members go about their normal activities paying little attention to the ritual action. The small rites are limited in the number of demons and ghosts which they address, and are usually the first treatment option of an exorcist and his clients.

The most simple and commonly practiced small rite is the **tel mantirima** (Wirz 1954:87-89). It is usually enacted in mild cases of demonic attack and involves applying coconut oil, over which seven curative charms have been intoned, to the patient's forehead. More complex is the **nul bandima** which, like the **tel mantirima**, can be performed at any time of the day or night. It involves the erection of a structure **(mal yahanava)** to the four Sinhalese guardian deities (Natha, Vishnu, Kataragama, and Saman), the giving of baskets of offerings **(tattuva)** to the demons, and the tying of protective threads **(nul)** around the wrist of the patient to guard against demonic attack (Wirz 1954:84-86). A frequently performed minor rite is the **preta pideni**. This is normally performed after nightfall and is designed to end illness caused by ghosts. There are three kinds of ghosts which cause illness and misfortune: the **mala preta** (ghosts of any deceased person), **gevala preta** (house ghosts, who do not stand in a kinship relationship to the living), and **gnati preta** (ancestor ghosts). An ancestor ghost is almost invariably implicated and named as underlying the illness for which this rite is performed. The **preta pideni**, while it is performed as a separate rite, is always part of any major exorcism to placate the demons (see Chapter 7).

The above rites are understood to be curative in themselves and do not, in the repertoire of exorcist practice, intend the performance of further rites. This is not so for the small rite known as the **apa nul**, or tying of the "security thread" (Wirz 1954:63-84) which always intends the later performance of a major demon ceremony. In the rite a thread is tied on the wrist of the patient and an offering given to the demon(s) held to be primarily responsible for the illness. The protection of the main deity or deities controlling the demon(s) is also invoked. The ritual places a limitation **(sima)** on the illness to a defined period during which it is held that the symptoms of the illness should abate. This period will vary from three days, seven days, and, according to Wirz (1954:84), up to a period not

TABLE 1*

Major Exorcism Patients: Sex, Age, and Occupation

Males			Age	Females				Occupation of Household Head				
Single	Married	Widowed		Widowed	Married	Single	Unemployed	Laborer	Other Unskilled	Skilled	Small Trader Business	Clerical
2			0-9			1		2			1	
2			10-19			4	3	2	1			
4			20-29		4	9	3	3	4	2	3	2
	6		30-39		7	1	1	6	2	3	1	1
	4		40-49		3		1	2	3	1		
	1		50-59		1			1			1	
	2		60-69		2			2	1		1	
		1	70+	3				1	1		2	
Total												
8	13	1		3	17	15	8	19	12	6	9	3

*Includes only patients who had one of the four following exorcisms: **Mahasona, Suniyama, Sanni Yakuma,** and **Rata Yakuma.** Information on the **Iramudun Samayama** is not included. As I have stated in the text, this exorcism often precedes the other major demon ceremonies.

exceeding three months.   The **apa nul** acts temporarily to alleviate the illness or, at least, to contain it, and, to the extent the symptoms of the illness abate, acts as confirmation of the diagnosis.   Theoretically, a major exorcism should be performed at the end of the period defined in the ceremony.   In an important way, the **apa nul** functions in a similar way to vows **(bara)** before the shrines **(devala)** to the deities.   It constitutes a promise that a ritual to placate the demon primarily causing the illness will be performed, the demon in return reducing his malign effect.   Failure to carry out this promise can, in the interpretation of specialists and laity, result in the reonset of the illness, perhaps with greater severity than before.   Should a remission occur, patients and their kin often forego a further ceremony.   But if illness recurs, it will be immediately connected with the earlier episode of illness, and there will be increased pressure to hold a major exorcism.

The major exorcisms which can follow the tying of the **apa nul** are, in contrast to the minor exorcisms, enacted in public before neighbors, friends, and acquaintances, and demand the attentive presence of household members and other kin of the patient.   Indeed, the patient's kin and others will be given roles in the performances of these rites, which is not an aspect of the smaller rites.   The major rites require the hiring of several exorcists skilled in a wide range of arts.   The major exorcisms are the most expensive rites, costing a household between 500 rupees and 1,000 rupees, which is well in excess of the monthly income of most of the working-class and peasant households which have them performed.[2]   The cost of a major ceremony includes the cash payment made to the exorcists, the buying and providing of ritual materials, and the provisioning of food consumed during the rite by those who come to witness the proceedings.[3]   Small rites such as the **tel mantirima** on average cost 10 rupees or less, whereas others like the **nul bandima** and **preta pideni** range between 20 rupees to 50 rupees.

Any of five major exorcisms can be performed following the tying of the **apa nul.**   The five ceremonies in order of the frequency of their performance are as follows: the **Iramudun Samayama** (for Riri Yaka); the **Mahasona** (for the Great Cemetery Demon); the **Suniyama** (for the sorcery demon); the **Sanni Yakuma** (for Kola Sanniya and the disease spreading **sanni** demons); and the **Rata Yakuma** (for Kalu Yaka and the seven illness-causing female demons).   This last rite is performed exclusively for female patients and addresses female-specific disorders, for example, barrenness, menstrual disorder, illness associated with pregnancy.   Children's illness is often directly linked to the mother and will thus frequently be treated in the context of this rite.   All the above exorcisms are regularly performed in the Galle area, although only a minority of those who fall victim to demonic attack are likely to have a major exorcism performed (see Table 4). Nevertheless, in the neighborhood in which I lived, hardly a week went by without the performance of a large-scale demon rite, and on one occasion I was able to attend three major rites on the one night.

The tables below present data on the patients and households for whom I observed the performances of major ceremonies in the Galle area over a twelve-month period between 1971 and 1972.   I have excluded separate information for patients and households who had the **Iramudun Samayama** which, with the **Mahasona**, was the most frequently performed rite.   This rite, which unlike the other rites is enacted during the day, is usually performed in conjunction with one of the other major demon ceremonies.[4]

Table 1 indicates that most large-scale exorcisms are performed at houses, the household heads of which are generally low in socioeconomic status. This table also shows that most of the patients are females (61.4%), although a significant minority are males (38.6%). This pattern, one which I

TABLE 2

Major Exorcism Patients: Sex, Exorcism Type, and Other Treatment

| Males | | | | | | Major Exorcisms | | Females | | | | |
| Previous consultation and/or concurrent treatment | | | | | | | | Previous consultation and/or concurrent treatment | | | | |
Deity shrine	Buddhist monk	Astrologer	Ayurvedic physician	Western trained physician	No.		No.	Western trained physician	Ayurvedic physician	Astrologer	Buddhist monk	Deity shrine
1	-	3	5	7	10	**Mahasona**	23	16	10	10	-	1
1	-	5	2	6	7	**Suniyama**	3	3	-	2	-	-
-	-	2	1	3	3	**Sanni Yakuma**	4	4	3	2	1	1
-	-	1	-	1	2*	**Rata Yakuma**	5	4	-	3	1	-
			Total males	22			35	Total females				
			% all cases	38.6			61.4	% all cases				

* The two male cases for the **Rata Yakuma** were infants, and their mothers were treated jointly with them.

will explore more fully in Chapter 5, is consistent with the views of exorcists and nonspecialists that major ceremonies are mainly performed for women. There is an exception to this, however, in the case of the **Suniyama**, where male patients outnumber female patients (see Table 2). The sorcery demon is mediated into illness by the malign thoughts or actions of others towards the victim. This is not an aspect of the intervention of other demonic figures who attack capriciously and directly without the mediation of human beings. Those who are most likely to activate the sorcery demon are those outside the household and immediate range of kin, typically persons with whom one is not related by kinship (but not necessarily), and with whom one is drawn into competition and conflict. Sinhalese men, relative to women, are considered to be highly prone to ensorcellment, because of their more frequent engagement in contexts external to the household and local community where competition and conflict is understood to be rife. This might be a factor accounting for a relatively large number of men to be treated in the context of the **Suniyama** ritual. Conflict at work or in the course of their business activity is often given by men as a reason for suspecting the agency of **Suniyama** in their illness.

Significantly, most of the patients are adults or individuals in their teens. This is possibly the effect of socialization into the culture of demonic illness whereby individuals learn, through social experience, illness displays appropriate to the recognition of demonic attack. It is also a function of the unwillingness of the exorcist to treat young children by a major exorcism, especially children who as yet have little language facility, who would be unable to follow ritual instructions, and who likely would be inattentive to the ritual events. Exorcists insist that major rites are of reduced effectiveness when the patient cannot understand the meaning of the various ritual episodes and fails to maintain an attentive focus on the ritual proceedings.[5]

Table 2 presents information on the engagement of exorcism patients with other specialisms for the management and treatment of illness and misfortune. It underlines the general point that exorcism is part of a wider complex of treatments, some of which are influential in leading patients to the performance of an exorcism ceremony. Many of the patients whom I interviewed had exorcism suggested to them by astrologers and **vedaralas.** I encountered no case where a medical doctor recommended exorcism but some patients were receiving western medical treatment concurrently with exorcism treatment.

In Table 3, I present summary data on those physical and other symptoms recognized by exorcists and their clients, and interpreted by them as the effect of demonic attack, for which the major ceremonies set out in Table 2 were performed. I have separated the symptoms of demonic attack recognized by patients and their household kin into two categories. Thus, on the one hand, are those symptoms of physical and mental or emotional disorder which are seated within the patient. On the other hand are those symptoms located in the social context of the patient. The table does not exhaust all the symptoms which were identified, as I have not included those recognized by others who were not members of the patient's household. The table shows, however, that a multiplicity of physical and/or emotional symptoms of individual distress indicative of demon attack were identified in the patients who had major exorcisms. Further, the table indicates that individual patient illness was connected with recognized disorders in the social relationships of patients and in the relationships of others in the patient's social context. Broadly, major exorcisms tend to be performed when a **variety** of symptoms indicative of demonic attack are present in the condition of the patient and in the wider social context encircling a patient and household.

TABLE 3
Patient Symptoms

Patient's physical and other symptoms (stated by patient and/or household kin)	Males	Females
Stomach disorder (pains, diarrhea, constipation, vomiting, etc.)	9	20
Body fever (hot and cold flushes, high temperature, shivering)	4	5
Chest complaints (difficulty in breathing, chest pains, congestion)	1	4
Headache	1	5
Swollen limbs, joints	3	4
Boils	4	1
Partial paralysis	2	2
Medically diagnosed congenital illness	1	3
Fainting (unconsciousness)	1	7
Trance (as a primary behavioral sympton of illness)	1	7
Listlessness (semiconsciousness, sleepiness, feeling of physical heaviness)	2	6
Violent behavior (physical assault)	2	7
Fear	2	5
Menstrual pains	-	2
Pregnancy disorder	-	6
Barrenness and illness after childbirth	-	2
	33	86

Problems in social context relating to patient's illness (stated by patient and household kin)		
Marital dispute	2	2
Disputes between kin	4	7
Disputes between non-kin	3	14
Land disputes	3	7
Work disputes	3	1
General problems affecting patient and household (e.g., trouble with police, debts, unemployment, recent bereavement)	5	7
	20	38

*This table only records information on those cases summarized in Tables 1 and 2. Note also that fear is an element of all cases of demonic attack. I have only counted it when sudden fear of fright was reported as the single major indicator of demonic malevolence from the outset, **and** seemed to outweigh other indicators of illness.

- Exorcists and their clients are concerned that exorcism rites alleviate the individual physical and mental symptoms of demonic attack. Following the performance of a major rite, exorcists will sometimes administer herbal decoctions to assist further in the alleviation of the illness, as well as engage in other forms of "post-ritual care." They will continue to visit the patient, and perhaps perform small rites like a **tel mantirima**. But exorcists stress the fact that the efficacy of their treatment is **the removal of demonic agency in illness** and not necessarily the alleviation or cure of the physical symptoms, for example, associated with demonic attack. They are quite willing to accept the idea that the cure of physical disorder may be dependent on treatment by **vedaralas** and medical doctors.   In client understanding, the persistence of physical and mental signs of patient disorder is usually taken as a sign that further ritual treatment, or alleviation in some other mode of practice, should be sought. Any exorcism can fail, and this is part of exorcist and client understanding.

Client opinion that a ritual has failed to end demon attack occurs most often after a minor rite. I seldom heard complaints regarding the efficacy of the large ceremonies. Minor rites, because they are rituals of first resort in a hierarchy of exorcism treatment, carry the expectation that they are likely to be less potent than the major exorcisms in dealing with demons.[6] Dissatisfaction, therefore, with minor rites is culturally prefigured and is a consequence of the cultural knowledge that there are bigger and better rituals. It is in the view of such knowledge that some patients will insist on a large ceremony and resist apparent attempts to be fobbed off with a small exorcism.

To some extent, the satisfaction with major rites is related to how patients are selected into their treatment mode and the fact that the large ceremonies, unlike the small rites, have their own "fail safe" mechanisms. While exorcists will deal with almost any kind of ailment in the context of a minor ritual, they are more selective in the case of major ceremonies. Exorcists sometimes refuse large exorcisms to patients widely acknowledged as terminally ill. They are wary of treating patients who are suffering from on overtly serious physical condition. I have heard exorcists say, when faced with such patients, that the demonic hold is so powerful that even a major exorcism will be of little avail and that the exorcist was called too late.

But, despite the care with which an exorcist might select the subjects of his science, he must often deal with "difficult" cases and these by major exorcisms. This is so if for no other reason than that these ceremonies are the rites of final appeal. One might reasonably expect major exorcisms to be highly exposed to the risk of client dissatisfaction. However, the large exorcisms contain their explanation for failure (what some scholars refer to as "secondary elaborations") in the structure of their ritual events. There are episodes in which the exorcist divines or, in trance "sees" indication of the likely outcome of the ritual action. Thus in the **avatara balima** episode of the **Mahasona** exorcism (see Chapter 7) an exorcist typically enters a trance during wich he may see a manifestation of the afflicting demon. I was told that if the demon appeared to block the exorcist's path then it was likely that the demon's power was too strong and that the ritual should be called off. I saw no occasions where this happened, but exorcists reported to me a number of instances when they had stopped a major rite following the appearance of a sign of continuing demonic control.

Quite apart from the above considerations there are good reasons why major demon exorcisms should be more effective than minor rites in ending demonic attack and relieving patient experience of disease. Such reasons should become more evident in my account of the **Mahasona** exorcism in later chapters. For the present, I stress the importance of the performance structure of large ceremonies and the capacity of major exorcisms to achieve public redefinitions of the patient's identity.

Small exorcisms do not present the nature of demonic illness (how demons organize the mood, subjective attitude, and how the demonic is revealed in the overt behavior of victims) as part of the structure of their performance. Major ceremonies, in contrast, elaborately define the character of demonic attack, and fill out and outwardly objectify the nature of a patient's subjective experience as this is culturally constructed. The movement of a patient from a condition of demonic control to a condition freed from the power of demons is presented and validated in the order of performance. The process of alleviation and cure, the effect of the rite, is carried **within** the structure of performance itself. This is not so much the case with the minor exorcisms. Their efficacy is not validated and shown in the organization of performance itself but rather in the nature of patient response following the performance. Major exorcisms are likely to be successful because they organize a context of experience and a context for the interpretaion of experience in which the demonic is destroyed and where the ability of the demonic to control action is demonstrably denied. Large ceremonies, at least in the moment of their performance, declare and evidence their efficacy.[7]

Major exorcisms are as directed to an audience of kin, friends and neighbors as they are focused on a patient. The curative power of major exorcisms is directly related to the fact that they are held in public and attract large audiences. The understanding that an individual is demonically ill is a social product, constituted in an intersubjective world. The recognition of demonic attack is not simply a fact of the individual patient's interpretation of the meaning of his or her own experience. The meaning of experience is intersubjectively formed and it is sustained in a social world which extends around a patient. Large public ceremonies act directly upon the attitudes and relationships of others towards a patient, and restructure these attitudes and relationships. In so doing major exorcisms reshape the world (and the person) of the patient and negate some of the basis upon which experience as demonic experience is sustained. Put another way, major exorcisms progressively reconstitute patient experience within a changed and alternative perspective upon the demonic, a perspective developed in the course of ritual action which is produced and maintained in relation to the body of the audience. The reciprocity of perspectives between a patient and others, that a particular experience is a demonic experience, is ritually broken, and the patient is drawn into and constrained within the ritually validated alternative perpective of others. Furthermore, the public statement which major ceremonies effect, that the patient is no longer dominated by demons, reduces the extent to which a patient can control the social definition of his or her illness, or continue to insist on demonic affliction.

Major exorcisms act upon demonic illness in the fullness of its manifestation in a patient and upon illness as it achieves a wider significance in a social context surrounding a patient. The effectiveness of large ceremonies and the general satisfaction with their performance, relative to minor exorcisms, is a function of this action. Large ceremonies are composite ritual forms and some of the ritual episodes they organize are performed as separate and smaller exorcisms. As composite forms, the major rites address the entire assembly of demonic forces. They confront the demonic in the full ordering of its power, but are so organized as to disrupt a demonic unity through the activation of more powerful forces contained in the cosmic order as a whole. They gain effectiveness in the public nature of their performance and, more than any smaller rite, deal with demonic illness in the depth of its cultural conceptualization and amidst a set of social relations in which illness receives its wide and various meaning and significance.

Sinhalese say that major exorcisms are performed in cases of serious demonic attack. Demonic illness can be serious in its current individual manifestation, in the cultural understanding of the likely projection of its course, and in the way the patient's illness experience signifies disorder in the social context of the patient. Any or all of these can be integral to an understanding of demonic attack as serious and can underlie the preparedness of exorcist clients to have a major exorcism performed.

Most patients who were the focus of large demon ceremonies during my fieldwork expressed clear prior signs of mental and/or physical distress (e.g., violent and uncontrollable behavior, refusal to engage in social interaction, swollen limbs, sores, severe stomach cramps, face and body paralysis). But I have witnessed the performance of major exorcisms after the patient has outwardly, at least, appeared to have recovered from a bout of illness. Some patients only exhibited mild symptoms. These were frequently of an everyday order manageable by Sinhalese outside the context of exorcism practice. Patients complained of headaches, colds, bowel irregularity, of feeling faint, and not wanting to eat. I am aware that these symptoms might relate to serious underlying disease in a Western biomedical sense. But the patients who complained of these disorders often had attended government or private medical clinics and had failed to have a more serious problem diagnosed. Exorcists themselves occasionally regard the physical symptoms of their patients to be instances of "false illness" **(boru leda),** though as a rule exorcists do not hesitate to affirm that such false illness is indicative of mental imbalance caused by demonic attack. The expression by a patient of physical and mental disorder is necessary to the performance of an exorcism of whatever kind, but the severity **per se** of these aspects of the illness is not essential to the performance of a major exorcism.

I stress the fact that the degree of severity of demonic illness is framed in terms of the cultural conceptualization of demonic illness and cannot be comprehended independently of such a conceptualization. The recognition by a patient and others of demonic agency in illness **is a factor in itself** which can lead to an instance of illness being viewed as severe and demanding the performance of a large scale rite.

Demonic attack has the possibility of death as its final projected outcome. The Sinhalese cultural awareness of this, and especially that of a patient who experiences the illness, is sufficient to generate some demand on the patient's part for a major exorcism. Demonic illness, therefore, can be serious both in its current physical and mental manifestation and in the likely projection of its course. The likelihood of death as a projection is signed by the degree to which the patient is considered to be subject to demonic control. There are several indications of this. One is the failure of previous ritual treatment to prevent the recurrence of mental disquiet or to allay the physical symptoms of the illness. Also the power of the demonic hold is suggested by the multiplicity of symptoms indicative of the demonic in the condition of the patient and in the wider social context of the patient. Particular demons are dangerous and threatening to the life of the patient in themselves. But their power is increased relative to the association of other demons in the illness. A multiplicity of symptoms indicates a gathering of the demonic and a concentration of the demonic power upon a patient, a power which is most effectively overthrown in the context of a major rite.

Demonic illness is polluting to the body of the patient and pollutes the house. The danger of demonic intrusion into the world of human beings is not necessarily ended with the disappearance or reduction of physical and mental disorder in the patient. Unless the malign attention of demons is broken, and the pollution this causes is negated, the malevolence of demons can be reasserted in the condition of a patient and even among those socially associated with the patient. This is a cultural motivation for the performance of exorcisms, and sometimes major ones, even in cases where patients have ostensibly recovered from the experience of their illness. Thus, I witnessed the performance of a **Mahasona** exorcism for a woman who had recently returned home following an operation for appendicitis. She and her relatives stated that unless the ceremony was performed, Mahasona would continue to realize his control over her, causing her further illness and possibly attacking other members of her household.

Demonic agency in illness can be dangerous to others as well as the patient. Demons can capriciously transfer their attention from a patient to others, especially those who are polluted through contact with the patient and the patient's household.[8] Knowledge that an individual is a demonic victim can lead other members of a neighborhood to reduce their interaction with a patient and a patient's household.

The cultural ideas surrounding demonic attack which become activated in the recognition of demonic illness mediate social relationships in the context of the victim. Attack by demons, therefore, can be serious in its social consequences. A stigma often attaches to patients suffering from demonic illness, so much so that they can become objects of fun and ridicule. This stigma and the embarrassment it can cause to those afflicted by demons can be further disruptive of the social context of illness and can lead to the illness being understood as serious.

The nature of exorcist diagnosis is biased towards generating a view that an instance of demonic attack is serious. The body as understood by exorcists is a single integrated system. Although some demons find their greatest effect in certain parts of the body, their influence can be apparent in other parts of the body and its processes. Symptoms overlap and indicate other potential symptoms, and this receives representation in the structure of the demon world. Thus Mahasona is conceived as being in a close structural relation with Riri Yaka, and the symptoms which indicate the effect of the former will usually suggest the activity of the latter, and **vice versa**. Therefore, exorcist diagnosis as this is constituted with reference to the demon world is oriented in application to the discovery of more than one demonic agent. The realization that a patient is subject to multiple demonic attack, and thus seriously afflicted, is a potential of the exorcist diagnostic system.

Exorcist diagnosis in itself can facilitate the construction of a patient's illness as a metaphor and a symbol of wider social problems extending around a patient. Exorcists probe the physical and psychological experience of the patient to discover the demons at the root of the illness, and simultaneously seek to validate the subjective experience of the patient by connecting it to external events and experiences encountered by others in the patient's context. The severity of demonic illness is emergent in such a process, for demons can be discovered as not only exercising control over a patient, but also to be engaged in ordering the experience and action of others.

The diagnosis of demonic illness by exorcists proceeds together with the more common-sense understandings of clients regarding the cause and nature of the illness, but it further acts to gather these understandings into a coherent view of the role of demons in a patient's affliction. This process varies from one situation to another and can be more fully explored through reference to particular cases.

The Definition of Illness and the Decision to Hold a Major Exorcism

It is a common anthropological and sociological observation that illness is culturally and socially constructed. The three cases of demonic illness I now examine provide further evidence for this and show how the illness experience of a patient can assume expanded cultural and social relevance which becomes a property of the illness as ultimately defined. I point to the definition and diagnosis of demonic illness as emerging dialectically in relation to its context. In this, both the illness of a patient and the social context of the illness can be transformed, each taking on new significance in relation to the other. Thus, the patient's illness can gather to it additional dimensions of meaning and significance beyond those which were initially recognized. The illness can begin to subsume or to incorporate aspects of its social context and as it does so can change or bring to clarity, through the focus illness provides, the nature of a context which it can increasingly come to symbolize. The way in which major demon ceremonies can come to act both on the experience of a patient and upon others in the patient's immediate context is inextricably tied to the process of illness definition.

I concentrate specifically on the process of the legitimation of demonic attack and the emergence of agreement as to the appropriateness of a major demon ceremony as a method of treatment. The legitimation of the definition of illness and treatment constitutes a problem for Sinhalese, particularly in relation to the staging of major exorcisms. This is so, if for no other reason, because of their expense. Patients (and members of their households) require the material support and cooperation of other kin and neighbors. Support is reduced if these others do not agree in some part with the need for the performance. In addition, Sinhalese are frequently skeptical. While the principles upon which exorcist practice is based are seldom denied, at least by the Sinhalese peasantry and urban working class, suspicion is often expressed as to the legitimacy of a diagnosis of demonic attack in specific instances.

The process whereby a particular definition of the situation in which an illness event receives widespread agreement, and becomes legitimate and plausible in the view of others, is a process of objectification. That is, the subjective view of the patient as displayed by external sign and action is understood by the others to be founded in the objective reality, as they see it, in which the patient is engaged. The process of objectification involves setting and interpreting the patient's condition in relation to those typifications of the social order in which the patient and others daily participate.

Berger and Luckman (1971), writing specifically on the legitimation of institutions, isolate two aspects of the process of objectification. These can apply equally, I consider, to the definition of the legitimacy and plausibility of a particular patient's role identity as a sufferer from demonic illness requiring particular treatment. Legitimation and plausibility have "horizontal" and "vertical" aspects. That is, the presentation by a patient as ill, the explanations and justifications for it, must be seen by others "to make sense" with reference to a wider set of current activities and involvements of the patient which extend laterally or horizontally into a general social context. Furthermore, the "totality" of the patient's life, the patient's biography, the vertical dimension of the patient's career, must permit successive phases or experiences in the patient's personal history to be endowed with meaning in relation to the specific illness episode (Berger and Luckmann 1971: 110-12).

These dimensions of legitimation bear a close connection with McHugh's (1968) criteria of "emergence" and "relativity" for the process of the definition of the situation. In accordance with these concepts, McHugh examines a process whereby an order and meaning is placed on the character of events in such a way as to generate agreement for common-sense action. Emergence, for example, "refers to definitions, and transformations in definition, of an event over time" (McHugh 1968:21), and "includes, in the present, the changing meaning of past events and future programs" (1968:35). McHugh attributes a number of dimensions to emergence, the most important for this argument being "theme" and "elaboration." Theme refers to the discovery of a meaning which interrelates a current event with past experiences and possible events in the future. But a theme cannot be said to exist unless it is portrayed, made apparent, "objectified." This is the property of elaboration whereby the theme "is compounded and elaborated by locating its particulars over a series of chronologically discrete events" (McHugh 1968:38).

In contrast with "emergence," "relativity" refers to the "definition and its transformation across space" (McHugh 1968:31).   The properties of relativity include among others "typicality," "substantive congruence," and "technical efficiency." There is a degree of overlap in these, and in the course of any particular definition only some might be present. Typicality is apparent in social interaction when others refer a specific instance of behavior to a general class of behaviors which are in some way comparable to it, and/or infer that the behavior is representative of some group or category of membership. Substantive congruency relates to the extent to which the assessment individuals make of their social context is "empirically" valid from the standpoints of others acting in the same context.   Examples of substantive congruency might be the publicly accepted valid pointing of the patient or others to the presence of social disturbance based in caste opposition, conflict at work, or competition over land or over status.   Such disturbance, in the cultural understanding of Sinhalese, can give rise to action resulting in the intervention of malign supernaturals.   Demons not only attack individuals who are "weak" but attack or can become manifest in social contexts which are weakened through conflict. Technical efficiency, the final property of relativity, is particularly relevant to the analysis. It involves the assessment by others (in a context where there is a great variety of alternatives) of the appropriateness of a specific method for achieving a desired end, in this instance exorcism as the technique for the alleviation of illness and misfortune. The formulation of a publicly legitimated and plausible role identity "fails when interactants agree on none of these components, as actors fail to interchange standpoints, they fail to communicate and become incapable of entering into the concerted actions that are characteristic of social order" (McHugh 1968:45).

I have selected three cases in terms of which major aspects of the argument and analytical approach outlined above can be extended. Two of the cases resulted in the performance of a **Mahasona** exorcism and one in the organization of a **Sanni Yakuma**. I deal with the first in greater depth than the others in order to avoid excessive repetition. The cases reveal aspects of the definitional process which are apparent, in varying degrees of specificity, in most instances of demonic attack resulting in major exorcisms which I have collected.

CASE 1: The Girl Who Heard Voices

The illness concerned Asoka (C,2), a girl of eight. Her family were members of a small community of the barber (panikki) caste and lived near

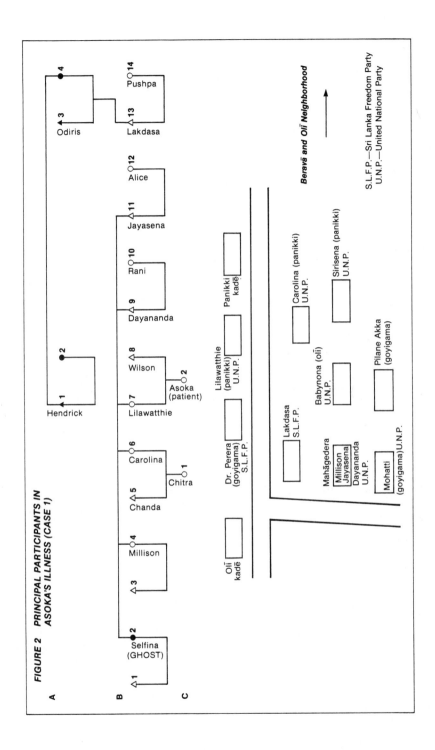

FIGURE 2 PRINCIPAL PARTICIPANTS IN ASOKA'S ILLNESS (CASE 1)

Berava and Oli Neighborhood

S.L.F.P.—Sri Lanka Freedom Party
U.N.P.—United National Party

the central market area of Galle town. The onset of the illness was marked by a singular event, close to midnight, when Asoka suddenly awoke, screaming. Amidst tears she complained of a headache and severe stomach cramp. Also, as reported by her mother, Lilawatthie (B,7), Asoka heard a voice. It sounded like that of her mother's elder sister, Carolina (B,6), who lived nearby. Lilawatthie played a key role in the initial identification of the cause of her daughter's illness and the establishment of a theme. Asoka's father was absent at the time in Beruwela, a town on the coast to the north of Galle, where he owns a small barber shop.

Lilawatthie quickly identified the ghost of her eldest sister, Selfina (B,2), as the main agent of her daughter's illness. According to Lilawatthie, her eldest sister had a voice similar to that of Carolina, and even looked like her. There are several reasons why Lilawatthie should have immediately thought of Selfina. The onset of Asoka's illness was almost a year to the day from the death of Selfina. Lilawatthie, with the help of other close relatives, had organized the giving of food to the monks (dana) in the local temple. She had also organized another **dana** three months later and, at the time of the onset of her daughter's illness, was again active in preparing for another **dana** for the anniversary of Selfina's death.

Both Lilawatthie's and Asoka's relationships with Selfina had been particulary close. Lilawatthie's mother had died when Lilawatthie was still a young child, and Selfina, as the eldest daughter, had taken her mother's place. Selfina had also shown an extremely close affection for Asoka, who would frequently play in Selfina's house.

In the everyday cultural understanding of Sinhalese, individuals are likely to become ghosts if they have an undue attachment to people and things of this world and if they express excessive worldly craving and desire. The close relationships of mother and daughter to Selfina were evidence of such attachment. Further evidence as to Selfina's likely ghostly affliction of Asoka was that although she had married, she had never borne children. It was understood by Lilawatthie and other relatives that Selfina had strongly desired children of her own. Indeed, their view was substantiated by Selfina's emotional closeness to Asoka and the fact that she had treated Asoka as if she had been her own child. Additional substance to Lilawatthie's opinion was given by her reference to a **dana** for Selfina. One specific aspect of such a **dana** is to assist the rebirth of deceased relatives and to prevent their being maintained in a ghostly limbo. At the time of her daughter's illness, Lilawatthie complained that her relatives were giving no support for the organization of another **dana** for Selfina.

Lilawatthie developed her own definition of the cause of Asoka's illness in accordance with her own culturally derived, common-sense understandings which were, potentially at least, substantively congruent with those of others in her immediate social context. On the morning following the onset of Asoka's illness, she summoned a local exorcist to her house. He supported Lilawatthie's interpretation in relation to his own set of diagnostic typifications and also elaborated it. He attached significance to the fact that Asoka had eaten a prawn curry in the evening before she was attacked. Prawns (isso), with other shellfish, belong to an impure food category and are attractive to malign supernaturals. Nonspecialist Sinhalese regard prawns, aside from their impurity, as particularly attractive to ghosts, as they are an expensive local food item. Ghosts crave expensive things. But the exorcist also opened the possibility of another malign agent in Asoka's illness, that of the demon Mahasona. This demon is associated with prawns and crayfish. Fishermen, when they are afflicted by demons, often report being attacked by Mahasona when they are fishing for prawns and cray at night. The exorcist inquired after Asoka's normal daily movements, and discovered that she passed a cemetery, a major venue of Mahasona, on her journey to school. There was thus room for disagreement about the primary cause of Asoka's illness.

Lilawatthie's older sister, Carolina (B,6), was also present at the initial diagnostic session with the exorcist. She seized upon the exorcist's suggestion that Mahasona was an agent in the illness and refused to accept Lilawatthie's opinion that Selfina's ghost was involved. When I interviewed Carolina alone she argued that for Lilawatthie to claim Selfina was a malign ghost was a source of embarrassment to her and other close relatives. It implied a moral condemnation of them by Lilawatthie as regards the obligation of the living to the dead and reflected poorly on the memory of Selfina.

The exorcist tied a thread (apa nul) to alleviate the effect of Mahasona and Selfina's ghost. It was to be effective for a period of three days. After he left, however, Carolina commented to Lilawatthie that demons and ghosts might not be involved at all. Asoka's obvious distress, she argued, simply might be the result of a serious physical disorder. Carolina insisted that Asoka be taken to a doctor trained in Western medicine. In response, Lilawatthie took Asoka to a medical practitioner who lived across the street. He advised that Asoka be hospitalized immediately for medical tests.

Asoka stayed in the hospital for two days. Here the doctors suspected meningitis and ordered a spinal tap. The result of this test and others proved negative. However, while Asoka was undergoing her tests in the hospital, Lilawatthie summoned another exorcist to her bedside. He was of the berava caste and highly reputed in the neighborhood. The first exorcist was not a member of this caste and was not widely regarded as a man skilled in most areas of exorcist practice. The new exorcist reconfirmed the initial diagnosis and tied a further thread to have alleviative effect in three days. Shortly after, Asoka left the hospital and returned home. Credence was given to the exorcist's diagnosis, and to Lilawatthie's interpretation, when the illness appeared to abate and when on the third day, after the second thread tying, Asoka again heard voices, and suffered a headache and stomach cramps. Lilawatthie again called in the second exorcist, and once more he tied a thread for three days. However, Carolina and some of the other relatives and neighbors were still skeptical as to the cause of the illness. They observed that the tests which Asoka had received in the hospital might, in themselves, have alleviated the illness, and not the thread-tying. Asoka was again admitted to the hospital and underwent further tests and a skull x-ray. The results were still negative.

At the hospital, and again at home, Asoka's symptoms momentarily abated. They were, however, to manifest themselves in all their severity on the occasion of the performance of a Mahasona exorcism at a neighbor's house. Asoka leaped out of bed and danced entranced to the house of the exorcism. She did so at the height of the major drumming and dancing episodes of the rite, when Mahasona is understood to be present in all his dangerous malevolence. The exorcist presiding over the ceremony was the one who was currently engaged in Asoka's treatment. He was called from the performance to attend to Asoka. In the course of his bringing her out of a trance, Asoka revealed that she had heard Selfina calling her to her world. Asoka's mother, Carolina and other close relatives were present. The exorcist declared to them that it was pointless to tie another thread unless Asoka had a large-scale exorcism to appease both Selfina's ghost and Mahasona.

One of the relatives present on this occasion was Millison (B,4), Lilawatthie's eldest surviving sister. She took a prominent role, elaborated the theme which Lilawatthie and the exorcist had identified and further substantiated it with reference to her own experience and the experience of other members of her family. Millison suggested that some of the recent illnesses and misfortunes which had befallen some of her kin could be accounted for by Selfina's ghost. She also raised the possibility of sorcery. Her own son had died three years earlier, and this she viewed as the result of sorcery. Millison indicated, furthermore, that Selfina's own death might have been the result of sorcery. She warned that unless a major ceremony was held for Asoka, then not only might Asoka die, but a similar fate could await other relatives.

Millison's open support for the diagnosis and a **Mahasona** exorcism was significant. She was the senior kinswoman among a local cluster of related households and her advice was frequently sought at times of personal and family crisis. She held important titles to land and property in which other kin held shares. Millison was largely responsible for managing aspects of the financial affairs of her kindred. Her seniority and influence with the family was symbolized by her residence in the family **mahagedara**. This is the house to which a set of relatives or kindred trace a common ancestral link. It had been built by her father, Hendrick (A,1), whose children and grandchildren now formed most of the panikki households in the area. Although Millison now lived at the house with her own husband, children, and the family of her youngest brother, it was also the house in which Selfina had resided. Millison promised her financial support for an exorcism and also stated that her house could be used as its venue. Millison's action not only provided legitimation for Lilawatthie's definition of her daughter's illness, but the intimations of sorcery and the choice of venue extended the grounds upon which others could lend their support.

More immediately, however, it is important to consider the patient's role in securing the legitimation of the diagnosis and the widespread agreement among her kin as to the appropriateness of an exorcism for Mahasona. Undoubtedly, an obvious factor was the persistence of the girl's symptoms and the apparent failure of other medical diagnoses and treatment. There were others of equal, and perhaps greater, importance. Young children are commonly regarded by Sinhalese as relatively innocent and devoid of guile.[9] I encountered, with this exception, no cases where children explicitly expressed that they were in need of exorcist treatment. It is part of everyday awareness that most sufferers from demonic illness are adults. Sinhalese do not normally expect children to falsify demonic illness. Asoka's behavior was, therefore, impressive. This was all the more so because she had become entranced precisely at that moment when Mahasona was understood to be present.

An important aspect of the above display was that knowledge of Asoka's demonic affliction was no longer restricted to a relatively small group of concerned kin. It was now the common knowledge of all those who had gathered to witness the neighboring exorcism. Such public knowledge can cause social embarrassment to the victim's household and other kin. There is a pattern for individuals with such knowledge to reduce their interaction with the household, for demonic attack is polluting and renders the victim's house dangerous. Moreover, if close kin do not attempt to end the demonic attack, they can be subject to widespread moral condemnation and, on some occasions, public ridicule. In an important sense this kind of public reaction to the presence of demonic illness might only effectively be countered by a public ceremony to rid the patient of demonic attack. It became apparent in the ten days which were to elapse between Asoka's entrancement and the performance of the **Mahasona** exorcism, that a number of problems which at the time beset Asoka's relatives became attached to her illness. Problems involving land and property, conflict among Asoka's kin, intercaste rivalry, the competition for status, and political affiliation, became important elements in the mobilizing of action focused on Asoka's illness and the progress towards the performance of the exorcism.

Asoka's relatives belonged to families whose members had been able to use their traditional caste occupation as barbers to advance themselves economically. Like the karava community, described in Chapter 2 (see also Kapferer 1977c; Roberts 1969, 1982), their fortunes had been affected by the former importance of Galle as a major port of call for trading vessels. In fact the panikki families resident in the area are descendants mainly of two men, Hendrick (A,1) and Odiris (A,3), both of whom were hired by karava engaged in the East African and Asian gem and curio trade. Hendrick and Odiris on their return from overseas moved from their natal village, located on the outskirts of Galle, into the town itself. They bought land, with the money they had earned in their trading ventures, from poorer members of the goyigama caste in an area bordering on a relatively large concentration of berava and oli.

The neighborhood in which these men settled is now the center of the largest panikki community in the town. The descendants of Hendrick have all maintained a strong caste identity and continue in their traditional occupation of barbering. Hendrick's sons run barber saloons in Galle town. His daughters also married barbers, all of whom, however, come from centers outside Galle and who own or work in shops in other towns along the coast.

The panikki, in terms of the cultural typifications of others outside their caste, are ranked low in the hierarchy of caste. They occupy a position proximate to other low-ranked castes, such as berava and oli, whose members comprise a substantial proportion of the households in the area. In fact, the various panikki families referred to the economic success of the founding members of the community in the neighborhood and their ownership of land and other property as grounds for claiming a higher caste rank relative to oli and berava households. Their relative economic wealth was also a basis for claiming social superiority over poorer goyigama residents in the area.

Various developments in Asoka's neighborhood affected both the presentation of the caste and social superiority of the panikki families over others in their immediate context. For example, when a neighboring oli household opened a small shop (**kade**) many panikki began to frequent it and, as so often happens, began to accrue debts. This economic dependence created difficulties for the presentation by the panikki of claims to higher status and caste position. It was partly solved when a panikki family opened a similar shop, which enabled the panikki concerned to shift their clientage to a member of their own community. But other factors had complicated the caste and status presentation of the panikki. Panikki families were no longer as clearly socially or economically dominant over other similarly ranked castes in the neighborhood as they had been in the past. In recent years members of the berava and oli communities have experienced some economic mobility. They have capitalized on occupations with which they are traditionally linked, astrology and healing, for which there is a continuing, and perhaps an increasing, demand in a situation of national economic recession. Some berava and oli, as described earlier, have become successful builders and carpenters, often through the sponsorship of wealthy and powerful goyigama with whom they have become politically linked.

The **Mahasona** exorcism, to which Asoka danced in a trance, was organized by an oli household. Many of the members of the neighboring panikki households viewed it as a display of status. In the discussions which centered on Asoka's illness, comments were passed by her relatives and members of other castes that the ability and readiness of the oli family to organize such a performance reflected badly on the panikki. Whereas the oli community could afford such an expensive exorcism, it appeared that the panikki could not.

The problems which the panikki had in their presentation of caste and status with reference to other households in their context also related to conflict and division within the panikki community itself. Some of the families descended from Hendrick had suffered a fall in economic fortunes. This was the case with Lilawatthie whose husband earned a relatively poor income and was away from Galle most of the time. More than this, however, there was a crisis developing among those households related to the patient, a crisis connected with disputes over land and property. The outcome of these disputes was likely to affect further the caste and status presentation of the families concerned.

The descendants of Hendrick held title to some of the land and property, specifically coconut trees, which had been owned by Odiris. When Odiris died his land and trees passed to his wife and only son Lakdasa (B,13). Odiris' wife in turn passed on some of her shares to her brother's (Hendrick's) children. Matters were further complicated by the subsequent actions of her son, Lakdasa. Lakdasa had not pursued the traditional caste occupation. Instead he joined the Sri Lanka army, in which he was eventually promoted to the rank of captain. Unlike other local members of his caste, who had married endogamously, Lakdasa married a goyigama woman whose natal area was in the Central Province of the island. Lakdasa's wife claimed that she was a radala, the highest ranked section of the goyigama caste and the one from which many of the Sinhalese kings had been drawn. She refused to associate with panikki women in the area and, instead, referred to them as low caste and uncivilized. Her airs and graces were a constant source of bitterness to other panikki men and women in the neighborhood.

This situation worsened when, upon Lakdasa's transfer to Colombo some three months before Asoka's illness, Lakdasa's wife began, as others saw it, to exert pressure on her husband to sell his shares in land and property. Although he had major shares in the tracts of land and trees involved, he did not have exclusive rights to them. He approached some of his relatives for their shares and began otherwise to define exclusive claims by building fences and denying access to the trees and produce in which his relatives had shares. Insult was added to injury. Not only did his wife constantly subvert the caste presentation of the panikki but Lakdasa's attempt to appropriate exclusive rights to land and trees struck at the material basis of panikki claims to a high socioeconomic status. A general aspect of disputes over land and property is that the various interested parties seek to mobilize support among their relatives for a particular definition of rights. They attempt also to secure the support of significant others who might be influential in the final outcome, particularly should the dispute reach the courts.

Lakdasa's wife claimed that she was a distant relative of Mrs. Bandaranaike, who is generally acknowledged as a radala. Both Lakdasa and his wife were well-known supporters of the then ruling Sri Lanka Freedom Party, of which Mrs. Bandaranaike was the leader. They insisted that through their political and social connections they could exert sufficient influence to win a favorable decision for their claims. Lakdasa and his wife associated on a regular basis with Dr. Perera, the doctor to whom Asoka was taken early in her illness. He was a goyigama and also an S.L.F.P. candidate for the local municipal ward. Lakdasa also had some association in the past with a prominent goyigama landlord, Mohatti. It was Lakdasa's relatively high occupational status and the caste of his wife which facilitated this association. However, the most significant feature of this association was that it had been Mohatti's father who had sold some of his land and property to Hendrick and Odiris. The name of Mohatti's father was recorded on the titles. Mohatti's statement on the history of the transactions could, as all the panikki involved recognized, be influential in a court decision should the dispute proceed to that level.

The support structure underlying Lakdasa's claims was not unambiguously in his favor. All the other panikki families were supporters of the rival party to the S.L.F.P., the United National Party, and although at this time this party was not powerful in the national political arena, it was important locally. The panikki families lived in a municipal ward held by a U.N.P. member. The ward was also part of an electorate which had returned a U.N.P. member to the national parliament. Furthermore, while individuals were conscious of the association between Mohatti and Lakdasa, they were also well aware of friction between the two. Mohatti had recently suspected Lakdasa's son of having a sexual liaison with his teenage daughter. Indeed, Mohatti had approached a brother of Lilawatthie, Dayananda (B,9), and had asked him to intervene and end the affair.

I have shown that Asoka's illness occurred at a time when there was considerable conflict within the panikki community, and when there was also a range of problems which affected the relationship of the panikki households with others in the neighborhood. The definitional process relative to Asoka's illness referred to this situation. Thus, Millison's intimation of the possibility of sorcery was substantively congruent with the recognition of social tension in the area. The general agreement which was achieved to hold the exorcism was not simply a consequence of the apparent severity of Asoka's physical symptoms. The decision was also reached because in many ways Asoka's illness reflected for her kin a set of other social difficulties which they were encountering.

The organization of an exorcism, quite apart from its curative effectiveness for a specific patient, affords the opportunity for others not only to express some of the social problems critically affecting them, but also the opportunity to resolve them, at least partially. This is precisely because of the public nature of exorcism performance, the fact that attendance is not restricted to close kin, and because it is held in the midst of the setting in which the various social, political, and other problems have emerged. Major exorcisms constitute events at which status can be displayed and where the nature of social and political relationships can receive public expression and legitimation. They are, in a significant way, household or domestic rites. Moreover, they are household rites which are capable of defining the nature of a household's or collection of households' structural articulation into a neighborhood and wider context.

The above can be shown by a description of the organization of social action which centered on the performance of the **Mahasona** exorcism for Asoka. I discuss first those who gave material and other support to the staging of the rite, and then examine briefly the organization of hospitality on the occasion of the performance. All Asoka's relatives, with the exception of Lakdasa and his wife, attended the performance and contributed, if not cash, at least some food and drink. Millison gave her house, the **mahagedera**, for the exorcism and also provided coconuts, coconut fronds, banana tree trunks, etc., used in the preparation of offerings and in the making of the ritual structures. Lilawatthie's husband (Asoka's father) and her two brothers, Dayananda (B,9) and Jayasena (B,11), among them contributed over 500 rupees towards the payment of the exorcists. Theirs was the greatest monetary contribution, and in the afternoon before the evening performance of the rite they supervised the gathering of materials for the building of the ritual structures. Lilawatthie and her sisters and Chitra (C,1), Carolina's daughter, engaged in the preparation of food to be given to the guests who would arrive.

Many non-kin also participated in the preparations. The most menial domestic chores, the collection of firewood, the washing of pots and pans, and the clearing of the house were carried out by Babynona. Babynona and her husband, both of whom were oli, stood in a subordinate relation to Lilawatthie's family. They rented a small wooden house from Lilawatthie's brother, Dayananda. Babynona's husband was a poorly paid casual laborer in the town. His household was frequently dependent on members of the panikki community for food and small loans of cash. Babynona's husband helped in the building of the main ritual structure. He was assisted by Sirisena, a member of the panikki caste but not a kinsman of Lilawatthie. Sirisena had worked as a cook in the British army during the period when it had been stationed in Aden. When he returned to Galle he invested his earnings in land, but, as a result of recently declining fortunes had been forced to sell some of it. He had been a close friend of Lakdasa and at one stage, in 1972, had even quarreled with Dayananda over land. On the eve of the exorcism, however, he was negotiating a price with Dayananda for the sale of his remaining property. Indeed, the ritual arrangements gave him an opportunity to demonstrate a changed social allegiance and his new dependency on Dayananda's support. During the exorcism he performed the role of the **madu puraya** (exorcist assistant), the most menial task associated with the ritual performance. The duties involve attendance upon the performing exorcists and the preparation of food offerings for the ghosts and demons. Another who assisted was a woman, Pilane Akka, a relatively impoverished goyigama widow. Like the others, she stood in a socially subordinate position to Lilawatthie's household. This was expressed in the nature of her participation, as she assumed the duties of washing the patient and the clothes in which Asoka was to be dressed during the rite. This task is ideally performed by members of the low-ranked rada caste, who also perform similar ritual duties on other occasions, as in the instance of a girl's puberty rite. Perhaps the most significant assistance was Mohatti's gift of a cock. In all exorcisms the cock is at the center of most of the ritual actions. The cock, a two legged domestic animal, is a symbolic victim, a patient surrogate. Exorcists transfer the patient's illness to the cock, use the cock to fool the demons, and make it, rather than the patient, the object of carnivorous demonic attention. Mohatti did not visit the performance of Asoka's **Mahasona**, but his gift of such a crucial object, vital to the curative project of an exorcism, signed his commitment to a return of Asoka's health and aligned him with Asoka's kin in their land dispute. At least this was the interpretation of Asoka's kin, who commented approvingly on Mohatti's gift. They also stated that it resolved the ambiguity of Mohatti's position in their current quarrel.

The immediate kin of Lilawatthie and her daughter attached importance to the extensive support they received in money, kind, and labor in preparation for the exorcism. On the eve of the rite a list of those who had given monetary or material assistance was displayed in the house. I recorded this practice at only a few exorcisms but it emphasizes, nonetheless, the significance which exorcism households in general attach to the public display of support from kin and others.

Asoka's exorcism drew an audience of over two hundred people. Throughout the performance food was offered to those seated outside (mainly men) and to those (mainly women) gathered in and around the doorway and front windows of the house. This food (tea, coconut milk, bottled soft drinks, oil cakes, sweetmeats, bananas) was given in accordance with customary Sinhalese rules of hospitality. But as at all the exorcisms I have attended the audience was not treated undifferentially. Thus persons of recognized high status received offers of food and refreshments in precedence to those understood to be lower down the social scale. Certain types of refreshment and food (coconut milk, bottled drinks, and bananas) also tended to be offered to those of high status instead of tea, oil cakes, and sweetmeats.

Invitations to dine inside the exorcism house, the order and acceptance of these invitations, most clearly reflect patterns of social differentiation, especially gradations of status, among the members of an exorcism audience. Indeed the social and political articulation of a household into its wider social and political context is defined by invitations to dine. Eating is viewed by Sinhalese as a most intimate activity and meals are usually eaten in private (Yalman 1972/3:287-89). To eat in another's house, to share the intimacy of a meal, is to imbue a relationship with great symbolic import.

It is common for a number of meal sittings to occur at an exorcism house, but not all members of the audience will be invited to share a meal. Typically, those invited first will be those of recognized high status. The best food will be provided and might be served by the household head if he is lower in status than his guests. This will be followed by other meal sittings during which the male household head might sit with the guests and be served by the womenfolk. Normally, it is males who are invited for meals, and they do not eat with the women.

The first to eat at Asoka's exorcism house was a prominent goyigama, indeed an eminent national and local political figure. He, and two important local business men, a shopowner and a gem and jewelry merchant, were invited inside the house and served food by the men of the household. They stayed only a short time. Senior members of the panikki community followed. Asoka's father and some of his friends and kin from the neighborhood were the last to eat in the house. None of the goyigama or oli members of the community considered socially inferior by the panikki were invited for a meal.

The organization of food and refreshments and of dining at Asoka's exorcism reflects the strong emphasis which Sinhalese place on status. This attention to status, and that in its smallest, most minute details, permeates almost every domain of Sinhalese life. Sinhalese are quick to note even the slightest affront to their status, and social relationships must be conducted with great care. A complex and often subtle cultural code of status is apparent in most social contexts and particularly in settings where the household is the focus. The status code is evident in the ordering of social precedence, as I have described, in speech, where personal pronouns indicate the relative status of the speakers, in seating arrangements, and so on. The Sinhalese concern with status is consistent with a culture which generally places a high premium on hierarchy and where hierarchy is the **sine qua non** of a social order and an embracing cosmic unity.

Food is integral in the cultural status code. Food is vital in the mediation of social relationships, in symbolizing their quality, and in signing the relative status of the parties to social relationships. In Galle, households of equal caste rank or status will exchange food of similar type, whereas those of unequal caste or status will exchange food of dissimilar type. For instance, a low-status household might give high status members of their caste community whole fruits but receive in return cooked curries. A similar significance to a pattern of food transactions has been widely reported for South Asian societies (Mayer 1960; Marriott 1968; Dumont 1970; Yalman 1967, 1972/3) and these transactions are variously tied to such general cultural principles as purity and pollution. In Sri Lanka whole fruits are considered a pure food category whereas cooked foods are relatively impure having been brought into contact with the impurities of human breath and hands.   When food is cooked for the gods (e.g. in the **gam maduva)** the person who prepares it must cover his mouth so that he does not contaminate the food and cause the anger of the gods. The Sinhalese concept of **indul** encodes cultural ideas concerning the relative purity and impurity of food and links it to status. Indeed, the Sinhalese concern with precedence at meal sittings may receive a cultural reinforcement in the concept of **indul**. To partake of food left by another is to eat **indul** and to sign an inferiority of status.

The symbolic properties of food (and also its mediating and regenerative power) receive their most intense and elaborate cultural meaning in ritual.   Supernaturals and their relational position in the hierarchy of a cosmic order are defined by the nature of the offerings they receive. The form of these offerings is also, to a degree, homologous with the form and character of the supernaturals to whom these offerings are given. Deities receive whole fruits and whole and fresh flower blooms. This symbolizes the purity of deities and signifies their capacity to unify and encompass relations at a higher level than demons in the cosmic order (see Chapter 6).   By contrast demons, whose form is often disjoint and fragmented, who bring the pollution of death and destruction and who are incapable of generating a cosmic unity, are given dead and torn flower petals, cooked curries, and sometimes marijuana and fecal matter. Within the deity and demon categories there are gradations of status and this is often signified by the order of precedence according to which particular demons and deities receive their offerings.

Exorcisms are occasions when food has a simultaneous ritual use and social use. This increases an awareness of the symbolic importance of food among those who have gathered to witness the rite. I have encountered a few people who have refused to take food from an exorcism household (parents sometimes warn their children against doing so) because they viewed the food as polluted by demons and hence dangerous, which is certainly a meaning of the food offerings given to demons within the rite. Individuals who accept food from an exorcism house symbolically reaffirm their association with the household and actively participate in the ending of the household's social isolation which is a condition of the demonic.

The ritual use and the social use of food at exorcisms have similar functions. In the ritual, food mediates relationships between human beings and the supernatural and is engaged in the active reordering of a cosmic hierarchy. In the social world which surrounds the exorcism performance, food mediates the social relationships of those who gather to witness the ritual events and is involved in structurally rearticulating a household into its social world. One might observe that the simultaneous ritual and social use of food points to essential parallels between the process in the ritual and the process in the surrounding social domain of an exorcism. Within the ritual events a cosmic order and its hierarchy comes into being while at the periphery of these events a social world and its hierarchy is formed, defined, and publicly communicated.

It is an anthropological truism that rituals give expression to the social and political dimensions of the context of their performance, and often function to resolve (as I have suggested in the description of Asoka's case) conflicts and problems emergent in the experience of daily life.   My discussion of some of the general cultural ideas regarding food and the role of food at exorcisms underscores such a widely accepted anthropological point, a point particularly well developed in various functionalist approaches to ritual. However, a problem with many of these approaches is that this is where they leave off. They often fail to establish vital connections between the culturally stated projects of rites and the inner logic of their ritual events, on the one hand, and the social and political ordering of relationships which is established or developed in the context of the rite, on the other. That is to say the articulation of social and political relationships at the periphery of a ritual performance can be an active property of the internal functioning of ritual events and also of their efficacy, and not a mere consequence of the occasioning of a rite (any rite) which must involve social interaction. Indeed, I propose that the apparently greater power of some rites relative to others to communicate, define, and express major aspects of their social context may be directly related to the degree to which dimensions of a social and political order are integral to the project and inner logic of such rites.

The healing project of an exorcism is to a large extent founded on the rearticulation of a household into an ordered mundane social and political world. Demonic attack gains force in the disruption and fragmentation of a social order and in the disarticulation of the relationships of a household within this order. I have located one of the important aspects of the social distribution and consumption of food at exorcisms in signing, symbolizing and actively regenerating an ordered social world around a household. To view the social use of food at exorcism as simply hospitality or to view the socially and politically ordered world which is created and defined at an exorcism as merely an expressive function of the rite, would miss the vital linkage of these features to the healing aim of exorcism.

The social and political world of human beings becomes possible as a direct logical function of the dynamic process of the ritual events of exorcism, as I will argue in later chapters (see Chapters 8 and 9). Indeed, I would go so far as to say that if the social and political realities of the everyday world are not generated in the course of a major demon ceremony, then critical dimensions of the underlying logic of exorcism have failed to realize their full force.

Exorcisms rebuild a cosmic order and it is the progressive subordination of demons in a cosmic rebuilding which makes the cultural and social world of human beings possible. Some of the main periods of social activity mediated by the offering and consumption of food occur at times of important expulsion and subordination of the demonic. A major break in the performance of large demon ceremonies is known as the **maha te** ("big tea") and it occurs immediately after the power of the gods has been asserted. Much important social activity occurs during this period which indicates the nature of the patient and household's social and political articulation into a wider social context. Therefore, the social and political import which many exorcisms appear to communicate and express is not merely functional in a significant but epiphenomenal sense, as seems to be the thrust of much general anthropological discussion of ritual, but it is integral to the inner process of exorcism.

Asoka's exorcism, in the opinion of her kin, was responsible for restoring her to health. Apparently she experienced no recurrence of her physical symptoms and she no longer heard voices. But Asoka's demonic condition threw into focus a great many problems which affected others in her social context. In an important sense the illness of Asoka was not reducible to the particular situation and experience of Asoka alone. Asoka's demonic attack became a catalyst for the management of a variety of problems which confronted others in her community.

Lilawatthie's deep emotional attachment to Selfina was given public voice in the events leading to the exorcism, and the performance of the

Mahasona satisfied to some extent Lilawattie's demand for a **dana**. Following the **Mahasona**, Lilawatthie proclaimed that Selfina had been released from her suffering as a ghost. She and others among her kin behaved in a way customary for a funeral. (After all, Mahasona is the Great Cemetery Demon, and his ceremony, perhaps more than the other major exorcisms, is heavy with the symbolism of death). A few days after the **Mahasona**, the important Buddhist festival of **Vesak** (which celebrates the birth, enlightenment, and death of the Buddha) took place throughout the island. Lilawatthie and her kin, claiming that they were in a state of mourning, refrained from participating in the celebrations.

Overall, the exorcism, held at the **mahagedera** of Asoka's kindred, defined for Asoka's kin their social position **vis à vis** others in the neighborhood, their unity at a time when their social and economic interests were under threat, and their powerful political and social connections in a moment of crisis. All Asoka's kin commented on the magnificence of the exorcism performance. Many remarked that it was more impressive than the **Mahasona** at the nearby oli house, and that, unlike the oli, the panikki had no difficulty in collecting the cash and materials for the rite and were able to hold it without delay. Asoka's kin were also well-satisfied that various prominent personages in the neighborhood attended or otherwise lent their support.

Asoka's case illustrates how the diagnosis and social definition of demonic attack, through a discourse engaging exorcists, a patient, kin, and others, both reflects a personal and social context **and** is actively constitutive of that context which it may be seen to reflect. A context is drawn into focus through the cultural aperture of the demonic and is shaped to the terms of the demonic as the demonic becomes formed and elaborated in the context of its recognition.

I have chosen the next case because it illustrates an event of demonic illness which failed to win the support of others in the patient's context. There was no disagreement as to the agent of the illness, but much divergence as to the nature of the social world relevant to the victim's demonic exposure. The case also raises issues regarding the relation of a paient's normal or routine social identity to a demonic identity.

CASE 2: The Delinquent Youth

This instance of demonic attack involves Sunil (C,2), a young man of eighteen. His family is goyigama and working class. Although Sunil had received some education at a prestigious Buddhist secondary school in Galle, the extreme poverty of his parents prevented him from pursuing his studies, and so he had left school when he was fifteen. Sunil, who is unmarried, lives with his parents in a small mud and cadjan thatched house at the edge of Galle town. He occasionally finds casual work as a laborer, but this often results in his doing the most demeaning work. He cuts firewood, plucks coconuts, clears drains and at times has dug latrine ditches for his wealthier neighbors. The neighborhood in which he lives borders on the area dominated by the panikki community which was the setting for the last case, and is highly socially differentiated. It contains many families of different castes and diverse socioeconomic status.

The onset of Sunil's illness was marked by his running wildly out of his house and accosting passers-by, babbling unintelligibly, and sometimes insulting them. He had no previous symptoms of physical illness. Sunil was a member of a youth gang, notorious in the area for many pranks and unlawful acts. His friends in the gang suggested that he might have been afflicted by Mahasona, for Sunil had come into contact with the ash from a

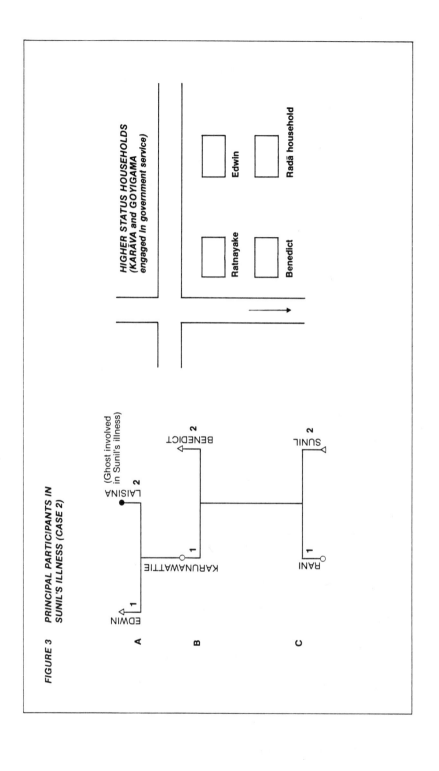

FIGURE 3   PRINCIPAL PARTICIPANTS IN
SUNIL'S ILLNESS (CASE 2)

funeral cremation which had not yet been purified by the sprinkling of **pirit** water. The gang, it turned out, had been pilfering coconuts on this occasion. Two goyigama men in the neighborhood, who were not professional exorcists, but who had some knowledge of curative mantra, were summoned. While they confirmed the suspicions of Sunil's friends and parents, they were not able to alleviate the illness. Sunil's father, Benedict, then summoned a berava exorcist who tied an **apa nul** to Mahasona. The symptoms abated and in a lucid moment Sunil compounded the theme of his illness as this had been identified. He stated that when he had cracked open a coconut, its flesh turned a deep blue black (the color of Mahasona) before his eyes and a great fear, a feeling of terror, surged through his body. He felt something heavy grasp him by the shoulder. The berava exorcist tied the thread as a protection for seven days, and the cause of Sunil's illness was further confirmed when, at the end of this period, Sunil was again overcome with madness. A thread was again tied for a further seven days, but this time with the explicit intention, as stated by the exorcist and agreed to by Sunil's father, that a large-scale exorcism for Mahasona would be held, preceded on the same day by a performance of the **Iramudun Samayama** for Riri Yaka.

Close relatives of the household assisted with some of the ritual preparations. They did this more out of a sense of obligation to kinsfolk than from any deep commitment as to the legitimacy of the illness. Some grumbled that Sunil was feigning demonic attack. Others noted that if Sunil was indeed suffering from Mahasona's malevolence then this had resulted from Sunil's own immoral action and that of the other gang members. It was even suggested that Sunil's contact with polluting funeral ash, was not accidental, but that Sunil had deliberately collected it for the purpose of sorcery. While they were prepared to help with the ritual arrangements, they claimed that all of them were too poor to make any cash contribution to the cost of the ritual. This did have some objective basis, for most of Sunil's relatives were engaged in ill-paid jobs as servants or laborers. None earned more than 70 rupees per month. But poverty, in many of the other cases I have observed, does not necessarily prevent relatives from offering cash support. I have recorded many instances where members of poverty-stricken households have pawned valuable items of property, a bicycle, a radio or jewelry, to help meet the costs of a relative's exorcism.

Sunil's parents attempted to deepen the emotional commitment of their relatives to the occasion and to assign to them some responsibility for Sunil's illness. His mother, Karunawattie (B,1) said that the ghost of her mother, Laisina (A,2), was afflicting the household and that this had made Sunil vulnerable to demonic attack. Karunawattie was the daughter of a mixed-caste marriage. Her father, Edwin (A,1), was goyigama but Laisina had been wahumpura, a lower-ranked caste.[10] Edwin's relatives had been against the marriage and for a time had no contact with him and his household. The important point, however, was that Laisina had been regarded as an outsider to Edwin's goyigama relatives in terms of both caste and kinship. That she was a ghost who had not yet been reborn was not their responsibility. If Laisina was now a ghost, so Sunil's goyigama relatives claimed, the responsibility for this rested only upon Edwin, his children and Laisina's wahumpura relatives.

Sunil's father attempted to link the illness with aspects of the immediate social context of his household. He indicated that sorcery might be involved in Sunil's illness and sought to legitimate this as an explanatory theme by referring to incipient caste hostilities in the neighborhood. He substantiated this by reference to the history of the settlement of his household and other relatives in the area. Benedict and his relatives began to settle in the neighborhood in the late 1950s, coming from their natal village on the outskirts of Galle. They chose the area because of its proximity to three major schools in the town. Benedict built his house next to a rada (washer) family on land owned by a goyigama lawyer. This family, together with a few other rada households in the vicinity, had arrived in their area some twenty years before Benedict. Benedict claimed that his next door rada neighbor was angered by Benedict's building a house nearby, for he had located it on land which the rada family had eventually hoped to buy. Benedict also declared that this rada household, and others, were jealous of his high position as a goyigama.

The rada caste is traditionally ranked low, and this is maintained in the urban context both by their tendency to follow the traditional caste occupation and by the nature of their continued traditional caste services in the domain of ritual. Thus, rada women are often employed to carry out the polluting tasks associated with exorcism ritual (the washing of clothes worn by the patient, cleaning the house) and are hired to wash the clothes and ritually bathe girls at their first menstruation. Benedict also stated that the rada members of the neighborhood had reason to be jealous of his household because his caste position as a goyigama meant that he and his family could more easily find employment in the wealthier households of the area. Many rada worked as house servants and could be seen as competing with poor goyigama for this work.

Benedict's understanding of the factors relating to Sunil's illness received little confirmation from others. Thus, Ratnayake, a goyigama neighbor, who was an electrician with the Municipal Council and whose wife was a secondary school teacher, openly objected to Benedict's claim that the latter's household had been ensorcelled by Benedict's rada neighbors. Ratnayake stated that the rada family and Benedict's family had, hitherto, freely associated on a friendly basis. He commented that they visited each other and that it was the daughter of the rada family who had run to fetch the exorcist upon the onset of Sunil's illness. The rada family members themselves drew attention to the many occasions in the past when they had helped Benedict's family. A pattern had developed in the neighborhood for households, particularly among the working-class residents and irrespective of caste, to engage in all kinds of mutual help. The women regularly visited each other. A number of them had organized rotating credit associations (sittu), a common feature of working-class areas, and these were multicaste in their membership.[11] Benedict's accusations threatened what they held to be neighborhood harmony. The accusations risked dividing those who had developed some dependence on each other, given their precarious and near subsistence economic circumstances.

Rather than accepting Benedict's allegations, most saw them as typical of his general "caste-minded" and troublesome behavior. His other next door neighbor, Charlie, a bus driver and a wahumpura, referred to the time when he had complained to Benedict over Sunil's having a sexual affair with his daughter. They quarreled and fought, spurred by Benedict's declaration that Charlie should be pleased that his daughter was friendly with a higher caste goyigama. Despite the lack of preparedness of others to accept Benedict's definition, Benedict maintained that the rada household was partly responsible for Sunil's illness. On the eve of the exorcism he told his rada neighbors, who offered their help in the ritual preparations, to leave.

The failure of either Sunil's mother or his father to win the support of their relatives or neighbors for their definition of the illness was largely responsible for the little assistance they received, in cash or help, for the exorcism. Both Benedict and Karunawattie were forced to depend on financial help from some of their more wealthy patrons. A retired karava station master, for whom Benedict did occasional jobs, gave 50 rupees.

Karunawattie borrowed 100 rupees from a local moneylender and her father borrowed a further 100 from the garage proprietor who hired him as a watchman.   Much of the cost was borne by the leader of Sunil's gang, Dharmadasa, a panikki who had recently opened a roadside shop.   Other members of Sunil's gang built the ritual structures and assisted with other aspects of the performance.   Apart from his immediate family, most of Sunil's relatives and neighbors commented that this was only right, as they considered that the moral responsibility for Sunil's illness lay predominantly with the gang.   Only a small audience gathered to witness the ritual events and Sunil, when it was over, was declared cured.   However, he suffered further relapses for which small, private, exorcisms were performed.

Exorcisms, and the diagnostic and definitional events leading to their performance, can backfire on patients and their households. This is so in the dual and interrelated sense of failing to provide some of the important conditions upon which a "cure" might be based and of failing to define and/or to redefine aspects of personal identity and of the social context which household members may view as integral to the illness.   While the diagnosis of demonic attack might reflect and refract that which is emotionally and socially problematic for individual members of a household, the diagnosis and the exorcism can intensify and by no means resolve the "demonic" nature of the situation —— the isolation of a patient and a household within a surrounding social world.   Sunil's case illustrates how an exorcism can backfire and leave a patient and a household little or none the better either in "health" or in the social world addressed through demonic illness and its treatment.

Sunil was a prime candidate for demonic attack.   His outburst of demonic behavior coincided with various difficulties which he was then encountering and which had recently come to a head.   These difficulties contributed to Sunil's increasing social isolation and, possibly, to a self awareness of the powerlessness of his present social condition.   Sunil was out of work and dependent on his family, itself impoverished, for support. His youth gang was breaking up.   The gang leader had opened a store, and two other gang members had found employment.   Three of his companions had recently married.   Sunil himself was of an age when young men typically assert their independence of the constraining authority of their parents. The demonic, as a symbol of human weakness and isolation, and its manifestation in the form of Mahasona was entirely appropriate to Sunil's situation. Perhaps it was too appropriate.

Sunil, although an excellent target for demonic possession, did not satisfy at least two conditions which can make demonic victims legitimate foci of sympathy and social support.   First, in Sinhalese cultural understandings demonic attack should ideally sign an **extraordinary,** out of the ordinary, change in behavior —— a relatively sudden transformation in identity and the way a person routinely goes about everyday activities.   The demonic as extraordinary in the Sinhalese imagination is explicit in demon masks, clay images, and paintings where demons are culturally represented in their extreme enormity and grotesquerie.   Second, a demonic victim ideally should not be seen as morally responsible or actively blameworthy for his or her affliction.   Demons are conceived of as intruding into their victims from outside, and this cultural view is consistent with a general attitude that victims are not directly responsible for their suffering. Asoka, in the previous case, became such a powerful symbolic focus of the problems of the panikki because, as an innocent child, her demonic experience was both extraordinary and no fault of her own.

Sunil's demonic possession did not mark his behavior as significantly different from his normal everyday activity. This was so in the sense that, like Mahasona who possessed him, Sunil was widely seen in his neighborhood as aggressive, bad tempered, occasionally violent, and unruly. The diagnosis of his attack revealed Sunil as to some extent blameworthy for his own affliction. Not only was he near a funeral place, a haunt of Mahasona, but some suspected he was collecting polluting funerary ash and, in any case, he was pilfering coconuts at the very moment he was attacked. Sunil either as a demonic victim or as unafflicted was not a person to whom many in his neighborhood could easily give sympathy or support.

Sunil's father did not help his son's cause. Benedict was seen by many others as being socially fractious. His accusatory behavior towards others upon his son's illness was viewed as further confirmation of Benedict's usual divisiveness, and interfered with the legitimating process of the diagnosis. The demonic implies social disorder and the presence of envy, jealousy, and conflict. Benedict's actions on this occassion were likely motivated by such a cultural understanding and they were certainly appropriate in a context ordered through an exorcist diagnostic framework. But Benedict did not develop his demonic understanding in close concert with an unfolding exorcist interpretation. He acted largely independently of the protective umbrella of a developing exorcist diagnosis. Perhaps this too was a factor which resulted in so little support for Benedict's household at their time of crisis.

Exorcism transforms a demonic identity into an identity where normal social roles can be reassumed. Potentially, exorcisms act upon personal identity in its widest social significances and as these significances are incorporated within the idea of the demonic. Exorcism returns and restores a person to the world. Sunil's case points to some of this potential, even in the tragedy of failure —— a failure possibly produced in the fact that the world which Sunil had entered through his demonic possession was little different from the world he had left. The circumstances surrounding Sunil's demonic attack suggest that Sunil, with the support of his parents, was seeking a retypification of personal identity as this had become defined in his neighborhood. Sunil's possession by Mahasona reflected in a heightened way his reputation as a local tough and petty criminal. By destroying Mahasona in an exorcism, Sunil by extension could also destroy aspects of a social identity which had become self-defeating and isolating as his gang broke up, as well as problematic for his family.

The following case examines further exorcism as a practice relevant to the routine organization of social identity in everday life. Additionally, the case involves a patient who had a long history of demonic possession and treatment by exorcism. Unlike the previous cases, therefore, this victim's condition had many of its aspects defined in advance of the current onset of demonic illness which I now describe.

CASE 3: A Chronic Illness

The patient, Indranie, (C,6) was an unmarried woman of thirty two. She lived in the house of her aged parents, who were goyigama. Her parents and many of her relatives were of recognized high socioeconomic status in the neighborhood in which they lived on the northern edge of Galle municipality. Her father, a prominent owner of land and property, was a retired government civil servant. Indranie's relatives held important positions in government bureaucracies or in private business and her recurrent illness was a constant source of embarrassment to them.

Indranie had been medically diagnosed as an epileptic and was in receipt of regular medical treatment at the government hospital. Even so, she and her relatives interpreted her condition as more than a physical problem and

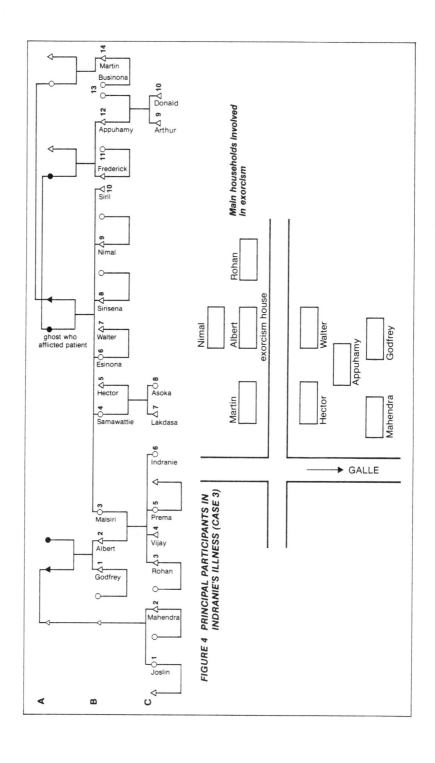

FIGURE 4 PRINCIPAL PARTICIPANTS IN
INDRANIE'S ILLNESS (CASE 3)

related it to the malign activity of demons. Her epilepsy had first made its appearance when as a girl of fourteen she had been admitted to a well-known and highly regarded girls' secondary school in Galle. She had fallen down in a fit and badly burned her hand, which became horribly scarred. Indranie and her family attributed this first experience of epilepsy and the burning of her hand to sorcery. She considered that she had been ensorcelled by a neighbor who was jealous of her success in being admitted to a school for which there was intense competition for entry. Indranie's mother had taken her to an astrologer, at some distance from Galle, who confirmed that someone in her area had performed a **kodivina** against her. Her mother also suspected the malign agency of Indranie's deceased maternal grandmother. Sorcery and ghostly attack were to be a recurrent theme in the understanding of Indranie's illness.

Indranie had, since the first epileptic experience, many epileptic attacks. These were signaled by extreme outbursts of temper, followed by convulsions. Her family and others noted that these frequently occurred after she had been involved in some kind of stressful situation, often when she had been insulted, engaged in a minor argument, or in some way personally humiliated. Indranie, because of her epilepsy, was regarded by others in her neighborhood as strange and abnormal. In many ways she was a figure of fun. Those who were not related to her would recount an instance when she had tried to post a letter with a used stamp and had been severely upbraided by the local postmaster. Humiliated, Indranie fell into a convulsive fit. Indranie's bouts of temper and convulsions were typical symptoms of malign demonic eyesight. She was known to be terrified of the world of demons. Most of her severe attacks were followed by minor exorcisms and more recently, in the last six years, her family had held three major exorcism performances for her. She had had a **Suniyama** and two **Mahasona** exorcisms. But it had been two years since the last performance of a major demon rite.

The onset of the present illness was marked by a large swelling on her throat. Indranie went with her mother to the local medical clinic and then to a **vedarala**. The latter drew his clientele largely from the middle class and had introduced a variety of innovations into his medical practice. The most remarkable was his use of "electrical" treatment. Thus, he would attach wires connected to a battery on the place where the patient was affected. Indranie received this treatment. In the evening, and while at home, her mother offered her rice to eat. Indranie threw the rice on the ground and in a violent rage ran out of the house and down the street. She screamed that she did not want rice but meat, and that she was going to the cemetery, where her grandmother was buried. Indranie's mother and other neighbors forcibly restrained her and, quietened, she returned to the house. In the view of her mother, Indranie was obviously being attacked by her maternal grandmother's ghost. The next morning mother and daughter went to visit an exorcist. He was the same exorcist who had treated Indranie on many previous occasions. He confirmed the mother's suspicions, but stated that it was inadvisable for him to stage an exorcism at this time. Instead, he suggested that Indranie, her parents, and other close relatives organize a **dana** to the monks at their temple on behalf of Indranie's grandmother. Indranie was not satisfied with this and declared that she wanted a large demon ceremony.

The next day Indranie argued with her next door neighbor. This neighbor, Businona (B,13), was the second wife of one of Indranie's maternal kin. Businona asked Indranie why she was sick, and Indranie replied that the ghost of a relative of the former wife of Businona's husband had attacked her. Indranie added that she suspected that her grandmother craved the wealth of her family and was jealous of their social position.   Indranie alluded to the important social connections of her family.   Her father, Albert (B,2), she said, was closely related to a prominent national politician, Mahendra (C,2).   At this, Businona flared up and insultingly told Indranie to leave (**"palyan pissi"** - scram, mad woman).   This event was followed, shortly after, by Indranie's experiencing a violent convulsive fit.   Indranie's mother summoned the exorcist, a goyigama, to the house and he tied a thread to Kalu Yaka.

Indranie was subject to considerable stress, which could have contributed to certain features of her illness display, independent of her anxiety at the swelling of her throat.   Her chronic epileptic condition, as I have said, made her an object of public fun and ridicule.   She was upset by the curiosity she caused in others.   Thus, she complained that on public transport people always commented on her scarred hand.   Indranie expressed a sense of isolation even in the midst of her own kin.   The angry insult by Businona was an objective instance of this.   Indranie complained that her elder brother, Vijay (C,4), who was single and lived in the same house, did not want to be seen with her in public.   It is possible that her selection of her deceased grandmother as an agent in her illness, now as in the past, expressed her need for support from her kin.   Indranie's father had married into the area, and her largest set of locally based kin was related to her maternal grandmother.   Her family at the time of the onset of her illness interpreted aspects of her insistence for a major ceremony as a plea for support.

The physical elements of Indranie's condition, which related to her own feelings of rejection, and which created her as an object of curiosity and sometimes ridicule, also contradicted her own opinion of herself as a person deserving respect.   She was conscious of her good education and the high status of her   family.   Her comment to Businona regarding her high-placed political connection   revealed aspects of this.   The angry rejection by Businona confirmed Indranie's discordant feelings.

Indranie's awareness of a disjunction between her social position and her public image was not assisted by the attitude of her close family kin.   Vijay's attitude was part of a general social embarrassment which Indranie's epileptic condition caused her family, an embarrassment of which she was acutely conscious.   Her brothers particularly were embarrassed by her repeated resort to exorcism treatment.   Indranie commented, and this was confirmed by their own statements, that they did not want her to have large publicly performed exorcisms.   This was a major reason why Indranie had not had a large demon ceremony for over two years, despite the fact that she had experienced a number of convulsive fits.   Indranie's brothers, and certain of her other kin, were devout middle-class Buddhists, who were of the opinion that belief in demons and exorcism were antagonistic to proper Buddhist thinking.   Indranie's close male relatives considered that if Indranie insisted on a major exorcism, such a public performance would communicate an image counter to the one they wished to present.   Her condition reflected poorly enough, in their view, on their own social esteem and that of their family.   Moreover, they referred to the earlier exorcism occasions, for which they had spent large sums of money.   Rather than ending her illness, they remarked, these exorcisms had confirmed further the public view that Indranie was controlled by demons.   At one exorcism, while in a trance, Indranie had climbed one of the principal ritual structures, which indicated the extreme degree of demonic control over her action.

Perhaps understandably, Indranie's brothers, were initially resistant to her pressure for another exorcism.   This intensified Indranie's feelings of rejection, which she expressed in violent outbursts of temper.   Their attitude, and particularly that of her eldest brother, Rohan (C,3), had all the more significance as Rohan was attempting to arrange a marriage for Indranie.   So far he had had little success, a fact which hardly could have assisted Indranie's own self-image.   Rohan stated that an exorcism now would further inhibit his efforts.   No one locally would marry his sister, and certainly not unless a large dowry was involved.   He was against any move to a major exorcism and stated that if Indranie refrained from an insistence on a large exorcism, then those in the area would forget the previous occasions.

Rohan was particularly concerned at the initial tying of the **apa nul** to Kalu Yaka.   He and other members of the family were aware of the negative public attitude regarding the nature of Indranie's condition which had developed over recent years.   This was that Indranie had a severe sexual craving, was consumed by erotic thoughts, and in fact had been attacked by Madana Yaka (the love or passion demon).   He is a form of Kalu Yaka (see Wirz 1954:103-104; Ariyapala 1956:218), who causes strong and immoral desire in young men and women.   The term **pissi,** used by Businona to Indranie, had the additional sense in the context of Businona's usage of attack by Madana Yaka and a madness caused by copulation with him.   In the more extreme views of some, Madana Yaka pollutes his victims and symbolically takes their virginity.   If an exorcism to Kalu Yaka were performed, this would legitimate some of the social stigma which attached to Indranie's condition and would further reduce her marriage chances.

Indranie, as an unmarried woman approaching middle age, was particularly vulnerable to such an understanding of her illness.   Most women tend to be married by their late twenties.   Her eldest sister, Prema (C,5), who was only six years her senior, had been married ten years previously. Indeed, Prema attributed Indranie's condition to a desire to be married and to jealousy at her (Prema's) own success.   Prema was married to a university lecturer.   Women who remain unmarried often become the subjects of gossip and are suspected of immoral sexual behavior, or at least intense sexual craving.   While Prema and her brothers were concerned for their sister's illness, they also expressed an attitude held by others outside the immediate family that Indranie was sexually crazed.

However, aspects connected with the process of the definition and legitimation of the illness made it difficult for Indranie's siblings, and particularly Rohan, to prevent a performance of a major demon ceremony. Moreover, they were caught in a vicious circle.   While the staging of an exorcism ran the risk of legitimating the opinion of others concerning the nature of their sister's illness, not to perform one meant that the public image of Indranie would in all likelihood persist.   There were elements which emerged in the definition and diagnosis of the illness, however, which did allow them to give more positive support.

Indranie's present illness could have been attached easily to previously legitimated instances.   The theme of her grandmother's ghostly attack was an agreed element of the current manifestation of the illness, as it had been of earlier ones.   Indranie's mother supported the opinion that the grandmother was an agency in her daughter's illness, even though some of her kin disagreed.   Indranie's father attached some of his own problems to her illness.   He argued that his wife's relatives might be envious of his social and economic position, a position that was thrown into relief by the emergence into political prominence of his own close relative.   This envy could be expressed in the malign attention of his deceased mother-in-law. More importantly, he was worried about the possibility of sorcery.   This was already a theme in Indranie's illness, one confirmed by the exorcist. Indranie argued that sorcery was an element in earlier instances of her illness and elaborated it further in relation to her recent experience. Thus, Indranie said that the failure of the traditional physician's electrical treatment, which was reportedly effective in other cases, was caused by **kodivina.** Indranie's father supported his daughter. He expected sorcery to be directed against him or his family because of his local prominence as a land and property owner. He had been involved in land disputes with his wife's kin, with whom he held land shares in common. He did not openly implicate his wife's relatives in sorcery, but it was well known in the area that there was internal dissension among the sets of kin related by marriage. One instance he did relate as possibly productive of sorcery concerned a recent occasion when he had been asked by a local fisherman to let one of the three houses he (Indranie's father) owned. He refused and an angry argument had ensued.

Indranie's own illness-behavior continued and caused increased embarrassment for her family and other kin. The exorcist was again called in, and he tied another thread, this time to Kalu Sanni Yaka. He diagnosed the swelling on Indranie's neck and her earlier rejection of rice as an attack by Sanni Yaka, who attacks the humor of phlegm. More specifically, it was Sanni Yaka in the form of Kalu Yaka, who primarily attacks women. It was agreed by Indranie's parents that a **Sanni Yakuma** to cut the malign effect of this demon be performed, together with a **preta pideni** for Indranie's grandmother and the cutting of an ash pumpkin **(puhul kapanava)** to break the spell of sorcery.

Indranie's **Sanni Yakuma** exorcism attracted a large audience from the neighborhood. Most of her kin were present and many traveled from other parts of the island. In all, over 500 people attended. The size of the gathering not only expressed the concern for Indranie's condition, but also reflected the social and political prominence of the household in the town and the wider context of the island. Her brothers took an active role in the ritual preparations, assisting in the building of the ritual structures. Rohan sat beside his sister throughout the night, comforting Indranie and giving offerings on her behalf to the demons and to the deities.

Indranie's illness, in its social construction, incorporated many of the problems which she and others encountered in their social lives. Their incorporation in the exorcist's diagnosis, and to some extent its resolution of the contrary attitudes towards the performance of a major exorcism by some of her close kin, facilitated agreement for a large-scale performance.

The most significant aspect of the case relates to the chronic nature of Indranie's condition. Exorcisms are sometimes repeatedly performed for those who suffer from chronic mental and physical disabilities: disabilities which, because of the negative cultural understandings which can attach to them, can disrupt the pursuit of a "normal" life in the everyday world of Sinhalese.[12] This points to the role of exorcisms in alleviating the effects of a patient's condition as this becomes socially problematic in the form of a negative and stigmatizing social identity. Through the idea of the demonic the identity of a patient as it has come to be socially conceived can be directly addressed, and shown not to be the personal responsibility of the patient, but occasioned by external and capricious demonic attack outside the patient's control. Exorcisms, by expelling demons who intrude their identity upon their victims, an identity which is not the patient's own, can change the relationship of patients to their social world and potentially free them, for a time, from the consequences of a condition which places limits upon their social action. In Indranie's case the diagnosis of her demonic illness itself involved a contradiction of some of the more popular views of her condition. Specifically, it confronted the opinion that Madana Yaka was an agent in the illness, stressing rather Kalu Yaka in his **sanni** form.

Demonic Attack, Identity and Context

A variety of perspectives has been developed towards traditional healing practices within the field of medical anthropology (e.g., see Fabrega 1971, 1972; Lieban 1967, 1977; Kleinman 1980). In general, anthropologists have stressed the sociocultural aspects of illness, although within this perspective there has been a long-term trend towards individual psychological and psychoanalytic frameworks of interpretation. The sociocultural emphasis is to be expected given the nature of the discipline and, with some notable exceptions (e.g., Kleinman 1980; G. Lewis 1975; Loudon 1976), the lack of training in Western biomedical science among anthropologists. I am in some agreement with Fabrega (1972:186) in relation to the problems set within medical anthropology that greater attention should be placed on the physiological process which might underlie patient disorder, and rather more with Kleinman, who criticizes a narrowness in perspective. Kleinman states that, "it is the **relationships** between different analytic levels (i.e., cultural, social, psychological, physiological) that are of special significance for understanding the healing process . . . these crucial interactions are precisely what the reductionist approach to healing avoids" (Kleinman 1980: 364). In relation to traditional healing practice, however, Kleinman places the greatest importance upon the understanding of illness in its cultural and social construction. I, because of my lack of specialist expertise, cannot precisely evaluate the physiological and psychological problems which might attach to patients understood to be demonically attacked, and thus cannot trace the complex interrelation between these and the sociocultural world in which patients live.[13] But I make only a limited apology for this. Demonic illness is above all a sociocultural construct to be understood first and foremost at this level and in its own cultural and social terms.

Central to my overall argument is that illness demonically conceived is not reducible to terms independent of its demonic conception. To sign an event of illness and suffering as the work of demons is to invoke some of the most powerful Sinhalese metaphors of destruction and disorder, and to point to death and cosmic disruption as ultimate possibilities. To recognize demonic agency is to constitute or to reconstitute an illness demonically (and in a way distinct from the construction of suffering through other specialisms in Sinhalese culture). I cannot overstress this. In the demonic idea articulated in practice coheres a particular accent upon the realities of patients, and others in their context, in which the demonic is as much **the** reality as it is reflective or symbolic of reality. Physical, mental, and social disorders can be themselves metaphors of the demonic, as the demonic may be the metaphor or symbolic representation of underlying physical, mental, or social disorder.

In other words, physical, mental, and social disorder can be the idioms of demonic maleficence and not necessarily the other way round. In the demonic conception, each implies the other, and it is integral to the logic of exorcist diagnosis that an individual's suspicion of a demonic experience be reflected and evidenced in emotional, physical, and social disorder. To raise the specter of the demonic as an agent of personal suffering is to generate its key idioms and to "create" the conditions for the further and elaborated recognition of the demonic.

When I say that physical, emotional and social disorders can be the idioms of the demonic this does not make them less real or vital in the patient's and others' experience and understanding; they exist as the totality of demonic experience and the basis of demonic terror.

A general implication of the above argument is that no particular theoretical orientation of, for example, a western medical, psychological, psychoanalytic or sociological kind, is privileged in the explanation of demonic illness. One further point: where the experience of suffering, realized as demonic attack, is rooted objectively in physical or mental or social disturbance, its comprehension as demonic transforms the meaning of the illness, and exposes it to all the potential significance of the demonic. A reduction, therefore, of the demonic to analytical terms which deny the integrity of the demonic as a phenomenon in and of itself, distorts and limits understanding.

The social definition and diagnosis of demon attack marks, as it can be instrumental in, a radical redefinition of the social identity of a demonic victim and the relation of the victim to her or his social context.[14] The term **aturaya** designates a victim of demonic malevolence, and patients during an exorcism will be addressed by the term. The victim is the center of demonic illness and pollution, and can assume the character of the demonic, as in all the cases discussed. Such individuals do not contain their disorder or sickness within an otherwise normal social identity. Their total identity is changed, or threatens a change, into the demonic. This change of patient identity signs, as it may actively convert, the sufferer into another and abnormal possibility of being which can alter the way an individual is related to and responded to by people in the surrounding social context. The diagnosis of an individual as a demonic victim suspends all other aspects of the victim's social identity. It isolates a patient as the vehicle and subordinate of the demonic, and reorients others to the victim in such a way as to deny a normal sociality, in effect the victim's normal social being.

The demonic identity of the patient is an integral aspect of the illness itself. The illness, then, is not simply a cultural expression of deeper-seated physiological or psychological or sociological troubles effectively translatable into the terms, for example, of a Western scientific discourse. I do not mean by this that the physiological and psychological difficulties of a patient, independent of a demonic conception, are not important to an understanding of a patient's condition. I insist, however, that the demonic is not just an idiom in which disorder and suffering is comprehended, or a medium for intersubjective understanding within a particular culture, it **is,** rather, the illness, its disorder and suffering.

I have concentrated on the definition and diagnosis of illness as a discourse which involves exorcists and their clients (those for whom the illness is problematic) and may engage, as well as the patient, household kin, other relatives, neighbors and friends. This discourse is enabled by the fact that exorcist knowledge is an abstraction and elaboration upon common-sense cultural ideas and typifications through which Sinhalese comprehend their action and experience in the world. The diagnostic categories of exorcists are not opposed to, or greatly distinct from, the cultural views of their clients, but they are extensions, or heightened, more esoteric and codified versions of those interpretational schemas variously employed by clients. The appeal of exorcist practice and the acceptance of the legitimacy of exorcist diagnosis rests both in its elaboration upon common-sense and in its framing of common-sense in terms which appear to rise above mundane, nonspecialist interpretation.

The diagnosis and definition of demonic illness, seen as emergent in a discourse, is not reducible either to a mechanistic consideration of the diagnostic categories of exorcists and the "rules" governing their operation, or to the specific situated circumstances of exorcist clients —— in which view, the diagnostic expertise of exorcists is reduced to an **ad hoc** exercise dictated by the "logic" or particularities of the client situation.

Exorcist diagnosis, as a system revealed in its practices, attaches significance to gender, age, time, and place of initial demonic experience, mental and emotional display, dreams, problems in a social and political world and so forth. These identify, within the framework of specialist understanding, possible maleficent agents. Also other factors relevant to exorcist knowledge —— the structure of the demon world, the underlying principles of a cosmic unity and hence of its disturbance, etc. —— organize exorcist enquiry. Exorcist knowledge (which is variable) to some extent defines the parameters of diagnostic practice, but it does not determine the diagnosis. The diagnosis is emergent in the conjunction of exorcist knowledge and the circumstances of its application. In this conjunction the meaning and experience of a broader social context become formed within a developing diagnostic structure articulated by an exorcist. The categories of exorcist diagnosis are infinitely expandable so as to incorporate within the single explanatory framework of the demonic most aspects of experience as this may be culturally realized. Moreover, as the cases of Asoka and Indranie illustrate, divergent opinions regarding the cause of illness can be contained, and to some extent resolved, within the framework of exorcist practice. Indeed, in the process of the discourse of an exorcist with clients, radically new definitions of the situation, and the meaning of experience within it, can emerge.

The definition and diagnosis of demonic attack, while constituted in context, is also constitutive of context. Illness, its demonic comprehension and the meaning of illness in relation to a wider social world, emerge together in a dialectical process, and take shape within exorcist diagnostic categories. Herein lies some of the power and potential efficacy of exorcism ritual, for it addresses and acts upon that which it defines and encompasses.

Demonic attack, while it finds its most acute manifestation in the individual person of the patient, can signal and symbolize problems in the experience of others associated with the patient. The presence of a single individual attacked by demons casts the shadow of the demonic over an entire context, and gives rise to the possibility of demonic intervention in the lives of others. Motivated by cultural ideas relating to demons (ideas articulated and brought to consciousness in the patient's problematic and the diagnostic process), others associated with the patient will search their own biographies for evidence of demonic malevolence. This was so, for example, in Asoka's case where Millison interpreted her own suffering as relevant to Asoka's distress; and in the case of Indranie, where her father was enlivened to the possibility of sorcery in his own experience. Not only may those who live in the presence of a demonic victim attach a demonic significance to their own experience, but also they may actively address their own problems through the body of the patient.

While demonic attack is an invasion of one person in particular, it is not necessarily to be interpreted by a reduction in analysis to the concerns of the individual in whom it is most clearly manifested. Demonic attack is a transformation of the identity of the patient and also potentially of a social context, its meaning and experience, as this context is inhabited by others. Indeed the acuteness of a patient's demonic distress, as I have witnessed it on numerous occasions, may be directly proportional to the distress and suffering of others, a distress and suffering which the patient can come to embody. The demonic illness of a patient can transcend the patient in the sense that its force and terror is also to be discoverable in the lives, experiences, and relationships of others who surround a patient. To return to an earlier point: an individualistic orientation to illness, one which focuses on the physical or psychological condition of a patient, may mislocate the root of the illness or undervalue its production in a wider structural context.

The case material I have discussed illustrates that the condition of a patient can bring to focus and can express social, economic, and political problems affecting a victim and others. It is important that this is not seen as merely some function of the strategic intent on the part of a patient or another to use personal suffering, or to fake physical and mental disorder, as a means of addressing other social and political difficulties. To do this is not only to impute to illness a motive which cannot be verified, it is also to deprecate the very real anguish which most demonic victims experience and display. Moreover, such a perspective would fail to see that the social, economic, and political import of demonic illness is produced as an integral aspect of its definition and diagnosis.

The incorporation of wider social, political, and economic factors in demonic illness is a propensity of Sinhalese cultural ideas of the demonic conjoined with the logic of exorcist diagnostic practice. I referred above to the "inter-metaphoric" dimensions of the demonic whereby, for example, it is manifested simultaneously in physical, mental, and social disorder, each signing and symbolizing the other. Once the idea of the demonic is introduced into the understanding of an event of individual distress, then it begins to resonate with, and open up numerous possibilities of the experiential context of a patient and others. The resonance of the demonic gains additional force in a discourse between exorcists and clients, which is directed to the determination and legitimation of the nature of illness. In such a discourse a subjective world of demonic experience receives objectification in a shared but problematic reality where economic hardship, political conflict, and public social slights and injuries can evidence a demonic disorder.

Exorcist diagnosis engages a principle of reciprocal validation: the common-sense of clients is authenticated in the esoteric domain of exorcist knowledge, while in turn the specialist determinations of exorcists are validated through a search of client experience and an establishment of substantive congruency with a common-sense interpretation of this experience. The principle of reciprocal validation is a key dynamic underlying the incorporative and encompassing features of exorcist diagnosis. In this dynamic a social, economic and political world is pulled within the boundaries of the demonic, and this world becomes defined in the identification of the demonic and assumes the disordered and distorted proportions of the demonic.

A social and political world embraced, and pointed to, in the demonic is integral to the logic and process of diagnosis and definition. Here also is some of the power of major demon ceremonies to effect a cure, for they address a world as it meets a patient and others in the fullness of the potential disorder of this world. More, as I discussed in reference to Asoka's case, major demon ceremonies actively restore an order and occasion the restructuring of social and political relationships in a way which is entirely relevant to a return to health. The social and political significance which the performance of major demon ceremonies may assume is vital in the logic and process of exorcism ritual itself, as this mundane significance is to the concept of the demonic and to the definition and diagnosis of demonic attack. The functioning of demonic attack and exorcisms in these ways is not a latent or even unintended consequence of them. Demonic attack, and its treatment, can come to have wide social and political import quite apart from any individual intent or motivation to use it in these ways.

If this chapter has raised some issues in the field of medical anthropology, it was not conceived as an exercise in this area of the discipline. I have been primarily concerned with providing information about the kinds of patients and the types of problems managed through exorcist practice and about the process which can lead to major exorcism performance. In the lives of Sinhalese, demonic illness and exorcism ritual have greater significance than just being seen as problems for medical anthropology or as parts of a system of health care. Demonic attack, and especially the major rituals which address it, take as problematic the principles upon which a cultural and social world and a wider cosmic unity are based. More specifically, the way demonic attack is conceptualized, diagnosed, and the situation of its relevance defined, creates exorcism as an important domestic or household rite. To neglect this aspect of exorcism ritual is to overlook one of its central features.

Exorcisms, and particularly the major rites, have their importance as household ritual highlighted when they are set in relation to the overall complex of rites available to Sinhalese centering on a household and its members. Most Sinhalese rituals held in the context of the house are limited to points in the life cycle and/or are restricted in the degree to which they present members of a household, and often a more extended range of kindred, before their wider community and in terms of their social articulation into it. Regular domestic ritual among Sinhalese focuses on the worship of the Buddha and the deities, but this typically is performed inside the house and away from public view. Family groups will visit the local temple on **poya** (full moon) days and observe the Buddhist precepts, but on these occasions the family and the household are subsumed in a community of worshippers. Girls' puberty rites (Winslow 1980), marriage ceremonies, and funerals are held at the house and, of course, reflect aspects of the social structuring of the household into a community which surrounds it. But these are life cycle rituals relatively limited in their occurrences for any one household.

Demons can attack anyone and strike without warning. So, too, conflicts, misfortunes, and a host of other difficulties can spring unplanned into the lives of Sinhalese, disturbing the equilibrium of individuals and rendering problematic the hitherto taken-for-granted ordering of their social world. The demonic tracks the ebb and flow of life in a mundane reality, upsetting and threatening its vital rhythms. The everyday world of experience and action is immediately relevant in the demonic, and the demonic takes its form and manifests its malevolence within it. The demonic encapsulates the abnormality of individual experience and the disturbance in an encompassing social world in which a patient and a household are set. Major exorcisms make the patient **and** the household the singular focus of a public ritual performance and establish a context in which the problematic nature of the social relationships of a patient and a household can be directly addressed. Exorcisms deal with the unplanned and the unexpected as this finds meaning in the articulation of individuals and their households into an everyday cultural and social world.

That major demon ceremonies are domestic and household rites, not limited to a stage in the life cycle or restricted to periods in a ritual calendar, is an understanding which allows us to proceed to the problem of the next chapter. Here my attention turns to the question of why it is that women are so often the subject of major exorcisms.

5. Exorcisms and the
Symbolic Identity of Women

It is a widely reported ethnographic phenomenon that women are more often the subjects of rites of healing and cults of exorcism than are men. Sri Lanka provides no exception to this observation. My initial purpose here will be to examine some of the well-known anthropological explanations for the phenomenon and to test their adequacy against my own Sri Lanka material. A major criticism which I offer relates to the anthropological discussion of the motivation of women to illness, and the management of illness within a particular cultural medium, which tends to reduce the motivation of women to individual factors, often psychological, or to their individual and category disadvantage in a practical economic and political world. Such perspectives tend to underplay the motivating power of culture itself, the organizing ideas and constructs of culture through which individuals interpret their action and experience to themselves and to others. Women, I argue, are subject to demonic attack as a function of their cultural typification, which places them in a special and significant relation to the demonic. With reference to this, I address the symbolic identity of women, and the logic of its constitution in Sinhalese culture, as critical in accounting for the frequency of their demonic attack and exorcist treatment relative to men.

Some Theories about Women

There have been many attempts to explain the relative frequency whereby women, in contrast to men, have recourse to possession states or other ritual means for the expression of problems which beset them. The solution has been sought variously by reference to the psychological characteristics of women; by reference to their structural position within a society; and by reference to the cultural attitudes and beliefs which relate to them. LeVine has argued that most anthropologists assume with varying degrees of emphasis "that there is some kind of adaptive fit between the personality characteristics of a population and the sociocultural environment of that population" (1973:98). In accordance with his view, most also assume "that individual personality, no less than the sociocultural system, is a functioning system with dispositions that manifest themselves in individual behaviour." These statements by LeVine as they stand might be unexceptionable, but their exercise in the hands of certain anthropologists is not without difficulties. Lewis' (1971) analysis of shamanism and cults of possession and the role of women is a case in point. He views the trance and possession states of Somali women to be a psychological release for the tensions which have built up in them as a result of their subordinate position in Somali society: as a means for expressing and rectifying their social grievances, and as a means for representing their social solidarity **vis-à-vis** men. Lewis extends this analysis to account for the high proportion of women engaged in similar cults of possession elsewhere in Africa and Asia and correlates this with their social and political peripherality. He states:

> In rural Ceylon . . . subordinate women are frequently beset by demons which cause sickness and voice the demands of the afflicted host very clearly. Here, as we have seen in some previous examples, there is also explicit evidence that women resent the position granted them by men: the partial alleviation which they achieve by possession does not exhaust their antagonism. Thus women frequently pray to be reborn as men and give other indications of their dissatisfaction with their lot as a sex (Obeyesekere 1970b). . . . It will now be clear, I think, that we are dealing with a widespread strategy employed by women to achieve ends which they cannot readily obtain more directly. Women are, in effect, making a special virtue of adversity and affliction, and, often quite literally, capitalizing on their distress" (1971:84–85).

In his reference to Sri Lanka, Lewis draws on the work of Obeyesekere. The latter explicitly states that for one village he studied in the Central Province of the island, "the social situation fosters antagonism between the sexes" (Obeyesekere 1963a:331). He also states that "Sinhalese culture places a high premium on male greatness and superordination, and female inferiority. Submissiveness, chastity, modesty are the prime virtues for women" (Obeyesekere 1970b:101). Obeyesekere's observation, cited by Lewis, that women often express a desire to be reborn as men relates to a belief that they are only able to achieve the general Buddhist life-ideal of **nirvana** once they become men in another birth. Obeyesekere further argues that general cultural evaluations in Sinhalese society and especially those pertaining to women produce psychological repressions and deep psychological conflicts concerning the awareness of self in women. A general view of Obeyesekere's is that there are contradictions in Sinhalese culture, as these focus on women, which produce in them "criticism, evaluation of, and dissatisfaction with the female role, and an envy of the valued roles of men (and often children); and they are all functions of the self" (1970b:102). In addition, Obeyesekere states, "On the basis of the psychological problems arising from the status-role situation of Sinhalese women we could draw certain inferences regarding demonic possession. The existence of hysterical predispositions in the personality make up of women could lead to a general propensity towards expressing conflict in terms of possession and towards **accepting** possession as a culturally constituted projective system" (1970b:102).

Leaving aside for the moment the question of whether women as a category are more predisposed than men to psychological hysteria and thus more impelled towards receiving exorcism treatment, there are important differences as well as similarities in the arguments presented by Lewis and

Obeyesekere. Both scholars see possession as the occasion for the release of psychological tensions. Obeyesekere, however, views psychological conflict, produced by the cultural attitudes towards women, and their structural position, as being primarily responsible for their seeking exorcism. He does not necessarily agree with Lewis that the reason for the greater involvement of women in demonic possession is directly related to their concern to express a social solidarity as women **vis-à-vis** men or a concern to reverse their normally socially subordinate position as women by participating in a ritual context in which they dominate or are the focus of attention. As a more psychologically based argument, even though derived from a set of culturally and socially located observations, Obeyesekere's position is difficult either to refute or to substantiate. A fundamental difficulty which such an argument poses, however, is that it is critically dependent on an assumption that general cultural and social processes will uniformly lead women rather than men to be predisposed to psychological hysteria, which is amenable to exorcism treatment. Obeyesekere's argument is also dependent on an assumption that demon exorcism functions primarily as a context for the release of various psychological hysterias and repressions and that there are few other alternatives open to women. But Obeyesekere's own evidence indicates that there are other alternatives open to them, and, furthermore, that women, far from repressing conflicts derived from their cultural and social position, air them publicly. Writing of intersex antagonism Obeyesekere states,

> Various manifestations, covert and overt, of such antagonism could be observed in the social structure. Such antagonisms are not ritualized as they are in some societies, but receive expression in culturally uncanalized directions. The most obvious manifestation of inter-sex antagonism is overt hostility, in the form of physical violence on the part of the male, and vituperation on the part of the female. Our field-notes show that all men beat their wives or, in the case of older women with grown-up children, have beaten them when they were younger. Most of the physical assaults are on wives who are capable of bearing children (those addressed as **kella** girl) and not on the older wives who are past the menopause (addressed as **pavula**) and have grown-up children. The younger the wife the greater the physical punishment she receives at the hands of her husband. Husbands often tell the anthropologist that the younger wives are beaten so often because they talk back to their husbands; they are so cocky and full of spirit that they have to be tamed in the first years of marriage (not at all a surprising fact). These physical assaults are sometimes quite serious, often causing bodily injury to the wife. Some cases called for hospitalization. The typical provocations for wifebeating seem to be (a) abuse by the wife; (b) failure to obey the husband or look to his needs, such as preparing his food at the right time; (c) suspicion of infidelity. **The wife, incidentally, is no passive recipient of assaults —— she often abuses her husband, particularly for idleness, and when she is beaten, out rushes a spate of filth and obscenity** (1963b:331, my emphasis).

My own data record similar instances but support my overall impression that Sinhalese women are often highly independent and are not prepared to adopt entirely, without a struggle, the submissive ideal espoused towards them by men. Indeed, in the presence of such vituperative women and given the male ideology, it is surprising that men are not more a complex of neuroses than the literature appears to suggest. Of course, physical beating might be productive of repression and lead women to resort to the protection of ritual means for the release of their anxieties. But repression as part of a general explanation for the frequency with which women resort to exorcisms is inadequate. Many women who have exorcisms are either young and unmarried or are older and past childbearing. These, in terms of the factors relating to the stage in their socialization into a culture, are at points in their life careers where in accordance with Obeyesekere's argument they are less repressed and, with reference particularly to older women, come to play a wider social and political role in their local communities.

Lewis' explicitly sociological argument is perhaps more amenable to refutation or substantiation than the more psychologically, or psychodynamically, grounded explanation presented by Obeyesekere. The validity of Lewis' thesis is expressly dependent upon the fact that women are opposed to men, as a function of their subordination to them, and that possession and exorcism rituals operate mainly as a means to circumvent their social position as women. This is not clearly borne out by my evidence. Women patients, in some of the exorcism rituals I have observed, will voice their grievances against men. I have witnessed occasions when women will express their marital complaints and in a state of trance pummel their husbands and publicly abuse their husband's kin. But just as often women will voice grievances which affect their households and their sets of relatives as a whole. There is no necessary correlation, therefore, between the type of grievances aired and the status and position of women as dominated by, and opposed to, men. Indeed, the process whereby illness is defined is one which can lead away from a particular focus on the problems which women, either individually or as a category, experience as a consequence of a subordinate social position. Furthermore, such a process can encourage the production of sympathy, of emotional and social support, not simply in terms of the patient's specific status as a woman, but rather in terms of the patient's and others' membership in a social group, inclusive of both men and women, which shares common difficulties and problems and for which the illness might represent a particular, objectified, instance of such problems.

Wilson (1967) has already argued that the opposition between the sexes and the subordination of females to males might not account for the frequency by which women resort to possession states. As an alternative hypothesis, Wilson posits that "spirit possession and similar states seem more closely correlated with social situations which regularly, though not necessarily give rise to conflict, competition, tension, rivalry or jealousy between members of the **same** sex rather than between members of opposite sexes" (1967:366). Wilson reanalyses Lewis' Somali data and seizes on the fact that it is mainly married women who become possessed. He argues that they are subject to status ambiguity and that this is especially so, as amongst the Somali polygyny is practiced. It is more in agreement with the ethnographic facts, he states, that possession be viewed as a means for overcoming status ambiguity produced in situations where men take on additional wives. Somali women become possessed in an effort to define clearly a status which is dependent on their relationship to men, but which has become threatened or rendered ambiguous by the further marriages of their menfolk. Possession is a means for the expression of jealousy and competition between women which has been engendered by the actions of men. Status ambiguity, then, is for Wilson the main explanation for why individuals have recourse to the public occasions provided by possession states. This, he considers, can be extended to explain the phenomenon in other societies. Wilson, however, recognizes that men might be placed in status positions just as ambiguous as those of women and that in some contexts men might experience possession as frequently or more often than women.   To explain this variation Wilson asserts that the factor of male/female interdependence might be relevant.   Thus, when men and women are dependent on each other economically and there is a potential for the interchangeability of social roles, then there is a likelihood for men to be possessed quite as frequently as women. He cites the instance of spirit possession in Haiti where men are possessed as often as women, where the household income is critically dependent both on male and female activity, and where men will occasionally perform female tasks such as cooking.

I find this argument to be generally more attractive than the one provided by Lewis. However, it is not without some difficulty when applied to Sri Lanka, and for some of the same reasons which are faced by the kind of explanation given by Lewis. These reasons are primarily methodological, and I will detail them presently. My immediate difficulty with Wilson's thesis is that most men and women can be understood as occupying social positions which are potentially definable as ambiguous. The thesis has its greatest explanatory force in relation to married women, and yet in Galle unmarried women are frequently the subjects of exorcist practice. In addition, when Wilson tries to explain the possession of men in male-dominated societies he is forced to accept a psychological explanation such as that provided by Lewis. Thus males who become possessed in Somali society are usually viewed as homosexuals in need of psychological outlet. Wilson, however, does modify this in terms of his argument, stating that homosexuals have a status ambiguity **vis-à-vis** other males.

These approaches, despite their differing emphases and the specific criticisms which could be addressed to each of them in turn, are all subject to at least one general criticism. This is that they all reduce unduly the multiplicity of factors which occasion the bringing of women within certain expressive modes of ritual action to a single or limited set of factors, which, although they might hold in a specific instance, cannot be generalized to incorporate or explain the pattern as a whole.

The problem of why women are predominantly the subjects of exorcist treatment inevitably raises the question of their motivation. Schutz has drawn our attention to the fact that "motive may have a subjective and an objective meaning" (Schutz 1967:70). This relates to his distinction between "in-order-to" and "because" motives. "In-order-to" motives are always in the future tense and refer to a preconceived goal or the attainment of some future project. The approach to an exorcist for treatment relates to the "in-order-to" class of motives in the sense that such treatment will enable the attainment of a future goal which is the alleviation or cure of an illness. "In-order-to" motives, as Schutz notes, are related to the inner consciousness of the actor. It is in this sense that they are subjective. Schutz, however, is concerned with the process of how the consciousness of the actor becomes inserted into, and interpreted within, the realm of his or her everyday world. This process is one of objectification and relates to the objective meaning of the act, in this case, for example, interpreting the meaning of illness and accounting for its cause. Objectification involves the actor and others consciously reflecting on their present action and experience in a way which locates the meaning of the act in their past experiences, and often relating these to future programs. This will be achieved also in terms of the typifications whereby they interpret action in their everyday world. "Because" motives relate to the process of objectification and constitute the objective meaning of the act as this is realized in the outer world of the actor's action. In the context of social action and interpretation, "in-order-to" motives become "because" motives. They thus become part of the temporal structure of the everyday world, which is an essential aspect of what Schutz terms "because" motives.

Critical to Schutz' distinction between "in-order-to" and "because" motives, is that the analysis of the motivation of actors to engage in specific action or to embark on particular programs must be rooted in the objective world as these actors intersubjectively construct it and act upon it. While the actor's private ("in-order-to") motives will spur the actor on in the course of ongoing action, it is the ability of these to be shared with other actors (of an individual actor to effect a "reciprocity of motives"), in effect to convert "in-order-to" motives into "because" motives, which enables individuals to realize their private concerns and perspectives in the social world. Schutz' social phenomenological approach eschews a discussion of the private attitudes related, for example, to the internal physical or psychological condition of individuals, independent of the external context. He is primarily concerned with the ways in which individuals intersubjectively arrive at their own subjective understandings through the constructions and typifications they share with others. As an extension of this, reference to the external social structural aspects of the world in which individuals act would be included in the understanding of their motivated social action only insofar as these are constitutive of the constructs and typifications whereby these individuals interpret, understand, and order their social world in relation to others.

I have argued for a distinction between the private, in this sense subjective, attitudes, intentions, and motivations to action of specific individuals, and the process of their public, intersubjective, or objectified, realization in a social context. The approach which I stress is one in which analytic attention is focused on the way in which the private attitudes of individuals are processed into the world of social action. This does not deny the significance of individual motives to action and the importance of the individual's inner consciousness of his or her physiological, psychological, and social condition. Indeed, as I have shown in the previous chapter, a variety of individual concerns emanating from within a patient and related to that patient's awareness of certain aspects of his or her social situation might be relevant to action within the exorcism mode.

A major pitfall of the other approaches I have discussed in relation to the question of why women are more frequently engaged in the framework of exorcist practice than are men involves precisely a neglect of the great variety of factors which might motivate individuals to action, whether they be men or women. Thus Lewis interprets the propensity of women to possession states and their treatment in the exorcist mode as expressive of their subordination in a male-dominated society. The great analytic danger here is that what might be a "real" privately understood physical or psychological disorder is reduced to the status of a mere presentational tactic for what Lewis independently deduces to be the primary motivation, the release of tensions and the expression of other social difficulties emanating from within a context of male oppression. The implications of the approaches of Wilson and Obeyesekere are not dissimilar. Wilson simply indulges in a clever functionalist modification of the Lewis argument, stressing the status ambiguity of women, as this emerges in the context of their relationships with men, as the major factor leading them to possession states. Obeyesekere emphasizes the culturally produced psychological condition of women and then argues that it is primarily this which brings them within the exorcist mode. I have no reason to doubt that in relation to specific instances such factors as feelings of oppression in a male-dominated world, a desire to overcome or to draw attention to this oppression, problems of status ambiguity, and inner psychological disturbance, among a host of others, might motivate women to exorcist practice. However, what I stress is that the explanation of why women **as a category** are more frequently drawn into the exorcist framework, rather than men **as a category,** cannot rest simply on the analysis of specific cases independently of the shared constructs and typifications which men and women have of themselves and of each other. It is possible that both men and women are the subjects in many cases of similar motives to action. I hypothesize that it is the property of the constructs in terms of which members of social categories interpret their action to themselves and to others which accounts for the frequency with which women, compared with men, receive alleviation and cure within the domain of explanation and expression controlled by exorcists (see also Stirrat 1977).   Regularity, and the frequency of response which is its index, is a consequence of the process whereby the attitudes of individuals, whatever their source, are objectified through the medium of relevant constructs into the social world of their action.

Approaches such as the ones I have discussed also fail to consider the time dimension —— the intervening period and process between the initial individual experience and display of illness, on the one hand, and the cultural and social definition and its treatment within the framework of exorcist practice, on the other. This has important implications for any explanation, like Lewis', for example, which accounts for the frequency with which women appeal to the exorcist mode in terms of male domination. The "because" motives of action which identify the cause of illness, for instance, in the physical, psychological, or social condition of the patient, are, Schutz argues, marginal to the awareness of individuals in their ongoing action. This ongoing action is dominated by "in-order-to" motives which are future and goal directed. It is only in the objectification of action, which emerges from within the individual, in the completed act —— in this context, its outward expression and acceptance that someone is ill as distinct from an individual's inner awareness of discomfort or illness —— that "because" motives come into play. These "because" motives, which are dominated by the past tense and which are engaged to explain the cause of the act, are introduced retrospectively. "As long as the actor lives in his ongoing action, he does not have in view its because motives. Only when the action has been accomplished, when in the suggested terminology it has become an act, he may turn back to his past action as an observer of himself and investigate by what circumstances he has been determined to do what he did. The same holds good if the actor grasps in retrospection the past initial phases of his still ongoing action" (Schutz 1967:71). All I wish to stress here is that the motivation to the act should be kept distinct from how this is explained and understood within the context of its completion and social recognition. That women might explain their illnesses with reference, for instance, to oppression at the hands of a husband or use illnesses to express feelings of frustration at their domination and powerlessness in the face of men in no way allows the analyst to assume that a woman has become ill as an initial consequence of these factors. This does not exclude the possibility, however, that aspects connected with the social condition of a woman patient as this involves her relationships with other women and with men might not become relevant as the definition, diagnosis, and resort to appropriate treatment for the illness develops.

This last point expands on the importance of the time dimension in the definition of illness and the difficulty it presents for the type of thesis developed by Lewis and others. The progressive definition of demonic illness and the move to exorcism treatment involves, as I have already argued at length, the attachment by others, both men and women, of their concerns to the objectified instance of the patient's illness. These others take an important part in the definition of illness and the decision for exorcist treatment. Indeed, it is the very engagement of the concerns of others in the understanding of an individual illness which constitutes an important dimension of the objectification of the illness. Any explanation of the frequency with which women resort to exorcist practice and the elaboration of symptoms, and the expression of these in the condition of the patient, must be able to take into account the motivating factors underlying the actions of these others as well as the patient.

There are additional methodological problems connected with the explanatory approach adopted by Lewis and others when it is related to my ethnographic data. The approach fails to account for the totality of the phenomenon of illness organized within the framework of exorcism practice. There are two related aspects to this. First, the approach of Lewis and others must be able to account for the instances in which men are the focus of demonic attack, as well as in those instances involving women. Table 4 includes information for males and females relating to treatment in the exorcist mode. The explanation provided by Lewis and Obeyesekere explicitly relates to women and not to men. Wilson's explanation is more satisfactory, but within the limits of my earlier reservations, in that it does purport to explain the action of the members of both sex categories.

TABLE 4
Proportion of Patients Receiving
Minor to Major Exorcism Treatment*

	No.	Minor exorcism rite	Major demon ceremony
Males	107	85	22
Females	147	112	35
Total	254	197	57

* I have excluded data on minor rites held by those who had major demon ceremonies performed.

Second, the approaches I have discussed should be able to explain the participation of women and men in all the healing rites related to malign supernatural attack practiced by exorcists. Table 4 shows that the highest proportion of all patients, for which I recorded information, receive minor ritual treatment from exorcists. This is significant, especially in relation to an argument such as Lewis' regarding the reason for female involvement, when it is understood that the minor rituals give relatively little opportunity to the patient to express problems of a psychological or social nature. The minor rituals are typically short in duration and engage the patient as a passive recipient of exorcist expertise. It is only during the major ceremonies that patients are likely to become "possessed" and are active otherwise in their treatment. Nevertheless, an exorcism of any type will create the patient as the focus of attention and thus provide a context in which the patient can deal with problems, for example, emanating from the structural position of the patient in a set of social relationships. But this is as true of male patients as it is of female patients. It is for this reason that

I stress that the approach developed by Lewis and others fails because it does not successfully explain, in their totality, appeals to the exorcist system.

An Alternative Approach

A major factor which brings women more frequently than men into the orbit of exorcist practice, an orbit in which demonic possession is a common mode of expression, relates to the typifications or cultural constructs which men have of women and women have of themselves. These constructs are critically related to a general understanding that women, rather than men, are more vulnerable to the attack of malign demons and ghosts. Irrespective of the internal motivations to the act (whether the engendering of action leading to the expression of symptoms indicative of illness is born of the patient's physical or psychological condition or the patient's feeling of dis-ease relating to an inner awareness of his or her social situation), the constructs in terms of which Sinhalese comprehend and interpret illness influence the frequency with which women are brought within the medium of exorcist practice. In other words, these cultural constructs are a major means whereby the "in-order-to" motives of individuals are transformed into the "because" motives of the patient and of others who are engaged in action and response to an individual who is recognized as ill. It is the relation of these constructs to the establishment of "because" motives that is highly important, not only for providing a context for the intersubjective understanding of an event of illness, but also for laying the ground for further action likely to lead to exorcist treatment.

Demons and ghosts are conceived of as being filthy and polluting creatures, who exhibit an undue attachment to the world of human beings. These features account for their low position in the hierarchy of the cosmological order. The ideas which describe the world of malign supernaturals also constitute understandings as to why certain individuals are more vulnerable to attack than others. Women as a category are understood by Sinhalese to be more vulnerable to demonic malevolence than men. They engage in domestic activities which bring them into frequent contact with the objects of pollution. It is women who do the cooking, and who clean up after children. At rituals women tend to preside over the more polluting tasks and to occupy the more dangerous and vulnerable positions. Funerals, for example, are occasions of great pollution and danger, and it is women who are most exposed to this, for customarily they sit around the body inside the house, while men usually sit outside and away from the corpse, which is a source of pollution. Histories of illness often trace the onset of demonic attack experienced by women to a moment during their attendance at, or return from, a ritual in which they were exposed to pollution - a girl's puberty ceremony or a funeral.

Menstruation and childbirth are both polluting activities. Women are generally viewed as more attached to matters of this world than men. This is reflected to some extent in the fact that the ghosts of former human beings, who assumed their ghostly form as a result of their excessive worldly attachment, are identified most often as deceased kinswomen. Women are conceived of as being more subject to emotional disturbance and excess, attachment to persons and relationships born of this world, as being more engaged in the pursuit of worldly desires, and as being mentally weak and more prone to worldly temptation. Such aspects comprise some of the ways in which women as a category are culturally typified, typifications which are shared by both men and women. What is important about these typifications is that they include the very aspects which are understood to attract demons and to enable their control over human beings.

Women as a category, therefore, are culturally prefigured in their identity **as women** as being vulnerable to demonic attack. That women are more prone to demonic malevolence than men is a widely held belief, which in itself is likely to contribute to their more frequent involvement in exorcism practice. This belief is validated by common-sense, a common-sense rooted in cultural typifications of women which create them as taken-for-granted objects of demonic attention. Men are also victims of demonic attack, but their culturally constituted identity **as men** is not one which predisposes them, in the common-sense understandings of themselves and women, to be the likely focus of demonic affliction. Men can encounter and engender the demonic in their action and experience in the world and as a consequence of the roles they play and the situations they enter, but their identity as male in itself protects rather than exposes them to the danger of demonic attack. Exorcists are males, and it is the power of their maleness which enables them to control the demonic. At major exorcism performances women are typically located inside the house and are understood to receive protection against the demonic by their confinement within its context. Men are typically located outside, in that area where the demonic assembles in its greatest power, but their male identity is viewed as a factor which reduces the danger which the demonic may present to them.

Female identity and the ground for the common-sense understanding of women's demonic vulnerability are constituted within a cultural context in which women are conceived of as subordinate to men. This cultural view, while it is widely shared by women and men, does not necessarily permit the relatively frequent participation of women in exorcism to be seen as an expression of female interests **per se**, independent of or opposed to the interests of men. Rather, the cultural conception of female subordination creates women as central symbols and as major vehicles and mediators for the expression and management of the concerns of both Sinhalese men **and** women in a world of action and experience which reaches consciousness and understanding through a variety of cultural ideas, ideas which also relate to the general cultural view of the subordination of women in Sinhalese society. The symbolic and culturally constituted position of women is one on to which men can play their own concerns and difficulties rather than **vice versa.**

In Chapter 4, I argued that the diagnosis and definition of demonic attack, and the exorcisms to treat it, are such as to encompass potentially a variety of problems affecting a patient, a household, and a more extended range of kin and others. Patients, as their demonic condition is understood, become symbolic of wider problems affecting others as well as themselves. I add to this that the symbolic identity of women as female when engaged in exorcism further empowers the illness to comment on the situation of the patient and others. This is a function of the culturally constituted symbolic position of women, a position of which they are made acutely conscious through their everyday participation in the world, which creates their bodies and selves as not only sensitive to disorders emanating from the world which surrounds them, but also leads women to incorporate these disorders as part of their own experience. Sinhalese women are vital symbols at once responsive to, and concentrating in their being, the forces and processes ordering and disordering the cultural and social universe of action and experience. The symbolic position of women and its relation to the cultural conception of their subordination, both influential in the selection by themselves and men into the realm of exorcist practice, can be elaborated by considering further factors of their cultural situation.

Ortner (1974) has approached the widely ethnographically reported phenomenon of the subordinate cultural position of women, and aspects of her analysis, though modified, are relevant to the argument I now pursue. I do not use it to account for why women might be socially, economically, and politically subordinate to men in their everyday world, a major thrust of Ortner's analysis. Why women are subordinated to men, or appear to play a less active role in the economic and political lives of many societies, has to do with historical processes which have placed them in a particular economic and political position within an ongoing structuring of relations, which is also occupied by men. The cultural ideas which men have of women and women have of themselves are the product of an historical process and are maintained, changed, or vary in relation to the structured position of women in the practical economic and political world. Cultural ideas concerning the subordination of women can function ideologically to legitimate the practical social, economic, and political superiority of men over women and may be reproductive forces of male domination. But the cultural ideas pertaining to female subordination do not in themselves have the power of determining the position of women relative to men in the practical workaday world. Their power in this regard, while influential in the ordering of everyday practices, functions primarily at the level at which they are constituted, at the level of ideas, and they have varying force in accordance with the way women are differentially structured, with reference to each other as well as to men, in the social, economic, and political relations of the society as a whole. In Sri Lanka, rules of kinship and inheritance give women, often on a par with men, access to and control over property and are factors in the ability of some women to exercise considerable power and influence (see Yalman 1967; Obeyesekere 1967). Women, particularly among the emergent middle class, often assume important positions in the economic and political life of their community and society. Rather than argue that the cultural ideas concerning female subordination cause their domination and devaluation in the real world (to do so is to force too strong a distinction between culture and society - the logic of one is contained in the logic of the other, and they are essentially inseparable in a single and mutually determining, but often contradictory, dialectical process), I emphasize the key role of these ideas in creating women as central symbolic figures for the manifestation and projection of suffering and misfortune which Sinhalese, regardless of gender, periodically experience.

According to Ortner, the widespread, but not invariable (e.g., see Briggs 1970), cultural devaluation of women is a function of the cultural definition of their gender-identifying physiological processes and gender role in the domestic context, the two being closely connected, which establishes women as **closer** to nature than men and as mediating nature and culture. Ortner modifies a simplified (even simplistic and inaccurate) view that women are nature and men are culture and states that "culture (still equated relatively unambiguously with men) recognizes that women are active participants in its special processes, but at the same time sees them as being rooted in, or having more direct affinity with, nature" (Ortner 1974: 73). The closer alliance of women with nature, Ortner stresses, is an understanding which, while it is not a cultural universal, is a product of culture (and I would add of its historical context, see Badcock 1975; Bloch and Bloch 1980; Rosaldo 1980:404-09), as is a nature/culture distinction itself. Women's physiological processes, e.g., menstruation and reproductive functions, are culturally conceived of as "natural" and bring them closer to nature than are men, as does women's major cultural identification with childbearing. Infants are themselves closer to nature as culturally understood, for they excrete without control, do not walk upright, cannot talk, and are otherwise unfamiliar with cultural practices.   All these culturally defined aspects of female gender are part of widespread Sinhalese cultural understandings.   Ortner continues that the domestic and the household, as the place where nature enters into culture, and the cultural association of women with domestic practice combine to reinforce and reproduce women and the domestic as closely allied with nature, and as at the base of a scale of relations and values formed in culture.   With reference to the domestic, for example, Ortner states that ". . . domestic units are allied with one another through the enactment of rules that are logically at a higher level than the units themselves; this creates an emergent unit - society - that is logically at a higher level than the domestic units of which it is composed" (Ortner 1974:79; see also Rosaldo 1974).   Men, not as closely allied with nature as women and not in their culturally defined identity associated with the domestic, indeed, culturally identified as primarily engaged in higher level relations and contexts external to the house, are thus conceptualized as superordinate to women.

As a general analytical approach purporting to account for why women are widely culturally conceived as inferior to men, Ortner's perspective has met with increasing criticism (e.g., see MacCormack and Strathern 1980; Quinn 1977). This has emerged from its failure as an explanation across a variety of separate cultures: its ethnocentric bias, its dependence, though modified, on the binary oppositions of, for instance, nature versus culture, private (domestic) versus public, among others. Despite these criticisms, however, aspects of Ortner's argument are, in my view, relevant to the Sinhalese context, though not necessarily in the form in which Ortner has baldly stated them.   My specific development of Ortner's argument here draws attention to the symbolic position of Sinhalese women as being related to principles of hierarchy involving a nature/culture dialectic; women as mediators between nature and culture; and, as I will discuss subsequently, women as transformational in the nature/culture relation.[2]

The hierarchy of the Sinhalese Buddhist cosmos, the ordering of relations between and within the various levels of a cosmic totality engaging deities, human beings, demons, and ghosts (see Chapter 6), involves ideas concerning the relation of nature with culture, important to the structuring of the Buddhist cosmos. Within the cosmic totality, nature and culture are engaged in a continual dialectic, and their dynamic tension is present at all levels, even at the highest —— with the exception of the Buddha, who, while supreme over the cosmos, is nevertheless outside or above the nature/culture dialectic and its potential for disorder and suffering. Gods in their own world (**deva loka**) and in their action in the mundane realities of men and women, as recounted in Sinhalese myth and legend, manifest culturally conceived natural emotions and passions: anger, desire, and greed.   Position in the cosmic hierarchy, as far as this is determined in accordance with cultural typifications relating to a nature/culture distinction, is not a simple function of the degree to which beings in the various modes of existence in the Sinhalese cosmos approximate, in their characteristics and actions, nature or culture.   Rather, position in the cosmic totality is an aspect of the degree to which culture controls and dominates the natural both in the internal constitution of being and in action. The domination of culture over nature is a central principle in the structuring of the cosmic hierarchy as a whole and in the ordering of relations of superordination and subordination within the various levels which Sinhalese distinguish within the hierarchy. Demons are subordinate to human beings and human beings to gods as a function of the extent to which the cultural dominates over the natural, or **vice versa,** in their being and action. Thus the characterization of demon personality and action presents them as the extreme disordering potential of nature incarnate, gaining power in culture through their domination of it. They present in their being and action all-consuming anger, lust, and greed, and as polluting and uncivilized creatures subvert the cultural order, disrupting and subordinating it to the ordered disorder of the demonic.

The normal and ordered Sinhalese Buddhist view of the cosmic hierarchy, and action within it, is not one which sees nature opposed to culture. They are in relative harmony, but this is a function of the subordination of nature to culture which, while structuring the relations in the cosmic hierarchy, is dependent on the power and ordered articulation of levels in the cosmic totality itself. The opposition of nature to culture is a potential of processes which condition all phenomenal planes of existence, where culture is inextricably intertwined with the natural and dependent upon it. Their opposition is threatened when the disordered and dangerous aspects of nature enter culture and/or when the power of culture to dominate nature is weakened as a function of disorder in the internal relations of culture, and most especially when the hierarchy of the cosmic order is subverted and, thereby, the power of culture to dominate nature lost.

Let me stress the idea that nature is not equivalent to disorder and culture to order. Order and disorder are emergent in the process interrelating nature with culture. In this process, culture also can be disordering of nature and nature of culture. This is an enduring possibility in their dialectic and gives rise to suffering at all planes of existence - even for the gods. Only through becoming removed from the chain of existence, by following the Buddha's Path and achieving **nirvana** (being freed from rebirth and a continued state of existence) can suffering ultimately be overcome. What is threatening to culture is **nature disordered**. This occurs as a process in nature, as an inevitable process of the movement from life to death, and as a process of culture and the action of culture upon nature. It is nature **decomposed** in culture, the fragmentation of the ordered unity of nature both in itself and in its relation to culture —— which can occur as a function of cultural action —— which is dangerous and disruptive to cultural relations. This is implicit in Sinhalese concepts concerning purity and pollution. Much of that which is considered polluting **(kili)** is the natural decomposed and not filth and dirt **per se.**

Death is polluting because it is the decomposition of the living form of Life. The human corpse is polluting because it is a unity in the process of disunification in decomposition. To kill is to decompose, and it is polluting to kill because of this and not just because it offends the Buddhist teaching. The preparation of food is polluting because the natural is decomposed in the process of its cooking. The purity of food is connected with the extent to which it is disordered, disunited, decomposed in its form. The foods which human beings typically give to the gods are whole fruits and flower blooms, at once symbolic of life, of natural unity, and of the wider unity which the gods represent in themselves as dominant in the cosmic order. In contrast, the demons receive cooked foods, nature decomposed through the action of culture, and receive such other objects as torn and withered flower petals or excrement —— symbolic of nature decomposed, disunited, and fragmented in itself. Herein, the kinds of offerings which the demons receive are the symbolic representation of the demonic. The demonic is nature disordered and outside the order of culture. Demons oppose the gods, not as nature to culture, but as disunity in opposition to the forces of unity whereby culture establishes an harmonious relation with nature. It is the demonic, as disordering and fragmenting of the unity of nature and of nature and culture in their ordered relation, which is polluting, as is the illness in which the demonic becomes manifest. Demonic illness is a disunification of the "wholeness" of the patient. The patient is subject or subordinated to the process of decomposition in the midst of life, internally disarticulated and, in turn, an agent through which the demonic can work to disarticulate or to fragment a wider and encompassing set of relations of which the patient is a part.

The primary weakness of culture, in Sinhalese Buddhist logic, is that it is premised on nature. Nature in culture (and nature is always present in culture and at all phenomenal planes of existence by virtue of the very condition of existence) realizes a danger to a cultural order, threatens its disruption, when nature is disordered and independent of cultural control and restraint. Disorder in nature produces disorder in culture. Alternatively, culture is continually threatened by disunity in itself as a function of action, conflicts, and oppositions, in accordance with divisions and differentiation in the order culture establishes. This disunity, which can be occasioned by action driven by culturally conceived natural emotion and passion, weakens the cultural fabric and the capacity of culture to subordinate nature, and can give rise to the dominance of nature disordered in culture — manifested and symbolized by demonic control. The disorder of nature refracts, and can be produced by, disorder in culture.

Female identity constituted in accordance with the typifications of Sinhalese culture is at the nexus of the culture/nature relation. Women, as conceived in culture are, more than men, a major point of articulation between culture and nature. Women are both closer to nature and closer to culture than men. They are culturally conceptualized as being closely attached to processes conditioning the human world and producing division and differentiation within it. It is women who are conceived by themselves and men to be more emotionally tied to the bonds of blood and kinship, and to life generally in the mundane world. Women embody and intensely symbolize, concentrate or condense in their identity, the dialectic of nature and culture and the dependence and foundation of culture upon nature. As males, men are ideally seen as less attached to the matters of this world and less polluted by the natural in them. Men are, in Sinhalese Buddhist culture, occasioned with greater opportunity to engage in practices theoretically removed from matters of the human world of existence. It is men and not women who can enter the Buddhist monkhood and, in modern-day Sri Lanka, it is men, especially later in life, who may remove themselves increasingly from matters of practical concern and give themselves to the practice and study of Buddha's teaching. As women symbolize within themselves the endless dialectic between nature and culture, they also can symbolize the suffering born of this dialectic both in themselves and in the everyday world as it extends around them, based as this world is in this dialectic.

Women concentrate within themselves the fragility of a world order as this is founded in the interrelation of nature and culture. In this sense they are "weak" in accordance with the logic of the cultural system in which they participate, and this is echoed in everyday common-sense understandings. Further, as points of primary articulation of nature with culture, women are the foci of "weakness" in the cultural order which encompasses them. Women, and the household which is culturally conceived of as their domain, are in their articulation vulnerable to emergent disorder and its agents in culture and in nature. They are responsible in their being for the entry of nature disordered (e.g., in menstruation) into culture. Women are the passageway for the entrance of nature into culture and the agents of the transformation of the natural into the cultural. This is so in their procreative role, their role in the nurturance and socialization of children, and in their domestic function as the preparers of food —— the conversion of the natural into the cultural.

Sinhalese culturally view points of transition in nature, transition in the nature/culture interaction and transition in culture, points and moments of articulation in structure, as weak and vulnerable to disorder. Additionally, disunity in a wider order concentrates and manifests itself at the sensitive and transitional points of articulation. Demons manifest their power at times and places of transition. They strike at moments of passage in the day and night; they dwell at river crossings, at crossroads, at waterfalls, and at cemeteries.

The idea of women as weak points in structure, as manifesting and reflecting disunity in a wider order and as canalizing agents of disorder —— though frequently passive and unintentional agents (see AmaraSingham 1978:114), instrumental in the production of disorder as the result of the disordering and natural emotional and passionate action of others around them —— is revealed in demon myth and in the routine of exorcism performance. Thus the chief of the disease-spreading **(sanni)** demons, Kola Sanniya, in one myth I recorded (see p. 123, also Obeyesekere 1969), was born of a queen wrongly accused of adultery by her husband, the King. The latter was engaged in a foreign war when he received the news that his queen had fallen pregnant. On his return, suspicious that his wife had committed adultery, the King had his wife disemboweled. A child, the King's son, born in this disordering of his mother and as a result of the disordered emotion of his father, took the form of a demon who eventually exercised terrible vengeance and suffering on the King and all his subjects. In another myth, the demon Mahasona is formed out of the giant general Jayasena's sexual desire for the wife of Gothaimbara, a fellow general in the army of the legendary Sinhalese folk hero of Dutugemunu. Personal combat ensued between Jayasena and Gothaimbara, during which Jayasena's head was kicked off with the little toe of Gothaimbara's left foot. The planetary deity, Saturn (Senasuru), had Jayasena's head replaced by the head of a bear, and so Jayasena, as ordered disorder, took the form of Mahasona.

In the main dance episodes of exorcisms, exorcist-dancers appear in the dress of women. In such guise, the dancers are understood to attract the demons to ensnare demons in their own demonic natural passion, and make them prisoners of their own lust. Exorcist female attire is symbolic of the mediation of nature and culture in the identity of the female and the vulnerability of women to the attack and control by the demonic. It is during the dance, held at a time when demonic power is in its ascendancy, that an exorcist-dancer will become possessed by the demon.

Men can be responsible for the disunity of culture with nature and can give rise to the disorder of their dialectical relation. Their action in culture, conditioned by natural emotions and passions, can disrupt culture, and their action outside the conventions, rules, and restraints of culture can give rise to the dominance of nature over culture and the disruption of the ordered hierarchy of culture. This is well illustrated in Sinhalese myth, where it is the action of males, typically in positions of kingly or princely dominance, which engenders the demonic. It is demons in the male aspect who are the most powerful and terrible, but this is consistent with the Sinhalese cultural principle of associating power with the male.

Sinhalese men can be weak in structure, in the sense I have discussed for women. As such they too are subject to the disorder of demonic attack. What I stress, though, is that their weakness or vulnerability is not a property of male identity as culturally typified, but rather of their location in a situation typically prone to demonic malevolence. My observations indicate that males who become demonically ill are often weak in structure or disordered in structure as a function of their **socially constituted situation** rather than as a function of this in combination with their **culturally constituted identity.** Thus there is a tendency for young men who are unemployed and/or are still dependent on their natal household to become victims of demonic attack. Some young male victims are members of youth gangs (see Case 2, Chapter 4) and engaged in petty criminal activity. Like demons they are at the margins of the cultural order and act to disrupt it. One youth who had a **Mahasona** exorcism was a notorious local gang leader and had recently been involved in a celebrated rape incident. He and his family attributed his illness to his anti-social behavior, behavior which brought him within the context of the demonic.

Men attract or engender the demonic largely through their conscious and intentional action in the world. When they are demonically afflicted, they often point to the malevolence of Suniyam (the sorcery demon) as the principal agent of their illness (see Table 2). Illness which is the consequence of sorcery is the result of the intentional action of another human being. Women can likewise attract demonic attention as a consequence of conscious and intentional action. But women also attract and engender the demonic as an involuntary aspect of their cultural identity as female, as a property of femaleness, and as a function of their cultural role as women (see also AmaraSingham 1978). It is in their cultural constitution as women, mediating in themselves nature with culture and as primary foci of articulation and transition of the natural into the cultural, which makes women vulnerable to demonic attack and which creates them as symbolic vehicles for the manifestation of disorder in the world around them.

It is the key points of articulation and transition in the structure of the cultural world of human beings, and of the articulation of the human world into an encompassing cosmic hierarchy, which are subject to the greatest ritualization and ritual control. In this the power of the hierarchical principle which orders the universe is invoked, as is the domination of culture over nature as a fundamental principle ordering relations in this hierarchy —— both of which are essential in the synchrony of nature with culture. Women and the house are the foci of intense ritual activity, both to ensure their own protection and that of other household members against the disturbing forces of the natural which threaten entry into women and the house, and to safeguard women and the home against the disruptive forces which can emanate within a cultural and social world extending around them. Women, and not men, are the subject of puberty ceremonies. Commonly, new houses have their foundations laid at an astrologically auspicious time, and in some instances a **pirit** ceremony will be performed by Buddhist monks to ensure the well-being of the household. In many houses pictures of the deities will be prominently displayed, often above the entrance to the house. Frequently, a picture of Sivali, who accompanied the Buddha on many of his journeys and who was the person always able to find him food, has pride of place on the doorway lintel. A daily practice in many houses, especially among the working class, is for women to carry incense through the house at dusk to purify and to protect the house against demonic and ghostly malevolence.

That women, and the house, are the subject of intense ritual activity continually points to them as the foci upon whom the forces of disorder can manifest their greatest effect. This is additionally significant, I suggest, for it contributes to the consciousness in women that their bodies and selves are likely to be factors in the disordering of the world as this centers upon them, and that the creatures of disruption are likely to manifest their power, in them. Women, therefore, are motivated in culture to incorporate in themselves misfortune and suffering which attach to men and to women in their household and among a wider range of kin. This is one reason why women are more prone to demonic attack. It also accounts for their more frequent involvement in worship which focuses on the shrines to the deities. At these shrines women not only seek help for their own specific problems, but also call for the help of the gods in protecting their menfolk from conflicts at work and from other dangers and misfortunes born of the everyday world and its exigencies.

Nature disordered is the central metaphor which relates to the Sinhalese cultural understanding of demonic illness. I have pointed out that nature disordered is also culture disordered. One logically follows from the other, for nature and culture are interrelated in a single dialectical process. Women are not only culturally conceived as the main agents in whom nature disordering and dangerous is most likely to be revealed. They are also the main agents for the transformation of nature into culture and through whom a threatened equilibrium in the cultural world of action and experience can be restored. Ritual, and I refer here specifically to exorcism, which takes women as patients, acts upon persons who in their symbolic construction are vital in the transformation of nature into culture and who are integral in the synchronous relation of nature with culture.

The cultural view that women are subordinate to men is of a piece with other conceptualizations which see women as primary points of focus in the articulation, and transformation, of nature and culture. In this, women, while they are "weak" in their internal constitution and are weak points in the cultural order which extends around them, are also central in the cultural order and the most sensitive to disturbances in it. The subordination of women within the hierarchical order of human beings and an encompassing cosmic totality is in effect constitutive of their "strengthening" by virtue of the power contained in hierarchy and the domination of culture over nature as a structuring principle of this hierarchy. Culturally, the subordination of women, their subjection to cultural control which is an aspect of subordination, averts the weakening of a cultural order which the forces concentrated in women can produce, and simultaneously "protects" women from forces of disruption often emanating from within the wider cultural order itself.

The subordination of women in culture is a function of their centrality in the nature/culture dialectic and in the cultural order. They are the linch pins of culture. But more than this, the cultural ideas relevant to female subordination are further integral in their symbolic construction as major vehicles for the expression of the widest concerns of men and women. This is so in the cultural association of women with the domestic and the view that their domain of action is ideally the house and neighborhood relations immediately extending around the house.

The domestic unit or the household does not stand opposed to the wider cultural and social order which surrounds it. Rather, it is, as Ortner argues more generally, subsumed within an embracing cultural and social order. The house culturally defined as the domain of women is at once also the place of men, who are symbolically dominant in its internal relations (the household head is typically male and it is men who eat first and are served by women at mealtimes). The house is the point of male social articulation with the neighborhood (as it is for women) and with the world of work beyond where men predominate, as this is culturally conceived and in social practice. The house, through the relations which center upon it, symbolizes the ordering of its members into a mundane cultural and social universe. This is so, for example, in the pattern of food exchanges between households, which define relative status, and in the social regulation of the entry of non-household members into domestic space. A set of kindred will sometimes define their bonds of kinship by reference to a particular dwelling (the **mahagedera**, see Case 1, Chapter 4). Occasionally, even political affiliation will be marked by the house which is painted with the party political color.

Women, strongly associated with the domestic, exchange symbolic significance with the house as an encompassing symbolic embodiment of the relations of all its members into an external world. That is, women in their association with the domestic are created as symbolic carriers of the set of relations which center on the house and which incorporate it within a wider cultural and social world. As such, a woman's disorder can represent, at a symbolic level of discourse, a disorder in the range of relations which extends around her. Furthermore, given the culturally constituted role of women in the mediation of relations which center on the house, a woman's disorder can actively threaten a disturbance in these relations, relations which take women, the domestic, and the house as their base. Exorcisms, as domestic or household rites, therefore, are highly appropriate to women, considering the range of relations which centers in the symbolic identity of women and the fact that their disorder is potentially disordering of the articulation of the household and its members into the wider community. This is so more than for men. Male identity formed in Sinhalese culture locates men's action primarily in the world outside the house, often at a distance from the neighborhood of the house. Their disorder is more likely to be linked with their relations in this world and not immediately and directly with the house and its internal order. This statement does not exclude such a connection, for their action and experience of suffering and misfortune can bring disruption to the internal relations of the house, and especially the local relations built upon it. But this is not a property of their male symbolic identity as such, as it is of female identity.

Numerous factors relating to the individual condition and social situation of men and women lead them into the framework of exorcist practice and to express what they and others conceive of as illness in the idiom of the demonic. What I have stressed is that the understanding of the frequency with which women, relative to men, are treated in rites of exorcism must be based on the terms whereby both Sinhalese men and women culturally comprehend and interpret to each other their experience of disorder and relate such disorder in the cultural world of their action. The cultural conceptions which Sinhalese have of demonic attack and of the likely victims of demon malevolence comprise what can be classed as "because" motives. These "because" motives, constituted in culture, form the taken-for-granted assumptions of everyday life, mediate and transform the internal and private or "in-order-to" motives for action into terms which establish the grounds for intersubjective understanding and the ordering of cultural action. "Because" motives and "in-order-to" motives interact in the process of experience and action so that understandings which might be classed as "in-order-to" motives become "because" motives, in their externalization and objectification at another point in a process, and **vice versa**. In this sense, individuals as part of their ongoing experience and action in the world can incorporate as a vital element of their self-understandings the "because" motives of the culture in which their identities are formed. Thus there is a continual dialectical interplay between the "in-order-to" motives which may give rise to individual experience and action in the world and the "because" motives —— the meaning and significance of experience, action, and the act for the individual and for others as these are objectified in an outer cultural reality.

Sinhalese women comprise in their symbolic identity the "because" motives relating to demonic attention and experience. I have examined certain aspects of the Sinhalese Buddhist cultural logic according to which some of the common-sense and taken-for-granted assumptions which men have of women and women have of themselves are formed. These assumptions relate directly to the symbolic identity and centrality of women in the Sinhalese cultural order. As a function of this identity, women are highly vulnerable to demonic attack and are sensitive to disorders in the world extending around them. They are likely to comprehend their experience of disorder, or to integrate to their experience the disorders which attach to others, as the result of demonic attack because of the way their being is culturally constituted. The symbolic identity of women is such that men, for example, can play onto women disorders which men experience in the cultural world of social action, disorders which the demonic can acutely symbolize. In the view I have explored here, men are part of the motivation of women to the demonic, but not necessarily in the sense elaborated by other anthropologists, which often treats such action by women as an expression of male/female opposition. Women are subordinated to men in Sinhalese cultural understandings. But this subordination cannot necessarily be seen as provoking opposition, nor can it be seen as placing women at the periphery of a world dominated by men. The subordination of women relates to their cultural **centrality** in the structures constituted in culture, and the subordination and centrality of women creates for them an identity and a role for the expression and management of some of the widest concerns of both men and women.

As I have emphasised, exorcisms are domestic or household rituals. The prevalence of women as patients in them relates directly to this fact. Women express in their bodies and selves the fragility of a cultural order, and in their identity as women are not only associated with the domestic and the house, but are major points of articulation of the household into its encompassing cultural and social universe. Exorcisms which take women as their focus, and especially the major ceremonies which place the household in a context of relations which extend out from and are built upon it, also take as a focus persons who are central to the order of the household and its wider integration. Moreover, exorcisms, by acting on women, are empowered (more, I suggest, than when men are patients) to restore and to transform a cultural order which has women and the house as its vital center.

6. The Demonic Illusion:
Demons and the Cosmic Hierarchy

Knowing that this body is fragile like a jar,
and making his thought firm like a fortress,
one should attack Mara, the tempter, with the
weapon of knowledge, one should watch him
when conquered, and should never rest.
Dhammapada, Chapter 3, verse 40

Sinhalese Buddhists who are the victims of attack by demons and ghosts, are understood by exorcists and other Sinhalese to have an abnormal and inverted view of the cosmological system; of the place of demons and ghosts within it, of the relation of demons and ghosts to human beings and to the vast host of other supernaturals which crowd the Sinhalese universe. The abnormal view of the demonically afflicted is one which "turns the world upside down."   While this is so, such abnormality is a constant potential of the normal —— of the way in which the cosmology should ideally be ordered by those who are not demonic victims. The marvelous and dense symbolic universe of deities and demons is riddled with the ambiguous and the illusory.   Only a thin veil separates the "real" from the "unreal." Buddhists, through right thought and action, and mindful of the virtues of the Buddha, can overcome the dangers of ambiguity and illusion and of placing alternative and mistaken constructions on reality in such a way that their minds and bodies become defiled, confused, and disordered.

Leach (1962) draws brief attention to the philosophic subtleties of the Hindu and Buddhist concept of **maya**, which has the connotation of illusion or "trick." In Hindu philosophy, which of course has affinities with Sinhalese Buddhism, **maya** is a "cosmic delusion which draws a veil across men's perception . . ." (Walker 1968:54; see also Devanandam 1950; Shastri 1911). I hasten to add, however, that among Sinhalese Buddhists, exorcists and lay people, ideas and terms related to the concept of **maya** are in everyday use and are not confined to the esoteric realm of theological discourse. Ames states that Sinhalese, in the southern provincial area of Sri Lanka where he worked, refer to "magic" as **mayama** in the sense of "illusion," "hocus pocus," and "jugglery." "They call magic things that only appear to be true, like circus tricks, pulling rabbits out of hats, or sleight of hand trickery" (1964a:37). Exorcists consider their healing rites to be elaborate tricks which they play on demons. The myths about deities and demons continually make reference to their trickery and their command over the illusory. The facility to change shape, to alter guise, and to transform into animals is a major aspect of demonic power, which can be used to fool both other supernaturals and human beings. In the same way, Sinhalese recognize the illusory, deceptive quality of everyday discourse and interaction. The term **mayam** is used in daily life to refer to the tricks and wiles which women specially play on men (see also Ariyapala 1968:70,302 for medieval Sri Lanka).

To be fooled and tricked, to treat the illusory as reality, is to be subordinated and subjected to the control of the prankster or trickster, be this a deity, a demon, or a human being. However, to see the reality behind the illusion, to be the unmasker as well as the masker, is to exercise dominance and superiority. The Buddha holds primacy in the Sinhalese cosmological order because he saw through all illusion and unveiled the tricks which were performed against him. A well-known and popular myth tells the story of how Gautama Buddha, while he was meditating beneath the Bodhi tree, became the subject of the powers of illusion of his major adversary, Mara,[1] who attempted to sway Gautama from his path to Enlightenment. Mara (Death) takes the form of Kama Deva (Life, the god of lust and pleasure) and then sends three beautiful goddesses, his daughters, and their retinues to dance for Gautama, to caress and to provoke him with desire and temptation. Ames gives a perfectly legitimate interpretation of this myth as pointing to the central Buddhist moral that for individuals to escape the suffering of this world, and to achieve salvation, they must forsake it "altogether for the other-worldly" (1964a:25). But I would add to this that it shows a further crucial aspect of Gautama's supreme wisdom: his ability to see through the illusory and to lay bare the truth underneath. In the myth, Mara cannot gain control or mastery over Gautama through his illusory powers and is forced to reveal himself in his true identity, as the harbinger of death. "He sends hordes of demons, hurls wind and rain, sand and flaming rocks, live coals and boiling mud at the seated Gautama . . . The demon hordes and their weapons are repelled by his virtuous serenity" (Ames 1964a:25).

Other myths and stories concerning Gautama or the previous Buddhas repeat a similar theme. They also indicate the authority and control which Buddha can exert over other beings through his power to unmask and expose the dissembler. A major dramatic act performed in the early hours of the morning in the **Rata Yakuma** exorcism, relates an event in the life of the first Buddha, Dipamkara, concerning the demon queen, Riddi Bisava and her daughters (Wirz 1954:65-66). The relevant myth tells how these demons were deprived of their authority from Vessamuni (Sk. Vaisravana), the lord of the demons, to afflict women with illness. They decided to appeal for help from Dipamkara Buddha and employed the ruse of weaving a cloth out of cotton which they had grown, spun, and woven, and which they then presented as a gift to Dipamkara in return for a renewal of their authority to afflict human beings. Dipamkara saw through the trick, understood the villainous intent which lay behind their action, and commanded them to bow to his authority and also to that of Vessamuni. In the dramatic performances of this myth (see Chapter 7) the cloth, supposedly a pure gift, is presented as used and rent with holes, and thus impure and defiling. The actor who plays the role of Dipamkara remains quiet while the exorcist whose role is Riddi Bisava abuses and sexually taunts him (Wirz 1954:69; Kapferer 1977a:106).

Illusion is a major force in the process of cosmic relations and expresses the essential changeable quality of these relations and the often ambiguous and unstable character of the gods and demons. The order of the Sinhalese Buddhist universe is not a static one, and the power of illusion, the ability of gods and demons to change form, is a vital aspect of this process. All modes of existence, as I stressed in the previous chapter, are conditioned in the dialectic which structures existence itself. This dialectic, in which life and death, nature and culture, purity and pollution, among others, are engaged in a single and enduring process, is constitutive of the ordering of the hierarchy of cosmic relations and the disordering of these relations. The power of illusion is inextricably connected with this cosmic process and is revealed as a force in the struggle between the gods and demons, in the ambiguity in the being and relations of gods and demons, and in the authority which demons can occasionally exercise over human beings. The stability of a universe which interrelates and orders gods, human beings, and demons in the one process, is ultimately dependent upon the Buddha and the power of the Buddha's teaching and thought. It was the Buddha, who in his Enlightenment and his release from the chain of existence, was freed from illusion and the danger and suffering it could bring. Exorcists call upon the power of the Buddha and invoke the gods —— who symbolize the power in hierarchy and whose power is dependent on hierarchy —— to restore the cosmic order, an order threatened by demonic malevolence and the illusion of demonic power. Exorcists insist that demonic victims concentrate on the purity and wisdom of the Buddha's thought and teaching, for it is through this that the illusion and disordering power of the demons can be broken.

Exorcists are the masters of illusion. Through their artifice and skill they can give rise to the illusory and disruptive powers of the demonic. But in their mastery of illusion they can also control the demons and expose the falsity behind appearances. The command and centrality of the illusory in the ritual work of exorcists is critical to an understanding of the logic of exorcist practice. For this reason alone it is important to discuss illusion as it is conceived of by exorcists and Sinhalese Buddhist laity. But more than this, an examination of illusion and other cultural ideas relating to it will enable a more complete understanding of the nature of demonic power. However, a discussion of illusion and its relation to processes integral to Sinhalese Buddhist cosmology is dependent on a more detailed outline of the Sinhalese cosmological system than I have given hitherto.

The Order and Ambiguity of the Sinhalese Buddhist Cosmos

The following account is based on exorcist and lay Sinhalese conceptions of the cosmic order collected in the Galle area. Locality is important because Sinhalese conceptions and classifications of the cosmic order are highly variable in their details, although they share much in common as to the principles which underlie them.

Several scholars, notably Ames (1966), Obeyesekere (1966), and Gombrich (1971a), have presented classifications of the supernatural beings who populate the hierarchy of the Sinhalese universe. Their classifications are in broad agreement with my own data. Broadly then, the Sinhalese pantheon is transcended by the Buddha, who is theoretically nonexistent. Beneath the Buddha, and composing the pantheon proper, is a number of superior deities who, as understood by Sinhalese, will become future Buddhas. These are known as **bosats** and are the Four Guardian Deities **(hataravaram deviyo):** Natha, Vishnu, Kataragama, and Saman. These deities are followed by a variety of other powerful deities **(devas)**, planetary deities **(graha devas)**, and minor deities **(devata, devatava)**. Below these deities is a horde of demons, including **raksas** and **yakku**, and lastly a variety of malign spirits **(kumbhanda)** and ghosts **(preta).**

Human beings occupy a position between deities on the one hand and demons and ghosts on the other. Sinhalese, both exorcists and laity, often refer to the cosmological system as being ordered into three "worlds": the world of deities **(deva loka)**, the world of human beings **(minis loka)**, and the world of demons **(yaksa loka)**. This is expressed in the design of a ritual structure, the **kapala kuduva**, erected at the beginning of the closing dramatic stages of major exorcisms. The structure is divided into three tiers, the top level being for the gods, the middle level for human beings, and the bottom level for demons and ghosts. These various worlds can be conceptualized as different planes of phenomenal existence, which, while separate, nonetheless interpenetrate. This is reasonably close to the sense which Sinhalese have of the cosmological system in which they act, and also to the Buddhist ideas and traditions in terms of which Sinhalese organize their everyday lives in relation to the supernatural.

It bears repeating that the principle of hierarchy is central to the order of the Sinhalese cosmic totality, and to the ranked relation of beings within and between the various planes of cosmic existence. The major ideas underlying the rank ordering of the cosmic hierarchy concern, **inter alia**, the extent to which the various supernatural beings are conceived of as following the Buddha's teaching or as committed to his Path, the extent to which they are given to the dominance of nature disordered in their being and action, and the degree to which they express this in their relative purity or pollution. Thus Natha is, for many Sinhalese, the highest of the deities. He is characterized as continually contemplating the teachings of the Buddha and as being so unattached to the matters of existence, that he is expected by Sinhalese to be the next Buddha (Maitri). The three other Guardian Deities, Vishnu, Kataragama, and Saman are all closely associated with Buddhism. Vishnu is conceived of as the protector of Buddhism on the island; Kataragama is closely linked with the ancient Sinhalese Buddhist resurgence against Hindu Tamil domination; and Saman is the god of Adam's Peak, a major center of Buddhist pilgrimage and the site of Buddha's footprint and the Buddha's first visit to Sri Lanka. The above Four Guardian Deities are considered to be the purest of the deities, with Natha being the most pure of them. Vishnu and Kataragama, however, are considered the most powerful, and are the most frequently represented at the deity shrines in the Galle area and throughout the island. Both are involved in matters concerning the human world and combine the ordering and disordering powers of the nature/culture dialectic in their being. Although Vishnu is the more benevolent of the two gods, in popular conception he is understood to assume demonic forms and the forms of other lowly creatures in the Sinhalese universe.[2]   Gombrich (1971a:159) notes the unusual but nonetheless interesting theory of a Buddhist monk in the Kandy area who stated that Vishnu is a "personification of nature." Kataragama is celebrated in myth and festival as a being both united with nature and as one who has nature's sometimes dangerous powers manifest in his person. Kataragama is the god whose passion for the beautiful Vaddha princess, Valli Amma (born of the union between a deer and a hermit and entering culture through her adoption by a Vaddha chief) attracted him to Sri Lanka. It is Kataragama who, as myth relates, slays powerful demons. In contrast with Vishnu and Kataragama, Natha has little power in the world of human beings. He rises above the nature/culture dialectic and, not being subject to the powers which reside in it, is himself less powerful in the lives of human beings.

Demons and ghosts are broadly conceptualized as being opposed to the Buddha's teaching (heretical, **mithya drsti**). But certain demons more highly ranked than others in their plane of existence are viewed as tending in the direction of the Buddha's teaching (**samyak drsti**). Major demons like Mahasona, Riri Yaka, and Kola Sanniya are viewed as opposed to the Buddha's teaching and are ranked below the other powerful demon forms of Kalu Yaka and Suniyam, whom exorcists see as tending in the direction of the Buddha's teaching. The internal ranking of demons is also in accord with the extent to which they are polluting, absolute representations of nature disordered, and of the extent to which they personify in their creation the disorder of culture. Exorcists state that Kalu Yaka is high in the demon hierarchy for he is the son of a high-born king. In exorcisms he does not receive the extremely polluting offerings of blood and cooked meats as do the other demons like Mahasona. Mahasona is the product of the sexual desire of a king for a woman of the lowly potter caste. He is born from the breaking of cultural convention.

As hierarchy structures the cosmic totality, hierarchy also orders relations in the demon world. Demons and spirits are largely classed into four main categories, each category being ruled over by a king. These four kings live at the sacred mountain of Meru in the Himalayas, and are the four "world guardians" (Gombrich 1971a:167). They command the four cardinal points, and are: Drhrtarasta, the god of the Eastern Quarter, who controls the **gandharva** demons; Virudha; who is king of the Southern Quarter and has the **raksa** demons subservient to him; Virupaksa, king of the Western Quarter who commands the **kumbhanda** (spirits) and **preta** (ghosts); and, lastly, Vaisravana, king of the Northern Quarter who commands the demons (**yakku**) and to whom all the other kings and the malevolent beings they command are subservient. Vaisravana is also Vessamuni —— the lord of the demons. The demons, according to verses uttered at the exorcism rituals are understood to enter the areas of human habitation from the eight points of the compass commanded by the four cardinal points. Vessamuni has his authority or warrant (**varam**) to command the demons from Buddha and Sakra (Indra of the Rg Veda). The demons in their turn have their authority to persecute and cause illness among human beings from Vessamuni. In being granted their warrant from Vessamuni all the demons are subject to limitations, and in general are not permitted to kill their victims. Vessamuni is understood to possess the eye of god Isvara (symbolically represented in decorative form on the **igaha** or arrow of Isvara which is used by exorcists in their rituals), its power being to smash and disintegrate recalcitrant demons.

The Sinhalese cosmos is populated by an almost bewildering array of supernatural beings. I consider that these multitudinous beings can be conceptualized as multiple refractions of the principles underlying the structuring of the cosmic order. The location of particular named beings in the hierarchy as a deity or a demon is a function of the degree to which they characterize in their manifest being and action a specific combination of factors, factors which in their combination are ordering of the cosmic totality and the articulation of its various levels in relations of superordination and subordination. Thus, as I have stated, particular named manifestations of deity or demon are ranked relative to each other and within their categories according to whether they are in accord with the Buddha's teaching, express the domination of culture ordered over nature disordered or express an ordered unity of culture with nature, and are relatively pure or impure —— all of which are interconnected. These principled attributes and their combination in any one named being are not absolutes, although this tends to be so at the extremes of the hierarchy.

Demons and ghosts tend to be the unmitigated representations of nature and culture disordered and of pollution.

The myriad supernatural beings which Sinhalese recognize can also be conceived in their manifest form as various combinations or possibilities of the ordering of substance in existence. As expressly stated by exorcists, deities, demons, and human beings, in fact all material forms, both animate and inanimate, are composed of, or related to, the five elemental substances, the **mahabhutas.** These substances, earth **(pathavi)**, water **(apo)**, fire **(tejo)**, wind **(vayo)**, and ether **(akasa)**, are fundamental in the Indian and Sinhalese medical traditions and are referred to in the Buddhist canonical texts (Karunadasa 1964, 1967:16-30). Exorcists relate them to the three body humors. Thus phlegm **(sema)** is connected with water **(apo)**, blood and bile **(pitta)** to fire and earth **(tejo** and **pathavi)**, and wind (Sk. **vayo,** Sinh. **vata**) to ether. Deities and demons are materializations of one or more of these substances and compose in their being the ordering or disordering and purifying or polluting potential of these substances. By extension, the innumerable Sinhalese deities and demons are inversions, refractions, or transformations of the possibility of each other, by virtue of their common constitution in natural substance and by the form they assume in culture, that is, the degree to which they are understood to act in terms of the rules and conventions of cultural life.

Deities and demons, as multiple refractions of the processes constituting form in existence, are also structurally interrelated in accordance with the substance constitution of their form. This is apparent in exorcist conceptions of the linkage between various deities and demons and in the manner by which exorcists symbolically present the beings concerned. Kataragama, for example, in his creation myth takes form out of the union of six fires and is predominantly associated with the substance of fire. He is linked to the planet Mars and its deity. These deities are related to Riri Yaka, the demon who effects an imbalance of the humor of blood and bile. Similarly, Vishnu is linked to the planet Saturn and its deity and to the demon Mahasona; all are specifically connected to the elemental substance, and the humor, of wind. Phlegm and the elemental substance of water are both linked to the deities, Natha and Pattini, to the Moon and its planetary deity, and to Sanni Yaka. Colors code these interconnections and symbolize the association: red is the color of Kataragama, Mars, and Riri Yaka; blue is the color of Vishnu, Saturn, and Mahasona; white is the color of Pattini, the Moon, and Sanni Yaka. These associations, and the symbols expressive of them, are clearly represented in the organization and content of exorcism rites.

An understanding that deities and demons are multiple refractions of each other and of the fundamental processes structuring being and the relations between beings in the cosmic system (which, in my view, increases an understanding as to why there should be such a multiplicity of deity and demonic representations) points to an essential ambiguity inherent in the cosmic order itself. This ambiguity is founded in the fact that deities and demons are constituted in a process whereby the forces of relative purity, of goodness, of fortune, of life, to mention but a few, are inextricably linked with the forces of pollution, of evil, of misfortune, and of death.

Before I look at ambiguity as a property of the principles in terms of which the Sinhalese cosmos is constituted, it is important to note that the ambiguity to which I refer is an aspect of particular beings as materially manifested, and not so much an aspect of their more abstract category membership as, for example, deities or demons. Ames (1966) and other scholars have shown that the structure of ritual prestations codes and marks the category membership of supernaturals and their positions in the cosmic hierarchy. Deities, for instance, receive pure offerings **(adukku)**, the lower planetary deities receive pure/impure offerings **(bali-bili)**, and the demons impure offerings **(dola)**. It is outside a ritual context and with reference to specific supernatural representations that Sinhalese often express difficulties in precisely locating various supernaturals in the cosmic hierarchy and sometimes in distinguishing between deities and demons. This is also reflected in the problems which most scholars encounter in reporting with precision Sinhalese conceptions of the order of particular beings in the cosmos. While this must be a function of regional variation linked with differences in historical tradition, I suggest that the many ambiguities and uncertainties are also inherent in the principles which underlie the cosmic order.

Gombrich (1971a:144-213), who presents for a Kandyan village perhaps the most sensitive account of a Sinhalese view of the cosmic order, expresses in his description some of the difficulties to which I have referred above. As might be expected, ambiguity is most evident in the middle range orders of the system. Thus, there has been some debate in the literature concerning the meaning of the term **devata**, frequently translated as "godlings" or "minor deities," and the particular beings which are classed by this term. Leach (1962:86) treats **devata** as comprising a secondary category in the cosmology, mediating between dangerous and powerful gods **(deva)**, which cannot be directly approached, and human beings. Gombrich (1971a:158 fn.16) disagrees and argues that the Sinhalese terms **deviyo** (god) and **devata** are synonymous. My own position is slightly different and leans more towards Ames (1964a:43-45), who considers the term **devata** to be applicable to supernatural beings who are transitional between the classes of deity and demon. Suniyam, for example, is commonly referred to as a **devata** and combines in his being the highly dangerous and polluting aspect of the demonic (in which case he is referred to as Suniyam Yaka) with the protective and purifying aspect of the deity (and when this is dominant, is referred to as Suniyam **devatava**). Demons, when they have broken free from their subordinate positions in the cosmic hierarchy and afflict human beings, are addressed in exorcisms as **devata** and not as demons. In its usage, **devata** is a term which is applied to beings who cross the deity/demon distinctions and who represent in their being a major point of articulation in the cosmic hierarchy. As a function of this, they are embodiments of its ambiguity and instability, which are properties emergent within the dialectic process of the entire cosmic order.

That deities can change into demons, and **vice versa**, as well as assume a variety of other forms, as can demons, contributes in itself to their often highly ambiguous character as they appear to everyday Sinhalese consciousness. In addition, the changeability of gods and demons, that they occasionally can manifest their ontological opposites, supports the general view expressed here that deities and demons constitute multiple refractions of the possibilities underlying the process of the cosmic unity. But most important, the ability of deities and demons to change form in appearance is a property of the power they hold in common —— the power of illusion. This power of illusion is a metaphor of the fluidity and process of the system in which deities and demons are composed and which is variously composed in them.[3]

There are numerous examples of the changeable and illusory character of deities and demons. I have already referred to Suniyam. Kalu Kumara (the Black Prince) can assume the form of a planetary demon **(raksa)**, the form of the lowly and terrible Kalu Yaka, the form of a woman, a dog, and a cow. Exorcists state that Deva Sanniya can be a god or a demon. He is a member of the class of disease demons which primarily attack the humor of phlegm and which are headed by the chief of the disease demons, Kola Sanniya. A masked representation of Deva Sanniya appears at the close of the major dramatic acts of large-scale demon exorcisms. Here he assumes the aspect of a god. Some exorcists explicitly refer to him as a manifestation of the goddess Pattini. Important demonic figures which appear in the dramatic acts of the **Rata Yakuma** exorcism are those of Riddi Bisava (the Cloth Queen) and her seven daughters. Their symbolic representation bears much comparison with Pattini, and exorcists explicitly make the reference. The myth of Pattini states that she had seven different births (Wirz 1954:143-45). She was born from a mango fruit, from a water lily, from the tear of a cobra, from fire, in a boat, from a dew drop, and, lastly, from the thigh of Isvara (Siva). Pattini has seven demonic attendants (demonic forms of herself) who spread sixty different diseases and epidemics over mankind.

Deities are not always benevolent beings, and this applies to some of the most powerful in the Sinhalese pantheon.[4] Thus Pattini has a malevolent aspect. Vishnu assumes the malign form of a **raksa** and is so represented at **bali** ceremonies performed by exorcists. Kataragama, perhaps the most frequently approached of the Sinhalese gods, can cause illness through possession, be invoked to cause others suffering and misfortune, and, according to Gombrich (1971a:174) is understood to sin through demon servants. Conversely, demons are not always entirely malevolent beings. Thus one group of demons, the **gara** demons,[5] who appear in the masked drama towards the close of the **gam maduva** ceremony to Pattini, both cause illness and prevent it.

Deities and demons are not only frequently ambiguous in themselves, but they also stand in an ambiguous relation to each other. This is evident in the above description which has drawn attention to the fact that deities can assume a demonic form. O'Flaherty (1976:62-65) argues generally in relation to Hindu texts and Buddhist Jatakas that deities and demons are indistinguishable from each other both in the often awesome powers they possess and especially in their powers of illusion. They are, she states, often only distinct in their opposition and in the fact that deities ultimately dominate, "the gods always win" (1976:64). The ambiguity of the gods and demons, their powers of illusion, and the eventual subordination of the demons to the gods and the Buddha, are illustrated by the myths presented below, which also fill out aspects of the demon character.

The Main Demons and Their Myths of Creation

Demons are both terrifying figures and beings which are absurd and ridiculous. They can be gigantic in proportion, or else, as in the case of Riri Yaka, growing from a finger's breadth in size to no more than a dwarf, yet possessing enormous strength. Demons are frequently the progeny of mythical kings and queens, but at the same time can be the result of mismarriages between those of high-born and lowly castes. Sometimes they are created through the divine power of the gods. Their births are marvelous and polluting. Demons at their births burst from the breasts of their mothers, take form out of their mother's menstrual blood, emerge from the blood spilt in war, and take form from funerary ash; their gestation is unnaturally long or else unnaturally cut short; they come from the womb too early and still unformed —— as lumps of flesh. Demons are fierce, bloodthirsty, full of sexual desire, and crave human flesh. Paintings of the demons, or their moulded clay images **(bali)**, portray them as the horrible creatures they can become. Demons are dark in color, they are covered with hair, their eyes bulge, their noses are gross and their nostrils flare, their lips are thick and protruding, and from out of their mouths curve

MAJOR DEMONS
(As Drawn By An Exorcist)

SUNIYAM
(In Deity Form)

KALU KUMARA

MAHASONA

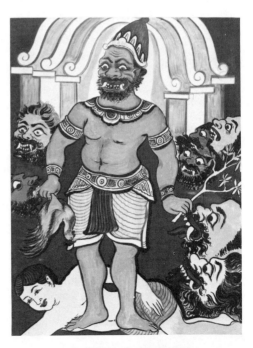

AVAMANGALE RIRI YAKA

gleaming white tusks. Kalu Yaka is depicted as carrying two headless children, whose heads he has bitten off and grips in his mouth (see p. 119). Demons are capricious and thieving, they delight in the playing of tricks.

There are numerous myths relating to each of the major demons and their various manifestations.[6]   Many of these, recited at exorcism performances (see Chapter 7), recount the births and mien of demons as I have presented them above.   Wirz (1954:27-47; also see AmaraSingham 1978:116-125) presents some of the versions of the mythical origin of the major demons, and these are very similar to the ones which I collected in the same area.   Obeyesekere (1969:181-87) gives excellent texts of the Kola Sanniya myth and this demon's conquest by Gautama Buddha. I have based the following brief descriptions of some of the demons who feature in the major exorcisms, and the stories connected with them, on verses uttered in the demon ceremonies, and on their myths as related by exorcists outside the ritual context.

Riri Yaka

Apart from his primary form, this demon has eight other manifestations. He is of such strength that he carries the Sun and Moon on his head. He has bloodshot eyes and red rays radiate from them. His face is blue, blood pours from his nostrils, and smoke billows from his ears.[7] His breath is foul and his mouth is filled with human flesh. Riri's body is red with blood.

In Wirz' (1954:27) version of his birth, Riri was formed in the clot of his mother's blood, which poured from her womb at the time of her confinement.   Shortly after his birth he began to develop evil habits, attacking people, biting their carotid arteries, and sucking their blood. He became so dangerous that the people whom he was terrorizing went to god Saman and implored him to help. Saman reasoned with Riri, but he became even more angry, claiming that he had a warrant to attack people from the lord of the demons, Vessamuni. Riri stamped his feet and, on this occasion, grew from a dwarf in size to a giant. Saman eventually bound him in irons and ordered him to be tied to the wheel of the sun-cart. Riri surrendered, and Saman let him go free on condition that he would not take life, and that he would satisfy himself with just making people ill. This Riri does at the three dangerous periods (tun yama), in the morning, afternoon, and evening.

Other myths tell how he was born from the blood of warring planetary deities, of his birth from the breast of Le Kali (blood Kali), whose breast he then ate. One version I collected explicitly connects him with Kuveni (see AmaraSingham 1973), the queen of the demons, who fell in love with Vijaya, the first Sinhalese king. Kuveni helped Vijaya conquer the demons, but later left him to return to her demon kin. These demons were so angered by her betrayal of them that they cut out her tongue. From the blood of her tongue, Riri Yaka was born.

The most dangerous form of Riri Yaka, Avamangalle (death time) or Maru (death) Riri, was created in the course of one event when he was hiding from Saman. He took cover in a thunder cloud, but he was so frightened that he screamed in terror. The god of Rain heard the noise and shot and killed Riri with an arrow. Riri was then reborn as Maru Riri and is understood as having a close connection with Mara or Maruva (the Evil One, the Harbinger of Death).

Mahasona

Mahasona, with Riri Yaka, is one of the most feared of all the demons. He is an enormous giant, tens of feet high and possesses awesome strength.

He rides a wild boar and carries an elephant upon his shoulders and drinks the elephant's blood from its neck. Mahasona has the head of a bear and smoke pours from his nostrils. He has seven other forms.

The main myth tells that he once was a giant, Jayasena, born from the union of King Parakrama-Bahu and a woman of the potter caste, at Pollonaruwa. He was a renowned military general, feared by the gods and by human beings.[8] Jayasena lusted after the wife of Gothaimbara, who was a human being of normal size. Gothaimbara heard of this and challenged Jayasena to mortal combat. Gothaimbara's followers warned him against the impending duel, fearing for his life against such a powerful adversary. However, Gothaimbara took no heed of their warnings and faced Jayasena alone and unarmed. The fight occurred at a cemetery ground. Gothaimbara avoided Jayasena's blows and then leaped into the air and kicked the giant's head from off his shoulders with a mighty blow from the little toe of his left foot. Jayasena's friend, the planetary deity, Senasuru (Saturn), was passing overhead at the time and took pity. He saw a bear caught in a thicket and instructed some nearby villagers to cut the bear's head off and place it on Jayasena's shoulders. This they did in great haste —— so much so that they placed it on back to front. Nevertheless, by this act Jayasena was reborn as the great cemetery demon, Mahasona.

Another myth tells how Mahasona was formed from ash. Bashman Asura (Ashes Giant) was the servant of god Isvara. He became Isvara's servant because he intended to perform a malicious trick against him. Bashman Asura wished to assume Isvara's powers, and he also lusted after Uma, the wife of Isvara (Uma is a pure and virtuous mother figure). Isvara had in his secret possession a marvelous spell, known as **Isvaradahana,** which if uttered to the palm of the hand empowered the hand to transform the head of anyone it touched into ash. Bashman Asura worked for Isvara for twelve years before Isvara eventually gave him the spell. At the last moment Isvara saw through his servant's ruse and fled. The god Vishnu, the brother of Uma in the myth, saw the plight of his brother-in-law, and now too that of his sister. Vishnu assumed the form of a beautiful woman, one aspect of the goddess of sexual attractiveness (Rati Devi). Bashman Asura immediately fell in love with her and begged Rati Devi to marry him. But Vishnu in the guise of Rati Devi turned Bashman Asura's own trickery against him. Rati Devi asked Bashman Asura to swear his devotion to her while placing his hands on his head. Without another thought, so enraptured was he with Rati Devi's charms, that he did so. Bashman Asura killed himself, and his head was turned to ash. It was from this ash that Mahasona took form. Out of this ash were also born the twelve wives or female demonic companions of Mahasona, one for each year of his false servitude to the god Isvara.

There are many other stories about the origin of Mahasona. He was born from a rock struck by a fiery arrow, from the womb of a king's mistress (a woman of the washer caste), he was killed by Vishnu, who was jealous of his beauty and power over women, and so on. These myths relate particularly to the various forms which Mahasona assumes.

Kalu Yaka and Kalu Kumara

This demon is depicted in the form of a **raksa.** His body is a dark blue black, and he has four arms and rides a black bull. He is often presented as devouring an elephant, with its bloody entrails hanging down his body. A cobra is wound at his waist. He spins a wooden club as he walks.

Kalu Yaka and Vata Kumara ("Round" Prince), are the main manifestations, of Kalu Kumara (Black Prince), Kalu Yaka being the most lowly form. The mythical stories concerning their origins are often the same. The most common myth of Kalu Yaka tells that he is the son of King Vijaya and the demon, Queen Kuveni. The young prince, Jivahatta, began to lust after women, and he would sleep with young girls at the cemetery. The people of the land complained to Vijaya of his son's sexual misadventures, and Vijaya exiled him. When Jivahatta died he was reborn as a demon and took his revenge on the men and women of Sri Lanka. An extension of this myth is also to be found for Kalu Kumara. During his period of exile, Jivahatta entered a strange and dark country (Istripura, country of women). These women all sexually desired the young prince. He was forced to sleep with countless young women every day.[9] Sexually exhausted, he died, to be reborn as Kalu Kumara or Kalu Yaka — in which form he began to avenge himself against all women for his death. In the version of Kalu Kumara's origin given by Wirz (1954:34-35), he was the son of a laundress adopted by a king of Anuradhapura. The boy was capable of amazing feats and once turned a huge club upside down (symbolic of power inverted), which hitherto only the King had been able to lift. Impressed, the King brought him into his household and conferred many honors upon him. Eventually he rose to the rank of a general in the army, which he then led victoriously against a king of North India who had enslaved many Sinhalese. While in India the prince encountered the country of women, and here he died to be reborn as Kalu Kumara or Kalu Yaka.

Other myths tell of different births of Kalu Kumara or Kalu Yaka. His parents are usually royal, and occasionally the myths comment that his gestation period was unusually long, ranging between ten and sixteen months. One origin myth states that he once was an ascetic Brahmin, who meditated for twelve years under a sacred tree. So deep was his meditation that snakes and the roots of the tree curled round his waist. God Sakra saw the Brahmin, and in character as a god who likes occasionally to exploit the weaknesses of mortals, had the idea to break the ascetic's concentration. Sakra assumed the form of a beautiful woman, and the Brahmin was filled with sexual desire. As the Brahmin approached, the disguised Sakra disappeared. The Brahmin forgot his meditational purpose and, maddened with sexual longing, wandered here and there. Sakra then created a lotus blossom with seven petals, and each of these petals became a beautiful woman. The Brahmin lived with these women until he died, when he was reborn as Kalu Yaka. Thenceforth this demon, assisted by his seven wives, who also assumed demonic form, enters the dreams of men and women, filling them with erotic thoughts and sexual passion. This myth is similar to that given by Wirz for Madana Yaka (1954:106-07). Exorcists consider Madana Yaka to be a form of Kalu Yaka.

The myth of Vata Kumara (the other major form of Kalu Kumara and Kalu Yaka) tells that his father was a **bhikkhu** who befriended Emperor Asoka, but who left the monkhood to become a minor king, known as Boksal. He married, and at the birth of his son, the astrologers proclaimed that the child, later named Siddhartha (which is also the name of the prince who later became Gautama Buddha), would become a monk. At the age of nine, Siddhartha entered a monastery. One day while he was climbing on the relic chamber or **dagaba** (which is round and hence his demonic name), he fell off and died. While alive, Siddhartha continually grumbled and was bad-tempered. Vessamuni, seeing his death, recreated him as a demon and gave him authority to persecute human beings. His first action as a demon was to travel to Anuradhapura, where he developed a deep sexual longing for the Queen. She became ill and was only cured after giving Vata Kumara a variety of offerings (see Wirz 1954:37-38 for a different version of the same myth).

Sanni Yaka or Kola Sanni Kumara

Sanni Yaka is a composite of eighteen different demonic forms (see p. 167). The chief of these demons is Kola Sanniya. Each of the demonic forms represents a particular disease or illness, and apart from the usual kind of demonic features, the nature of this illness or infirmity is often expressed in the contorted facial masks worn to represent them. The myths I collected relating the origin of Kola Sanniya are very similar to those reported by Wirz (1954:40-47) and Obeyesekere (1969:181-187). I summarize the main events in the myth.

In the first age **(kalpa)**, at the dawn of civilization, lived a beautiful princess. The rays of the Sun, Ravi, entered her, and she became pregnant. These rays polluted her and forced the foetus in her womb into a single formless ball of flesh. It was to this that she gave birth. The people were alarmed at the evil portent of the birth, and they placed it in an earthen pot and floated it down a river. It floated past a bank where Buddha (in a previous birth) was meditating. He took the pot out of the river and placed it beside him. When he looked into it, he saw two children (twins) — a brother and a sister. Later they married, and from this union the people of Lichchavi sprang and multiplied. But the bad **karma** of their origins was to catch up with them.

Much later in the city of the Lichchavi (Visalamahanuvara) lived King Sankapala. He had sixteen queens, but his senior queen was Asupala. Shortly after she conceived, Sankapala left his capital to engage in a foreign war. While he was away jealousy developed in the royal court, and when Sankapala returned to his pregnant queen, he was told that she had committed adultery. Asupala denied the accusation and claimed that she had slept throughout the King's absence. Despite her protestations of innocence, Sankapala had Asupala tied to a tree and tortured. Eventually she was executed by being cut in two. A male child fell from her rent womb, and Sankapala called his astrologers to see what he should do. They examined the young prince's horoscope and declared that he would bring ruination to the city. But against this advice the King took his son into his palace and had him suckled by seven princesses. When the prince was eighteen he learned the story of his mother's death. Overcome with grief and anger, he swore to wreak his vengeance on his father and all human beings. He left the palace and wandered the countryside, collecting eighteen different poisonous plants with which to kill his father. These plants were in three groups — **vata, pitta, sema** (wind, bile, phlegm) — and out of them were created the eighteen **sanni** demons. In the company of these demons, and with five thousand other followers, the prince sacked his father's city and committed great slaughter. The prince, now in the form of Kola Sanniya, slew his father and ate his flesh and drank his blood. Terrible famine and awful pestilence followed the destruction of the city. The stench of death and putrefying flesh filled the air.

Buddha (the myths name both Dipamkara Buddha and Gautama, the present Buddha) saw the fate of the city with his Divine Eye and took pity upon it. He approached the city in the company of five hundred followers, deities and human beings. It was so polluted with death that he did not enter it. Instead he called on the gods to cleanse it with torrential rains, a rain of flowers. The city was now purified, and Buddha entered the city and threw all the demons out. He scorched them with the bright rays of colored light which emanated from him and sprinkled pure water **(pirit pan)** upon them. He then asked his follower, Ananda, to search the city for any

demons remaining in hiding. Kola Sanniya was found lurking by the city gate
(kadavata). Buddha spared his life because he was the son of a king, but only
on condition that he limit his attacks on human beings by making them sick
rather than killing them. After expelling Kola Sanniya from the city, he
placed Natha at the right and Saman at the left of the gates to guard
against the entry of the demons.

The Logic of Hierarchy and the Power of Demonic Illusion

The power of the Buddha and his teaching and the authority of the gods
are thematic elements of the demon myths. Demons cower, hide, and flee
in the face of the Buddha, and are bound, beaten, and killed by the gods.
While the gods are vulnerable to demonic illusion (e.g., Isvara's experience
with Bashman Asura), they are able to see through the ruse and the trick and
to avert the threatened demon usurpation of their powers. The myths
repeatedly assert the hierarchical principle which orders the Sinhalese
cosmos. It is in the assertion of hierarchy that the terrible disruption and
disorder which the demons personify, and which is at the source of their
birth, can be averted. I examine further the hierarchical principle for it is
in relation to it that the powers of gods and demons are constituted, powers
which are distinct despite a surface similarity. Demonic illusion emerges in
the failure of hierarchy and works against the order of hierarchy. The
illusions which demons create around themselves are more properly
delusions (moha) in the sense that both demons and the human beings the
demons afflict are deluded by a power which is false. In contrast, the
illusion of the gods works in accordance with the hierarchical principle, and
through it they display a possibility of their being as this is constituted in
the hierarchy of the cosmos.

The hierarchy of the Sinhalese cosmic system is based on a principle
whereby each successive level of supernatural beings is subsumed in and
subordinated to the next. The ranking of specific supernaturals in the
hierarchy is dependent on that level in the cosmic totality at which they
receive their most complete and coherent manifestation. Thus the most
powerful of the deities - the Four Guardian Deities - achieve their most
completed form at the apex of the hierarchical order. These deities, in
their complete form, restructure elements constitutive of being at a lower
level and achieve a higher level and more encompassing ordering of
relations.[10]

Essentially, each successive level in the cosmic hierarchy, and the
supernaturals which compose their form at each level, is a transformation
into a higher structural ordering of the level beneath it. A logic of
transformation, built into this hierarchical order, governs the movement or
passage of supernaturals through the structure of hierarchical relations.
This logic is one which permits movement of supernaturals from higher
levels of structure to lower levels and back again. Such movement is
consistent with the hierarchical principle of the cosmos. Thus, given that
deities conceived as high in the rank order subsume lower orders in their
being, it follows that these deities can manifest themselves at those various
levels which they subsume.

As I have described, deities can manifest the demonic. This is a major
dimension of their danger. The manifestation of the demonic is inherent in
the deity as constituted in accordance with an hierarchical principle
whereby lower levels of being are incorporated and subsumed into higher
levels. But as lower orders of being are carried, though transformed, into
the higher forms of manifestation of the deity, the reverse is also true.
Thus, while the demonic is immanent in the divine, the divine is also a

possibility of the demonic. Contained in this logic is a key aspect of the ambiguity of the deity, but also a key aspect of its vital power. Deities in their manifest forms can symbolize both the order and disorder of the cosmos and the corresponding condition of the world of human beings as this is constituted within the encompassing cosmic order. Deities determined by the same cosmic forces which affect the lives of human beings, nonetheless in their power of transformation can change a threatened disorder into order. The transformation of the deity into a higher and more ordered form has the symbolic power of transforming the context of a human world in which the deity appears. This is the purpose of much ritual work in Sri Lanka which focuses on the deities and which acts to transform the deity into a higher structural mode of being. By acting upon and through deities, ritual can restore an order, the disorder of which can be symbolically represented through the appearance of a deity in a lower manifestation.

Demons, like deities, can assume higher and lower manifestations of form. But, unlike deities, they cannot transform the essence of their composition into progressively higher orders of structure in the cosmic hierarchy. They can only disguise or mask through their appearance to perception their true demonic identity. Demons are determined by principles which constitute the base of the hierarchy, and this is so in their highest and most complete manifestations, even though this might appear otherwise. Deities, however, compose in their highest manifest forms those combinations of principles which order higher-level relations in the cosmic hierarchy. The hierarchical principle of the subsummation of lower into higher modes of being describes the major and most powerful demons, but it is a subsummation without transformation. Thus the major and most feared demons, like Kalu Yaka, Kola Sanniya, Mahasona, and Riri Yaka compose within themselves a variety of disorders which have distinct, named demon representations. For example, Mahasona has seven other subordinate forms of himself, and Riri Yaka has eight. These minor forms coalesce in the dominant overarching forms of the major demons. The major form of demons is an aggregation at the level of the demonic. It is not a transformation in the sense achieved by deities who in their change of appearance transform lower levels of structure into a higher-level ordering. Rather, the higher manifestation of the demonic is a joining of separate disorders into a more expanded and unified disorder.

It is part of exorcist understanding that the main afflicting demons, for whom exorcisms are performed, are incapable of enforcing a high-level order. Suniyam is the exception to this, but he loses his demonic aspect in transformation, becoming benevolent and protective. For the other major demons, however, there is a strong sense that once a demon, always a demon.

It is important to note that the major demons, in the conception of exorcists, control and dominate through form in appearance. This power of illusion, while similar to that of the deities (both demons and deities can fool each other and human beings, e.g., the deity Sakra is portrayed as constantly tricking human beings as one of the above Kalu Yaka myths illustrates), is also distinct. Demons in their illusions of form mask what in actuality they are. Their disorder is always present and lies hidden behind their disguise. In Sinhalese ideas of the cosmic order, control and domination over others is a function of the ordering capacity of the being concerned and by extension of the forces of order in the encompassing cosmic totality. Control and domination in disorder is a contradiction in terms. Through their power of illusion, demons hide this contradiction, achieve a false resolution in form, and cover up the fundamental absurdity of their claim to authority and domination. The power of demons is in their surface appearance, and those who are not subject to the demonic illusion of form can withstand the destructive and disordering potential of the demonic. Gothaimbara was the mere size of a normal human being, but opposed unarmed a terrible and fully armed giant. Nonetheless, not fooled by appearances, Gothaimbara prevailed, and with the weakest part of his body.

Demons who are essentially untransformed but yet assume a dominating position subvert the hierarchical principle of a cosmic order where dominance is a property of transformation, a transformation which is an ability to subsume **and** restructure lower levels of order at higher and more encompassing levels. Demons transgress the rules of movement through the cosmic hierarchy, which is dependent on both a transformation in appearance **and** a transformation in the attitude and essence of their being. The apparent movement of demons up the hierarchy through the tricks they can play on the senses attacks the principle of hierarchy and the other principles structuring hierarchy (such as the power of the Buddha's teaching and the domination of culture ordered over nature disordered), and inverts the structure of determinations in the cosmic order. Lower beings and the disorder they compose become determinate of higher levels of structure, and the cosmic order begins to twist and to collapse on its axis. This inversion is clear in the iconography of the demonic (see p. 119). Thus Riri Yaka stands astride a human being, and Mahasona rides a boar which, in exorcist understanding, is a manifestation of Vishnu.[11]

The power of demons and their ability to control through appearance arises when they are outside the cosmic hierarchy. Demons are weak in structure and manifest their extreme disordering power when they are freed from a subordination in the structure of hierarchy. This differs from the situation of the deities. Deities achieve their greatest power in structure and become weakened and dangerous when the structural order fails or becomes disordered. Here is a logical reason, consistent with the ideas of Sinhalese Buddhist culture, which accounts for the location of shrines to the deities in the grounds of Buddhist temples. The Buddha, while theoretically nonexistent, nonetheless is paramount in defining the hierarchical structure of the cosmos and ensuring the relative stability of relations formed within it. The association of the deities with the Buddha is not simply a function of their greater purity and their non-opposition to the Buddha, but also relates to the fact that their own power, a power derived in hierarchy and structure, is dependent on the Buddha.

When I state that deities are weakened outside structure, I refer to their loss of a critical dimension of their power —— the ability to order relations at a higher level in hierarchy. The incapacity of deities to do this reduces the deity/demon distinction and is productive of ambiguity in their relation. Such an incapacity is an inherent possibility of the cosmic process which conditions all modes of existence and upon which the cosmic hierarchy is established. Thus, for instance, nature in its process, upon which all modes of existence are constituted, can become disordered —— especially in its transitions (e.g., in seasonal shifts as culturally conceived) —— and this renders the higher-level orders established upon it vulnerable to disorder. The image I have is of a cosmic totality in constant expansion and contraction, one continually imploding upon itself. The weakening of hierarchy and structure in such a process, the appearance of disorder in a cosmic unity, is refracted in the decomposition of the deity, who may begin to assume a lower and more disordered and dangerous form. In Sri Lanka, seasonal festivals and other calendric rites directed to the deities can be interpreted as occurring at points in the weakening of structure, or at moments of structural transition, and as being concerned with the restoration of the power of the deities to unify at a higher plane of their being and existence.

Deities are distinct from demons in their opposition. This opposition and the power of deities to prevail over the demonic, and in fact the very constitution of the divinity, inheres in the hierarchical principle. The failure of hierarchy moves the deity towards the demonic, and demons now no longer subordinated in structure can emerge to dominance and power. In an important way the depiction in myth of the struggle between deities and demons is a metaphor for the assertion of hierarchy. Once hierarchy is restored, through the overcoming of the demons by the deities, the power which the demons had threatened or gained is lost. Weakened in structure, they no longer oppose its order.

The ability of demons to control and dominate through illusion is contained in processes which resolve the contradiction between the apparent order of their form in appearance and the disorder which lurks behind it. This resolution of the demonic contradiction occurs when the context the demons enter is itself disordered. In this, the demon claim to power and domination is capable of realization, for they are the "ordered" personifications of disorder **par excellence.** Demons, as conceived by exorcists, are dispersed, divided, and fragmented by the power of hierarchy and structure. They are scattered to all points of the compass. It is when demons are no longer subordinated in hierarchy that the demonic can assemble in its greatest power, and in its assemblage fragment, rather than be fragmented.

Human beings are subject to demonic power and the illusion of demonic control when they are disordered in themselves and in their relations. Further, human beings are deluded by the illusion of demonic power when their perception of a wider cosmic unity, its hierarchy and principles of order, is obscured or restricted. It is through a conscious and reflective awareness of the hierarchy of the cosmic order and the further principles according to which the cosmic hierarchy finds its essential unity, that the demonic illusion and the power of demons can be broken.

Major exorcism rituals find their structure in performance in accordance with the cosmic principles I have outlined. Exorcists create, in their organization of ritual action and in the aesthetic of performance, the conditions for a demonic unity and a restricted standpoint upon an encompassing cosmic totality. But exorcists also reconstitute a cosmic order as it ideally should be conceived. They reestablish the hierarchy of the cosmic totality with the subsummation and transformation of lower levels of order within higher levels. Exorcisms in their succession of ritual event and action "rebuild" the cosmic order and so structure standpoint upon it that the mystifying illusion of the demonic is shattered.

Demons are tricksters. The falsity of the illusion they spin is implicit in popular understanding of the meaning of the name of Vessamuni, the demon lord, as "false face." I stated at the beginning of this chapter that to be tricked —— whether this be in the events told in myth or in everyday life —— to be fooled by the disguise or by the mask, to be trapped by appearances, is to be under the control of the trickster and the dissembler. But to see through illusion, to apperceive correctly what is directly hidden from perception, is to dispel the illusion and to assert mastery over the trickster. This is the power of the Buddha in his confrontation with Mara. It is the power of the Buddha and his teaching and the power of the principles of the cosmic hierarchy and of the hierarchy itself, which enables the removal of the illusion of the demons and their resubordination in structure. Dominated and ordered in structure, demons lose their terrifying aspect and are reduced to their proper absurdity. As Obeyesekere (1969:189) notes, for example, Kola Sanniya expresses in his very name his absurdity, for **kola** has the connotation of "comic." Much of the skill of exorcists rests upon their ability to trick the demons, to trap them in their own morbid jest, to uncover the reality behind the demonic illusion and so revealing it, use this reality, dominated and controlled as it is by the Buddha and the deities, to ensnare the demons, to dissolve them, as did Vishnu of Bashman Asura, and banish them to their own lowly plane of existence.

7. The Exorcism of the Great Cemetery Demon: Event and Structure in Major Exorcisms

Mahasona is one of the most feared of the Sinhalese demons, and his exorcism, except for the smaller daytime rite for Riri Yaka (the **Iramudun Samayama**), is the most frequently performed in the Galle area. The description of this chapter and the analysis in those to follow focus on the exorcism for Mahasona. This rite, its main events, and their sequencing and action, broadly follow the cultural paradigm of the other major exorcisms. All the major exorcisms gradually elaborate the dominating disorder of the demonic, confront the demonic with the greater power of the divine, confine and subordinate demons in the structure and hierarchy of the cosmic order, and reduce demons to absurd, foolish, and ultimately powerless figures. All the major demon ceremonies begin with episodes summoning the demons, succeeded by the elaboration of supernatural power in magnificent episodes of dance and, aside from the **Iramudun Samayama,**[1] move to their conclusions through the medium of comic drama.

Major exorcisms are extraordinarily complex occasions. But their complexity is guided by the cultural principles discussed in the preceding chapters, especially by those relating to the order of the Sinhalese cosmos. The main demon ceremonies can be conceptualized as a structured combination of a number of specific rites, many of which can be performed independently of a major exorcism. Generally, these specific rites address separate or less powerful manifestations of the principal demon for whom a large ceremony is performed, as well as those other demons who are associated with the main demon addressed in the exorcism and/or linked to this demon through the mediation of the patient. Thus, a major exorcism is an encompassing ritual form which corresponds to the encompassing nature of the principal demon it addresses. As the major demon gathers or subsumes other demonic forms into his being, so a major exorcism is a gathering or subsummation of a collection of rites into an overarching order. The hierarchy of the Sinhalese universe is also engaged in the sequencing of ritual events —— the early rites in an exorcism are to the ghosts, followed by rites to the demons, then minor and major deities, concluding with salutations to the Buddha. The hierarchy of the Sinhalese cosmos is also stressed in each particular ritual event ordered into the ritual progression as a whole.

The major demon ceremonies, nonetheless, are markedly distinct, despite their similarity in overall structural form and the fact that they include in common many specific rites to the demons and deities. They are chiefly distinct in the main ritual edifices which dominate the ritual space and in their defining ritual episodes of dance and drama. This is especially so with the **Suniyama** exorcism which, in its organization of ritual space, its ritual "buildings," and in its major dances, bears a close resemblance to village deity ceremonies (e.g., **gam maduva, devol maduva**), even though it is generally classed by exorcists as a **yak tovil** rather than a deity rite (**deva tovil**). In my account of the **Mahasona** exorcism I will indicate some of the distinguishing features of the other exorcisms and briefly describe their main distinctive episodes. My attention here will be directed to the **Rata Yakuma** and **Sanni Yakuma** and not so much to the **Iramudun Samayama** or to the **Suniyama**. The **Iramudun Samayama**, with the exception of its concluding episodes (see Wirz 1954:92-94), is with some alteration incorporated into the structure of the other major exorcisms. The **Suniyama**, while similar to the other exorcisms in its overall structural form, represents such a departure in its central episodes from the other rituals as to demand a separate description. Wirz' (1954:73-83) description broadly corresponds with my own observations, and I refer the reader to his account.

While particular central episodes of dance and drama distinguish one type of major exorcism from another, these episodes are not necessarily exclusive to that ritual with which they are principally associated. This is most notable with the masked drama of the **sanni** demons, which is enacted towards the conclusion of the **Sanni Yakuma**. The dramatic acts of this episode, in the Galle area at least, are often enacted as part of the other major exorcisms, except the **Iramudun Samayama**. In the exorcism traditions in which I studied, the drama of the **sanni** demons is now an integral part of the **Mahasona**. I was told that this was not so in the past and that it is an innovation, although comic episodes relating to the demons were enacted earlier, but without masks. This is an example of exorcisms as developing forms which build from the materials of Sinhalese culture, but at the same time order them to the logic of the ritual process within which they are included.

My account of the **Mahasona** exorcism is not based on one particular observed enactment.[2] I have witnessed some eighty **Mahasona** exorcisms, and there is variation from one performance to the next. The factors which relate to this variation range from the particular condition of the patient (which can lead to the inclusion of certain rites not presented on other occasions) to the knowledge and skill of the performing exorcists. Nevertheless, there is broad agreement among the exorcists in the Galle area as to the ritual events which ideally should be performed and their appropriate sequencing. I describe the **Mahasona** in terms of exorcist views as to which ritual events should be presented, and their appropriate location and timing in the structural progression of the ritual. In all the **Mahasonas** I witnessed, only one performance radically departed from the sequencing of ritual events as widely accepted by exorcists. The ritual concerned dissolved in confusion leaving the exorcists, the patient, and members of the patient's household dissatisfied with the performance.[3]

I describe in some detail the **Mahasona** as typically conceived. The analysis of the rite as a performance is left to the succeeding chapters. Nevertheless, it is essential for the analysis of later chapters that the reader gain some feel for the ritual as it is enacted. For this reason, I fill out my description of particular ritual events with accounts of their enactment on the specific occasions I witnessed them. Although I have selected, especially in relation to the major episodes of comic drama, those performances which I and my Sinhalese companions considered to be among the best examples of the exorcist art, the manner, style, and mood of major exorcisms is similar for most enactments of the rite that I have witnessed. The photographic record of the **Mahasona** at the end of this chapter is intended to assist the reader's visualization of the main exorcism events.

Ritual Preparation and the Organization of Ritual Space

Preparations for the rite are well under way at the ritual household **(tovil gedera)** by the time the exorcists arrive, usually in the morning. Well before the day of the performance, the presiding **gurunanse** —— who has already played a prominent role in the diagnosis of the illness and whose responsibility it is to organize a group of exorcists for the performance —— gives the household head a list of materials which will be used in the ritual and which should be provided by the household. Many of the exorcists in the Galle area have printed itemized lists which are given to their clients. Most materials used in the rite, with the exception of clothing, masks, and drums used by the exorcists,[4] must be provided by the household. These materials include those used for the construction and decoration of the ritual structures (wooden poles, banana tree trunks, coconut palm leaves, etc.), in the weaving of offering baskets, in the preparation of offerings, and so on.

When the exorcists arrive, the presiding exorcist is greeted by the male household head, who offers the exorcist a glass of water and some betel, customary modes of Sinhalese greeting. The exorcists, with the assistance of the other male members of the household, other male kin, neighbors, and friends, then begin the task of building the ritual structures, weaving offering baskets, making a variety of ritual objects to be used in the ritual episodes, and preparing food and flower offerings. The cooking of the food offerings for the ghosts and demons is normally done by a member of the exorcist group, the **madu puraya** (exorcist's assistant).[5] During these activities, the women of the household busy themselves in the preparation of food for the guests who are expected to attend the rite.

A space is cleared in front of the house for the rite. This space, which varies according to the amount of room available, is known as the **sima midula** (see Figure 5). Most of the ritual action is confined to this area, and it is demarcated by a variety of ritual structures. Once the ghosts and demons enter this ritually bounded space, they are understood to be confined or bounded **(sima)** by it, a property of the power of the ritual structures which encircle the perimeter of the performance area. The idea of the containing and restricting of demons is a recurrent thematic element of all major exorcisms.[6]

All the large-scale exorcisms, with the exception of the **Iramudun Samayama,** have one major structure which is located opposite to where the patient is usually seated on the front porch of the house.[7] This structure, the "palace of the demon(s)" **(yak vidiya),** or **atamagala** (eight-cornered house) in the **Suniyama,** dominates the ritual setting and is elaborately and magnificently decorated. It takes most of the day to build.

The design of the **yak vidiya** differs according to the type of exorcism being performed. The **Mahasona vidiya** (the palace of the Great Cemetery Demon), which is constructed only for the **Mahasona** exorcism, is a large, roofed, quadrangular structure which is approximately six feet high. Theoretically it should, as with the **vidiyas** for the other exorcisms, be built

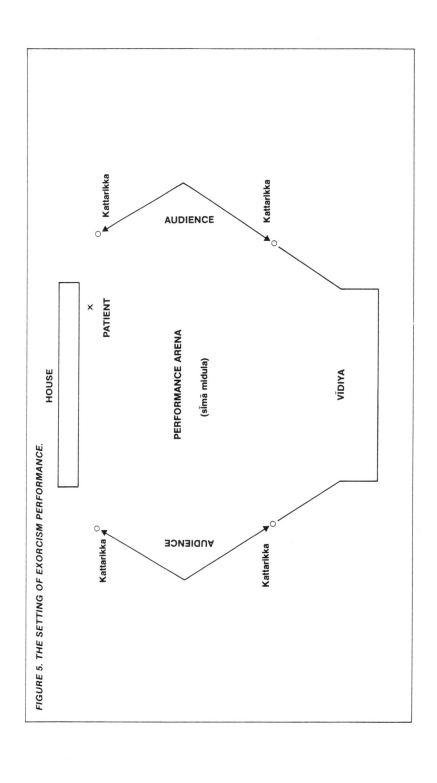

FIGURE 5. THE SETTING OF EXORCISM PERFORMANCE.

HOUSE

PATIENT

Kattarikka

AUDIENCE

Kattarikka

PERFORMANCE ARENA

(sīmā midula)

VĪDIYA

Kattarikka

AUDIENCE

Kattarikka

in accordance with precise measurements based on the traditional Sinhalese unit of a **riyana** (approximately eighteen inches).[8]   This rarely occurs in practice. At each of the four corners of this structure are large panels **(torana)** made from flattened-out banana tree trunks which are decorated with a latticed pattern.   This crossed design, which is also a major decorative form on similar panels in the **vidiyas** of other exorcisms, has the magical property of blocking or restraining demons. The four **torana** are considered to be the points where Mahasona or specific forms of him enter the **vidiya**. They are also regarded by some exorcists as the "rooms" of these demons. At the center of the **Mahasona vidiya** is a structure known as the **pancha massa**.[9] At the top is the offering table **(massa)** for Mangara Deviyo, the deity who is in immediate control of Mahasona. Here is placed a small pot - out of audience view - which is covered by a white cloth (symbolic of purity), in which are contained offerings to Mangara. The front panel of the **pancha massa** has the form of Mahasona painted upon it. He is colored a deep blue black **(kalu pata)** and has the head of a bear. He carries an elephant across his shoulders and is depicted with a sword opening a wound in the elephant's neck and drinking its blood.[10]

At the base of the **pancha massa** and the four **torana** are placed small earthen pots, in which are kept coconut **(pol mal)** and areca palm flowers **(puvak mal)**. These pots are for Bumi Devi or Polova Mahi Kantava, the goddess of the earth. She is a symbol of purity and, in one of the **Jataka** stories (tales of the previous lives of Gautama Buddha), protected Buddha against his major adversary, Mara. The power of the pots is to contain the demons within the **vidiya**. Flowers are also placed in the corners of the **vidiya**. The corners of the demon palace are conceptualized as the 'fortress' of the gods **(devata kotuva)**, and the flowers are offerings to them. The gods primarily concerned are Isvara (Shiva) and the Four Guardian Deities of Sri Lanka (Natha, Vishnu, Kataragama, and Saman).   The entire structure is splendidly decorated with a variety of leaves. Ideally seven different types of leaves must be incorporated into the decoration of the **vidiya**.   These leaves are from trees which have symbolic connection to the Buddha and the deities and also have medicinal properties in traditional Sinhalese herbal medicine **(ayurveda)**.[11]   Young coconut leaves **(gokkola)** decorate the structure and hang from its roof and walls. Their tips are frequently cut or tied in a manner to represent the weapons **(avuda)** of the gods, and most often the trident **(trisula)** of Isvara who exorcists say is the deity who created exorcism. This is common decorative practice for the **vidiyas** in all the major exorcisms. The overall roof plan of the **Mahasona vidiya** matches that of protective **yantra** drawn to ward off attack from this demon.

Although generally similar, the demon palaces of the **Sanni Yakuma** and **Rata Yakuma** exorcisms are distinctive in their designs. Thus the **vidiya** for the **Rata Yakuma** is quadrangular in shape, enclosed by walls on three sides, with the side facing the patient remaining open. Around the inner walls of the enclosure are placed seven **torana** (three on each of the side walls and one in the center of the rear wall facing the patient). These **torana** are for the seven princesses, or queens, who are the daughters of Riddi Bisava (the Washer Queen), around whose myth are organized many of the ritual episodes performed in the **Rata Yakuma**. Several of my exorcist informants have stated that these **torana** are the points of entrance of the princesses into the **vidiya** and can be interpreted as their "bed chambers." Each **torana** is a place of offering at which is placed a small lighted torch **(vilakku)** or lamp and also flowers, areca palm blossoms, rice, and sandalwood.   The central **torana**, known as the **mudun male**, and set in the rear wall of the **vidiya**, is of principal focus in the **vidiya** and is specifically for Riddi Bisava. The **vidiya** for the **Sanni Yakuma** tends to be less elaborate in its decoration when compared with those for the exorcisms already described. The palace for Sanni Yaka (the collective noun for the **sanni** demons) is also enclosed on three sides, and has nine **torana** decorated for the eighteen **sanni**, or disease spreading demons.

Various other structures are also erected at the ritual site. At every major exorcism, including the **Mahasona**, an offering stand (**mal yahanava,** flower fence) is placed to one side of the demon palace. The stand is made from flattened banana trunks with the same crossed design as on the **torana** of the **yak vidiya.** The table itself is covered by a canopy decorated with coconut leaves. On the table are usually placed six lamps with flower offerings. These are to the Buddha and the main deities, and are normally set in the following order: Buddha, Vishnu, Kataragama, Saman, Natha, and Isvara. At the side of Mahasona's palace is erected another structure known as the **Suniyam** or **Pillu vidiya.**[12] This is square in shape (approximately four feet by four feet) and is designed in accordance with the **yantra** for Suniyam, which is also the design for the **atamagala** in the **Suniyama** exorcism. The **Suniyam vidiya** is divided into nine sections (**gabe),** divided by sheaves of banana trunks, the inner concave parts of the sheaves being turned face up. These dividers are conceptualized as the offering plates (**aile)** for Suniyam and his followers. Flowers and rice offerings are placed in them. The nine divisions are understood by exorcists to be for the nine planets and for Suniyam and his followers. The central division is for Suniyam. This structure has the magical property of containing Suniyam within it and of protecting the patient from sorcery, or the use of Suniyam by other persons who wish to harm the patient. The **Suniyam vidiya** which I have described is usually erected for all major exorcisms.

At some **Mahasona** performances another structure, the **Kumara vidiya,** will also be constructed (in addition to the **Suniyam vidiya** or sometimes instead of it) and placed to one side of the demon palace, typically the northwest side, the main direction from which comes the demon who resides in the structure. The structure is considered to be the palace of Kalu Kumara but prominence is given to Vata Kumara, one of the main forms or associates of Kalu Kumara. It is erected at a **Mahasona** only for female patients, and is always present at a **Rata Yakuma.** The top platform of the structure, like the **Suniyam vidiya,** is divided into nine sections for the nine planets and for Kalu Kumara and his various associates. A pole rises from the center of the platform, and two yellow coconuts (**tambili)** are hung from it, together with coconut flowers. The pinnacle of the structure is for Vata Kumara, and it is connected to the four corners of the platform by plaited strips of coconut leaves which hang down the sides of the structure and have their tips tied in the shape of the **trisula.**[13] Ideally the leaves from nine trees must be used in the decoration of the structure, and these have symbolic connections to the Buddha, the main deities, and the planets —— some also have medicinal properties. The overall shape of the structure is that of the **dagaba,** from which the boy-monk Siddhartha fell to be reborn in the form of Vata Kumara.

Between the main demon palace, the lesser **vidiyas** (the **Suniyam vidiya** or **Kumara vidiya),** and the place where the patient is seated, are placed four offering tables (**massa, kattarikki),** which are situated at the four corners of the **sima midula** and essentially demarcate the performance arena. They are made by lashing four poles together so that they cross. Offering baskets for the demons are placed in them during the performance.

I have described the principal structures which are erected at the site of an exorcism, and which are in position at the start of performance. One other structure, the **purale,** requires description. The **purale** is the central structure for the **Iramudun Samayama,** but can also be important for the major all night exorcisms which the **Iramudun Samayama** frequently precedes. The **purale** is not built at the main ritual site.[14] It is located well away from the patient's house, usually in a clearing at the edge of the neighborhood or village, and sometimes near a pathway intersection or a small stream. Exorcists state that it should be constructed in a "wild" area away from human habitation —— in other words, in a place where demons are most likely to exert their malign effect. The place where the **purale** is erected is conceptualized as a cremation place or graveyard. Indeed the **purale** is often built in an area where Sinhalese cremate their dead. Typically the **purale** is a small fenced enclosure decorated with areca palm in a manner similar to that which is built at a graveside. On occasion, but seldom in the Galle area, a raised platform will be constructed with a small ladder leading up to it. It is at the **purale,** or on the **purale** platform, that a straw effigy will be burned during the **Iramudun Samayama,** but sometimes also in a major exorcism which follows. At the peak of the midnight watch and at the end of the morning watches of a large-scale demon ceremony, an exorcist, dressed as a demon, will run to the **purale.** At the end of the performance of an **Iramudun Samayama** or after the conclusion of another major exorcism which usually follows it, the offering baskets to the demons and the other ritual structures are placed at the **purale** and destroyed. On the few occasions of a large all-night exorcism when a **purale** is not erected, the various ritual structures, offerings baskets, etc. will be thrown into an area not inhabited by human beings, sometimes at the edge of the neighborhood or in a deep drainage ditch.

Various themes developed in the course of an exorcism performance are present in the organization of ritual space, in the design of the structures which mark out this space, and in their decoration. Victor Turner (1967, 1968, 1974) has written extensively about the multivocality of symbols. This multivocality is most apparent in the structures erected at the ritual site and their ordered positioning. Demons and ghosts are polluting and dangerous. The structures themselves and the space which they surround are also polluting and dangerous.[15] The one exception to this is the **atamagala,** the major edifice built for the **Suniyama.** This "building" is dominated by Suniyam in his protective form as a deity, and in the course of this rite the patient must move from a situated location outside the **atamagala** to a position inside it. This models the transformational process of the **Suniyama** rite. The patient when outside the **atamagala** is in a relation of opposition to Suniyam, who manifests his demonic aspect in the patient's affliction. However, when the patient moves inside the structure, Suniyam in effect changes from his malevolent aspect and becomes protective of the patient, reordering the patient in accordance with Suniyam's own higher-level ordering as a deity. This is not so in other exorcisms, should the patient enter the **vidiya** of the main afflicting demon. In the other exorcisms the movement of the patient inside the **yak vidiya** is indicative of an intense disorder of mind and body, for as I explained in the previous chapter, these demons cannot transform or be reconstituted at a higher level in the cosmic hierarchy, but can only intensify the chaos of lower-level orders of the cosmic whole. The ritual action in the **Mahasona, Sanni Yakuma** and **Rata Yakuma** exorcisms is explicitly organized to prevent the entrance of the patient into the demon palace. This important difference between the the **atamagala** in the **Suniyama** and the demon palaces in the other exorcisms emphasises the distinction which I have already stressed between the **Suniyama** and the other large-scale demon ceremonies.

The ritual buildings and the space which they mark out are dangerous and polluting because demons enter and congregate in them. Further, and in a critical sense, the structures, and the space which is demarcated by them, express key contradictions and oppositions which are evident in the illness of a patient and which are thematically developed in the performance of an exorcism. Thus the "house of demons" confronts the house of the patient. The world of nature disordered in all its potential malevolence, represented by demons and their places of residence, opposes culture, represented by the house of the patient. Other linked oppositions are implicit in this: death, a potential outcome of demonic attack, opposes life; pollution opposes purity (the house of the patient is ritually purified before any major exorcism begins); disorder opposes order. This last opposition, and in particular the association of the demon palace with disorder, is indicated by the term, **vidiya**, for the demon palace. Thus as Wirz (1954:48 fn) notes, **vidiya** has the connotation of street or house on a street. It is designed as a place where a number of streets, traveled by demons, intersect. The demon palace, therefore, as a "street" or "house at the intersection of streets" opposes the house of human beings. In Sri Lanka, the streets, and especially crossroads, are conceptualized as potentially dangerous, disordered, and chaotic. It is at crossroads that shrines to the Buddha are typically erected. Thus, at a point of great danger is located the source of greatest protection — a shrine to the Buddha.

The organization of the ritual setting and the deployment of ritual structures within it, as representative of fundamental contradictions and oppositions underlying and emergent within exorcism performance, also has implicit within it the basis for their resolution — the domination of Culture over Nature, of Purity over Pollution, and of Order over Disorder. The relation between deities and demons, and particularly the control and domination of the former over the latter, is present in the decoration and design of the ritual structure. Overtly, for example, the **vidiya** is the house of the demons, and exorcists state that one purpose of its magnificent decoration is to make it attractive to demons. But the design of the **vidiya** also indicates the presence of deities; offerings to the deities are placed around the structure and encircle the demonic — indicative of the control and the encompassment of the demons by deities. This is also suggested in the decoration of the **vidiya,** hung as it is with the symbols of the power of the deities. In the **Mahasona vidiya,** the offering table **(pancha massa)** to Mangara, the deity who is the superior of Mahasona, is above the picture of the demon. Immanent in the demonic is the divine.[16]

Demons and ghosts are most dangerous when they roam freely outside the control and restraint of a cultural and cosmic order. Consistent with this, demons are most threatening when they congregate at the exorcism, but outside the structures which have been prepared for them. The entrance of the demons into the various ritual structures exposes them to control and subordination at the hands of human beings, with the assistance of the deities and the power of the Buddha's thought and teaching. While the ritual structures, when they come to contain the demonic, are dangerous and polluting, they are also a major means whereby the threatening presence of the demonic can be controlled and ultimately expelled from the world of human beings. When the demons are contained in the ritual structures, the space which they haunted becomes free of their presence, purified, and made safe once more.

In an important sense, the major ritual structures erected at an exorcism are elaborate traps. Indeed, a decorative form hung from the roof of the demon palace represents the "iron" net of Maha Brahma. The demons when they enter are "caught" in its mesh, and so imprisoned become further subordinated to the will of human beings and their gods.

It is late in the afternoon when the preparations for an all-night exorcism are finally completed. Benches, chairs, and mats are set out on either side of the performance arena, between the patient's house and the demon palace, and relatives, friends, and neighbors begin to arrive. Lighting is not required in the twilight of the late afternoon, but as night advances the whole scene is lit, with electric lights if available, but otherwise with hurricane lamps. At approximately 5:00 P.M. the first events of the ritual begin.

The Order of Events in Demon Exorcisms

Each of the major exorcisms, with the exception of the **Iramudun Samayama**, is divided into three periods: the evening watch **(sandayama)**, the midnight watch **(maduyama)**, and the morning watch **(aluyama)**. The evening watch begins with offerings to the Buddha and the major Sinhalese deities, followed by further ritual events which summon the demons to the ritual occasion. The order of these events, and the actions prescribed for them, is similar for the **Mahasona**, the **Sanni Yakuma** and the **Rata Yakuma**, the exorcisms with which I am principally concerned in this description. The evening watch ends at around 9:30 P.M. and, after a break, usually of half an hour during which the exorcists often take light refreshments, the period of the midnight watch begins. It is during the midnight watch that the awful reality of the demonic reaches a climax. The midnight watch concludes at about 2:30 A.M., when the exorcists again take some light refreshments in a period known as the **Maha te**. At 3:00 A.M. the period of the morning watch begins, and it is during this time that the major dramatic acts are presented —— with the exorcists wearing the masks representative of various demons. The whole performance ends at daybreak, in much the same way that it began, with salutations to the Buddha and the Sinhalese Guardian Deities. Table 5 presents a listing of the main events of the **Mahasona** exorcism and the approximate time of their enactment.

The Evening Watch: The Summoning of the Demons

The first ritual event involves the giving of offerings to the ghosts **(preta pideni)**, usually the ghosts of dead kin **(gnati preta)**, and is performed at all major exorcisms. A specially constructed offering basket **(preta tattuva)** is placed on the ground before the front porch of the house. This basket has four sticks lashed together (in a manner similar to the offering stands for the demons, the **kattarikki**) which rise from it so that the basket is at the base. At the top of the sticks is placed a coconut **(kurumba)** covered by a brightly colored cloth. The offerings placed in the basket should include, theoretically, but not always in practice, twenty-five kinds of mixed meat and vegetable curry **(pas vissi malua)**, five kinds of sweetmeats **(pas kavili)**, five kinds of fruits **(pas paluturu)**, curd and treacle, various intoxicants (toddy, arrack, marijuana, and sometimes opium), stimulants such as beedis, cigarettes, cigars, and betel nut; and a cup, saucer, and plate. Clean water **(kasapan** - strained through a cloth) is poured into the cup, which also contains the five metals - gold, silver, copper, lead, and iron. The metals (coins or thin metal strips) are representative of the earth **(pathavi)**, one of the five essential elements of matter **(pancha mahabhuta)**. The five elements of matter are an important aspect of the logic of offering and the organization of ritual enactment.

Placing the offering basket on the ground is indicative of the low status of ghosts relative to, for example, demons, whose offerings, as I will describe, are set on chairs conceptualized as offering tables. The crossed

TABLE 5

Approximate Time of Event	Major Events of the **Mahasona**	
5:00 P.M.	Offerings to Ghosts	
6:00 P.M.	**Namaskaraya** to Buddha and Guardian Deities	I
	Seating of patient	Evening
	Offerings to demons	Watch
9:00 P.M.	**Avamangalle** (Death Time)	
10:30 p.m.	Major dances	
	Mahasohon samayam pade (gathering time dance of Mahasona)	
12:00 P.M.	**Avatara balima** (the appearance of the demon)	II
	Adavv dances	Midnight
		Watch
12:30 P.M.	**Mangara pelapaliya**	
	(presentations in honor of god Mangara)	
2:00 A.M.	**Kalu Vadi paliya** (The appearance of the hunter of demons)	
2:15 A.M.	**Mahasona dapavilla** (The appearance and death of Mahasona)	
2:30 A.M.	**Maha Te** (refreshment break)	
3:00 A.M.	**Ata Paliya**	
	Dahaata Sanniya	III
	(the apppearance of the 18 sanni demons)	Morning
		Watch
6:00 A.M.	**Dekone Vilakkuva**	
	(double torch presentation of demon)	
	Final homage to Buddha and Guardian Deities	
	Destruction of ritual buildings	

sticks have the symbolic power of restricting the ghosts to the basket. One exorcist maintained that the four sticks used were for the four main cardinal directions from which the ghosts come. The offerings to the ghosts, as the list I have given suggests, are considered to be highly polluting. Thus, impure intoxicants and stimulants are included in the offerings. The curries do not have to be specially cooked, as in the case of food offerings to the demons, and some exorcists maintain that they can be bought already prepared from local shops. The offerings are understood to be attractive to ghosts, who crave the food and luxuries of the human world.

The presiding exorcist blows on a bamboo whistle (**vasdanda**, poison pipe)[17] and smokes incense (**dummala**) over a brazier (**anguru kabala**). At the same time he intones seven mantra. The first mantra, as Wirz (1954:188-90) records, tells of the age of a former Buddha when some priests sinned in the preparation of food to be distributed at a ritual meal. For this they were transformed into ghosts. The following mantra summons the ghosts and asks them to take the offerings prepared for them. In the course of these mantra, the names of the Buddha and the deities are uttered. After the mantra are completed (usually after about half an hour), the offering basket is taken inside the house and placed in a room, which ideally should not then be in use. The exorcist then goes through the house and flames **dummala** (a powdered tree resin) in order to purify it. Exorcists claim that a purpose of this rite is to draw the ghosts away from the area in which the exorcism is to be performed. If this is not done, there is a risk that they will take the later offerings for the demons. The acceptance of the offerings by the ghosts traps them in the basket, renders them subject to human control, and facilitates their removal as agents in the patient's illness.

In Chapter 4 I discussed the fact that most instances of demonic attack also recognize the malign agency of ghosts. The placement inside the house of the offering basket to the ghosts symbolically expresses the subordination of ghosts to the cultural order of the Sinhalese household and their connection with it. Often, and in the course of events later in the evening, the offering basket will be examined for any indication of disturbance. If it is disturbed, this suggests that the ghosts have accepted their offerings and thereby removed their malign effect.

The offering to the ghosts, although invariably preceding all major exorcisms, is not regarded by exorcists as part of the demon ceremony itself. Theoretically it is not part of the first period of an exorcism, the evening watch. This period begins at around 6:00 P.M., after the offering to the ghosts and after the exorcists, seated on mats in the performance arena, have been served food by members of the patient's household. Members of the patient's household and others who have come to attend the exorcism will also be served food prior to the beginning of the major exorcism.

Immediately before the first events of the evening watch, the performance arena is purified with pure water (**handun kiri pan,** unused water mixed with sandalwood, coconut milk, and turmeric), contained in a new earthen pot (**kotale**). The water is sprinkled on the ground with areca nut flower. Lamps are lit at the **mal yahanava** for the Buddha and the Guardian Deities. This is most often performed by an exorcist, but occasionally the patient will assist in this. A **namaskaraya** (verses in salutation of the Buddha and the main gods) is uttered, and the Buddha and the gods are asked to help in the curing of the patient. Exorcists state that the patient must focus his or her thoughts on the Buddha and the power of the deities for the work of a cure to be effected.

The patient is then seated on a mat, often reclining comfortably against pillows.[18] The patient is dressed in white clothes which have been washed by a woman usually of the rada (washer) caste, who traditionally performs this ritual service for other castes on the occasion of exorcisms and other rituals. On the mat before the patient are placed five objects: a leaf of the **tolabo** lily **(Crinum asiaticum)**, a length of the hiressa vine **(Cissus quadrangularia)**, a coconut, a wooden rice pestle **(mol gaha)** which contains an iron ring, and a fistful of unhusked rice **(vi)**. These objects are understood to have curative and protective powers for the patient and to provide a barrier between the patient and the demons who will be called to the ritual scene. For example, demons are afraid of iron, and the pestle containing the iron ring is viewed by some exorcists to be representative of the **axis mundi** and the pole of Maha Brahma, the creator of the universe, with which he batters and subdues demons. At the end of the exorcism, the rice is scattered on the ground to be eaten by birds and animals: a merit-making **(pinkama)** activity which is further protective of the patient, and accords with customary Sinhalese Buddhist practice. The objects, with the exception of the rice, relate to a myth concerning Vijaya, the first Sinhalese king of Sri Lanka, who was afflicted by illness caused by the demon queen, Kuveni, whom he married but subsequently deserted. The objects were used in the healing of Vijaya and also of his successor, Panduvas, who was also attacked by Kuveni (see Seneviratne 1978:105-7).[19] Ideally, the five objects should be placed at the patient's feet by a close male relative. I stress that these objects are regarded as not only protective of the patient, but also of the entire household.

Chairs are placed in front of the patient in preparation for the major episodes of the evening watch —— the offerings to the main demons. A curtain **(kadaturava)** of white cloth is held between the patient and the chairs, blocking the patient's view of the proceedings which immediately follow. The curtain is usually held by two male kin of the patient. The whiteness of the cloth, also symbolic of purity, is intended to promote an emotional and mental quiet **(saumya)** in the patient. Exorcists also state that it functions in much the same way as the iron net of myth, ensnaring demons and preventing them from consuming the patient.[20]

In the **Mahasona** exorcism, five offering baskets are now placed on the chairs before the patient. These, in their ordering for female patients and from the patient's left to right, are: the **Mal bulat tattuva**, the **Kalu Yaka tattuva**, the **Riri Yaka tattuva**, the **Suniyam tattuva**, and, lastly, the offering basket for Mahasona.[21] The **Mal bulat tattuva** contains flowers **(mal)**, betel leaves **(bulat)**, a small pot of turmeric water **(kahadiyara)**, in which is placed some areca flowers **(puvak mal)**, and a thin lighted torch **(vilakku)**. The contents of the basket are for Buddha and the Guardian Deities, and in a few exorcisms I have witnessed the basket is an alternative to erecting the **mal yahanava**. The **Mal bulat tattuva** is protective of the patient, and, unlike the other baskets is kept by the patient throughout the performance. The water contained in the pot will be used to purify the performance area, and be used to bring the patient and exorcists out of trance.

The offering basket to Kalu Yaka is divided into five sections (see Figure 6) and has the design of protective **yantra** drawn against the effect of this demon. Each of the sections is for the five forms which Kalu Yaka assumes, including that of Kalu Yaka himself, who occupies the central section. The offerings include husked rice **(hal)**, mixed with seven different kinds of pure vegetables; five kinds of roasted **(pulutu)** grains; five kinds of sweetmeats made from oil and rice into which five colors have been mixed; nine kinds of flowers; betel and sandalwood paste. The offerings contained in the basket are indicative of Kalu Yaka's high rank relative to other demons, like Riri Yaka and Mahasona, who are considered to be low in the

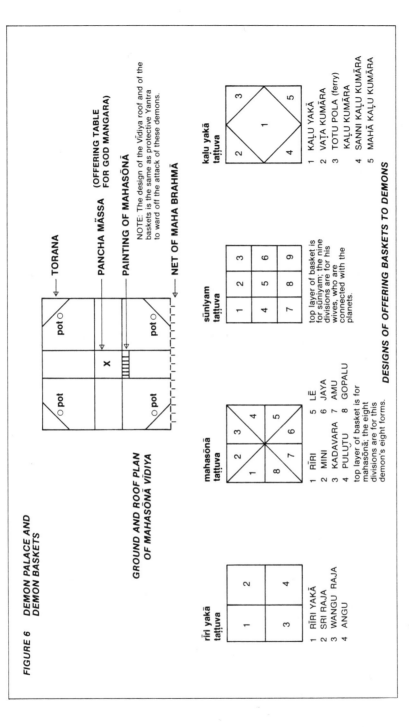

FIGURE 6   DEMON PALACE AND
            DEMON BASKETS

GROUND AND ROOF PLAN
OF MAHASŌNĀ VIDIYA

→ TORANA

→ PANCHA MĀSSA   (OFFERING TABLE
                   FOR GOD MANGARA)

→ PAINTING OF MAHASŌNĀ

NOTE: The design of the Vidiya roof and of the
baskets is the same as protective Yantra
to ward off the attack of these demons.

→ NET OF MAHA BRAHMĀ

riri yakā
tatṭuva

| 1 | 2 |
| 3 | 4 |

1 RĪRI YAKĀ
2 SRI RAJA
3 WANGU RAJA
4 ANGU

mahasōnā
tatṭuva

	2	3	
	1	4	
	8	5	
	7	6	

1 RĪRI   5 LĒ
2 MINI   6 JAYA
3 KADAVARA 7 AMU
4 PULUṬU   8 GOPALU

top layer of basket is for
mahasōnā; the eight
divisions are for this
demon's eight forms.

sūnīyam
tatṭuva

1	2	3
4	5	6
7	8	9

top layer of basket is
for sūnīyam; the nine
divisions are for his
wives, who are
connected with the
planets.

kaḷu yakā
tatṭuva

2		3
	1	
4		5

1 KAḶU YAKĀ
2 VAṬA KUMĀRA
3 TOTU POLA (ferry)
   KAḶU KUMĀRA
4 SANNI KAḶU KUMĀRA
5 MAHĀ KAḶU KUMĀRA

DESIGNS OF OFFERING BASKETS TO DEMONS

hierarchy of the demon world. Unlike Riri Yaka and Mahasona, Kalu Yaka receives relatively pure vegetables and grains and no meats. A small torch placed in one corner of the basket completes the offering.

The basket for Riri Yaka also has a shape similar to that often found on protective **yantra** and is normally divided into four equal sections (see Figure 6), one for Riri Yaka and the others for each of three of his followers, or other forms of himself. The food and flower offerings are essentially the same as for the **Kalu Yaka tattuva** with the addition of roasted meats from land and water creatures **(godadiyamas)** and blood **(le)** drawn from the comb of a cock.

Suniyam Yaka's basket is more elaborate than any of the former. It has nine divisions for the nine planets; there is a raised section of the basket (indeed it is conceptualized as having two "floors"), the central part of which is a hollowed-out piece of banana trunk that contains offerings to Suniyam Yaka and his wives. The offerings in each of the sections and in the raised central part are similar to those in the basket for Riri Yaka, with the exception of blood from the cock and roasted meats.

The last offering basket, which is to Mahasona, is divided into eight sections, one for each of the forms which this demon can assume. As with the **Suniyam tattuva** it has a raised section, the central part being made from half a coconut shell (symbolic of a skull) in which are placed offerings to Mahasona. The contents of this basket are the same as for Riri Yaka. The offering baskets I have described for the main demons are the same for all the exorcisms. With the placement of the offering baskets, the main ritual events of the evening watch begin.

In the Mahasona, and in all the other major exorcisms, **dummala** is smoked over the baskets and over a live rooster, placed beneath them. The smell of the **dummala** incense draws the demons to the rite and attracts them to the offerings. **Dummala** is a resin from the **sal** tree, the tree under which Gautama Buddha was born. Thus in its use, the power of the Buddha is invoked in the bringing of the demons to the ritual scene.[22] A cock is an indispensable part of every exorcism. It is regarded as the main sacrificial victim **(billa)** of an exorcism, and the demons are invited to take it rather than the patient or an exorcist. The cock is an equivalent of a human being, and stands in a significant relation of similarity and contrast to a human being. It walks upright on two legs and is a creature of culture and the domestic. These essential similarities enable exorcists to play a trick on the demons, who are led into taking the rooster rather than a human being.

While the baskets and the cock are being smoked, the exorcist blows on the poison pipe. The shrill of the **vasdanda** is the sound of the demons, and it calls them to the ritual scene. The exorcist-drummers, seated a short distance away from the offerings and facing the patient, roll a drum rhythm (known as the **magul bere** and played at most important ceremonial occasions) which announces the start of the major offering episodes.

Spells and songs are now chanted and sung at each of the offering baskets, beginning with the first demon in the ordering —— Kalu Yaka or Suniyam Yaka. There are three main kinds of verse form which are employed at the presentation of each offering basket. These, in the order in which theoretically they should be performed, are: **mantra**, which summon the demon and command the demon to take the offering; **kannalavva**, or an invocation to the Buddha and the gods in which will often be inserted the name of the patient; and **kavi**, or songs about the demons and the deities.

The mantra intoned contain Sanskrit, Tamil, Sinhala, Malayalam, Telegu, and even Persian words (Tambiah 1968:177). This linguistic mixture, coupled with the considerable speed with which the mantra are uttered, limits the extent to which they can be comprehended, either by the patient or the ritual audience. However, their utterance is often preceded by the presiding exorcist's informing the patient and audience in Sinhala that he is about to summon all the demons and their controlling deities. Each mantra begins with the phrase **Om Namo,** understood by exorcists to be a salutation to Buddha and/or Isvara. **Om** is the creative cosmic sound of the universe and symbolic of Isvara.

The presiding exorcist, who utters the main mantra, approaches the offerings and carries over his right shoulder the **igaha** of Isvara, which is the appropriate position for this object of divine power and demon destruction. The **igaha** is a stick, approximately three feet in length, decorated at one end with young coconut leaves and areca flowers in the shape of an arrowhead, interpreted by exorcists as the destructive eye of Isvara. A coin offering **(panduru)** is tied with a strip of white cloth halfway down the shaft. From time to time the **igaha** is drawn down the patient's body and towards the offering baskets, an action which removes the demonic illness from the patient and transfers it to the baskets. The **igaha** was given to lord Vessamuni, and by its power he smashes and subjugates the demons.

The first mantra **(yaksa disti kirima)** refers to the cosmic order and the subservience of the demons to the Buddha and the deities. This theme, already stressed in the **namaskaraya** which begins the exorcism, is repeated in many of the following poems and songs. When the demons are referred to in the mantra and the other verse forms they are addressed as **devatava** (god or godling), which signifies their ambiguity of status and the higher powers which they have usurped as a result of their control over the patient. The power of the opening mantra and of those to follow is to bring the demons to the ritual site, force the demons to accept their offerings, and also to confine and trap them in the offering baskets.

The poems and songs of the **kannalavva,** which follow the mantra, invoke the gods and entreat them to assist in the cure of the patient. They also call the demons and recount aspects of their myths. They are sung predominantly in Sinhala, and thus are potentially comprehensible to the patient and to the members of the ritual gathering. The patient is explicitly enjoined to attend, by the exorcists and often by close male kin who are seated nearby. Nevertheless, as I will argue in the next chapter, the organization of ritual performance places a limitation on the degree to which the patient and members of the ritual gathering attend to the details of the utterances. Like the mantra, the **kannalavva** are considered to have curative properties.

Various **kavi** are also sung at each offering basket to the demons. These are mainly in Sinhala, but employ a large number of words not in daily use. There are five main named types of **kavi,** and, in the order in which I was told they should ideally be presented, are: the **asirivada kavi,** which relates aspects of the myths relating to the demons and praises their powers and also the powers of the deities; the **ambun kavi,** which tells how the offering baskets and other ritual structures are made; the **yadini kavi,** which is basically similar to the **asirivada kavi,** and which tell of the ancestry and origin of the demons; the **atakona kavi,** which calls the demons from the eight directions; and the **sirasapada** (head-to-foot) **kavi,** which is principally curative and is sung to remove the illness from the patient.

Exorcists state that the songs **(kavi)** should evoke in the emotional state of the patient the prevailing mood of their content, and that the style of their presentation should be consistent with this mood. Some of the older exorcists described the appropriate style of presentation and the mood which should be evoked in terms of the concept of **rasa** (taste, mood, sentiment). The **rasas** to which the exorcists referred are those documented in the great Sanskrit aesthetic tradition. For example, the dominant mood of the **yadini** and **asirivada kavi** sung at Kalu Yaka's offering basket should convey a sense of his lustful and erotic **(srngara rasa)** character as well as his terrible **(bhayanaka rasa)** nature. Likewise, the mood for the songs describing Mahasona should express his furious **(raudra rasa)** and terrifying mien, but should also give a sense of the heroic and dynamic energy **(vira rasa)** of the event of Gothaimbara's overpowering of Jayasena. Songs which recount the power of the gods and their capacity to control the demons should also give rise to the sentiment of **vira rasa** and also to the compassion **(karuna rasa)** of the gods. The mood of the **sirasapada kavi** should be that of **karuna rasa,** and in its removal of the illness should produce a feeling of calmness and quietness **(santi rasa)** in the patient. These and other **rasas** should also be expressed and evoked in the music which accompanies the **kavi** and in the later events of music and drama. In the drama which concludes an exorcism, for instance, the demons should be presented, not so much as awful, raging, and terrifying, but as loathsome and disgusting **(bibhatsa rasa)** and as comic **(hasya rasa)**, evoking in the presentation of the demonic this feeling in the patient.[23]

There is often considerable repetition and overlap in the content of the various songs. An example of the songs typical of those often sung at exorcisms is the following **asirivada kavi** for Mahasona which I recorded.

> In prosperous Sri Lanka, beyond the seven seas,
> At the city of Pollonaruva,
> Lived Gaja Kumbakari, a woman of the potter caste,
> Mahasona was born from her womb.
>
> Day by day he grew,
> On the third month of his birth, he was named Jayasena,
> His face was like a mirror,
> His body was white, and he shone in the darkness.
> People were in terror of him,
> He threw stones and sand at them,
> He shouted loudly and caused people to fear him,
> He comes in many forms, as a dog and as a pig.
> He journeyed to Vessamuni
> And asked permission from him to terrify the people as a demon,
> Vessamuni gave him permission after Jayasena had worshipped him,
> On his return he saw the wife of Gothaimbara.
>
> Jayasena was attracted to her great beauty,
> But she resisted his advances.
> Angry, Jayasena caused her to become ill.
> Gothaimbara discovered the harm that had befallen his household.

The poem continues and relates how Gothaimbara killed Jayasena in a duel by kicking off his head, only for the demon to be brought back to life by Senasuru (Saturn), who placed the head of a bear on his shoulders. The song concludes with a list of the offerings which should be given to Mahasona.

The **sirasapada kavi** typically concludes the sequence of mantra, poems, and songs intoned at each of the offering baskets to the demons. It is during this song that the **igaha** is drawn down the patient's body removing the illness, placing its demonic essence in the baskets. The downward (from head to foot) motion of this action is consistent with the exorcist understanding that demonic illness leaves through the patient's extremities, particularly the feet, but also the hands. A major aspect of the **sirasapada kavi** is that it invokes the power of the Buddha:

By the blue color of the Buddha must all the sickness of your head
  go,
I have given all my pearls, gold, silver, and other riches,
By the power of the Buddha's light all the sickness must end . . .
By the power of Buddha's red color all the illness must vanish,
The Buddha's light spreads everywhere,
The patient's sickness must leave from the feet and from the
  fingers.

When the mantra, poems, and songs for each demon basket are
completed, the basket is taken by the exorcist and passed three times
(signifying the **tun dosa,** the three humors) over the patient's head. The
patient is then expected to touch the basket, and to wipe his or her face
three times, and to place flowers, betel leaves, and rice in the **Mal bulat
tattuva.** This action (**Mal bulat dima muhuna atha pisa damima** —— flower
betel face wiping offering) is capable of multiple interpretations. It is an
offering by the patient to the demon, but is also an invocation to the gods
represented in the **Mal bulat tattuva.** It transfers the demonic illness of the
patient to the offering basket. As an offering to the demon it signifies the
patient's subordination to the demonic will, but also indicates the freeing of
the patient from demon control, and the subordination of the demons to the
deities. Exorcists normally interpret this action as simply concluding the
offering to a particular demon, as indicating that the demon has been
successfully summoned to the ritual occasion, is now taking the offering and
is being contained in the basket, and that the patient is in the process of
being relieved of demonic control and illness. During this event the exorcist
will also take the cock and hold it before the patient, smoking it with
dummala. The cock is then thrown on the ground beneath the offering
chairs. At the close of each offering to the demons, the exorcist will
announce that the offering is completed (**tindui nivaranai),** and members of
the household cry, three times, **"Ayubo"** (**ayubowewa,** Long life). The
patient is often in a state of semitrance throughout much of the offering
episodes, and is assisted in the concluding events of the demon offerings by
a close kinsman who is seated nearby. The entire sequence of offerings is
generally considered by Sinhalese to be highly dangerous and to provoke
extreme anxiety in the patient. A kinsman who is usually seated with the
patient will comfort the patient throughout the proceedings.

After all the demon offerings have been completed, the exorcist will
then take a torch (**pandama)** and throw burning **dummala,** which billows in
balls of orange flame, at the cloth curtain (**kadaturava)** which divides the
patient from the offerings. This action (**killa gahanava,** pollution hitting), in
the view of the exorcists, purifies the curtain which has become polluted by
the demonic presence. The curtain is then removed, and the offerings to the
demons are taken away and placed on the offering stands (**kattarikki)** at the
perimeter of the performance arena.

These events of the evening watch last approximately three hours, until
9:00 P.M. The mantra, poems, and songs are highly repetitive in theme and
content and are presented with great rapidity. Thus, for example, mantra
and song which are recognized as distinct by exorcists merge in
performance. Other exorcists, who sit on the ground at the side or behind
the presiding exorcist facing the patient, also accompany the presiding
exorcist in the uttering of the spells and in the singing. Their role is more
prominent when the presiding exorcist must break his flow of chanting or
singing to engage in actions connected with the offerings to the demons.
Rhythms (**kavi** or **bera tala)** are played on the drums by exorcist-drummers
in accompaniment to the poems and songs, but not usually to the mantra.

During the mantra the exorcist will rock from foot to foot, and this develops into a more recognizable dance for the poems and songs. The steps of the dance are those which become more elaborately presented in the major dance episodes of the midnight watch.

In the **Mahasona** a short break of ten minutes or so follows the offering of the baskets to the demons, during which the exorcists often take refreshments. A major episode now begins —— the **avamangalle** (death time). This bridges the evening and midnight watch periods. It is the time when Maru Riri Yaka (the Death Blood Demon and the most terrible form of Riri Yaka) is considered to be at his most powerful. A rolled reed mat is brought out. A drum roll is beaten, and the exorcist sings a song about the history of the mat **(padura upata)** while it is smoked with **dummala** to attract the demons:

Padura Upata

I take refuge in the Buddha.
I take refuge in the Dhamma.
I take refuge in the Sangha.
With my mind on the Buddha I recite the history of the mat.

The Seven Queens, the Seven forms of Pattini went to collect rushes.
They went to make a mat.
Prince Dhammeti had an illness but there was no mat upon which he could lie.
The gods told the Seven Queens to bring a mat.
They went to Dumbara pond (a dwelling place of Mahasona) but found no rushes.
They asked everywhere.
They went to the Sun Moon pond where they found many rushes.

I take the mat in my right hand.
I make the breasts of the Seven Queens full of joy.
I lie down upon the mat to remove the sickness.
I have permission from the gods.

The mat is then laid out on the ground, a short spell is uttered, and the exorcist stretches out **(dapanava)** upon it. He is covered by a red cloth, its color being symbolic of Riri Yaka.[24] The exorcist's head is at the foot of the patient while his feet, which point to the **Mahasona vidiya**, rest on the folded end of the mat, which is where the head would otherwise lie in a normal sleeping position. The exorcist lies in the manner of a corpse and thus portrays the central theme of this ritual event —— the exorcist's offering of himself as a corpse to Maru Riri Yaka. The exorcist blows on the poison pipe **(vasdanda)** while offerings are placed on the ground to Riri and the other major demons to be summoned. This is done by the exorcist's assistant **(madu puraya)**, who places the offerings at the head, stomach, and feet of the recumbent exorcist. The interpretation given by exorcists for this is that the offerings should be prepared at the three points of the body where the mat is tied around a corpse. A cock is also placed at the feet of the exorcist and smoked with **dummala**.

I have stated that the offerings are primarily for Maru Riri Yaka. In the **Mahasona** exorcisms I have witnessed, however, the offerings are given to three forms which Riri Yaka takes - Maru Riri, Totupola Riri (the Ferry or River Crossing Blood Demon) and Sohon Riri (the cemetery blood demon).

This varies for the other two exorcisms, where Sohon Riri is replaced by Sanni Riri (in the **Sanni Yakuma**) or Rata Yakum Riri (in the **Rata Yakuma**). Two other demons also given offerings are Mahasona and Suniyam. All the offerings are eventually placed in a basket (generally known as the **avamangalle pideni tattuva**) which is typically set on the exorcist's stomach.

The offerings during the **avamangalle**, which are the same for the three exorcisms, include rice in packets or **gotu** (placed at the three points down the exorcist's body), seven types of vegetable curry, five types of roasted grain (**pulutu**), land and water meat (**godadiyamas**), nine types of flowers torn into small pieces, and sometimes human excrement and marijuana. At the feet of the exorcist an egg is cooked in the cranium of a human skull. This is a most significant aspect of the **avamangalle** episode and evokes frequent comment by those who gather at the occasion. The cooking of the egg is regarded as the destruction of a life, and as such it attracts demons. But further, it is conceptualized as an action in which a life (the egg) is exchanged for the life of the patient. The danger to the patient, as a demonic victim, is removed by presenting the egg as a victim (**billa**) in the patient's stead. The preparation of the offerings during the **avamangalle**, and, indeed, this entire episode, is viewed as highly dangerous and polluting. Sinhalese exorcists and laity refer to the preparations of the offerings in this episode (and especially the cooking of the egg) as "low caste" (**nicha kula**). It is explicitly understood as standing in direct opposition to rightful Buddhist practice. Indeed, Maru Riri is generally regarded by exorcists and audience as a manifestation of Maruva (Mara) who, as I described earlier, is the chief adversary of the Buddha.

During the preparation of the offerings and their presentation to the demons, mantra, poems, and songs are uttered in much the same sequence as in the earlier offerings given to the demons. In the **avamangalle** episode of the **Mahasona** exorcism, mantra are first intoned to the forms of Riri Yaka, then to Mahasona, and finally to Suniyam. This is followed by an invocation to the gods (**kannalavva**) which includes a plea for their aid in curing the patient. Poems and songs are sung about the demons, which call them from the eight directions, relate their history and the types of ailments they cause. The exorcist commands them to take the offerings and to accept his body instead of the patient.

Avamangalle Samayam Kavi

All the demons come to this place.
Come from across the seven seas, the seven mountains, the seven ponds, the five rivers, the five crossings. Come from the city of the demon rock.
Come the demon who dwells at the burial ground.
Come the demon who lives where the Vaddas dwell.
Come the demon who makes this patient ill.
I give the cock. I give its blood for you to drink. Come quickly.
Come the demons who scream in the sky.
Come the demon who eats dead bodies.
There are many things to eat here.
Come the demon who must seek permission from Vessamuni.
Oh Mahasona come.
Come and take the cock instead of the patient.
Come Mahasona who is commanded by god Saman and the Guardian gods.
Come the cruel demon who has caused such illness.
The power of god Natha spreads throughout Lanka.

The demon of death has come and struck my chest with his sword.
Oh god. I am dying. Riri has cut my leg and is drinking my blood.
I cannot live. I cannot bear my suffering.
Oh demon take my life and not the life of the patient.
Riri has come as the demon of death.
He carries a club and a rope.
Oh demon eat my flesh and drink my blood.

In return for these offerings the demons are asked to remove their illness-causing effect upon the patient. When the **sirasapada kavi** begins, the exorcist lying on the mat takes the **igaha**, as he did in the offering events preceding the **avamangalle**, and draws it down the patient's body. He then touches the offering basket placed on his stomach, and then the cock lying at his feet. These actions, which are repeated three times, draw the illness out of the patient and transfer it to the offering basket, and then to the exorcist's body, and thence to the cock. The patient is then asked to wipe his or her face with the cloth which covered the exorcist. This is done three times, and the cloth is placed in the offering basket, which the patient is asked to touch, again three times. The exorcist then takes a lighted torch, revolving it three times over the patient's head, and then gives it to the patient who blows on it. These actions remove the illness from the patient's body: the wiping of the patient's face, the touching of the basket, and the revolving of the torch remove the three illnesses, or the disorders of the three humors, caused by the demons. The blowing on the torch releases the fever and heat **(usna ginijal)** of illness from within the patient's body. These actions are enacted similarly at the end of the **avamangalle** period in all the other major exorcisms.

Flowers and betel leaves are then placed in the **Mal bulat tattuva,** either by the patient or a close male relative, to secure the protection of the Buddha and the main deities. They must be placed in the **Mal bulat tattuva,** for the deities are pure and their offerings should not be mixed with the impure and polluting offerings to the demons. A final action performed by the patient is to give a ring to the exorcist, who places it on his finger. This action has a number of connotations. Exorcists stress that the ring should be valuable, for its value both attracts and encourages the demons to remove their ill effects. The ring symbolizes the bond, the "marriage," between the patient and the demons, and represents the thread **(nula)** which is tied at the diagnosis of demonic illness. The giving of the ring from the patient to the exorcist, therefore, both signifies and symbolizes the breaking of the bond which unites the patient with the demons.

Upon the completion of these actions, **dummala** is ignited and thrown near the patient. This action is purifying and repels demons, in contrast to the smoking of the resin **(dung allanawa)** which attracts demons. While this is being done, members of the patient's household cry, "Long life, long life, long life." The exorcist is now rolled up in the mat and burning **dummala** is thrown over his body. Male kin of the patient come forward, and crying in "mourning" carry the exorcist's body to one side of the demon palace. The patient is instructed by the exorcists to look away for, exorcists say, the patient would witness an aspect of his or her own "death." Indeed, as I discuss more fully in Chapter 8, in the ritual events leading up to and including the **avamangalle**, the patient's self is no longer constituted in the "normal" and healthy everyday world. The patient has a demonic self, and the transference of the illness, the essence of the demonic, to the body of the exorcist, is metaphorically a "death" of this demonic self.

Exorcists state that the offering basket used in the **avamangalle** should then be taken to the **Suniyam** or **pillu vidiya** (or to the **Kumara vidiya** in the case of a female patient). Here mantra and songs are uttered to protect the patient from sorcery. The basket used in the **avamangalle,** and the others previously offered to the demons, is then taken to the **purale** (cemetery place). Occasionally, however, the removal of these baskets to the **purale** occurs after the enactment of the major dance episodes of the midnight watch.

In the ritual events I have described, a demonic reality is constructed in which the patient is understood by all those gathered to be immersed and subjected. This reality, which is dominated by the dangerous, disordering, and polluting aspects of the demonic, is emergent, nonetheless, in a context where the Buddha and the deities are also present. The demons are controlling and dominating, but yet they are subject to the control of the Buddha and the deities, and by human beings who act through the deities and enlist their divine aid. As I described for the major ritual buildings or structures, in the midst of the demonic is the divine. The disordering aspect of nature, which the demonic expresses, is itself ordered and subordinated within an overall cosmic and cultural unity surmounted by the Buddha and the deities. The luring and tricking of the demons is particularly evident in the **avamangalle** during which the exorcist presents himself as if he were a human corpse, "fooling" the demons into taking the cock as a human surrogate. The demonic, as both nature and culture disordered, is summoned from the outer regions of the universe and from places marginal to, or outside, culture —— as sung in the **atakona kavi:** "from the mountains, from the waterfalls, from the streams, from the cemeteries, from the crossroads." Powerful and threatening as the demons are, they are ensnared and trapped within culture and are rendered subject to the control which resides in its ordered hierarchy. This is so in a very real sense. The offering baskets are "magical" designs, the power of which, when combined with mantra and song, holds the demonic within them. The demons actually, as well as metaphorically, are placed within structure, and are exposed to the control of human beings. Contained and constrained within the baskets, their malign connection with the patient can be broken and their demonic illness dispelled.

The Midnight Watch: The Dance and Death of Mahasona

The events of the **avamangalle** are normally completed between 9:30 P.M. and 10:30 P.M. During its closing stages, the exorcist-dancers have been preparing for the major dances, collectively referred to as the **Mahasohon samayam pade** (the gathering time dance of the Great Cemetery Demon), or less usually the **Mahasohon natuma** (dance of Mahasona). Typically, two or three dancers perform the dance sequences.[25] The dancers are dressed as women.

The dress of the dancers is magnificent. Each dancer wears a red and black banded conical cap **(samayam toppiya).** Around the base of the cap is a "diadem" cut from banana trunk and decorated with coconut leaves. At the ears are large multibanded rings **(todu)** shaped from young coconut leaves. From either side of the cap fall long hair tresses **(pita varala),** which reach almost to the knees and which are also made from young coconut leaves. The faces of the dancers are powdered white, accentuating the eyes, under which the black from a pot is applied, emphasizing the effect. A large ornament **(tali)** is hung around the neck. According to the exorcists, this is symbolic of marriage and also is the ornament of Isvara. A tight-fitting bodice **(kabaye),** made of black, red, yellow, and white cloth, is also worn. A white sarong-type dress **(hela)** is wound at the waist and tied by a wide band of red cloth **(pachchawadam)** in such a way that the white cloth of the dress must appear above the red.   The red and white here are specifically associated by some exorcists with Kataragama and Pattini, respectively. A frilled cloth (inahede), patterned in black, red, and white, is also tied at the waist —— as exorcists state, to heighten the beauty of the hips. Two similar strips of cloth (rali patiya) are tied just above the ankles. Silver bangles (valalu) are worn on the arms, and on the lower parts of the legs are fastened strips of leather to which are attached small bells (gejji). Silver foot bracelets (silambu) are also worn.   The bangles, bells, and foot bracelets give out a jingling sound during the dance —— a sound which exorcists state is attractive to demons. The colors of the headpiece, bodice, and dress are those of the three humors unbalanced by demonic attack. The black eye shadow also signifies the demonic. But, as elsewhere, hierarchy, order, and the divine are represented in the dress of the dancers as well. For example, the foot bracelets are understood to be the ornaments of the powerful —— of kings, of gods, and also of demons. Exorcists consider them to be the ornaments of Pattini, a goddess who figures prominently in much ritual, including exorcism.[26]

I was unable to elicit from the exorcists a clear and consistent account for why the dancers assume the dress of women.   (It should be noted, however, that the dress is not exclusively female. Traditionally, bangles and foot bracelets, for instance, could be worn by males.) Exorcists are acutely aware of the multivocal qualities of the symbolic articles which are displayed in the course of exorcism performance.   One exorcist with extreme care, pointed out to me that the symbolic references of various articles depends on the context in which they are presented. Some exorcists argued that the female dress of the dancers is a continuation of a tradition formed in the historical past, when women danced at exorcisms.   Others stated that the dress refers to Pattini. My own interpretation is that the dress is consistent with the association of the demonic with the female, and particularly appropriate to the dance context of exorcism where the demonic manifests itself in some of its greatest intensity.

In Chapter 5 I argued that the female mediates the demonic, a thematic aspect of the demon myths. The dancers, then, dressed as women, mediate the demonic into the world of human beings. Indeed, the demonic becomes manifest in the bodies of the dancers, and they often become entranced and "see" the demons, as they perform the elaborate and magnificent dances of the midnight watch.   While the dancers appear as "female," it must be stressed that they are males in female attire. It would be a mistake to interpret the exorcist-dancers as assuming some kind of transvestite role. In the dancers, the strength and authority of the male lies behind and within the female. During the dance, the demonic enters into the male body of a dancer dressed as a female. Trapped in a male body, which is also healthy and nonafflicted, the demonic can be controlled and expelled. The illusory, the play on appearances and form which is such a constant theme of major exorcisms, is thus present in the dress of the dancers.

A slow rhythmic drumming announces the beginning of the major dance sequences. The dancers gather before the mal yahanava and a namaskaraya is intoned to the Buddha and the Four Guardian Deities. A lamp is lit to Isvara, the lord of the dance, in the mal yahanava. This is usually done by the principal dancer. Lamps are also lit by the exorcists at the base of Mahasona's palace, to the goddess of the earth, Bumi Devi or Polova Mahi Kantava. The dancers then move to where the patient is seated and offer their salutations, bowing to the head of the household and also to the patient. They will similarly greet the drummers seated on a mat at one side of the performance arena and then move around the perimeter of the arena giving their salutations to the audience. A ceremonial drum rhythm (magul bere) is then beaten in honour of the Buddha. **Dummala** is smoked on a brazier, and the dancers inhale the fumes. This action is explicitly intended to attract the demons to their bodies. Several named dances now follow and typically are: the **samayam pade** (gathering time dance); the **aile pade** (offering plate dance); the **vata pade** (whirling dance); the **anguru kabala pade** (brazier dance); the **kukulu pade** (cock dance); the **vilakku pade** (torch dance); and the **igaha pade** (arrow dance). Some of these dances might be excluded or others added in any particular performance of the **Mahasona**, but generally the first dance and the last three were included in the **Mahasona** performances I have observed. All these dances, in performance, tend to merge into one continuous flow of movement and increase in their intensity.

In the beginning dance **(arambha pade)**, which is a feature of all exorcisms, the dancers present the basic steps **(pada)** and body poses **(matra)** of the various dances to follow.[27] A typical opening pose is that struck by Shiva **(Isvara)** as the lord of the dance. Specific rhythms are played for each successive dance, each of which begins slowly and heavily **(barata)** and then quickens **(kadinama)** in its tempo. The drum rhythms played are intended to evoke a sense of the divine and the demonic. Specific demons have associated drum rhythms which are incorporated into the music of the major dances. These rhythms will also be played at the offerings to the demons and later in exorcisms when certain demons make their masked appearance. At the start of the major dances, the lead drummer will often call the tune (e.g., **ring gadi gada gadi gada gada gadita**, etc. —— the rhythm of the **samayam pade**) and then beat it on the drum, while the dancers match to it the appropriate steps.

A description of the dance episodes of the midnight watch of the **Mahasona** on one occasion I attended will give some impression of the nature of these episodes. There is considerable variation in detail in the organization of any dance performance but, in general, the events I describe for one performance are likely to occur in others.

During the first major dance of the **Mahasona**, the **samayam pade**, a mantra is intoned, followed by a song which calls Mahasona, and his other forms, to come from the eight cardinal directions. A dancer blows on the poison whistle to summon him. The dancers, holding lighted torches, then move anticlockwise from the demon palace around the perimeter of the performance arena. The direction of their progress is appropriate to the demonic but is opposite to the direction in which Sinhalese typically move in their everyday worship at the temples **(vihara)** and shrines **(devala)** to the Buddha and the deities.[28] One by one the dancers enter the arena, until all are dancing together. As the tempo of the dance increases, the dancers leap, swirl, tumble, and wheel around the arena (this swirling and wheeling is known as the **vata pade**, and is a motion used in all the dance episodes as well as a separate episode of dance in itself). Further songs are sung by the dancers and the drummers which call Mahasona but also his controlling deity, god Mangara. The demon Mahasona is now understood to be present at the scene. One dancer grasps the roof of the demon palace and shakes it vigorously, an action which signifies the coming of the demon into his ritual abode. The **samayam pade** lasts about thirty minutes and is one of the longest of the dance sequences.

The **aile pade** is now performed. It develops in much the same way as the preceding dance. The songs of the dancers and the drummers announce that the dance is in honor of Mahasona. The dancers move before the patient and juggle their torches in the air. They request Mahasona to take their dance as an offering and to remove his hold upon the patient. This dance leads into the **vata pade**. The dancers swirl their long tresses of "hair," and then spin faster and faster around the arena, their torches carving fiery circles in the night air. The increasing tempo of this dance, and the others, according to the exorcists, signifies the gathering power of the demonic. The **vata pade** is followed by the **anguru kabala pade.** One dancer takes the brazier and dances slowly around the arena, finally coming to the patient, over whom he smokes **dummala.** This action, as elsewhere in the exorcism, attracts the demonic eyesight to the patient. The cock, until now on the ground near the patient, is picked up and thrown into the arena. This marks the beginning of the **kukulu pade** which is specifically for Mahasona in his Le Sohon (blood cemetery) form.

One dancer takes the cock. He blows on the poison whistle. In his right hand he holds a lighted torch and the **igaha.** He moves in front of the patient, accompanied by the other dancers, and infuses the cock with **dummala** smoke. This is intended to transfer the demonic eyesight from the patient to the cock. A mantra is intoned demanding that Mahasona take the cock. The dancers then move back to the demon palace, and the dancer who holds the cock places it over his head so that one wing of the cock falls over his face, partly obscuring it. He then dances back and forth between the patient and the painting of Mahasona at the demon palace. Other dancers leap and tumble around the arena. They each take hold of the cock in turn and dance in a manner similar to the first. Finally, one dancer takes the cock, enters the palace, then suddenly reemerges backwards and throws the cock over his shoulder at the patient's feet. This action was regularly performed at the exorcisms I observed. It is interpreted by the exorcists as being extremely terrifying to the patient, who often recoils and cries out in alarm. Exorcists understand the action to so jolt the patient that the demonic grip on the patient becomes loosened, enabling Mahasona's hold to be broken.

The **kukulu pade** concludes with more leaping and swirling. Each dancer swirls once (**ek wattama**), twice (**dek wattama**), and then thrice (**tun wattama**). At the end of each turn, one dancer takes a lime, cuts it in two, and throws the pieces into the air. This action is a divination, the purpose of which is to determine whether the patient will be cured. If the lime halves fall face up, they indicate that a cure will be effected. This auspicious falling of the limes invariably occurred at the exorcisms I attended. One dancer moves in front of the demon palace and, facing the central part of the structure, the **pancha massa**, sings a **kavi** in praise of Mangara. Meanwhile, another dancer confronts the patient, picks up the cock, and asks Mahasona to accept it as an offering. He then waves the cock three times (for the **tun dosa**) over the patient's head. The cock is then thrown on the ground and **dummala** is flamed and flung towards the patient and at the cock. All the while the steady beating of drums resonates around the arena. With the burning of the **dummala,** the area around the patient is purified and the demon repelled. Members of the patient's household cry, "Long life, long life, long life."

Two shorter dance sequences follow, the **vilakku pade** and the **igaha pade.** In the first dance, the exorcists enter carrying small torches (**vilakku**) and circle the arena. Their chests have been sprinkled with pure turmeric water, and a mantra has been intoned, to protect the dancers against the fire of the burning torches which they hold against their chests. This action, known as the **gini sisila,** is interpreted by exorcists as a demonstration of divine power, the power of the goddess Pattini and Devol Deviyo.[29] Following this, the dancers gather up the larger torches, leap and tumble round the arena, juggle the torches in the air, and burn **dummala,** which billows in fiery orange bursts above the performance arena. One dancer rushes inside the patient's house and runs from room to room, burning

dummala. These actions are generally understood to purify the house and, again, the performance arena which has been polluted by the demonic presence. It is concluded by the dancers placing five small torches at the five **torana** of the **vidiya.**

As in the other dances, the exorcists retire into the demon palace and then reemerge, one dancer carrying the **igaha.** This begins the **igaha pade,** and a rapid rhythm is beaten on the drums. The dancer carrying the **igaha** enters the patient's house, while the other dancers, executing a high-stepping dance, move around the arena. The exorcist with the **igaha** burns **dummala** inside the house and then returns to the front of the patient. He and the other dancers offer their salutations to the patient and similarly to the drummers, to whom they give betel leaves. The dance ends with a dancer taking the **igaha** before the demon palace, suddenly leaping and swirling in the air, and finally stopping before the patient. The members of the household again cry, "Long life." The theme of this dance, as stated by the exorcists, is the removal of the demonic from the patient and the house and its transference through the power of the **igaha** to the **vidiya.** The **igaha pade** essentially concludes the major dance sequences of the Mahasona.

In the **Mahasona,** and in all the other exorcisms, an event known as the **avatara balima** is enacted at the hour of midnight and is usually performed before the **vilakku pade** and **igaha pade,** although I have witnessed **Mahasonas** where the **avatara balima** occurs after these dances. It involves the appearance of an exorcist in the masked manifestation **(avatara)** of the main afflicting demon. The mask (see illustrations) is essentially a mouthpiece made from woven coconut leaves, with a red hibiscus flower as the protruding lips of the demon. The face of the exorcist is blackened. Occasionally, a lighted torch will extend out of either corner of the mouth; these represent the demon tusks **(dala).** The wearing of the double torch is more usual, however, in the similar event which occurs towards the end of the morning watch and which is known as the **dekone vilakkuva.** In the **avatara balima,** the exorcist first inhales **dummala** smoke, and then directly confronts the patient to the deafening accompaniment of the drums. Ideally the exorcist should become possessed by the demon and evoke a similar response in the patient. The masked dancer then runs through the house purifying it with flaming **dummala** burned on torches **(pandam)** that he carries in either hand. He then runs to the **purale** during which the demon may appear to him and block his path. This can indicate that the patient is beyond the help of even a major exorcism ceremony, and I was told that should the demon appear in this manner, the rite should be called off (see p. 59). It is common for patients to become possessed either before the masked dancer's run to the **purale** or close upon his return.

The **avatara balima** is an episode of extreme tension. I have seen members of a patient's family wait anxiously for the return of the dancer from the **purale** and grapple and fight with the dancer, who on these occasions is entranced and understood to be the demonic incarnate. The mood of this event and of the dances preceding it is described by some exorcists as evoking the awesome and the miraculous **(adbhuta rasa),** for in them the full power of the supernatural is created.

The major dances and the **avatara balima** occur at a key transitional point in the ritual process, when the demonic both reaches its greatest power and begins to weaken. Exorcists and lay Sinhalese understand the power of demons to grow and to become the most threatening as the sun declines in the heavens. The power of the demons increases from midday to midnight, and weakens after midnight as the sun begins its ascent. This view underlies the organization of the ritual events in all exorcisms. The most powerful mantra and songs are concentrated in the midday to midnight

period.   The songs elaborate the terrible and frightening strength of the
demons.   In the dance, too, the terrible sense of the demonic builds in the
quickening rhythm and tempo of the music and the movement of the
dance —— in the **Mahasona** from the **samayam pade** through the **kukulu
pade** —— and often culminates in the demonic possession of the patient, who
typically dances entranced towards the **yak vidiya**. Following this high point
of the demonic, which according to exorcists should be achieved at the hour
of midnight, the power of the demons begins to weaken and to give way to
the power of the gods.   Thus the main concluding dances —— the **vilakku
pade** and the **igaha pade** —— give rise to the power of the deities and their
control over the demons.   The enactment of these dances is often one of
levity (indeed, of the comic, **hasya rasa**) and, as I will describe in the
following chapter, the dancers begin to "play" with the dance and to break
up its dynamic flow and tension.   This is particularly so in the short dances
(**adavv**) which come at the close of the major dance sequences in all the
large demon ceremonies, and after the **avatara balima**, should it be the final
episode of the dance.

   The **adavv** dances are performed for the patient, the household head, and
other individuals in the audience, usually prominent and relatively high-
status members of the local neighborhood.   These dances each last no more
than a few minutes.   Typically one of the exorcists will announce the person
for whom he will dance a short number of steps and then approach the
person so "honored" for a small monetary payment.[30]

   With the conclusion of the **adavv** dances, the drummers, who have been
standing throughout the performance, now seat themselves on mats at one
side of the performance arena.   One drummer plays a light rhythm (**hin tala**)
while songs are sung invoking and praising the god Mangara.

Mangara Kannelavva

   I give homage to God Mangara.   I give my salutation to the god
   king.
   Your fame has spread throughout Ruhuna.
   By your power remove the illness and the darkness.
   Oh!   Mangara who has brought your followers across the sea to
   Lanka with this power help the patient.
   Oh! God Mangara you have destroyed the banyan tree
   Where the demons kept their treasure. You have broken the power
   of the demons.
   Oh! God Mangara you have tied the wild buffalo.
   The buffalo that threatened the lives of the people.
   Oh! God Mangara who has killed the crocodile of God Saman.
   Oh! God Mangara who has killed the deer of God Saman.
   Oh! God Mangara who has caught and tamed the elephant.
   By these six powers remove the illness from the patient.

   The dancers execute short dance steps in front of the **pancha massa** in
the demon palace.   It is now approximately 12:30 A.M., the major dance
episodes having lasted nearly two hours.   The next main event of the
midnight watch, the **Mangara pelapaliya**, or presentations for god Mangara,
is now about to begin.

   The sequence of dramatic acts, the **Mangara pelapaliya** or **Dolaha
pelapaliya** (twelve presentations), begins between 12:30 A.M.   and 2 A.M.

These dramatic acts are:

1. **Pavada watatira paliya** (cloth presentation)
2. **Kude paliya** (Umbrella Presentation)
3. **Kodiya paliya** (Flag Presentation)
4. **Sesat-Chamara paliya** (Fan Presentation)
5. **Horana-Kombu paliya** (Horn Presentation)
6. **Dawul-Tammattam paliya** (Drum Presentation)
7. **Hevisi paliya** (Ceremonial Band Presentation)
8. **Vina-Nadiyak paliya** (Stringed Instrument Presentation)
9. **Li-Keli paliya** (Stick Game Presentation)
10. **Atmana paliya** (Lime Juggling Presentation)
11. **At Bandima paliya** (Elephant Tying Presentation)
12 **Mi Bandima paliya** (Buffalo Tying Presentation)

These acts should be performed at all **Mahasona** exorcisms and constitute dramatic episodes which distinguish the **Mahasona** from other exorcisms. They are never performed in the other large-scale demon rites; however, variations on the acts as they appear in the **Mahasona** are performed in the major community rites to the deities, the **gam maduva** and the **devol maduva**. In these rites, the acts are usually referred to as the **Dolaha pelapaliya**.[31]

Exorcists state that twelve acts must be performed in the **Mangara pelapaliya** of the **Mahasona** exorcism. These acts involve dramatic dialogue together with the presentation of various symbolic articles associated with each of the acts. This whole performance is conceived by exorcists as an entertainment for god Mangara who, as stated previously, is the deity who is the immediate superior of Mahasona. The acts are designed to amuse and please Mangara so that he will give his assistance in the cure. The start of each act is announced by the playing of a short drum rhythm, and songs are sung in praise of Mangara. The songs and the dramatic acts should be comic and are intended by exorcists to evoke a sense of the comic from the audience. The drumming and singing stops when one of the exorcist-dancers enters the arena from the **vidiya** and engages a drummer in dialogue. This dialogue is replete with puns, spoonerisms, profanities, sexual innuendo, and obscenity. In the course of the dialogue, the dancer and the drummer (who plays a role very similar to the "straight man" in vaudeville) discuss what must be enacted and presented. Comic reference is often made to the patient, to aspects of Sinhalese customary tradition, to well-known events in the daily lives of Sinhalese, and to the preceding episodes of the exorcism rite. As the dialogue develops, the meaning of the symbolic article presented is divulged. If the dancer does not have the object with him, he reenters the **vidiya**, takes the article, and presents it to the audience. He then circumambulates the performance arena carrying the symbolic article and performs a variety of comic actions in relation to it. At the end of the dramatic dialogue, drumming starts once again and the actor-dancer breaks into a short dance. He moves rapidly between the **vidiya** and the patient. The tempo of the dance increases in such a way that the dancer appears to be out of control. Sometimes the article which is presented is crumpled or destroyed in the course of the action. Each act concludes with the dancer going before the patient and waving it three times (for the **tun dosa**) over the patient. The article carried or presented is then placed on top of the **vidiya.** A short song in praise of Mangara is sometimes sung, and the next act begins. For some of the acts, members of the audience, usually young boys, are invited into the arena to assist the dancer with the performance. The entire sequence of acts normally lasts a little over an hour and is usually completed shortly after 1:30 A.M.

In specific performances of the **Mangara pelapaliya** there are likely to be variations in the content and ordering of the acts (see Kapferer 1975), and some of the acts might be excluded. I describe a sequence of such acts from one performance of a **Mahasona** which I witnessed and which was repeated in much the same way at a number of others. I have included in this description some necessarily brief excerpts from my tape transcriptions of the comic dialogue. The twelve acts are introduced with the reading of a document of authority **(sannas patraya)** that the **Mangara pelapaliya** must be performed. For much of the action, the dancer treats the document of authority as if it is a horoscope. This is the basis of much of the humor. The dancer, standing at one side of the **vidiya**, holds a strip of coconut leaf. He turns towards the drummer who is standing near the front porch of the patient's house.

Dancer:	(to the drummer) Buddha, copulate with your mother! Seven Deaths! Where did you come from? You fat, small, skinny man.
Drummer:	I came the day before yesterday.
Dancer:	Really! May the Buddhist dispensation shine in glory **(Budu sasuna babalewa)**.
Drummer:	**Budu sasuna ibewa** (a nonsense response).
Dancer:	What's to be done with this pineapple **(annasi)**?
Drummer:	Not a pineapple —— a document **(sannas)**. It's a letter which must be posted.
Dancer:	Here we are two half people, not knowing what to do.
Drummer:	Yes, yes —— I know —— I am very small . . .
Another dancer interjects:	We are dancers and very small —— but that drummer is huge and fat.
Drummer:	Shut up you rest house bum, you German madman (a reference to German tourists in the area), you piece of valueless metal.
(The drummer now sings a drum rhythm, **ring gada gada gadun.**)	
Dancer:	Stop that . . . eei, eei . . . it's been a long time, so many months since we tied the security thread **(apa nul)**. We tied the security thread and made a **yantra** to bind this patient to this place this day . . . to remove the darkness and illness from this sick person. Ah (looking at the coconut leaf "document") this seal **(muddara)** must be broken and the letter read.
Drummer:	The urine **(muttara,** a play on **muddara)** broken and the letter read.
Dancer:	It's not urine . . . the seal must be broken. We'll have to break the seal and see.
Drummer:	What is it?
Dancer:	It looks like a monkey resting its head on a walking stick (a reference to Riri Yaka who has the face of a monkey and like other demons carries a club).
Drummer:	Ahh no! That's **ayanna** (the first letter in the Sinhalese alphabet).
Dancer:	What's this next thing . . . looks like a crab.
Drummer:	That's the letter **sri.**
Dancer:	**Riri** letter? (He makes a pun on the utterance **sri.** There are many possible puns here, among them Riri Yaka, blood, and also defecation.)

Drummer:	Early morning?
Dancer:	Not early morning —— shitting on the beach on the way home in the afternoon.
Drummer:	Is that true?
Dancer:	These days we don't get a chance to go to the beach (a common practice among the Sinhalese working class and especially fishermen is to perform the morning ablutions on the beach). Time is so short these days that we can't go to the beach —— we don't even have time to shit at the roadside.
Drummer:	Don't read it letter by letter you fool. You must make words of those letters and then read the words.
Dancer:	Then listen as I read it. Taking twenty-one and a half paces at midnight . . . midday, Friday, Wednesday in the Sacred year, one thousand, one hundred and fifteen, at noon, started a journey towards the west staring upwards.
Drummer:	To start that journey you would have to go on the main road.
Dancer:	Why the main road?
Drummer:	Because you are lying on your back.

(The last four exchanges of dialogue make reference to the **avamangalle** episode of the rite and comment on Sinhalese funeral practice whereby funeral processions take the main roads. The dancer's opening reference to this makes fun of the mantra and **kavi** of the **avamangalle** period, which describe the nature of the actions which should be performed in it. To face west signifies death, and it is one of the main directions from which the Cemetery Demon comes.)

Dancer:	I didn't say "lying on your back."
Drummer:	It didn't sound correct. Read the other side.
Dancer:	(presents his behind to the drummer): Is this the other side?
Drummer:	I didn't mean your anus (used the word **aparagoyane.** This is the name of the city in which the ruler of the demons of the Western Quarter lives. It has the meaning of "West" and is used colloquially to refer to "anus.")
Dancer:	Then?
Drummer:	The other side of the document.
Dancer:	Aaah! Here it is **Saka biyan** (a reference to the first words uttered by astrologers when reading a horoscope).

The dialogue continues in this manner, and the actors make puns on the names of the planets. One pun leads into the subject of lotteries in Galle, and the dancer lists three prizes he would like to win: a triangular bull and an octagonal ox-racing cart, a coffin, and some cadju (cashew) tree sap. These prizes are discussed in such a way that fun is made of the magical designs of the ritual structures. The coffin is treated as an object of great fortune and luck, and not misfortune. The cadju sap is described as being used by newlyweds on their marriage night. The reference is to semen, and the joke is contained in the property of cadju sap (semen) to cause the skin to peel and produce great discomfort. Further puns and **doubles-entendres** follow as the dancer continues his reading of the document. Eventually the meaning of the document is fathomed. The dancer announces "For God Mangara to come to the **vidiya** we must raise a canopy and place a cloth on the ground. Now we must describe and demonstrate what the letter tells us." The drummer strikes a tune on his drum, and both he and the dancer, accompanied by the other exorcists, sing a song. The song is for Mangara and requests his aid in curing the patient's illness. A white cloth is then presented (**Pavada Watatira paliya**) to the patient and the audience by the dancer and placed on top of the **vidiya**. The cloth is symbolically multivalent, at once, for example, indicative of the canopy held over sacred objects carried in procession and of the cloth spread beneath the coffin bearers at funerals.

Five acts or presentations now follow in relatively quick succession. They are: the **Kude paliya** (umbrella presentation); the **Kodiya paliya** (flag presentation); the **Sesat-Chamara paliya** (fan presentation); the **Horana-Kombu paliya** (horn presentation); and the **Davul-Tammattam paliya** (drum presentation). They are each part of the procession to honor Mangara. Each act, like the first, involves elaborate comic action and dialogue. Thus the dancer enters from the **vidiya** with the umbrella (made from banana trunks and covered with white cloth —— it is in the shape of a commercially available umbrella, and even folds up). Comments are passed that it looks like a bat, then like the umbrella that schoolmistresses carry —— not at all like what it should be, the umbrella carried above sacred objects in procession. During the **Kodiya paliya** the dancer and drummer engage in extended discussion concerning the nature of the vests worn by men and women in everyday life. The word for flag (**kodiya**) is confused with the colloquial term for vest **bodiya** and then linked to the sacred Bodhi tree. Mention is made of current economic hardships and that if the cloth of the vests get any thinner the whole population will be placed in prison for indecent exposure.

The **Sesat-Chamara paliya** involves the dancer's entering the performance arena carrying the fan or sun shade upon which is drawn the symbols of the Sun and Moon. The drummer enquires what it is, to which the dancer responds that it is a **sesat**. "What?" says the drummer, pointing to a drawing of a hare (the symbolic representation of the Moon), "a **sesatek**?" He has confused the word **sesat**, with the term **satek** or creature. Both actors then discuss the poverty in which people live and how there is not enough money to feed human beings, let alone animals. The drummer, after telling the dancer that he has been confusing him, announces what the object truly represents. He adds that it is also the **chamara**, or sacred yak's tail. This is interpreted as **demmala** (Tamil) by the dancer, and a discussion ensues about Tamils —— how they have advanced in life, grown rich, and are no longer lowly people in everyday life.

In the **Davul-Tammattam paliya**, the dancer comes out of the **vidiya** playing a small double-drum (**tammattam**). It is slung around his waist but, as the action proceeds, rises to his chest. The drummer comments that the drum looks like a woman's breasts. Much ribaldry follows. As in all the other comic dialogues the theme quickly turns to the subject of filth and excrement. "What are those sticks (**kadippu**)?" the drummer asks. "Did you say **kadi puka** (ant's anus)?" responds the dancer punning on the word for sticks. This is developed, and the dancer contends that he is not playing on an ant's anus at all, but on the anus of a squirrel. Clear reference is made to the skin of the drum and how it is polluting. More discussion ensues, and the drummer insults the dancer by suggesting that the latter does not wash his anus properly after the morning ablutions. The dancer catches up the theme of "playing" and states that he is not playing a drum, but the **pol**

paliya (a Sinhalese ritual coconut-throwing game for the deities, see Wirz 1954:168-76). The **tammattam** is likened to a pair of coconuts similar to those included in the earlier offering episodes to the ghosts and the demons. The act concludes with the drummer playing a furious rhythm on his drum, which the dancer attempts to match on the **tammattam.** The dancer's arms, sticks, and drums become hopelessly entangled, so much so that the **tammattam** begins to crumple. The drumming stops, and the dancer looks down at his drums. "Look what has happened to my drums. The patient's illness must have entered the **tammattam** —— all that evil eye, evil mouth, evil thought, envy, and longing. Let the patient's illness be destroyed like the **tammattam**!"

The above acts are followed by six more: the **Hevisi paliya** (ceremonial band presentation); the **Vina-Nadiyak paliya** (stringed instrument presentation); the **Li-Keli paliya** (stick game presentation); the **Atmana paliya** (lime juggling presentation); the **At Bandima paliya** (elephant tying presentation); and the **Mi Bandima paliya** (the wild buffalo tying presentation). For the **Hevisi paliya**, the dancer goes among the audience and selects five young boys to assist him. They take up the various objects already presented and, coming out of the **vidiya**, walk in procession behind the exorcist-actor, who carries the umbrella, to the accompaniment of drumming. More comic dialogue passes between the exorcists, and they mock a religious procession **(perahara)**, a regular event in the lives of Sinhalese villagers and townspeople on sacred days in the Sinhalese Buddhist religious calendar.

The two final acts (the **At Bandima** and the **Mi Bandima**) are of particular interest. While their comedy expands upon earlier comic themes, dominant in them are the themes of control, tying, and taming. Objects of nature are explicitly related to culture, disorder confronts order and is eventually controlled through the actions of human beings.

The **At Bandima** begins with the dancer's entering the arena carrying a mahout's hook **(henduva)**. "What's that?" the drummer asks. "It's to tie a great tusked elephant," replies the dancer, "a **henduva**." "Did you say a **sembuva** (bronze pot)?" queries the drummer. "No! It's an iron hook and with it I will tie an elephant," states the dancer. "Prove it," demands the drummer. A lengthy discussion then follows, during which the dancer says that he must be brought some refreshments, for in order to prove his claim, he must tell a long story about his experience with elephants. He then recounts how he journeyed into a jungle near Kandy. On his journey he crosses a bridge which passes **under** a ditch **over** which a river runs. Suddenly he espies an elephant basking in the sun, but its legs are pointing up in the air (as if dead) and from its trunk (he uses a colloquial term for penis) dribbles stinking pus. Thus seeing the elephant he immediately tethers it with an iron chain. "Seven Deaths!" exclaims the drummer, "That's a wonderful story." At this point the dancer goes inside the **vidiya** and returns with an "elephant," performed by a young boy who walks bent over holding two sticks for front legs. His body is covered by a white cloth and he wears a mask modeled as an elephant's head.

Dancer:	Here is the elephant I spoke of. Do you know what I like most about this elephant?
Drummer:	No . . . what?
Dancer:	Its trunk. See, look where it is . . . near the mouth. (He goes to the rear of the elephant and lifts its tail, which is made of cloth.) Look! It's between the two cheeks . . . it's dripping.

Drummer:	I see no cheeks. That's the tail. Don't talk like that - can't you see that it is an innocent child.
Dancer:	Seven deaths! Buddha's mother! My tusker can't have sexual intercourse!
Drummer:	Talk to it in elephant language.
Dancer:	**Tette kide aliya . . . buru, buru aliya** —— kneel down elephant.
Drummer:	What if it lies down and refuses to kneel down? (The elephant kneels down.)
Dancer:	Elephant —— lift your leg so I can mount. (He climbs onto the back of the elephant). **Billa, billa . . . bili aliya, bili, bili.** (The words make reference to the cock as a sacrificial victim in the earlier episodes of the exorcism.) Now we'll have to make a cross and put the elephant into the ballot box. (The elephant is a symbol of Sri Lanka's ruling political party, the U.N.P.)
Drummer:	Spoil your vote . . . tear the elephant up.
Dancer:	This elephant is worthless. It's worth no more than the bottom card in the pack.
Drummer:	Don't cause this poor elephant any more trouble.
Dancer:	Why not?
Drummer:	That elephant is the tusker which god Mangara tamed.

The act ends with a song which relates how Mangara tames the elephant. The dancer and the elephant return inside the **vidiya**, after they have both presented themselves in front of the patient. Another song is sung which recounts how Mangara tamed the wild buffalo. The dancer and the boy (now as the buffalo) enter the performance arena and the **Mi Bandima paliya** begins.

Dancer:	See my elephant . . . all tuskers are the same.
Drummer:	Come here, come here tusker . . . don't you want some arrack?
Dancer:	That's not right.
Drummer:	Yes . . . why, am I wrong?
Dancer:	It's a tusker.
Drummer:	No . . . it's a very wild buffalo.
Dancer:	Seven Deaths! This buffalo has footrot/marriage sickness **(hira leda).**
Drummer:	This buffalo hasn't got marriage sickness.
Dancer:	What's the stupid beast got then?
Drummer:	Footrot **(kura leda).**
Dancer:	Footrot, marriage sickness . . . what's it matter? If it's not got marriage sickness now it will get it in the future.
Drummer:	We must do something about this sickness. In my area to cure footrot we tie (**bandinava,** a word also used colloquially with reference to marriage) the buffalo up in a muddy paddy field.
Dancer:	That's foolish . . . why, if you tied the beast in the mud the footrot would become worse.

Drummer:	No, no. The mud draws out the poison (**vas**, a word also used in reference to demonic illness).
Dancer:	I don't think it could work. We don't have this custom in our area. When we have a buffalo with footrot, we bury it with its four legs pointing upwards. A good remedy . . . eh? Within three days the buffalo is all dried up, like leather.
Drummer:	No . . . our way is the right one. All the people do it my way where I live near Ambala jungle.
Dancer:	But someone would untie it there. Seven Deaths! If you tie it at an inn (**ambalama**, a play on "Ambala") someone will untie, it and the illness will become worse.

At this point the dancer pushes the buffalo away, takes off his belt and begins to whip it. He chases the buffalo around the performance arena. Finally he puts a rope (the rope of Mangara) around its neck and leads it into the **vidiya**. A verse is sung which tells that the buffalo belongs to Mangara. This act completes the **Mangara pelapaliya**. The objects used in these acts are placed, for Mangara, at the **pancha massa**, in the **vidiya**.

Exorcists state that the acts of the **Mangara pelapaliya** are to please god Mangara, and thus to invoke his aid in breaking Mahasona's hold over the patient, but they also stress the importance of its comedy —— its vital role in amusing the audience, and for mentally soothing the patient by directing the patient's thoughts away from an overriding focus on a malign and terrifying supramundane reality conjured during the preceding events of the exorcism.

The comedy of the **Mangara pelapaliya** is appropriate, exorcists say, to the lowly and marginal character of the god Mangara. He is a deity who mediates between human beings and gods and demons. Mangara's character, his ambiguity and the uncertainty of his powers, is in accordance with his mediating position. Mangara plays tricks on the gods who dominate the pantheon and, like the demons, sometimes tries to deprive these gods of their powers. One myth relates that he was once a human being, a magician in possession of marvelous spells, who upon his death became a deity. Mangara's major role is as a destroyer of demons, but he is subject to the destructive power of the demonic. He is killed by the wild buffalo, whom exorcists interpret as the demonic manifestation of Yama, the god of death in the Vedic tradition. Pertold (1973:111 fn. 1) records that Mangara is a benevolent deity, the custodian of the ways and pathways, associated with the **gara** demons whom he controls. This would account for the enactment of dramatic acts for Mangara in the **gam maduva** and **devol maduva** deity ceremonies where the **gara** demons make their appearance.

Mangara is transitional between demons and deities, and in his very being constitutes a finely balanced conjuncture of major disjunctive forces in the cosmic whole —— forces of generation, degeneration, and regeneration. The comedy of the **Mangara pelapaliya** explores and reveals what is encoded in Mangara. As it does so ritual definitions and redefinitions of the relation between the divine and the demonic are effected. I examine this in Chapter 9 and the critical transformational role of the comedy of the **Mangara pelapaliya**.

The character of Mangara both as a killer of demons and as a deity opposed to, and controlling of, Mahasona (and, too, the **Mangara pelapaliya** as a major transitional episode in the **Mahasona** exorcism as a whole), are clearly indicated by the ritual events which should immediately follow the enactment of the **Mangara Pelapaliya:** the **Kalu Vadi paliya** and the **Mahasona dapavilla** or "death of Mahasona."

The **Kalu Vadi paliya** (which in some exorcist exegeses is seen as part of the **Mangara pelapaliya**) is usually enacted by the dancer who presented the **Mangara pelapaliya.** He takes the **igaha** and a bow. Occasionally, the exorcist-actor dresses in the masked guise of Kalu Vadi. Following the uttering of verses and a brief dance, Kalu Vadi "fires" the **igaha** at the cock which is placed on the ground before the patient. Typically, it is at the third attempt, after a lime has been cut and a mantra uttered at the forehead of the patient, that Kalu Vadi succeeds in striking the cock.

Several interpretations are given by exorcists for this episode. Kalu Vadi is the servant of Mangara and a hunter who searches the jungle fastness for demons whom Mangara then kills.[32] This is the subject of the song which usually begins this episode. Exorcists state that Kalu Vadi's eventual striking of the cock with the **igaha** represents the discovery of the demon and its impending destruction. The attempts at "shooting" the cock refer to an event in the Kalu Vadi myth, when Kalu Vadi hunted a deer. Sorcery prevented him from hitting his mark, and it was only when the spell was broken that Kalu Vadi gained his quarry. Exorcists generally interpret the act as signifying the final removal of any sorcery which might impede the cure of the patient.

A rapid beating of the drums closes the Kalu Vadi episode. Cries are heard from within the demon palace, and the whole structure shakes. Mahasona is about to make his appearance. An offering basket to Mahasona is placed on a chair before the patient. A dancer swirls around the performance arena and moves between the patient and the **vidiya.** Mantra are uttered and songs are sung to Mahasona, calling him to accept the offerings which have been placed for him and to remove his hold over the patient. At this point the patient sometimes enters a trance, and shivers and sweats. Three limes are drawn down the body of the patient to remove the illness. They are cut at the three points of the body affected by the illness, at the head, at the stomach, and at the feet, and placed in Mahasona's offering basket. A white cloth, **(kadaturava),** as in the earlier offering sequences, is held by male relatives of the patient, screening the patient off from Mahasona's offering basket and the events which are about to be enacted.

An exorcist dressed in the guise of Mahasona and wearing the mask of a bear now enters the performance arena. He burns great clouds of **dummala** on a torch, and the flames momentarily envelop him and the demon palace. Typically the demon examines his portrait at the foot of the **pancha massa,** moves around the performance arena, and then stealthily moves towards the patient. Suddenly he bursts through the cloth curtain and onto the patient, and nuzzles and strokes his victim. Mahasona then steps back, takes his offering basket and returns to the demon palace, where he places the offering basket on the roof of the **vidiya.** He beckons to the **madu puraya** to bring the brazier and then deeply inhales **dummala.** Exorcists say that through this action Mahasona is brought within the body of the actor who is presenting the demon. Indeed the actor often becomes entranced, becomes Mahasona. After inhaling the **dummala,** the actor goes inside the **vidiya** and reemerges carrying a pot and a staff, Mahasona's club. A mat is laid out before and in the full view of the patient, the cloth curtain now having been removed. A deafening sound of drums fills the arena. Mahasona places the pot at the head of the mat, moves back to the **vidiya,** and then rushes forward and breaks the pot with his club. At the same time he falls down on the mat and is carried to one side of the **vidiya.** This is done by close male relatives of the patient, who cry in mock mourning.

These actions, according to exorcists, enact the death of Mahasona. Exorcists say that the pot carried by Mahasona is the demon's "head" which Mahasona then smashes —— an action symbolic of his "death" and the removal of his effect upon the patient. Mahasona's demonic essence, which is removed from the patient and transferred to the offering basket, is conceived of also as passing into the pot. It might be noted, too, that Mahasona was born of a woman of the potter caste. The pot, therefore, contains the demonic essence and at the same time is symbolic of his birth. Mahasona dies shattering the vessel which symbolizes that which gave him life.

With the death of Mahasona, the offering basket to the demon is presented again before the patient. It is held by the presiding exorcist, but sometimes by a close kinsman of the patient, and is revolved three times over the patient's head, signifying the removal of the demonic illness. The episodes involving the death of Mahasona end at about 2:00 A.M., and with them the period of the midnight watch concludes. Exorcists consider that the major curative work of the exorcism is now completed, the malign demonic eyesight connecting the patient to the demons and exposing the patient to demonic control having been largely severed.

The flow of ritual action, is now broken by the **Maha te,** during which the exorcists and members of the audience receive food and refreshments. The period of the morning watch begins at 3:00 A.M. In this period the major comic episodes which are collectively referred to as the **Dahaata paliya** are then performed. Before I describe these, however, I will give some brief indication of the main variations which occur in the midnight watch of the two other major exorcisms which are otherwise similar to the **Mahasona,** the **Sanni Yakuma** and the **Rata Yakuma.** This is important: while the analysis I present in the chapters to follow focuses on the **Mahasona,** I do claim that the overall logic of my argument is applicable to the **Sanni Yakuma** and the **Rata Yakuma.**

Variations on a Theme: Major Episodes of the Midnight Watch in the **Sanni Yakuma** and **Rata Yakuma** Exorcisms

The episodes of the **avamangalle** begin the events of the midnight watch in both these exorcisms. The **avamangalle** has essentially the same organizational form as in the **Mahasona.** However, where the **Sanni Yakuma** and **Rata Yakuma** exorcisms principally differ from the **Mahasona,** and from each other, is in their major periods of dance drama.

The **Sanni Yakuma**

As in the **Mahasona,** the major dance episodes of the **Sanni Yakuma** (collectively known as the **Maha samayam pade** —— the great gathering time dance) follow the **avamangalle** and begin with the ceremonial beating of the **magul bere.** The **kadaturava** is held in front of the patient, and the exorcists sing about its history and its connection to the goddess Pattini and the **sanni** demons. Mantra, poems, and songs follow, invoking the demons, praising their powers, and recounting their mythical history. Four main dances are performed. These, in order, are: the **samayam pade** (gathering dance); the **aile pade** (offering dance); the **torana** or **vidiya pade;** and the **pandam pade.** The overall style of the dances is similar to that of the **Mahasona.** The first dance announces the arrival of the demons; the second, the offerings which have been presented; and, the third, which is the most elaborate, the entry of the demons into their palace. During the **torana pade,** the patient frequently becomes entranced. The final dance item, the **pandam pade,** purifies the performance arena with the burning of **dummala** on the torches. The **igaha** is used, and songs are sung, to remove the illness from the patient. As in all the major exorcisms, the dances are concluded by shorter items, **adavv**, in honor of the household members and selected individuals in the audience, in return for small monetary gifts.

After these dances, a dance-mime is performed. A dancer appears in the magnificent guise of the Lichchavi kings, and in the gestures of the dance mimes the story of the Lichchavis and the disaster which befell them at the hands of the **sanni** demons (see Chapter 6). The songs which accompany the dance also relate this history and the birth of **Kola Sanniya** and the eighteen **sanni** demons.

The **Rata Yakuma**

The major items of dance, which follow the **avamangalle**, in this exorcism describe the arrival of Riddi Bisava and the seven princesses at the ritual site and their entry into their palace. The dancers are dressed in white, but their other ornamentation is similar to their attire for the major dance episodes of the **Mahasona** and **Sanni Yakuma**. The main dance events, in the order of their performance, are: the **samayam pade**; the **vilakku pade**; the **torana pade**; **anguru kabale**, **dummala pade**; and the **igaha pade**. The **adavv** dances conclude the events. During the dances the exorcists sing the myth of Riddi Bisava and how she and her daughters came to afflict women. After the performance of the **adavv**, an offering basket is presented to Riddi Bisava, her daughters, and to Kalu Yaka, and they are asked to remove their malign influence. Further poems and songs follow, recounting the myth of Riddi Bisava and how she and her daughters tried to fool Dipamkara Buddha with the gift of a white cloth and how they eventually bowed to his authority.

Major events of comic mime and drama now begin. According to the exorcist tradition with which I worked, seven **paliya** must be performed. These, in the order of their presentation, are as follows:

1. **Viyan Redde Paliya** (Cloth Presentation)
2. **Mudun Male Paliya** (Presentation to Riddi Bisava)
3. **Nanumura Paliya** ("Toilette and Dressing" of Riddi Bisava Presentation)
4. **Kapu Upata Paliya** (Cotton Spinning and Weaving of the Cloth Presentation)
5. **Daru Nalavili Paliya** (The Washing of the Baby Presentation)
6. **Dalumura Paliya** (Betel Presentation)
7. **Chamara Paliya** (Fan Presentation)

The first two acts are performed during the main dance sequences. Thus towards the end of the dance, one of the dancers takes a white cloth and spins around the performance arena, finally placing it above the rear central section of the demon palace —— the **mudun male**. At the close of the dancing, all the dancers gather in front of the **mudun male** and give their salutations to Riddi Bisava and her daughters. The **nanumura paliya** follows, with the principal dancer sitting before the patient with a basket filled with various objects of dress and toiletry. All these are made for the occasion from coconut leaves, banana trunk, and flowers. Exorcists state that ideally twelve acts (**dolaha paliya**) must be included within the **nanumura paliya**, though many more are frequently enacted.[33] These acts mime the dressing of Riddi Bisava. In the first, the actor applies **nanu** (a paste made from limes, coconut oil, turmeric, and sandalwood) to the hair. The face is then washed, the body scraped of dirt, and soap applied. This soap, according to tradition, is made from tree wax, but in the performances of one exorcist group I witnessed, is presented as an ordinary piece of domestic soap, with the letters L U X boldly etched into it. The dancer's hair tresses are then combed out, oil applied, and a hair pin and comb set in place. Earrings and necklace are then worn and bracelets placed on the arms. Eye shadow is applied, and the body is perfumed with sandalwood. The dancer then stands up, places a diadem on his head, and tightly winds a white dress at his waist. The mime is completed by the actor taking a chew of betel and proudly admiring himself in a mirror.

The mimed dressing of Riddi Bisava is then followed by the **Kapu upata paliya.** The exorcists sing about the growing and spinning of the cotton and its weaving into a white cloth, which Riddi Bisava presents to Dipamkara Buddha. The exorcist actor sits on a mat before the patient and opposes either another exorcist or an individual drawn from the audience, who plays the role of Dipamkara Buddha. The actor accompanies his various actions of growing, spinning, and weaving the cotton by attempting to engage "Dipamkara Buddha" in comic dialogue (see Kapferer 1977a:106), while "Dipamkara Buddha" remains silent. The dialogue is full of ribald humor which pokes fun at aspects of the myth and also events in everyday life.

When this is completed, the **Daru Nalavili paliya** starts. The exorcist-actor goes to the **mudun male** inside the demon palace and brings out a doll. It is a male child. Here I describe one performance of this episode which I observed, one which was enacted in essentially the same manner in all the **Rata Yakuma** exorcisms I witnessed. The dancer sits on a stool in front of the patient and begins to wash the baby in a basin of water. He splashes the audience. He then takes the baby onto his lap and carefully dries it — particularly the genitals and the buttocks. The actor holds his nose, as if offended by the smell. **Nanu** is applied to the head and oil rubbed into the body. He mimes, in effect, the washing of a newborn infant. The actor then lifts his bodice and mimes suckling the child. He complains that one breast is dry and places the baby on the other, but howls in surprise for the baby has "bitten" his nipple. The entire act, as the one before it, evokes great amusement from the audience. The act ends with the actor presenting the "baby" to the members of the audience and finally giving it to the patient, who gives a small offering to the actor in return. The whole sequence symbolizes the removal of one of the chief blights of Riddi Bisava and her seven daughters, their abilities to cause barrenness and to bring harm to women and their children.

In the **Dalumura paliya** the patient gives the actor betel, mixed with sandalwood paste, flowers, and coins. These are taken to each of the seven **torana** in the demon palace and finally to the **mudun male.** Songs accompany these actions, which call on Riddi Bisava and her daughters to remove their illness-causing effect. The last act, the **Chamara paliya,** is very short and involves the fanning (the cooling) of Riddi Bisava and her daughters at the **torana** or their "bedchambers." The midnight watch of the **Rata Yakuma** is now essentially over.

The Morning Watch of the **Mahasona:** A Comedy of Demons

Extended episodes of comic drama characterize the morning watch in all large-scale exorcisms performed throughout the night. In the **Mahasona, Sanni Yakuma,** and **Rata Yakuma,** they are known as the **Dahaata paliya,** or eighteen presentations. In the **Suniyama** exorcism they are performed after another comic act, the **Vadiga patuna** (see Wirz 1954:80; also Chapter 9). The **Dahaata paliya** is similar in the **Mahasona, Rata Yakuma,** and the **Suniyama,** but concludes differently in the **Sanni Yakuma.** Thus in the **Sanni**

Yakuma, an exorcist-actor as a masked representation of Kola Sanniya, the chief of the disease-spreading **sanni** demons, makes his appearance, but has his path blocked to the patient by two exorcists (or individuals drawn from the audience), who cross two rice pounders **(kadavata)** which act as a barrier to the demon (see Obeyesekere 1969:192). Kola Sanniya does not appear in the **Dahaata paliya** of the other exorcisms. Instead, the conclusion of the comic acts is marked by the masked appearance of the actor as Deva Sanniya. No comic dialogue accompanies the presentation of Deva Sanniya, which contrasts with the comic dialogue of the Kola Sanniya act.

Each act of the **Dahaata paliya,** in all major exorcisms, involves the appearance of an exorcist-actor in the masked guise of a specific apparition or demon. The **Dahaata paliya** is in fact a combination of two distinct sequences of dramatic acts. These, in the order of their performance, are: the **Ata paliya** (eight spectacles or presentations) and the **Dahaata Sanniya** (eighteen disease-spreading demons). The acts of the **Ata paliya** involve the masked presentation of demonic apparitions who present the major symbolic articles used repeatedly throughout the preceding episodes of the exorcism. These apparitions are: (1) Pandam Paliya (torch-bearing apparition); (2) Salu Paliya (cloth, or shawl-bearing apparition); (3) Kendi Paliya (water pot - bearing apparition); (4) Kalas Paliya (earthen pot-bearing apparition); (5) Tambili-dalumura Paliya (orange coconut/betel leaves-bearing apparition); (6) Anguru-dummala Paliya (brazier/**dummala**-bearing apparition); (7) Igaha Paliya (**igaha**-bearing apparition); and (8) Kukulu Paliya (cock-bearing apparition). In all the exorcisms I have observed the **Ata paliya** starts with the appearance of Pandam Paliya, followed by Salu Paliya. The sequential ordering of the other acts varies from performance to performance, although the Kukulu Paliya tends to be the closing act. Any one performance might exclude the appearance of one or more of these specific apparitions, although as a rule Pandam Paliya, Salu Paliya, Kalas Paliya, and Tambili-dalumura Paliya are performed.[34]

I have referred to the figures who carry the various symbolic articles as apparitions. In the view of exorcists, the demons of the **Ata paliya** are not demons in the same sense that Mahasona, Riri Yaka, and Kalu Yaka are demons. Some exorcists stated that the masked presentation of the **Ata paliya** is a relatively modern innovation, and that formerly it was a brief episode, not performed with masks. Wirz writes of the apparitions: "They play the parts of servants. . . They represent no particular individuals and hence bear no names. The group as a whole symbolizes the demon army of Vessamuni-rajjuruvo, ready to receive and execute his orders" (1954:58-59). Obeyesekere (1969:188) states that each of the apparitions is one of the guises of Sanni Yaka or Kola Sanniya, the chief of the disease demons. This does not agree with the exorcists on the Galle area, who nonetheless recognize the **paliya** to be linked to the **sanni** demons, if not specific guises of them.[35] For exorcists and audience, each **paliya** is treated as a demonic figure who in their entrance "on stage" immediately prior to the **sanni** demons, appear to herald the arrival of these demons. Against the exorcism as a whole, it is possible to view the **Ata paliya** as having some structural equivalence with the **Mangara pelapaliya** and the Kalu Vadi episode. This is so in that the **paliya** mediate the demonic and the divine, and in their enactment sign dimensions of the demonic/divine relation.

The articles carried by the demonic figures of the **Ata paliya** are those symbolic objects which are engaged centrally in the transformational work of the ritual, and are vital in the control and expulsion of the demons. The carriage of the symbolic articles by demonic figures may be seen as signifying the incorporation by the articles of aspects of that which they are designed to control, their conversion from pure objects of divine power,[36] for example, into objects of pollution as a function of their ritual use. I take as most significant for later analysis, however, that in the **Ata paliya** demons "play" with the objects of their control. In this play is explored the relations of the divine and the demonic to each other and to the world of human beings. I suggest that the **Ata paliya** not only heralds the **sanni** demons, but establishes a context for their destruction.

The **Dahaata Sanniya** (eighteen disease demons) sequence of acts follows immediately upon the performance of the final act in the **Ata paliya**. Exorcists differ in their listing of the **sanni** demons which could theoretically appear in any performance. If I were to combine the **sanni** demons named by exorcists whom I interviewed, my list would be considerably in excess of eighteen. The list given by Obeyesekere (1969:189) is in broad agreement with those I collected and contains the **sanni** demons which were listed most often by the exorcists in the area I researched. The following list of the **sanni** demons and their associated symptoms is based on that given by Obeyesekere:

Sanni demon	Major symptoms of patient afflicted by demon
1. Bita Sanniya	obscenities, confused behavior, timidity (**bita,** timid)
2. Buta Sanniya	nonsensical talk, or **vabuta**
3. Abuta Sanniya	humorous nonsensical talk, or **kolam**
4. Olmada Sanniya	babbling
5. Kala Sanniya	patient cannot eat, gets thin
6. Jala Sanniya	excess of phlegm, dysentery (**jala,** water)
7. Deva Sanniya	sees beautiful people in dreams, a sign of disease
8. Demala Sanniya	performs pranks and utters nonsense that sounds like Tamil (**demala**)
9. Naga Sanniya	sees snakes in dreams, aching body, bloodshot eyes.
10. Bihiri Sanniya	diseases of the ear (**bihiri,** deaf)
11. Maru Sanniya	deliriums, death
12. Vata Sanniya	rheumatism, stiff joints
13. Avulum Sanniya	difficulty in breathing, pains in chest
14. Vevulum Sanniya	shivering
15. Gulma Sanniya	diarrhea, vomiting, inability to eat food, nausea
16. Vadi Sanniya	sees guns and shooting in dreams (also causes body sores)
17. Kana Sanniya	in seeing (**kana,** blind)
18. Ginijal Sanniya	excess of heat, bilious diseases

In any performance of the **Dahaata Sanniya,** seldom more than eight, and usually fewer, **sanni** demons, make their appearances. Each is presented by an exorcist-actor who wears a mask appropriate to the demon presented. As a rule, Maru Sanniya is the first of the **sanni** demons to enter the performance arena. He is the most terrible of the **sanni** demons, and is a manifestation of the demon of death or the Evil One (Mara) in his **sanni** form. The last demon to appear is either Kola Sanniya, in the **Sanni Yakuma** exorcism, or Deva Sanniya in the other major exorcisms. The masks for both these demonic representations sometimes incorporate miniaturized forms of the other **sanni** demons; both Kola Sanniya and Deva Sanniya, dependent on the type of exorcism being performed, unite the **sanni** class of demons within their respective forms.

The nature of the comic drama of both the **Ata paliya** and **Dahaata Sanniya** and their relations to other concluding events in an exorcism can best be understood by describing one performance, as I witnessed it, in a **Mahasona** exorcism. The acts I describe are from the same **Mahasona** in which was enacted the **Mangara pelapaliya** I recounted earlier.

Immediately before the start of the **Ata paliya**, a rectangular box-structure is erected in front of the demon palace and before the painting of Mahasona. This is the **kapala kuduva**. It is mounted on a rice pounder which passes through its center and which is set in the ground. The **kapala kuduva** is placed in such a manner that it can spin on the axis provided by the rice pounder. Generally, exorcists understand the **kapala kuduva** to be the "offering nest" for Sanni Yaka. It was described to me as having three levels. The top level is representative of the world of the deities (**deva loka**), the middle level of the world of human beings (**minis loka**), and the bottom, the world of demons (**yaksa loka**). The rice pounder is conceptualized as the staff with which Maha Brahma battles and subdues demons. It is also understood as the **axis mundi**. As each demon enters or leaves the performance arena, he will shake the **kapala kuduva** and spin it on its axis.[37]

At approximately 3:00 A.M. a loud drumming announces the appearance of Pandam Paliya. Chairs, on which offering baskets will be placed, are moved in front of the patient. Cries and shouts are heard from inside the demon palace and the whole structure shakes. Pandam Paliya enters wearing the mask of a lion and holding two torches. Great orange flames of burning **dummala** precede him. There is no dialogue. Pandam Paliya stares at members of the audience and assumes a variety of grotesque postures. He then moves up to the patient, waves his torches three times before the patient, and moves back inside the demon palace to cries of "Long life" from the patient's relatives.

The drummers seated on mats to one side of the performance arena begin to sing in praise of Pattini. Salu Paliya enters from the **vidiya**, wearing a white cloth around his neck. It is the same cloth (**kadaturava**) held in front of the patient earlier in the ritual as a protection against the demons, and was the sacred canopy in the **Mangara pelapaliya**. Now it is symbolic of the shawl of Pattini. A drum rhythm is beaten which is specifically for Salu Paliya. The demon dances around the arena, stopping every so often to break into a shoulder-shuddering laugh. Salu Paliya hides his face, points at the patient, laughs, and then engages the exorcist-drummer, as "straight man," in conversation. "**Anee puta** — Alas my son, my son." "I am not your son," replies the drummer in mock anger, "You are my younger brother." An argument ensues between the demon and the drummer concerning the proper mode of address they should use to each other. Eventually, the drummer traps the demon into agreeing that he, the drummer, should be called by the superior term, "father." This evokes laughter from the audience, which continues throughout the following short interchange.

Drummer:	What brings you here?
Salu Paliya	(breaks into song) I give my hand to receive all truth. My grandfather's anus is huge . . .
Drummer:	Aaa . . . correct. That's not simply an anus you are singing about. That's a night soil truck (**gu lorry**). Your grandfather's anus is as big as three hectares. (Salu Paliya laughs.) You laugh like a striking cobra. What's that you carry around your neck?
Salu Paliya:	I am off to the cinema hall.
Drummer:	Why . . . that looks like a cinema screen you have there.

Salu Paliya:	Not a cinema screen, but the cinema curtain . .
Drummer:	Or else the fine dress of an attractive woman.
Salu Paliya:	Hah! No really it is a nylon sarong.
Drummer:	Yes. I can see that you are wearing it like one of the local ruffians . . . hitched high above your ankles.

More dialogue follows, during which the drummer elaborates on the lowly and filthy nature of the demon. Salu Paliya then breaks off the interchange and confronts the patient. "What's wrong with you? You've been attacked by a demon, eh? Well, it's not me!" Salu Paliya then returns to the drummer, reaches under his jacket and carefully places some coins in the drummer's hands. The drummer demands higher payment. The episode draws to a close with Salu Paliya again approaching the patient and breaking into song which parodies that sung by the exorcists when he first entered the arena.

Salu Paliya:	The quality of your chastity is dazzling. The quality of your chastity is dazzling. This man (pointing to the drummer) smells of excrement, ha, ha, ha.
Drummer:	Your (**umba**, a term used to address status inferiors, and often insulting)bowels will be washed white from uttering such filth . . . sing another poem.
Salu Paliya	(to the drummer) **Gurunanse**. Can it be true that this daughter (the patient) is sick? If she is sick, then the sons must be very healthy.

Salu Paliya then passes his shawl three times over the patient's head and returns inside the demon palace.

The actor returns in the mask of Kendi Paliya and carries a pot, understood to contain the pure water from the sacred Himalayan pond of Anotattavilla. It is the water which purifies the patient and the exorcists of the polluting effect of demons; this water was used in the earlier ritual episodes to bring the patient and the exorcists out of trance. The mask is that of an old man; Kendi Paliya leans on a staff and stumbles and staggers around the arena. Kendi Paliya makes a sound as if he is breaking wind and furiously stirs the contents of the pot, which he says contains excrement. He spits into it and mimes drinking its contents.

Drummer:	What have you brought?
Kendi Paliya:	Pure water **(pan)**.
Drummer:	If that's so then you must say a mantra. (Kendi Paliya responds by blowing into the pot and then trips, "spilling" the water.) Buddha's mother! Water is going all over the place. Still it doesn't matter. Your mantras are useless. Say a good mantra.
Kendi Paliya:	How about a **"Mottapalu bandima."** (**Mottapalu** has the connotation of simpleton —— "tie a simpleton" —— and is a pun on **godappalu**, which refers to a mantra used to cut sorcery.) I take my refuge in Mottapalu. The 330 million gods who rule this world command Queen Mottapalu. May this sick woman's fever, headache, dysentery, and smallpox be cured by these gods.

Drummer:	Good. The government is vaccinating everywhere against smallpox.
Kendi Paliya:	I pour the water from the golden spout (the word used for spout also has the meaning of penis) so that this woman will be cured of all sickness.
Drummer:	Good . . . now wipe your face (refers to an earlier curative action employed by the patient when mantra are uttered).
Kendi Paliya:	When I say this mantra you will become sick. Your face will be covered in sores. I will come to your funeral. **Om namo.** The Sky is tied by a thread. The ground is tied by a string of coconut leaf. The sea is tied. . . What is the sea tied with? Aah . . . a fishing penis.
Drummer:	What a fine way to tie the sea.
Kendi Paliya:	The sea is tied with a fishing net.

Kendi Paliya presents the pot to the patient and returns inside the demon palace. Kalas Paliya now enters the arena. He wears a mask which represents that of a young woman. He is dressed in a tightly fitting and brightly colored skirt.

Drummer:	My sweetheart, my darling, my little lollipop . . . what should I call you?
Audience Member:	Karunawatthie (a name meaning a pleasing "kind-hearted" girl).
Drummer:	Not Karunawatthie she should be called Bakalawatthie (bow-legged woman). Seven Deaths! She is already trying to tempt someone. (Kalas Paliya has seated "herself" on the lap of a member of the audience).
Kalas Paliya:	Annee, annee . . . you are ugly.
Drummer:	Look at that! She's wriggling so much that her backside looks heavier than her top.
Kalas Paliya:	(to the drummer) Annee . . . you're ruining my reputation.
Drummer:	Really . . . we can all see that she's been ruined (deflowered) by the shape of her arse. Come here my little one.
Kalas Paliya:	Leave me alone!

The drummer implores her to come to him, and at last Kalas Paliya goes and embraces him. The drummer struggles free and exclaims that she is a whore and a slattern, to which Kalas Paliya responds with loud sobbing cries.

| Drummer: | What are you wearing? It's a mini-skirt. You're a corpse (**mini**) demon. (Here the drummer puns on the English and Sinhalese meaning of the word "mini.") How do you worship at the temple in such a short dress? How can you board a bus? |

(Kalas Paliya squats on the ground in demonstration and reveals her crotch.)

| Drummer: | Won't you cause impure thoughts to enter the mind of the priest (**bhikkhu**) if you do that, my darling? |

(More dialogue follows until the drummer demands that Kalas Paliya reveals who she is.)

Drummer:	Why did you come disguised as a woman, as a whore?
Kalas Paliya:	I came to meet my lover in Galle. He promised me some Gunasiri toffee. (The reference here is to a radio commercial in which a father gives Gunasiri toffee to his children. The commercial is presented to the tune of a popular song which extols the beauties of the modern girls of Bombay.)
Drummer:	Not that.
Kalas Paliya:	I have come dressed as a woman because I am the goddess of the earth (Polova Mahi Kantava) who once defended Buddha against Maraya.

More **paliya** now make their appearance, including Anguru-dummala Paliya, Tambili Paliya, Dalumura Paliya, Igaha Paliya and Kukulu Paliya. The comedy of these acts is similar to those I have described and employs much ribald humor which pokes fun at various symbolic objects and actions used and enacted in the previous ritual episodes. Acts which properly belong to the **Dahaata Sanniya** are now performed. The first **sanni** demon to appear is Maru Sanniya. He wears a black mask and a skirt of **burulla** leaves, as do all the subsequent **sanni** demons. A white cloth (**kadaturava**) is held in front of the patient, screening off an offering basket to Sanni Yaka which is placed on a chair.

A rhythm is beaten on the drums. Shouts are heard from within the demon palace. The whole edifice shakes. Maru Sanniya sneaks out of the **vidiya**, spins the **kapala kuduva**, and creeps back inside the palace. The demon reappears and stealthily moves around the arena, staring at and fixing individual members of the audience in his gaze. As he moves he starts to sprout teeth —— first one tooth, then suddenly another, and another, until he displays four. Maru Sanniya then approaches the patient, but somersaulting backwards, breaks through the audience, scattering a small group of card players. Now on all fours, the demon stalks towards the patient, suddenly leaping through the curtain and onto the patient. The patient, a woman, recoils in terror, but her brother seated beside her holds her head and forces her to look at the demon. Maru Sanniya takes hold of the rice pounder (**mol gaha**) at the patient's feet and makes stabbing motions in the air. Relatives of the patient cry, "Long life, long life." The demon goes before the **vidiya** and, to the beating of drums, executes a short shuffling dance. Maru Sanniya then returns to seat himself beside the patient, takes a strand of her hair and mimes paring her toenails. He takes a torch and "cooks" and "eats" them, all the while grotesquely licking his lips.

As Maru Sanniya gets up to leave the patient, the drummer asks him where he is going.

| Maru Sanniya: | I am off to Maradana (a suburb of Colombo) by a first class express bus. |
| Drummer: | You must do a lot of traveling. Why, what was it I saw you doing only yesterday? You pissed near the sacred Bodhi tree, then shitted on the |

	temple grounds, after which you stole a monk's robes. What else have you done? Why, you also stole a ration book and visited the barber shop to have your head shaved.
Maru Sanniya:	You **peretaya** (ghost)!
Drummer:	Aaah ... you're just a crazy demon, beneath contempt.

More mutually insulting exchanges follow, which become more and more obscene, to the obvious delight of the audience. This is ended when Maru Sanniya suddenly points to the patient.

Maru Sanniya:	**Gurunanse,** the patient is showing some signs of amusement. (The patient at this time was recoiling in evident fright.) Look here (Maru Sanniya addresses the patient), look at my face, show a bit of movement. If you don't speak I will beat you on the head.
Drummer:	Stop that.
Maru Sanniya:	Look! The patient is beginning to giggle. Now she is starting to behave more like a young woman. (The patient was holding her hands over her face, but occasionally opening her fingers to steal a peek at the demon.) Look here! You must look at my face. Simply move those hands away. If you don't look at or talk with me ... I will beat you on the head.
Drummer:	Stop that.
Maru Sanniya:	Come on woman ... Smile.
Drummer:	(to the patient) Open your eyes. (to the audience) He (Maru Sanniya) wants the patient to say out aloud what has caused her illness. He would go if she laughed.
Maru Sanniya:	Patient ... I will cook and eat one of your fingers (he blows into the patient's ear).
Drummer:	Speak up. (To Maru Sanniya, who seemed to be whispering to the patient.)
Maru Sanniya:	Buddha's mother! This is like trying to get an audience with the D.R.O. (The District Revenue Officer is one of the most important locally based government officials. Individuals must be registered at his office for such matters as entering their children in school and receiving their rice rations.) I have sent something like twenty petitions to this woman, and I still haven't got a reply. I'm off to send her a telegram!
Drummer:	Lead her on a little. Talk to her as if you know what has caused her illness.
Maru Sanniya:	(to the patient) If you have suffered from a sickness .. . say so, ha, ha, ha, ha . . . (patient shakes her head).
Drummer:	Use your mouth, don't shake your head. Say out loud whether you had an illness or not, we can't hear you.

| Maru Sanniya: | (to the patient) Seven Deaths! If you had an illness, can't you say so? What were the symptoms of your illness? |

Further exhortations to the patient from Maru Sanniya and the drummer follow, but to little avail. Maru Sanniya then leaps away and somersaults through the audience. He runs outside the ring of spectators and around the patient's house. Eventually he climbs on top of the **vidiya** and glares down at the audience. The act concludes with Maru Sanniya coming down from where he is perched and taking the offering basket for Sanni Yaka, which has been placed in front of the patient. The patient then puts two rice packets **(gotu)** in the basket, which is revolved three times over the patient's head. As the patient's relatives cry "Long life," Maru Sanniya replaces the offering basket on a chair before the patient and returns inside the demon palace.

Three more demons make their appearance in the performance arena, Demala Sanniya, Bita Sanniya and Gulma Sanniya, and engage the drummer in comic dialogue. Each act begins with the singing of a short poem to the demons concerned and concludes with their receiving offerings from the patient in a similar way to Maru Sanniya. I present some of the dialogue in the act involving Gulma Sanniya.

The exorcists sing a short song to Gulma Sanniya. During this the demon enters the arena wearing a blue mask. Its mouth is set in a contorted grimace. Gulma Sanniya leans on a staff. He finds difficulty in walking and gasps for air. His belly is extraordinarily bloated.

Song for Gulma Sanniya

When Gulma Sanniya casts his eyesight he causes stomach trouble.
If he is given food, he will not eat our stomachs.
Oh! Gulma Sanniya, come and take the offerings. Accept our rice.
By the power of Vishnu remove the illness caused by Gulma Sanniya.
Vishnu look upon the patient. See the patient's sorrow.
Oh! Vishnu heal the illness of Gulma Sanniya.

The song ends, and the demon is engaged in conversation by the drummer.

Gulma Sanniya	(crying as if in agony) **Ammaa, ammoo.**
Drummer:	What!
Gulma Sanniya:	**Apoi!** Buddha's mother! Buddha's father! **Apoi!** I can't bear it!
Drummer:	What, my son?
Gulma Sanniya:	Mother come here. **Apoi** . . . stroke this part (pointing to his behind).
Drummer:	I can't touch someone's **gu lorry** (night soil truck).
Gulma Sanniya:	Buddha's mother! Buddha's father! Riri's mother! (Emits a loud "raspberry," the flatulence of stomach ailments; the demon howls as if in alarm.)
Drummer:	Howling, crying. That stomach won't be getting any food.
Gulma Sanniya:	Buddha's belly never hurt like this. What's happened to my belly? **Apoi! Gurunanse,** my friend. What's happened to my belly?

Drummer:	How am I supposed to know? Why **yodayo** (giant)? Don't you know?
Gulma Sanniya:	At night I get drowsy, and the rice smells bad.
Drummer:	Rice smells bad?
Gulma Sanniya:	Buddha's mother, my belly is kicking. Has such a thing happened before?
Drummer:	Does the pain come from the back towards the front?
Gulma Sanniya:	My belly is kicking terribly.
Drummer:	You aren't sick. Seven Deaths! You can't die from that sickness. Why . . . you should be happy that such a thing is happening to your belly. Don't you know what it is? You are about to have a baby. You have **dola duka** (pregnancy suffering or cravings).
Gulma Sanniya:	No. I have **gedara duka** (house suffering). There is no way I can escape from suffering. Younger brother **(malli)**, go to my home and take my wife. Go to Hapugala . . . it's only fifteen cents on the bus. Tell them that your elder brother sent you to take his wife.
Drummer:	Yes, yes . . . this is what must happen if we are to share in brotherly love.
Gulma Sanniya:	Oh, oh. I must lie down. Like in the **mala darahava**. (He makes a reference to the earlier episode in the **avamangalle**, when the exorcist offered himself as a corpse to the demons.) You settle down with my wife.
Drummer:	That skinny bitch. She is thinner than an areca tree.
Gulma Sanniya:	**Apoi.** That leg is kicking. You said I have a baby in my belly.
Drummer:	Not that. We must stop the fooling. I will play no more tricks **(mayam)** on you. Dawn has broken. We must finish. Your stomach is bloated because it has a ball of **pulutu** (fried grains, included in the demon offerings).
Gulma Sanniya:	Seven Deaths. Is there a Veda Mahattaya **(vedarala)** here?
Drummer:	I will do. We will pour medicine down your nostrils. Not that . . . we will do an operation, like the hospital doctors. We can cut that lump out with a pen knife . . . no, a chain saw would be better.
Gulma Sanniya:	**Ammo, amma.**

The demon kneels down on a mat. He sneezes loudly, and the drummer exclaims that this is a bad omen. Gulma Sanniya then smacks his belly, breaking a pot which he has concealed beneath his clothing. He howls as if in agony, and a number of objects tumble out before him. These include a coconut, some sweetmeats, a small quantity of fried rice, and a piece of dried fish. The demon and the drummer poke through them and engage in a mock diagnosis.

Gulma Sanniya:	**Apoi!** The **pulutu** has burst. What's this? (Points to the coconut.) Oh . . . **duka, muka, puka.** (Suffering, mouth, anus)

Drummer:	This means that you must have had boils in the anus. How is this so? Did the boils come to the anus from the stomach?
Gulma Sanniya:	I must wash my hands and throw it away. What else is there here?
Drummer:	Now we can see what the patient has eaten.
Gulma Sanniya:	Buddha's father. I see the patient has eaten corpse (**mini**) sweetmeats, Riri sweetmeats, **pulutu**, cuttlefish. **Apoi**. The patient has eaten all these things?
Drummer:	There's no doubt . . . the woman (the patient) had a **pulutu** boil in the stomach. Eeee. After eating this food the boil must have grown. Now the boil has burst. We must give two packets of rice with **pulutu** and be off.

The episode concludes with the patient placing these offerings in the basket to Sanni Yaka. The demon takes the basket, passes it over the patient's head, and returns to the demon palace. Deva Sanniya now appears. There is no comic dialogue. The demon takes Sanni Yaka's offering basket, and after receiving offerings from the patient, places the basket on his head and then returns to the **vidiya**, putting the offering basket on the **kapala kuduva**.

The **Dahaata Sanniya** is now over. The audience begins to break up, either returning to their homes or setting off to work. The exorcists begin to drum and sing, and a dancer performs the **dekone vilakkuva** (double torch). Wearing the double torch (symbolic of demonic tusks) and the plaited mouth-mask, he dances around the arena. He rushes into the house burning **dummala** and then runs to the **purale**. By this action the dancer purifies the house and transfers what remains of the polluting presence of the demons to the cemetery ground. The final act of the exorcism (but performed only for female patients) involves the patient walking in procession around the **mal yahanava**, and sometimes the **Kumara vidiya**, while the exorcists sing the praises of Buddha and the Guardian deities. The exorcism concludes in the same manner as it began. The various ritual structures are now pulled down (**kapanava**, cut) and thrown at the **purale**. They, together with the other ritual objects made for and used in the ceremony, are understood to have absorbed the polluting essence of the demons and must be removed from the area of the house. The only exception is the **igaha**, which is placed in the ceiling of the patient's house. It continues to provide protection for the patient for as long as it has "life" and power, that is, until the materials from which it is made dry up.

Exorcism ritual is its own exegesis. The mantra, songs, and poems all explicitly relate their purpose; they call the demons, demand that the demons take their offerings, and tell that the illness which the demons cause is removed. They call on the purity of the Buddha's thought, on the Buddha's teaching, and on the power of the gods to dispel the sickness and impurities brought by the demons. In the poems and songs, the cultural meaning of the various symbolic articles and actions employed in the ritual are elucidated. So, too, is the mythical basis for the organization of symbolic action in the ritual. The poems and songs continually reiterate the cosmic order and the lowly position of demons within it. These themes, and others, such as the negation of pollution by purity, are evident at all points within the ritual process. Thus, the cosmic hierarchy, its generative and inherent powers, is present in the design and decoration of the ritual structures built for the ritual occasion. Aspects of the poems and songs are elaborated in the extended episodes of dance and drama. The comic drama has, as one of its principal elements, the presentation of the demonic as filthy, polluting, and lowly. The demons are shown to be illegitimate intruders into the world of human beings. They become figures of fun, tricksters who are caught in their own jest, specters subject to the powers of those whom they sought to usurp, dupes trapped in the snares set by those whom they strove to delude. These and other aspects of the comic drama and of the dance will be of central analytical concern in the chapters to follow.

Exorcism rituals remove the demonic and eradicate the dangers, pollution, and illnesses which are caused and manifested by the demonic. Nonetheless, they reveal the terrible potential which is ever-present in the worlds of action and existence. Exorcism rites develop on the ambiguous and the illusory. They present as if real a dominating and powerful world of horrifying demons and ghosts and then "unmask" it and subordinate it within an order and a reality as this should be typified and understood by the normal, the healthy, and the unafflicted. But the roots of demonic and cosmic disruption, integral to, yet contradictory within a cosmic process, maintain an awful potential even in the midst of their expulsion, subjugation, and reordering. The Maru Sanniya act within the **Dahaata Sanniya** is an example. Maru Sanniya is a demon who opposes life. In the views of exorcists and lay Sinhalese, he is one form of Mara, the Harbinger of Death. In the act he is typically presented as absurd, filthy, polluting, and inferior. But he is also terrible. He leaps and tumbles through the audience and encircles it, simultaneously fragmenting, scattering, and encompassing the audience. He threatens the domination of his terrifying and powerful aspect over those who gather to witness the performance and threatens to unify them within the terrible and disordered order he portrays.

In my description of the major demon ceremonies I have stressed that alternative constructions, different and opposed possibilities of the cosmic totality, and the relation of human beings within it, are present in each of the main ritual episodes. The whole is immanent in the parts and the hierarchy of the cosmic totality realizes its power in the progression through each of the ritual events. Exorcism places the constituting principles of the universe into the process of their dynamic tension and creative force. Successively more powerful, ordering and disordering, manifest possibilities of the cosmic whole are engendered at each moment in exorcism, which in the course of its action is nothing less than the cosmic totality in the vital, life-giving and life-taking, motion of its creation. The various orderings which comprise the cosmic encompassment are, in exorcism, collapsed, compressed, telescoped, one in the other. The ritual process of exorcism is one in which these orderings spring forth, Jack-in-the-box-like, disclosing their powerful world-making and world-destroying capacities.

Each ritual episode reaffirms, elaborates, and either deepens or alters the key thematic of the one before. They project backwards and forwards: back to the terrifying reality of the patient, dominated as it is by demons, and forward to a world purified and cleansed of demonic malevolence, transcended by the Buddha and ordered and controlled by the deities. As the exorcism proceeds from one episode to the next, and through the phases of the evening, midnight, and morning watches, the terrible world of the demons first intensifies, threatening to override the forces of control and order, and then becomes progressively subordinated in the cosmic order, as this order is progressively rebuilt and comes to encompass the demonic. The dialogue of the episodes of comic drama, for example, comments on the malign demonic reality conjured in the earlier phases of the exorcism, subjects to ridicule many of its objects, and provides a means for the distancing of the demonic from the reality of normal, unafflicted, human beings.

I have been able to describe only a fraction of the immense symbolic richness of exorcism. Sound, song, smell, dance, and drama combine into what can only be described as a marvelous spectacle which engages all the senses. Exorcists understand their rituals as composing the five essences of sound (**sabdha**), visual form (**rupa**), touch and feeling (**sparsa**), taste (**rasa**), and smell (**gandha**). These are the essences which are "materialized" in the five elemental substances (**pancha mahabhuta**). It is out of these essences that the exorcists conjure and create both the divine and the demonic. One exorcist referred to the essences collectively by the Sanskrit word **skandha**, or impermanent conditions. The term relates to the Buddhist concept of impermanence (**anicca**) and conveys the sense of constant change and flux, of continual forming, re-forming, and dissolving (see Ling 1973:111). While not claiming that the term is part of the everyday vocabulary of those non-specialist Sinhalese who attend exorcisms, I nonetheless consider that it conveys a crucial quality of exorcism performance: formed in the color, music, song, and the sounds of magical incantation; in the smell of incense; in the movement and gesture of dance; and in the masked presentation of the demonic, an array of images appears and disappears, forms, re-forms, and dissolves in the kaleidoscope of an exorcism performance.

A more complete sense of the process of an exorcism than I have presented so far, requires a change of analytic focus. I have described the organization of symbolic action within particular ritual episodes and the sequential ordering of episodes within the ritual as a whole. The description and the underlying logic of exorcism ritual has proceeded in accordance with the interpretations given by exorcists and in terms of what they consider should be performed in exorcisms of a specific recognizable type. In the analysis to follow I will stress, more than hitherto, ritual as performance. It is in performance that ritual gains its efficacy, and, in my view, reveals itself as essentially the "hermeneutic" of culture - a method whereby culture analyzes itself. Exorcism transforms a patient from illness to health by engaging a patient and others in the logic and process of its own hermeneutic. What this hermeneutic is and the way in which it may achieve vital transformations in experience and interpretations of experience is the concern of the following chapters.

THE CEREMONY OF THE GREAT CEMETERY DEMON:

A PHOTOGRAPHIC DESCRIPTION

(PHOTOS COURTESY OF GEORGE AND MARIE-CLAUDE PAPIGNY)

RITUAL PREPARATIONS AND PRELIMINARY EVENTS

CONSTRUCTION OF MAHASONA VIDIYA

This **vidiya** is of the most "traditional" design. The central **pancha massa** (for Mangara) is connected to the four outer **torana** by arches (**arukku**) hung with coconut leaves.

THE MAKING OF SYMBOLIC ARTICLES

The exorcist on the left makes the **igaha**, while the person on the right weaves an offering basket.

THE TOOLS OF DEMON MASTERY

The **mal bulat tattuva** (on chair), **igaha** (right), **dummala** (in tray under chair), rooster, and torches (left rear).

DANCE SCENE IN IRAMUDUN SAMAYAMA

A white cloth -(**kadaturava**) screens off the patient as a mock funerary bier (foreground) is being prepared. The exorcist-dancer will enter the bier and attract Iramudun Riri to his person. An offering stand (**kattirikka,-ya**) is at the left with the Riri Yaka **tattuva** placed upon it.

THE PURALE

An exorcist climbs the **purale** platform at the close of **Iramudun Samayama** to burn a straw effigy.

THE PRETA TATTUVA

Offering to ghosts given just prior to the main exorcism ceremony.

NAMASKARAYA AT MAL YAHANAVA

A mother and her sick child light oil lamps to the gods.

THE SUMMONING OF THE DEMONS

The shrill of the demon pipe (**vas danda**) and the smell
of **dummala** brings the demons to the ritual place. The
madu puraya (at left) assists.

THE AVAMANGALLE

Exorcist withdraws demonic
illness by "head to foot"
motion of **igaha**.

NICHA KULA

An egg is cooked in the cranium of a human skull
during **avamangalle**.

THE DEMONIC ILLUSION

A demonic figure (Mahasona) appears to the patient through
the smoke of **dummala**. Demons are understood to take form
in the smoke of **dummala**. This was performed at the close
of an **avamangale** I saw and was observed by me on only a
couple of occasions. There was no dialogue, the demon
simply appearing and then disappearing.

A DANCER DRESSES

The **Vata Pade**

The **Vilakku Pade**

The **Kukulu Pade**
A dancer summons Mahasona

THE DEMON IS THE DANCER

With the cock "masking" his face the dancer advances
on the patient. Note the demon net above the dancer on
the **Mahasona vidiya**.

PANDEMONIUM

Two members of the audience become possessed during the **igaha pade** (woman in sarong and youth in checked shirt). The exorcism was disrupted and was only restarted after the possessed left the arena following promises that separate exorcisms would be held for them.

ENTRANCING A PATIENT

An exorcist himself moving into trance confronts the patient in an effort to engender the patient's trance.

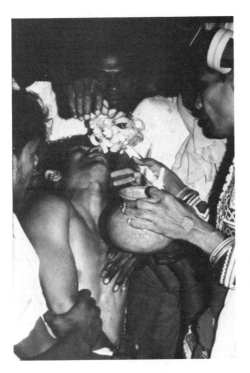

THE DEMONIC COOLED AND SUBDUED

The demonic is withdrawn from an entranced patient through the power of the **igaha** and the cooling and purifying properties of sacred water.

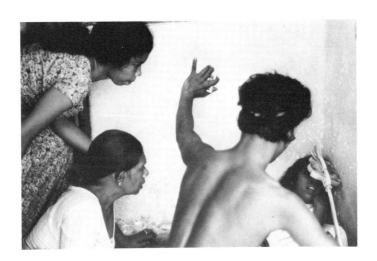

A MOMENT OF ANXIETY

An exorcist draws a patient back to consciousness, while a worried mother and sister look on.

AVATARA BALIMA
The powerful abstract consistency of the demonic.

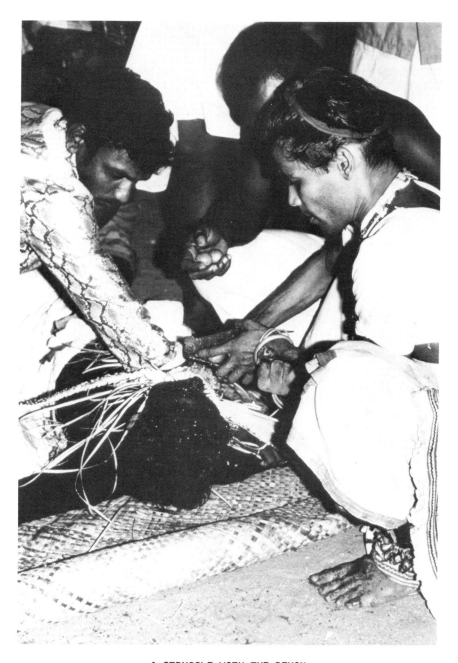

A STRUGGLE WITH THE DEMON

The exorcist entranced has just returned from the
purale. He has collapsed on the ground and a relative
of the patient (left) and exorcists (right) struggle
to restrain the demon possessed and prostrated exorcist.

THE MANGARA PELAPALIYA

SANNAS PATRAYA

TAMMATTAM PALIYA

HEVISI PALIYA

MI BANDIMA PALIYA

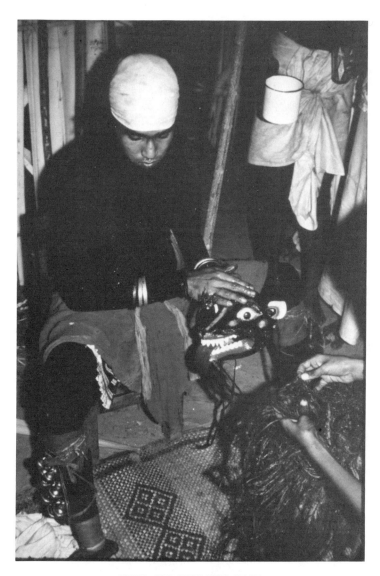

ACTOR AND MAHASONA MASK

While the **Mangara pelapaliya** is being enacted an
actor prepares for his role as Mahasona at the rear
of the demon palace.

MAHASONA REVEALED

The audience watches as Mahasona moves to his death. Note the mixture of facial expression among the audience members.

THE MAHA TE

Exorcists take food seated on the ground.

PANDAM PALIYA
The **kapala kuduva** is at left

SALU PALIYA

SALU PALIYA AND DRUMMER SHARE A JOKE

KALAS PALIYA
"My sweetheart, my darling, my little lollipop."

KALAS PALIYA AND HER LOVER

KENDI PALIYA

The apparition expresses his relief from an extreme
attack of flatulence.

MARU SANNIYA SPROUTS TEETH

AND STEALS TOWARDS THE PATIENT

MARU SANNIYA GAZES CARNIVOROUSLY AT PATIENT

Most commonly this demon is presented with curved tusks. The face is blackened, and except for the hair, tusks, and moustache, no mask is worn.

AUDIENCE AWAITS PATIENT RESPONSES

An exorcist showing concern on his face stands behind the
two boys.

"BUDDHA'S MOTHER!

This is like trying to get an audience with the D.R.O."

DEMALA SANNIYA CONSIDERS A POINT

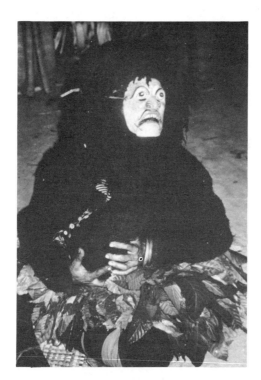

GULMA SANNIYA: "Apoi.
The **pulutu** has burst".

A DEMONIC UNITY IN FRAGMENTATION: DEVA SANNIYA

The eighteen **sanni** demons are represented in miniature
at the top of the mask. Exorcists say that the carved
style of the mask (the eyes especially) is appropriate
to the deity form.

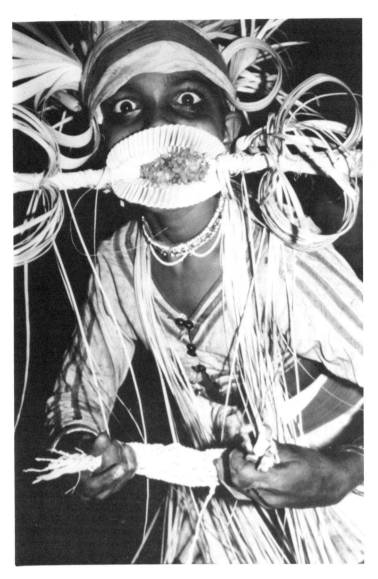

DEKONE VILLAKOVA
An exorcist twelve years old takes the demon role.

A SPENT DEMONIC FORCE RETURNS TO THE SCENE OF HIS
DESTRUCTION: THE EXORCISM IS CONCLUDED.

SELECTED EVENTS FROM THE RATA YAKUMA, SANNI YAKUMA,
AND SUNIYAMA EXORCISMS.

THE RATA YAKUMA

THE DANCE OF THE SEVEN QUEENS

THE TOILETTE OF RIDDI BISAVA

The queen struggles to open a bottle of perfume. This
and other episodes of the toilette are mimed.

RIDI BISAVA TAUNTS DIPAMKARA BUDDHA

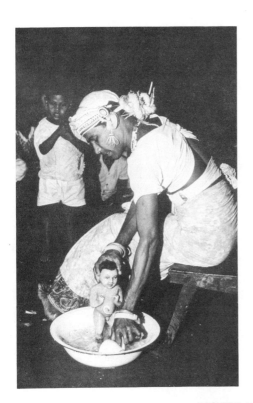

WASHING THE BABY

Notice the growing delight
on the small boy's face.

THE DANCE OF THE LICHCHAVIS

The **Lichchavis** are understood to have translucent skins and this is indicated by the style of dress.

KOLA SANNIYA AT THE GATES

Male relatives of the patient with crossed rice pounders. The episode refers to the **kola sanniya** myth where Buddha placed Saman and Natha as guardians at the gate of Visalamahanuvara. The episode is highly comic.

A DANCER IN SPECIAL DRESS FOR THE SUNIYAMA

This style of dress is not used for the other exorcisms. Sometimes it will be worn at other ceremonial times for the deities, or rites marking an auspicious occasion.

A PATIENT INSIDE THE ATAMAGALA

In this situation the patient is freed from Suniyam's malevolence and now is placed under Suniyam's protection.

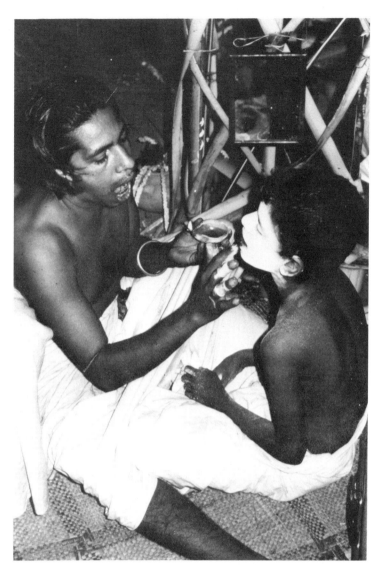

A YOUNG EXORCIST IS MADE-UP FOR HIS ROLE IN THE VADIGA
PATUNA COMEDY

A COMEDY OF BRAHMINS

Three Brahmins find themselves in the midst of the **Suniyama**. In the course of the comedy they reveal the history and the meaning of the rite. This particular episode involved two of the Brahmins vying for the sexual attention of the young "novice" Brahmin. The **Atamagala** is in the background.

8. Music, Dance, and Trance

Between the poles of the conscious and the unconscious,
   there has the mind made a swing:
Thereon hang all beings and all worlds, and that swing
   never ceases its sway.
. . . .
All swing! the sky and the earth and the air and the
   water; and the Lord Himself taking form:
. . . .
Songs of Kabir, trans. Rabindranath Tagore, 1915

Sinhalese exorcisms are artistic forms. But their art is turned to the practical purpose of acting upon the problems which affect the lives of human beings in a mundane world. Exorcists take pride in their art and recognize the importance of the aesthetic —— of music, song, dance, and drama — in the curing of demonic illness. This and the next chapter concentrate on the aesthetic of exorcism and its role in ritual performance. The thesis I develop is that transitions and transformations in meaning and experience are communicated, received, and engendered among ritual participants through the dynamic properties of the major aesthetic modes of exorcisms and by the way participant standpoint or perspective is ordered in ritual action. More generally, I approach the issue of the relation of artistic form to meaning and experience. Thus my analysis is based on the assumption that possibilities for the ordering of experience and its meaning inhere in the structure of artistic form. In other words, individual experience and the meaningful interpretation of it is a possibility of the way the context of action and experience is moulded and mediated in artistic form. Art, as T. S. Eliot wrote, is an "objective correlative," a formular of experience and emotion which can also evoke among those who are embraced by it a subjectivity appropriate to the emotion and feeling which art formulates.

Exponents of the arts and scholars in the East and the West have long related artistic forms to their roots in ritual. But anthropologists, despite an enduring interest in the aesthetics of the cultures they describe, have given insufficient attention to the significance of aesthetic form in ritual. Sinhalese demon ceremonies permit no such avoidance. Exorcists locate and elaborate particular aesthetic modes at various stages in the ritual process, and the patient's progress in it. Demon ceremonies, therefore, provide one opportunity not only to explore the practical importance of the aesthetic in one type of rite, but also to examine, within a given cultural setting, the way in which specific aesthetic modes order experience and give rise to certain possibilities of meaning in and about experience.

Exorcisms are transition rites which have the classic structural form described by Van Gennep (1961) and extended upon in the work of Victor Turner (1967, 1969, 1974). Indeed, their division into the time periods of the evening, midnight, and morning watches could hardly make this more apparent. In these, respectively, the patient is separated from the mundane world, then placed in a liminal world of the supernatural where demonic and divine forces are fully elaborated and joined in struggle, and then replaced within the paramount reality of everyday life in which the patient is freed from demonic control and returned to normality. Transition rites, such life crisis rites as those concerning initiation, death, installation to office, and healing, are understood in many cultures not only to mark a change of identity but actively to transform one identity into another. It is in their transformational capacity that members of specific cultures often recognize the efficacy of the rites they perform, and it is the explication of the transformational process of exorcism as this is achieved through performance which is a principal analytical task of this chapter and the next.

Terence Turner (1977:53-70) has developed a general abstract model of the transformational logic of transition rites which is applicable to major demon ceremonies. Broadly, in accordance with the model he outlines, they effect a passage between two states of the person, these two states being constituted in the one overall matrix of relations. This passage is a movement from a lower possibility of being to a higher. This is so in the movement from illness to health in exorcism, which is a passage from a lower demonic possibility of being to a higher nondemonic being in which normal everyday social roles and identities can be reassumed. Essentially this is a movement in hierarchy and is effected through transformational operations which govern movement through a cosmic order in which demons, human beings, and deities are constituted as beings within the one cosmic totality or matrix of relations. Exorcisms as a whole and in their sequential ordering of events, as well as in the internal structure of these events, model the vertical order of relations in the cosmic hierarchy along a horizontal plane. As the patient moves through the rite, he or she is progressively reordered in terms of principles which structure relations at the apex of the cosmic hierarchy. A transformation in identity, in my usage here, occurs when the elements comprising an identity at one level within a matrix of relations are recombined to form another identity, or identity state in which a variety of roles and associated identities might be relevant, composed at a higher level in the same matrix. A transformed identity or identity state is that which subsumes an identity previously excluded from it or, in the case of exorcism, is a negation of a prior established identity.

Exorcisms in their logic proceed by developing the demonic to a point where it assumes its most encompassing form, but is unable to transform in the sense of being able to compose itself in a manner consistent with those orderings of relations at a higher plane of cosmic existence. The demonic becomes disordered by the deity, or reordered and weakened as it is subordinated to it, and the patient, through the power of the deity to recombine elements at a higher level in hierarchy, is transformed into a higher nondemonic mode of being. In exorcism, the peak moment of transformation is in the midnight watch, when the greatest power of the demonic is revealed and brought into conjunction with divine powers. This is a period of major transformation in the cosmic matrix, a "pivoting of the sacred," when one organizational possibility of cosmic relations gives way to a higher, more encompassing, and reordered form. It is at this moment that the contexts relevant to everyday life can be reconstituted (what may be regarded as the paramount reality as distinct from a finite province of meaning which is the world of the patient apart from the everyday), in which patients can rediscover themselves and their identities in a normal social world. In the Sinhalese cultural view, such a world and its order is dependent upon the domination of the Buddha and the deities in the cosmic system. The triadic phasing and character of the events in exorcism is consistent with its hierarchical transformational logic, and comprises what I consider to be the objective structure of major demon ceremonies. The separation phase (the evening watch) encompasses a period when the demonic is largely dominant and, because demons constitute a low level of ordering, cannot constitute the everyday world of human beings within it. With the emergence of the divine in the liminal or marginal period of the midnight watch, the reconstitution of an everyday world within the context of ritual action becomes possible. This is fully realized in the reaggregation phase (the morning watch), which objectively asserts the dominance of the divine and the subordination of the demonic.

An understanding of the transformational logic of exorcisms, or any rite of transition for that matter, still leaves open the question of how its transformational efficacy is communicated to and made part of the experience of participants. Terence Turner (1977:63) claims that this is achieved in the "iconicity" of the symbolic forms of the rite with its objective structure, its progressive modeling of the transformations and transitions occurring within it. The symbolic forms of the rite are the media by which ritual participants become subjectively oriented in the ritual process. They link the inner experience of the subject with the objective structure of the rite. Through the manipulation of these mediating symbolic forms, the inner experience of the subjects can be made to parallel the transformations taking place in the objective structure of the rite. This is essentially the perspective of Victor Turner's work, as well as that of others, such as Munn (1973), whom Terence Turner cites.

However, the above process, essentially the objectification of the subjective, has still to be demonstrated, and it is for this reason that I concentrate on the structure of performance and the nature of the aesthetic it organizes. In Chapter 1, I argued that ritual performance is more than the enactment or execution of a "text."[1] Ritual performance is a structure of practice emergent in a context which itself is ordered through the process of performance. It is in the structure of practices which comprise a ritual performance that meaning and the world of its experience is constituted. The meaning of exorcism is progressively disclosed in its performance, and it is the engagement of participants in the progress of this disclosure which is central to an understanding of how a ritual communicates its meaning and also to an understanding of how it may achieve its transformational purpose as this is realized by the participants. What ritual communicates, and the transformations it may effect as these are revealed to participants, occurs on at least two planes: that of experience, the immediately felt individual subjective encountering of a context of meaning and action, and that of the conscious reflective grasping of this experience in terms of idea constructs and typifications of the culturally objectified world.

What is experienced and the capacity to reflect upon experience is a property both of the media of performance and of the way individuals are positioned in relation to central ritual events organized within the various performance media.   All major exorcisms, with only slight variation, systematically position individuals (and focus their gaze) differentially in relation to the central events and systematically change their positioning in the course of performance. Exorcism performance develops a complex and changing communicational field, and this constitutes a vital aspect of how exorcisms do their work.   A consideration of the positioning of ritual participants points to the importance of the audience in ritual, those who are not the central focus of the ritual action or are bystanders looking in upon the action. With the exception of Geertz' (1972) study of the Balinese cockfight, the role of the audience in ritual has largely been ignored.[2]

In exorcism, the category of audience is problematic, with individuals moving in and out of the central action, alternately standing apart from it and being directly engaged in its process.   This oscillation between engagement and nonengagement produced in performance has the potential of exposing individuals to the subjective experience of the rite, and then removing them from such experience so that they can objectify the nature of that into which they passed. This is part of how exorcism communicates its import. The patient is also made to oscillate in a similar manner, and I suggest that some of the curative efficacy of the rite may be connected with this oscillation. Further, the process whereby the audience is involved in the rite, especially in the midnight and morning watches, is integral to the transformational project of the rite. Through it important alterations in the meaning of experience and the nature of an objective world are facilitated.

It is the aesthetic of exorcism, its music, dance, and drama, to which I attach the greatest significance in analysis, but always in relation to the positioning of ritual participants.   The form of exorcism aesthetic has inherent possibilities for experience and meaning. By form here I do not refer to the outer shape of the aesthetic, but to its inner structure, the organizing principles which affect the degree to which it unites with its subject. "The form is less the shape of an object than the shape of the system which the subject forms with the object, of that 'rapport with the world' which expresses itself unfailingly in us and is constitutive of both the object and the subject" (Dufrenne 1973:231).   In their form, the music, dance, and comic drama of exorcism organize perception in distinctive ways and, through this, the meaning and experience of what is presented in them. Essentially, music and dance have their meaning constituted in the directly revealed experience of them. Their form is such that they can potentially achieve an existential unity with their subject.   They can produce in experience what is already integral to their form. Exorcists are concerned to construct in ritual that which they aim to transform. Music and dance have the capacity to engender in experience that which is objective in the rite and, at the same time, subject those who are embraced in their realm in a process of change which the rite intends. However, the unity which the musical or dance object achieves with its subject can place that which is directly revealed or disclosed in subjective experience beyond the objective grasp of those who are engaged in the immediate process of experiencing music or dance. Hence the movement to comic drama in exorcism. Drama, and comic drama in particular, places the object at a distance from its subject and, further, in its specific dynamic, as I will show in the next chapter, tests and explores the objective truth of that which was revealed directly to experience in the music and dance.

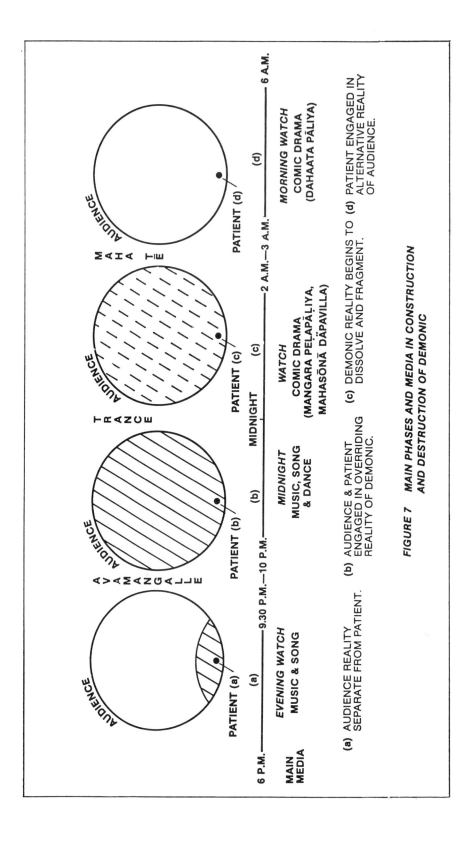

FIGURE 7   MAIN PHASES AND MEDIA IN CONSTRUCTION
AND DESTRUCTION OF DEMONIC

Exorcists are concerned to restore the body and the mind of the patient to a healthy equilibrium. They do not conceive body and mind dualistically. A disturbance of the body is also a disturbance of the mind, and **vice versa.** For either one to be restored to its proper balance, so must the other. Exorcists understand their music, dance, and comedy to act directly upon the body and mind of the patient. In the context of music and dance, the exorcists restore the physical equilibrium of the patient and withdraw the essence of demonic disturbance. In the comedy, they restore a balance of mind, destroy the demonic illusion, and draw the patient back from isolation into a social world.

The following analysis in this chapter and the next is based on the largely "textual" description of the **Mahasona** in Chapter 7. I do not examine a particular enactment of the **Mahasona** (see, however, Kapferer 1979a), but rather concentrate on those repeated aspects of enactment which constitute the regular performance structure of the **Mahasona** and, also, the **Rata Yakuma** and **Sanni Yakuma.** My observation of over eighty major demon ceremonies indicates a marked similarity from one enactment to the next. Some variations in detail which occur, in general, do not contradict what I analyze as the performance structure of exorcism. Within the exorcism tradition in which I worked there is wide agreement as to the style of presentation of specific ritual episodes, the roles which the patient and others should adopt within them, and so on.

The Performance of the Evening Watch

The start of the evening watch of all major exorcisms is characterized by a differential positioning of the ritual gathering in relation to the central ritual events. The positioning of ritual participants also corresponds with variations in the focused attention to the central ritual events, and the meaning and action context which they develop. These variations are systematically produced by the performance rules, whereby the exorcists "produce" an exorcism performance. The way individuals are positioned and focused in the setting of the rite provides the basis for the development of contexts of meaning and action which are alternative to or outside of the immediate context constructed around the patient. It is from standpoints formed within such alternative contexts that different accents upon a reality developed in the patient's context can be generated. Overall, the ritual action of the evening watch progressively elaborates a contrast between the finite province of meaning of a demonic victim and the paramount reality, its multiple contexts of meaning and action, of the nonafflicted. In effect, what is produced as part of the performance structure of the evening watch are the two reality states of the demonic and the everyday, a transition between which exorcism is directed to achieve, in the sequential order of event and action.

Figure 7 indicates the positioning of ritual participants at major exorcisms and the area in which the central ritual action is concentrated during the watch periods. In the evening watch, the ritual action is tightly organized in an immediate area extending a few feet outward from the patient.

The performance rules governing the positioning and focusing of the patient's attention in the evening watch, and throughout an exorcism, impose a restriction on patient movement. The patient must remain seated on the house veranda (a liminal space) facing the **vidiya.** Except when vitally necessary the patient cannot get up, move away, or talk with friends and acquaintances in the ritual congregation. Patients are enjoined by the exorcists to focus their attention on the demon offerings and the action surrounding them. The patient is virtually isolated in a world charged with the force and power of the supernatural which the exorcists are conjuring. Demonic victims understood to be in a state of physical and mental aloneness (**tanikama**, see p. 50) are indeed, to all intents and purposes, positioned alone within the rite.

Members of the patient's household are typically clustered a few feet away from the patient. In the case of female patients, a senior male household relative usually will sit close to the patient, occasionally comfort the victim, and sometimes place offerings in the demon baskets. It is the patient's relatives who cry "Long Life" at the end of each offering episode, and thus mark the ritual progress of the patient. The household kin have few roles directly connected with the ritual action, but their positions in the ritual setting, and an expectation that they should attend focuses them on the ritual process. It should be stressed, however, that unlike the patient, no restriction is placed upon their movement. Like the rest of the ritual congregation during the evening watch, they can move around freely, talk with friends, and occasionally assist with the serving of drinks and sweetmeats.

Most of those who attend the exorcism (relatives of the household, friends, neighbors, and other acquaintances) are positioned away from the central ritual action. Their numbers gradually swell, often to well over a hundred, and sometimes to two hundred or more, as the evening watch proceeds. As they gather, they sit or stand at the perimeter of the performance arena and continually move around it. Most gossip about their daily experience, some drink, and others play cards. Their attention is hardly focused on the patient's context at all, except when the presiding exorcist (**gurunanse**) occasionally announces the start or close of a particular ritual episode. Sometimes individuals pass between the exorcists and the patient **en route** to the house, but the exorcists pay them no notice.

Exorcists contribute in their ritual action to the separation of the patient's context from those of the audience. Thus, they tend to cluster tightly around the patient, obscuring the view of the audience. While not engaged in the ritual action, they will converse with members of the patient's household and others in the ritual gathering. They mediate between the understood world of the patient, which they are constructing, and the everyday contexts around them, in which they also actively participate. Occasionally they will explain publicly before the audience what they are about to do.

The social order of the everyday world, those factors which divide, differentiate, and stratify Sinhalese in their daily experience, is everywhere in evidence in the total situation of the rite. Exorcisms, as I described in Chapter 4, are occasions when food is given to the ritual guests. Invitations to eat inside the house tend to follow the lines of rank and status. Chairs are reserved for high-status and influential members of the community. Men gather outside the house, while women congregate inside the house, stand in the doorway, or else peer out of iron-grilled windows at the ritual scene which unfolds before them. For most of the ritual gathering, the cultural and social order of Sinhalese daily life is accentuated. It is a "celebration" of it. This everyday world encircles the ritual context of the patient, but does not encroach upon it. An invisible frame or boundary seems to mark off the world of the patient from the other realities which engage most in the audience.

Those individuals positioned outside the patient's context, insofar as they attend to its ritual action, look in upon the patient's world from standpoints within everyday contexts established in the ritual setting. So positioned, they are variously enabled to apply rational or common-sense understandings born of the paramount reality of daily life and its ordering. The patient's reality is external to their own. While it is peripheral to their attention, the context of the patient is made to appear to the audience as organized in accordance with the objective structure of the cosmic order as this should normally be conceived by Sinhalese Buddhists. The constant message of the exorcists is that the demons are being summoned by the authority of the Buddha and the deities, and that the demons are being controlled by the power of the divine.

The patient is presented with the same overt information, and is explicitly exhorted to concentrate on the purity and power of the Buddha and the deities. What freqently occurs, however, is that the patient can be seen to enter a quasi-trance indicative of demonic control. This is expressed by the patient's sweating and a shivering and trembling of the body and limbs. Undoubtedly the patient is predisposed to demonic experience. The diagnosis and definition of illness are likely to confirm a self-understanding among patients that they are demonically attacked. In their expectations they are opened to the demonic experience, and this is especially so when the objects of the demonic are presented, the baskets of offerings, the smoke and smell of the **dummala,** and the shrill of the demon pipe. But a demonic experience in the patient is also a possibility of the patient's positioning and other aspects of the performance.

Everyday contexts are withheld from the patient, and the patient is located and fixed within a context to which the demons are summoned. The patient is able to look out upon the interactional contexts of others, but these are filtered to the patient through an immediate context in which supernatural powers are immanent. The patient cannot stand apart from context, except through an act of his or her own will, by engaging actively in interaction with others in terms of alternative standpoints outside the central ritual events. Different accents upon the one supernatural reality are developed within the patient's context, but these are held in a progressively unstable relation. The normal everyday attitude of demonic subordination to the divine, while the logic of exorcism, is uncertain in the context which envelopes the patient.

Within the patient's context the powers of demons and of deities are presented in dynamic relation. Each offering episode asserts the power of a particular demon, and this is conveyed through song. This gives way to the counterassertion of the controlling and subjugating powers of the Buddha and the deities only to dissolve once again in the reassertion of the power of the demonic and the presentation of yet another basket. Demonic disorder is overcome in the order of the divine, and the essence of the patient's illness is progressively removed from the patient's body, but a demonic disorder is reestablished in the summoning of another demon.

A white curtain, the **kadaturava,** is held between the patient and the demon offerings, and the patient is exhorted to take strength in the knowledge of the Buddha. The whiteness of the curtain, symbolic of purity and the power of the divine, is intended to protect the patient from devouring demons and also to produce a mental peace and emotional quietude. It partly obscures the patient's view of the ritual action, but all the while the patient is assaulted with the sound and smell of the demonic. The cloth is removed with purifying bursts of flaming **dummala,** which is a conversion of the smoke and smell of demonic substance into the substance of the divine. But the removal of the curtain reveals the baskets of the demons and their pollutants, to which the patient signs his or her relation by placing offerings in them.

The patient's context oscillates between the disorder of the demonic and the order of the divine, with demons giving rise to deities, and **vice**

versa. The patient, in the midst of such a context, is further opened up to its dynamic movement by the media of music and song. Embraced in a musical realm, the patient is further removed from the paramount reality of everyday life, and the objects of experience, the divine and the demonic, take form in the organized flow of music, and in this are enabled to unite with the subject of the patient. The nature of exorcism music requires examination, for the quality of its form may indicate what is potential in the patient's experience and, therefore, what is disclosed directly to the patient as the meaning of the ritual world in which the patient is set.

Music and Song

Music and song, which is the musical flow of words, have what Langer considers to be a central feature of all art, ". . . a tendency to appear dissociated from its mundane environment. The most immediate impression it creates is one of 'otherness' from reality —— the impression of the illusion enfolding the thing, action, statement or flow of sound that constitutes the work" (1953:45). This is so for those who, as Hofstadter so aptly notes, are not in the "grip of the aesthetic" (1965:160). Those who are opened up to the aesthetic and have their perception structured by it are nonetheless engaged in a context charged with all the reality the aesthetic composes in its form. The world which is potentially disclosed in aesthetic form is ordered by the way it immediately appears and enters through the senses. In music this is through sound. Music, however, is not sound or even tone but is **made** out of sound and intonation and the dynamic movement of its elements. Its meaning or the possibility of meaning in experience is vital in its internal structure. Music is **par excellence** a temporal art, and I attend here principally to its internal time structure. It is this which gives to music a particular significance in exorcism (and perhaps in ritual generally), which is directed to bringing cosmic forces into play and which is concerned with conducting a patient into the realm of the supernatural and exposing the patient to its transformational powers.

Lévi-Strauss understands musical time to be distinct from that of the mundane world. He states that

> . . . music transmutes the segment devoted to listening to it into a synchronic totality, enclosed within itself. Because of the internal organization of the musical work, the act of listening to it immobilizes passing time; it catches and enfolds it as one catches and enfolds a cloth flapping in the wind. It follows that by listening to music, and while we are listening to it, we enter into a kind of immortality (1970:16).

While musical time may be a synchronic totality and enclosed within itself, it is far from static as explicit in Lévi-Strauss' phrase that "music immobilizes passing time." Rather, music is time in the dynamics of its movement. Music is movement in time.

Musical time has many of the features of phenomenologically described "originary" time and constitutes an objective correlative of time in an existential or experiential dimension. It suspends the time scale by which human beings apprehend time as passage in consciousness through reference to objects in an external world. The objective time ordering of mundane life subdues the quality of time as it is experienced, and it is this quality which may be recovered in music, but made distinctive in the particularity of musical form.

In the phenomenological view, time (and space) is **a priori** the consciousness of it. Time (and space) is foundational of being and consciousness in the world and as foundational, is "originary" time. Briefly, originary time, the "lived" experience of time, or time as prereflective (before it is fixed as an object in consciousness) is a continuous flow of instants, of "nows." These form a unity in a "continuous present," a present which is its "past" and which is even now becoming its "future." Originary or lived time is continuous movement; human beings in their experience of it are perpetually in flight and are not fixed at any moment. By way of contrast, objective time, which always has implicit within it originary time, is a temporality imposed by consciousness. Through this the instants of lived time are interrelated through objects in an outer world and realized as themselves objective pasts, presents, and futures. Objective time is a relentless forward succession through distinct blocks of time. It does not have the reversibility of lived time, of time prereflectively experienced, which projects both forwards and backwards. Husserl distinguishes "cosmological" or objective time from originary time which "is not to be measured by any state of the sun, by any clock, by any physical means and generally cannot be measured at all" (1952:235). The "flux which **we are**" in originary time becomes, in objective time, "a time which we have" (Dufrenne 1973:246).

Musical time is a measured time; its progress is marked in its beat. This beat, however, is the foundational schema integral to the development of musical rhythm. The beat of musical time, more than marking time, establishes intervals of duration. From these intervals of duration and repetitions and variations in them emerges the vital rhythm of music and its dynamic movement. Ultimately, the rhythm of music is filled out in the harmonic and melodic quality of the sound, which also become the quality of the duration and movement of the music (Dufrenne 1973:259-61).

In the music of exorcism, the harmony and melody is provided by the singing, while the drums primarily produce the beat. Occasionally songs are sung without the accompaniment of the drums, but they include the timing of the beat of the drum played prior to them or as voiced by the songsters, and **vice versa.** Skilled drummers are able to play a variety of notes of different timbre and tonal quality on their drums, and thus the drumming itself can assume a melodic quality. Measured time, as a property of all music, is contained especially in the sounded beat of the drums. But this is not the measured time of objective or "clock time" which marks a progression through invariant units of time. In exorcism drumming, the beats change their tempo and produce varying intervals of duration which alter the rhythmic structure of the music. The musical time of exorcism is manipulable and reversible. What Schutz has to say of this in the context of Western music, and of the possibility for the listener engaged in it, seems to me equally applicable to the music which exorcists play on their drums. "The hearer . . . listens to the ongoing flux of music, so to speak, not only in the direction from the first to last bar but simultaneously in a reverse direction back to the first one" (1964:170).

When I state that music has some of the aspects of the originary time of the phenomenological reduction this is not to say, as Langer does, that music is the "image of passage, abstracted from actuality to become free and plastic and entirely perceptible" (1953:113). Music is not necessarily a particular abstraction of the world as lived and experienced, as Langer argues, or a reflection of **duree,** of "inner time" in Bergson's (1910) sense (although it might strike such a chord). However, like all art which is directed to a subject, **music demands the living of the reality it creates.** Engaged in music, a listening subject is opened up to the experiential possibility internal to its structure, its duration, change, and movement through successive and repeated nows, and to a sonorous past continuous with the present and moving to its future. The listener in time with the music is in the flight of its process and perhaps this composes the "kind of immortality" which Lévi-Strauss discovers in the musical experience.

Exorcists understand both the creative moment of the universe and beings within it to be composed in sound. **Om,** the first word of the mantra, is the creative sound of the universe and **ring,** the first drum note is its equivalent. In Chapter 7, I described the rhythms of the drum music as formed in the combination of five basic sounds which are equated with the five elemental substances **(mahabhutas)** of all matter. In their combination is "materialized" the demonic and the divine: specific rhythms, for example, are explicitly associated by the exorcists with specific demons. The style of musical presentation is intended to evoke the mood appropriate to the character of demons and deities, as too should the musical organization of words in songs which describe these beings, their powers, and the events of their myths.

The music of exorcism already cognized in culture as the music of the supernatural, and carrying this association in song, is generative of the demonic and the divine. The movement of music sets the supernatural into the process of its formation. The drum rhythms and the songs as they are presented at each offering basket in the evening watch move from those associated with the demonic to those of the divine. Thus they develop in accordance with the hierarchical logic of the cosmic order. However, they tend to be interlinked in one continuous flow of sound. Although there are shifts in the tempo of the beat as the music changes out of the demonic (the tempo slowing and the sound decreasing in volume), the music can be conceived of as having the one overall rhythmic structure united by the beat. This, and the fact that the music is composed from the same basic set of sounds (and played on a single type of instrument), means that the demonic and the divine, while constituted in the one totality of the musical structure, are essentially in unstable relation. The deity can emerge from a rhythmic recombination of sounds evocative of demons but equally, through a quick combinational change, the music can revert to the demonic. Indeed, exorcists alternate rhythms, moving quickly back and forth between the divine and the demonic. Broadly then, exorcism music creates demons and deities as part of the one totality, gives expression to them as alternative possibilities of it, and produces them in uncertain dynamic interrelation.

The music of the evening watch is largely for the patient alone. Seated on the ground, the drummers face in towards the patient. The music envelops the patient and, through the organized rhythm of its sound, can enter into a direct, and internally experienced, relation with the body. It is in the body that music is heard, and it is with the body that the dynamic movement of the music may be expressed. Musical rhythm, its beat, harmony, and melody as an organization of sound can enter into a correspondence with the inner rhythm of the body. It follows that the supernatural, manifested and perceived in the rhythmic sound of music, can enter directly into and become consubstantial with the body of the patient. In other words, through music the meaning of the demonic and the divine is revealed in the direct experience of them, an experience potentially constituted within the body itself.

What this meaning is, is partly given by the form of the musical medium. Thus the demonic or the divine is potentially experienced as different durations and rhythmic movements contained in the time structure of exorcism music. The instability of a supernatural world in which deities and demons are in violent struggle is also a possibility of the music, for these beings emerge in different relations and qualities of sound and are made present in its reversible world. The oscillation of the musical rhythms by the exorcists between the demonic and the divine can, I suggest, produce an experiential instability in the patient at any moment, for what has passed is also a potentiality of a future and is a potential in the present.[3]

Patients during the evening watch frequently indicate in their expressed action the inherent possibilities of exorcism music and its capacity to become the direct experience of the body. When the demon rhythms are played, patients often move into a quasi-trance, but move out of it with the slower tempo and more varied beat of the music of the divine. Sometimes patients continue to shake, tremble, or appear dissociated and are only brought back into apparent consciousness when the exorcists stop their music altogether.

Music, for those cast into its realm, has the tendency to deny reflective distance. This is so in the capacity of the musical object to enter directly into the experiencing subject and to form a unity with the subject. Reflection, in the sense I use the term, on the meaning of the object is dependent on an act of consciousness whereby the subject can hold the object at a distance and thereby expose it to the analysis of thought. Exorcists command the attention of their patients to the meaning of the verses of the songs. They demand that their patients exercise the rationality of thought. In the exorcist view, individuals, by subjecting the objects of perception to thought, can overcome the illusions wrought on the mind through perception and can reestablish a unity of mind with body, with the mind in the dominant relation. The verses of the songs, as texts, clearly explicate the inferior nature of demons and their subordination to the Buddha and the deities. The ability of the patient so to comprehend this message, however, is limited by the fact that the patient is embraced by the music. While the verses of the songs may hold the patient in a reflective attitude, they also can deepen the direct experiential possibility of the music as a whole. Thus, for the patient, the songs carry the affect of the music and intensify the sense of the demonic and the divine and their dynamic interrelation. Patients reported after exorcisms that during the evening watch they were filled by the fear of the demonic and had difficulty understanding the words of the songs.[4]

Major exorcisms, from the start of the evening watch, develop their course in accordance with cosmological or objective time. The sacred time of the rite is a linear succession of stages ordered in blocks of time which mark the ritual progression of the patient towards a cure. Each ritual event is enacted at a time when demons are understood to be powerful, and also in accordance with the moment when deities are understood to exercise their greatest power. Exorcists reckon the timing of ritual episodes by reference to their own wrist watches or to those of others in the ritual congregation. Traditionally, the ordering of the ritual events is in terms of the movement of the sun and moon across the heavens, the demons gaining strength from the point the sun begins its decline, but weakening as the sun starts its ascent. Demons are fixed in time at particular moments in its linear progression. Thus, specific demons attack at certain times of the day and night. However, by their control over a patient they subvert time and, in effect, are time out of joint. Exorcism rituals, in following the course of cosmological time, essentially rebuild time and in so doing refix demons in time (as well as in space). They reestablish the objective unity of time and also the hierarchy of the cosmic order which is founded in this unity.

The sacred or cosmological time structure of exorcism is time in forward and irreversible movement. It incorporates secular or ordinary social time and is distinct from social time only in the sense that it constitutes a higher transcendent ordering of time. Leach (1961) argues for transition rites generally that they alternate in their development between sacred time and secular time, the former being a stopping of ordinary social time. For exorcism this is never the case. The alternation between different time structures which Leach detects is, in exorcism, an alternation between the "inner time" of the rite — the qualitative movement of time as process and in the experience of its rebuilding — and its "outer time," where movement as the passage through time receives objectification.

In the evening watch the patient limited to the central ritual action is placed in musical time which constitutes the "inner time" of the rite. The patient can be conceptualized as in something like originary time, during which the powers of the universe are in play and cosmic time is in the process of its movement and dynamic tension. Revealed directly to the patient in the music, the demonic and the divine are not held apart from the patient as objects necessarily knowable in reflective consciousness. Rather, they are knowable to the body in their direct presence through the medium of music. The patient located in the inner structure of the rite is withheld from its objective outer ordering, where the relation of deities to demons is clearly apparent. This is not to say that the patient is not made to move towards the objective or outer structure of the rite, ordered as it is in cosmological time. At the end of each offering to the demons, the music and song momentarily stops. The exorcists announce that the demon summoned has arrived and that his illness-causing essence has been removed. The patient is made conscious of having passed through a stage in the curative process, a stage which is irreversible in the objective cosmological time structure of the rite, and the everyday world. But the patient is immediately plunged once more into the inner process of the rite and the objective structure of the cosmic order which the patient is made to experience is obscured. Such an objective view is largely only available to the audience, insofar as they attend, whose members are at the outer structure of the rite and are able to interpret the meaning of the patient's experience in terms of an objective ordering which is also part of their common-sense rational world. The frequent expression by patients of an apparent fear of the world they are made to experience confirms before an audience the meaning of the demonic as this is culturally understood to be the subjective condition of a demonic victim.

The Performance of the Midnight Watch

In the midnight watch, both the patient and the audience are brought together within the inner time and inner structural process of the rite and subjected to a greater unity of the demonic. This unity is eventually broken by the divine, and the context in which the patient assumes a demonic identity begins to transform in accordance with the order of the deities.

My analysis here concentrates on the episodes of the dance and trance and leaves the significance of the drama of the midnight watch to the following chapter. I focus explicitly on some of the aesthetic properties of exorcism dance, its relation to the entrancement of exorcists and patients, and its role in the construction and destruction of a reality in which demons dominate.

Before the dances of the midnight watch begin the audience becomes more directly focused on the central ritual events (see Figure 7). This occurs during the events of the **avamangalle,** which immediately follows the demon offerings. More of the ritual space is used, and the exorcists do not cluster so tightly around the patient and obscure the view as before. The **avamangalle** is generally recognized by Sinhalese who attend exorcisms as an awesome occasion. Exorcists consider that the presentation of themselves as a "corpse" to the demons is dangerous. Such aspects of the **avamangalle** probably contribute to the greater focused attention of the ritual gathering.

It is upon the start of the music for the major dances, however, that the repositioning and refocusing of the audience in relation to the central action is made formally part of the rules structuring performance. Two or three drummers stand at the perimeter of the performance area and beat the demonic rhythms of the dance to follow. These are louder and their beat more insistent than in the preceding episodes, and they flood the whole setting. Music and the context it organizes are no longer at the periphery of other contexts of meaning and action. The sound, tone, and the dynamic rhythm of the music dominates. As the dancers begin, they circle the arena and face towards all those seated or standing at its edge. The whole performance area now becomes filled with the ritual action. In effect, the ritual context of the patient is taken to the audience, whose movement, talking, and card playing comes to a stop. The mood is expectant, for it is part of the general knowledge of the spectators that the full power of the demonic will be manifested — the exorcists and possibly the patient becoming possessed by Mahasona.

The ritual congregation is unified in its common focus on the ritual action, but it is an individuated unity. Individuals are not engaged in the kind of social interaction characteristic of the evening watch, and everyday contexts of meaning and action are suspended. In a way, the members of the audience are made alone and isolated and are in a similar relation to the ritual action as is the patient.

The repositioning and focusing of the audience prepares them for the aesthetic of the music and the dance. The audience, its everyday contexts now suspended, is placed in readiness to be recontextualized in the supernatural world of the patient and placed **in process** with the patient. Further, patient and audience placed in relation through the music and dance are brought into something approximating what Schutz terms a "pure We-relationship." For Schutz, a pure We-relationship (the total inter-penetration of self with other whereby each directly and sympathetically shares the one experience) is largely outside the possibility of the everyday world and, perhaps, is only attainable in love and music. In the social relationships of everyday life, human beings enter the subjective experience of others indirectly through cultural and social typifications, objectified constructs which mediate intersubjectivity, which describe experience but do not constitute experience in its experiencing (see also Natanson 1970).

The aesthetic object, as my earlier discussion has indicated, can enter into a direct relationship with its subject, and the nature of individual experience is given in this relationship. The aesthetic object frames individual experience, sets it in motion, and establishes the context of its experiencing. Unlike the constructs, objectifications, and typifications by which individuals interpret and describe their experiential worlds, the aesthetic object creates experience in the direct experience of it. Those who share in the culture of the aesthetic and are placed in essentially the same relation to it experience the same object, are united in it, and have their relationships to each other mediated through it. This, however, is not to say that they reflect upon or interpret their experience of the aesthetic object in the same way. Nevertheless, to the extent that individuals do reflect in the moment of their experiencing, what they reflect upon in the aesthetic object is an organizational aspect of the aesthetic object itself.

It is in accordance with the above thesis that I consider that members of an exorcism gathering when brought into a common relation to the aesthetic of music and dance are both engaged with the patient in the one context of experience and are potentially united in something approaching a pure We-relationship. That this might be so and that it is generated by the music and dance is perhaps of some functional importance in the curative project of the rite. How the patient experiences the demonic is also directly revealed to the audience. In this, the objective meaning of what it is to be a demonic victim is fleshed out and receives additional validation. Furthermore, the changes which exorcisms are intended to effect are made part of, and authenticated by, the direct experience of the rhythms and movement of music and dance. The audience is made partner in the buildup and flowing away of demonic force in the patient and is made capable of feeling this as integral to its own experience.

The Dance of the Midnight Watch.

The costume of the dancers, marks their bodies as included within and subject to the forces contained in the cosmic order. Their bodies are ornamented with the symbols of the gods and their power, and thus implicit in exorcist dress is the hierarchy of the cosmic totality. The "crown" headdress is interpreted by some exorcists as associated with Maha Brahma, Isvara, and Kataragama, whose authority and powers are at the head. The exorcists wear the ankle bracelets of the goddess Pattini. The items of dress are located at the twelve points of the body influenced by the signs of the zodiac and the planets. The dressed bodies of the dancers, therefore, as well as indicating the cosmic order, also point to its temporality.

If the totality of the cosmos and its unity with the body is present in the dress of the dancers, it is in the dances of the midnight watch that the cosmic order and its temporality is set in the motion of its formation. The movement of dance has been generally described as form-in-the-making (Sheets-Johnstone 1980:36). The dance of exorcism is the process of the cosmos and the beings within it taking form. All the dances are composed out of the combination of five basic steps, which are equivalent to the five sounds of the drum, and are linked to the five elements of all matter in the universe. In the combination of the steps of the dance are created the demonic and the divine, and the movement of the dance sets them in the dynamic and tension of their relationship.

The dances of the **Mahasona,** and the other exorcisms, follow a similar logic of progression as do the music and other ritual actions in the evening watch. Thus, in the view of exorcists there is a movement from the creation of the demonic to the emergence of the divine. In the **Mahasona,** an overriding power of the demonic builds until it is manifested in the masked presentation of the demonic in the **avatara balima.** This occurs simultaneously with the emergence to dominance of the controlling power of the deity, which subdues and repels the demonic.

The exorcists' understanding that their dances constitute the greatest elaboration of supernatural force is a specific cultural recognition of what might be intrinsic to the dance form as a more general phenomenon (see Hanna 1979:114-20). Dance is an extension of music; this is explicit in exorcist theory. It is a visualization of the duration and dynamic rhythm of exorcist drumming, the dancers deliberately matching their steps to the beat of the drums and then moving beyond it in their leaping and swirling motion. This visualization is an externalization of the existential properties of music and is the process of music's being made into an object present to outer observation. Through dance the possibility of that which is internally revealed to an audience and patient through the music is extended before them, and what they may variously "read" in the music as their direct experience of it is constrained to the patterned motion of the dance. In this sense, dance is an objectified interpretation of the potential inner experience constituted in music.

But dance is not an object which necessarily stands apart from those who witness it. Dance, like music, can draw those who are attentive to it into the realm of its creation. I hasten to add that this is not a property of dance alone, but of the unity it achieves with the music. I have commented that the drum rhythms upon which the dance builds are insistent and regular. This is more so than in the evening watch, when the rhythms of the demonic and the deity alternate. The music of the evening watch is also filled out in the harmony and melody of song. There is usually little singing in the midnight watch until the conclusion of the main dances. Dufrenne states that "music, when it makes its form infinitely flexible, nevertheless retains . . . a character of proportion and objectivity which is imposed on the listener. The listener is **before** the melody and not inside it, whereas the dancer is **in** the fox trot, or the regiment **in** the military music" (1973:515). The music of the evening watch has a degree of flexibility which can move the patient in and out of the demonic, a movement which nonetheless is productive of instability in the patient as externally witnessed. The demonic music of the dance, however, loses its flexibility and is dominated by the beat.

The movement of dance spatializes the temporal structure of music; this is integral to dance as a symbolic form objectifying the existential properties of music. Music, of course, has a spatial quality, its volume occupies space, but it does not define or delineate it. This is an aspect of dance, however, which defines the space which music occupies. The spatialization which dance, and certainly the dance of exorcism, can effect is not simply limited to the space, the performance area, already made for it. "A dance creates its own space within and beyond the boundaries of the stage area," states Sheets-Johnstone (1980:54) in relation to Western dance. The space of dance is qualitatively defined in a three-dimensional areal pattern which is continually moving and changing (see also Williams 1978). The exorcism dancers, in the tensional flow of their body movement, in their leaping, swirling, and tumbling, extend the space which they create both vertically and laterally. The space of their dance is above and around the audience. While swirling and tumbling, the dancers will at times brush with the audience and break through them. The spatializing movement of the dance places the audience not so much at its margin, but embraces and includes the audience in the reality dance constructs.

The elaboration of the demonic is appropriate to the dance form by virtue of its externalization of the inner world of the demonic as formed in music and by its capacity to spatialize the movement of the demonic. In these two aspects dance is iconic with the logic of exorcist practice. By the midnight watch the exorcists understand that they have summoned the demons and that they have withdrawn their essence from the patient's body. The demons are now gathered in full force in the midst of the ritual assembly. Dance as the externalization of the existential carries this import. Additionally, exorcists have a concern to present the demonic in the terms of the culturally understood reality of the patient, as a controlling and dominating unity. This is an aspect of the spatializing properties of dance which unify space in movement (the demonic is no longer dispersed and scattered) and which encompass the audience and the patient in the space dance creates.

The motional energy of the body in dance has been described as the primary illusion of dance, which is the illusion of force (Langer 1953:181; Sheets-Johnstone 1980, chapters 3 and 4). In dance the body is made the focus of creative force and is the center from which the energic qualities of force in movement (e.g., in the flexive tension of the body, in the lineal projection of the dynamic line of the body, in the areal patterning of movement) spring and develop in continuous flow. The dancers, their bodies marked by their costumes as the centers of cosmic force, create this force in the dynamics of their motion. They sign their entry into a supernatural world by placing areca palm flowers under their feet, indicating their removal from the mundane. The dancers inhale the demon smoke, inducing the demonic to enter their bodies. They begin the dances by each dancing separately while the other dancers look on. As one follows the other, each of the dancers repeats and elaborates the patterned motion of the preceding dancer. There is a competitive aspect to the dance, each dancer striving to exceed the skill of the other. This creates a generative building of the dance as a whole, and the dance reaches its greatest elaboration when all the dancers are moving together throughout the performance arena.

The dancers are understood by the exorcists and the audience to become one with the forces they generate. They present in the continuous and fluid motion of the dance a cosmic unity in the process of its creation, are virtual embodiments of its force, and, as the dance builds towards its peak as the hour of midnight approaches, are understood to be the demonic and subject to its experience in themselves. Exorcists claim that during the dance they sometimes "see" visions of the demonic. They see the illusion of the demonic and are united with its form in illusion. This receives its absolute objectification in the **avatara balima**, when an exorcist-dancer assumes the manifest form of the demonic illusion and, as regularly presented, enters into a trance. This signs and symbolizes both the identity of the demonic with the dancer and the completion of the demonic, as illusion, by the dance itself.

In the dance, and in the process of appearing to become what they create, exorcists end one aspect of their mediatory role characteristic of their action in the evening watch. While they mediate the demonic through their bodies into the ritual context (which incidentally is a theme of the **avamangalle** episode extended into the dance), they end their mediation between the finite meaning province of the patient and the external contexts of the paramount reality. This contributes to the further decomposition of alternative contexts of meaning outside the demonic and is a factor in potentially reordering audience experience within the terms modeled in the motional form of dance.

Langer draws attention to the power of dance to draw within its realm those who are focused upon it. She cites Mary Wigman's statement that dance has the "magnetic power of transmission which makes it possible to draw other persons, the participating spectators into the cosmic circle of creation" (Langer 1953:207). I have observed this apparent power of the dance in exorcism performances. On a few occasions, at the height of the dance, members of the audience have become entranced and have danced within the performance arena. The overriding of alternative contexts of meaning by the dance, and the fact that the exorcists no longer mediate the ritual action which maintains the audience as separate from the ritual action, reduces the ability of individuals to reflect on what is performed before them in terms of external rationalities, independent of that which they retain or protend in themselves. Exorcism dance can draw audience members into the immediate experience of its realm because it subverts those contexts whereby reflective distance can be achieved and sustained.

The hand, limb, and body postures which exorcists strike in the flow of dance are loaded with the cultural meaning of both the demonic and the divine. The dances typically begin with the exorcists' adopting the posture of Isvara as the Lord of the Dance. The hand and finger positions are those of the Buddha and the deities represented on the images in every temple on the island, but are also those represented in the sculptures and paintings which exorcists make of the demons or demonic manifestations of the deities. The gestures create the sense of cosmic powers in dynamic tension. The flaming torches which the dancers carry, juggle, and touch to their chests communicate the purifying power of the deity but they also communicate a general sense of demonic power. The demonic as presented in exorcism builds its awesome appearance in the fire of the torches. The meaning of the gestures in dance is a property of the whole form of dance. It is contained in the flowing structural unity of dance and the context it develops. This, in the dances leading to midnight, is dominatingly that of the demonic, although the power of the deity is waiting to rise within it. The leaping, swirling, and tumbling motion of the dance, while the extreme of force in movement, is also a metacommunication of the turbulence of the demonic.

By the gestural organization of dance, exorcists strive to present the sense or feeling of that which they present. Exorcists model mood in the dance and state that, as in the drumming and song, the **rasa** appropriate to the fury or sensual character of the demonic should be produced in their movement (see p. 144). The organization of dance-gesture is a "feeling form" (see Sheets-Johnstone 1980:60-63). That is, it is a culturally recognizable modeling of emotion or feeling in relation to which a patient and an audience can cast or reflect what they directly experience in the perception of sight and sound. Dance as a feeling-form, a model for the reality of experience, is essentially what Langer means when she distinguishes dance as virtual gesture from the natural gesture of ordinary experience.

> Every being that makes natural gestures is a center of vital force, and its expressive movements are seen by others as signals of its will. But virtual gestures are not signals, they are symbols of will. The spontaneous gestic character of dance motions is illusory, and the vital force they express is illusory; the "powers" (i.e., centers of vital force) in dance are created beings — created by semblance gesture (1953:175).

The progression in most performances of the **Mahasona** and other exorcisms is towards the conjunction of natural gesture (i.e., emotion and feeling as the direct, unconsciously reflected or prereflective, immediate and spontaneous expression of experience) with virtual gesture (the culturally modulated symbolling of emotion and feeling). That is, the rhythm and movement of dance extends until a point is reached when the virtual gesture of dance is no more simply a symbolling of emotion and feeling, but is the direct and spontaneous expression of the feeling-form which dance presents. The point at which natural gesture appears to overcome its virtual symbolling is in the trance of exorcists and, frequently, of patients.

Trance as a programmed event of exorcist performance is the peak moment in the formation of the demonic and is that point when the object of the demonic enters into direct communion with the subject. Trance is the dissolution of any subject/object distinction, and in exorcism emerges as natural gesture out of the virtual gesture of the dance. It is in trance that the nature of the object as directly experienced discovers its validity, a validity which is defined in the subjectivity of the subject. "The world to which the subject is related, and which is at once his destiny and his own act — like a mirror in which he recognizes himself — is proportionate to his being. Its consistency and reality increase as the subject gains depth and authenticity: We could even say that its objectivity is measured by the extent of the subjectivity in the subject" (Dufrenne 1973:449).

Dance and Trance

Exorcism trance is a structural analogue of dance. That trance also emerges in the context of dance in a variety of cultures indicates that the properties intrinsic to the dance form might be generally productive of the trance experience. With specific regard to exorcism, I argue that trance is a possibility of the structure of the dance context and that when it occurs in patients it marks a transformation into a demonic self. Further, dance is directly productive of trance by its inherent capacity to limit perception and to inhibit the subject's ability to reflect upon himself or herself as an object at a distance from the object created in dance.

Exorcist and patient trance is distinct. An exorcist-dancer almost always appears to enter a trance in exorcism, and particularly during the **avatara balima.**   The onset of trance is sudden and follows the deep inhalation of demon incense, amidst the loud, rapid, and regular beat of the drums. It is often signed by the exorcist's giving a loud roar and rushing through the performance arena. His action is iconic with the cultural understanding of demonic control; it images both the suddenness of demonic attack and its turbulence. While it is virtual gesture, however, it is also presented as natural gesture. That is, exorcists are concerned to present their trance behavior as both a modeling of demonic possession and as the actual and direct experience of the exorcist who is in the role of the demonic. The audience, too, is generally concerned with the authenticity of exorcist trance, and much discussion usually follows concerning whether or not the demon actually entered the exorcist's body. After the entranced exorcist runs to the cemetery place, taking his demonic pollution with him, he then returns to collapse. Before he collapses, he will sometimes grapple with members of the audience and resist the attempt of his fellow exorcists to restrain and purify him. In effect, the demon opposes the controlling powers of the divine, which the other exorcists invoke to end the trance. The entranced exorcist generally collapses on the ground and usually shakes and shudders for some time. This is interpreted by exorcists as indicating the extreme of demonic control and that the entranced exorcist was close to death, the ultimate outcome of demon attack. The "drama" of the exorcist's demon possession tends to be more extreme than the demon possession, when it occurs, of the patient. This is especially so when exorcists do not expect their patients to enter a full trance.

Just over fifty percent of the patients observed entered a full trance. Exorcists do not consider patient trance to be essential for a cure, and a thorough attempt to produce it is usually only made in cases of chronic demonic attack or if patient trance was a prior symptom of demonic malevolence. The possibility of the extreme of demonic attack is already indicated by the exorcist's trance, and the experience of the demonic and its progressive tension is carried in the music and dance. Most patients I observed appeared to be in a quasi-trance at the height of the danced creation of the demonic. Ideally, exorcists seek to constrain the full trance of a patient to that period when the exorcist enters a trance and to the time period around midnight, when the powers of the deity are beginning to increase. A full trance, in the exorcist view, is potentially dangerous to the life of the patient and should occur not only when the demon is at its most powerful, but also at that moment when the power of the deity is about to

take over. It is only with divine power that the demon can be controlled and
the patient drawn back from his or her course towards death, which is the
passage of demonic possession.

The trance of the exorcist and of the patient are often placed in direct
relation, the trance of the former so presented as to induce a trance of the
patient. Thus the exorcist in trance, or in the demon role, will crouch
before the patient, fix the patient in his gaze, and furiously shake his body
in time with the drum rhythm.[5] The intention is not just to model the
demonic before the victim, but to effect a transfer of the demonic into the
victim. Vital connections between exorcist presentation and patient
experience, though less extreme, are a regular feature of exorcist action
towards a patient throughout exorcisms. What exorcists continually strive
to demonstrate is that the demonic or nondemonic possibility of the reality
they construct is also part of the real experience or attitude of the patient.
For example, in the **kukulu pade** which usually precedes the entrancement of
exorcist and patient, an exorcist-dancer approaches the patient with the
cock, one of its outspread wings obscuring his face (see p. 152). The patient
typically recoils when the cock is thrown, signing in vital movement a fear
of the demonic illusion. In the dancer, whom others see as a human being,
the patient sees the demon.

The full trance of a patient is characterized by the patient's rising and,
in time with the music, dancing towards the demon palace. As the patient
does so, he or she begins to fall out of step as the exorcists attempt to
purify the patient and draw out the demon. The patient is prevented from
entering the demon palace, for this, if it occurred, would indicate the
failure of exorcists to master the demon and also communicate, contrary to
intention, that the demon was beyond the control of higher powers in the
cosmic order. The patient, although sometimes violent at the moment of
demonic withdrawal, and occasionally at the onset of trance, often presents
the trance in a way which is fluid and graceful — more in keeping with the
dance than is the trance of the exorcist.[6]

There is a correspondence between full trance in exorcism and dance.
The entrancement of exorcist and patient externalizes and spatializes the
demonic rhythm of the music. The exorcist-dancer runs through the
performance area and beyond to the cemetery ground. The patient moves in
time with the music and marks out the space of the demonic in the progress
towards the demon palace and establishes in this his or her vital connection
with the demonic. Further, the trance gesture is also that of the virtual
gesture of the dance, but now as natural gesture. Dance fills out the
meaning of directly communicated experience and makes it open to common
observance. This is so for trance, especially when it occurs in the meaning
context established by dance, but with one key difference. Trance is also a
condensation and a reinternalization of the outwardly projected space, time,
and vital force of the demonic made apparent in the dance. The diasporatic
dimension of the unified totality of the music and dance of the created
demonic is grasped by the bodies of the patient and exorcist "in one swoop
of the intentional arc" (Merleau-Ponty 1945:164). In the trance, the
demonic achieves its greatest and most intense unity.

Obviously, the correspondence I have noted between trance and dance is
due to the fact that trance develops out of the dance. But, trance, by
taking the form of dance, adopting its feeling-form and realizing the virtual
as the natural, is enabled relatively unambiguously to carry the full weight
of the cultural import of the demonic.

It is conceivable that the process of contextual formation in music and
dance is generative of trance and in accordance with the terms these forms
establish. Most anthropological studies have viewed trance as a state and

have largely confined themselves to describing its internal properties (e.g., Bourguinon 1965; Prince 1968; Wittkower 1970). Trance is described as an altered state of consciousness, a state of dissociation, a state of unawareness, etc. These descriptions are often static and leave us little the wiser as to what this state is and how it is produced. The weight of discussion in this latter regard focuses on specific factors (the role of drugs,[7] rhythm in music, etc.) and isolates them from the overall process in which they are located and interrelated. I approach trance here as both produced in a particular culturally constituted structural process and as taking its character and significance in this structural process. My extension of this approach in the following analysis seeks to explore further the role of trance within the overall curative project of exorcism. Specifically, I address the problem of trance and its relation to the transformation of patient identity and to the patient's experience of self.

Regardless of whether or not a trance occurs, the structural movement of exorcism until the peak moment of the demonic in the **avatara balima** can be viewed as a systematic reversal of the process whereby a self is constructed in everyday life. The logical outcome of this reversal is, I suggest, the trance experience, which is an experience in which the individual can cease to objectify or have a consciousness of self as an object independent of his or her experience. Sinhalese recognize this as an aspect of their trance experience. Patients who entered a complete trance repeatedly reported to me that they had no awareness of their own action or the actions of others around them. Their minds, they said, were a complete blank. Some did comment that the only things of which they were aware were demonic or ghostly figures, experiences which are consistent with cultural expectations. The reported lack of consciousness by patients of course absolves them of responsibility for their actions. Some entranced patients abuse and attack their relatives. However, lack of consciousness in the way patients indicate is entirely possible given the way the demonic is contextualized in music and dance and the way patients and audience are ordered within their context.

Mead's (1934) theory of the self provides some additional theoretical insight into the possible experiential process leading to trance in exorcism, and to the transformational structure of exorcism as a whole as this affects a patient.[8] I prefer Mead's approach to some of the more psychodynamically oriented ones of other anthropologists interested in similar problems (e.g., Hallowell 1955; Bourguinon 1965; Spiro 1967; Obeyesekere 1970b). This is not because they might be any the less valid, but because they are less sociologically oriented than is the one developed by Mead. Thus, many of the other approaches seem to pass immediately from cultural ideas to the inner working of individual psychology, and back again, without much attention to intervening social interactional processes. Mead argues from the position that society is prior to the individual and that the construction of a self is emergent from the interactive insertion of individuals into their social world.

For Mead, the self arises in social experience and emerges in accordance with the individual's ability to treat himself as an object. The individual has a self which is developed indirectly through taking the attitude of the other towards himself as object. More complexly, the self is emergent from a process whereby the "I" interacts with the other, who reflexively produces a "me," the objectified subject "I," or the attitude of the other towards the "I". Mead argues that there is a reciprocal interpenetration of the self with the other, whereby the self intrudes into the other, and the other intrudes into the self. Conceptually, the point of intersection between the self and the other is the "me." The self is constituted out of the interaction between the "I" and the "me," which is in Mead's terms a conversation of gestures or symbols, without which it is impossible to have either thought or a conception of self. The "me" always presupposes the existence of the other.

There are two further points, central to the ensuing analysis, and to the analysis of comic drama in the following chapter, which should be noted. First, the existence of a self implies a distance between the "I" as subject and the "me" as object. Without such a distance the individual cannot enter into himself from the perspective of the other. In other words, the individual is restricted from looking at himself from alternative standpoints outside himself. Moreover, should the "I" and the "me" be identical, there would be no way in which the individual could engage in that inner process of self-reflection or the conversation of gestures which is, according to Mead, basic to conscious reflective mental activity. Second, Mead refers to what he terms the "complete" self, or the fully developed self. This self is constituted out of multiple selves which are structured in relation to each other. The selves which are activated in social intercourse are continually changing relative to the particular social context, and the process of ongoing social experience. The complete self is rarely, if ever, activated in any one social context of experience.

A principal concern of Mead's is with the process which leads to the genesis of a self. The first stage in the process is taking the "Attitude of the Other." The second stage is the development of what he calls the "Generalized Other." Essentially, the Attitude of the Other involves an individual's taking on the identities or roles which others adopt in relation to him — of "father," "postman," "doctor," etc. The Generalized Other develops when the attitudes relating to role others are generalized in terms of social and cultural typifications, and are interrelated so that the individual recognizes the appropriateness of certain attitudes in an unfolding social process, and acts accordingly. The distinction between the Attitude of the Other and the Generalized Other is cogently made by Mead in relation to "play" and "game." Thus, in Mead's terms play involves moving from one role to another without consideration for interrelation or appropriateness. This is an example of the Attitude of the Other. A "game," which illustrates the Generalized Other, involves the recognition of specific roles or identities as standing in particular relations one to the other, the individual adopting or changing roles appropriate to context.

The above aspects of self, which are in a continual process of development and modification, are crucial, in Mead's conceptualization, if the individual is to insert himself or herself in the everyday world of action and/or engage in what Schutz and other social phenomenologists term a "reciprocity of perspectives," which enables concerted social action.

The self, as constituted in the everyday world, is likely to be transformed and potentially negated if processes are established which interfere with or reverse aspects of the above. Critical to the argument I present is the ability of an individual to experience himself or the outer social world of his action indirectly. Both forms of indirect experience are dependent on the emergence of a "me." The loss of a "me" — the ability of an individual to take his own standpoint towards others and the perspective of others towards himself in terms of the Attitude of the Other and the Generalized Other — results in the direct experience of self or other. Such direct experience has the effect of negating the capacity to reflect on self or other or to have an awareness of self or other as objects.

Major demon ceremonies are occasions whereby those who are at the focus of the organization of ritual action and the media of performance (especially the patient) become vulnerable, potentially, to the loss of the objective "me." In the course of this, the individual enters into a direct experience of himself or herself. A process is established in which there is a loss of distance between what Mead terms the "I" and the "me," and, therefore, the possibility of a failure of the individual to have a self consciousness or awareness of self.

Looking at the rite overall, in the evening watch the patient is progressively separated from alternative contexts in the paramount reality of everyday life by action in which the individual can adopt the Attitude of the Other and act appropriately in accordance with the Generalized Other. In effect, the patient is inhibited from adopting alternative standpoints towards himself or herself which are constituted in the outer world of social action, and which can lead to the emergence of a self as a composite of multiple selves, organized one to the other in a process. The patient is confronted with a single and determinate property of self, the demonic, and through the organization of ritual action and the media of performance is relatively restricted from taking an alternative perspective to it, as can the other members of the ritual gathering. The culturally understood and presented demonic attitude of the patient is continually reasserted in the finite meaning province of the patient's context.

It is possible to regard the ritual construction of the demonic (the nature of demons, the kinds of activity in which demons typically engage, the way demons interrelate with other beings) as an alternative, if perverse, Attitude of the Other and Generalized Other, to use Mead's terms. I think this would miss a fundamental aspect of the demonic as this is culturally typified. Rather, it is more accurate, in my view, to consider the ritual construction of the demonic in the events of the evening and midnight watches as the "Attitude of the Subjective" and the "Generalized Subjective." If this is accepted, then it follows that the episodes leading up to and including the major dances establish processes which are directly counter to the construction of a self which can engage in interaction in the everyday world. To an extent, the patient in the ritual is denied everyday typifications and is prevented from having an objective self independent of the direct subjective experience of the demonic. Exorcists and others in the ritual gathering establish interaction with the patient in terms of what they understand the patient subjectively to experience. The patient is acted towards in the ritual as a demonic victim (aturaya), at least until the close of the midnight watch, and other identities which the patient might have in everyday life are suppressed. Such action as the patient does engage in does not demand intersubjectivity on his or her part. Thus the patient is encouraged to interact with others, the exorcists, for example, in the terms of the patient's own subjective experience of the demonic, as this is culturally understood, and not from alternative perspectives on the demonic which others might possess. This permits the patient to become submerged within a personal subjective reality, indeed to withdraw, which is a widely reported feature of the trance process. This withdrawal, especially in the music and dance of the midnight watch, is not counteracted in the ritual by the patient having to come out of himself or herself to engage with others on the terms of their alternative attitudes, or their own subjective standpoints.

I stated that exorcism ritual establishes a process whereby the objective "me" can be lost. This is so, using Mead's terminology, because the subjective "I" of the patient is brought into precisely the same relation to the demonic as is the objective "me." Therefore, the "I" as subject is identical to the "me" as object. The "me," then, is redundant and can be totally incorporated within the "I." Put another way, the fact that there is no real distance between the "I" and the "me" enables the latter to become the direct experience of the former. This is different from the relation between the "I" and the "me" in everyday life, where they are not constituted in the same experience. In the normal social action of the mundane world, individuals stand in different relations to each other and to the institutional structures which order daily life. These different relations are to some extent a property of the "me," formed as it is out of the interrelation of the self with the other. I add here that the consciousness of a self, formed out of the interaction of the "I" with the "me" is constantly changing and being modified as a result of individuals constantly coming into association with others in different contexts.

In the episodes of the evening watch, many of the conditions are present for a loss of distance between the "I" and the "me," but not the total "collapse" of the latter into the former. This is because of at least two features of the regular performance of demon ceremonies. First, the construction of alternative contexts of meaning and action, connected with the paramount reality in the setting of performance, maintains the patient in some contact, if an extremely tenuous contact, with the Attitude of the Other and the Generalized Other. These operate at the periphery of patient perception, contained as the patient is in a ritual context in which the finite meaning province of the dominantly demonic is created. Second, ritual action, and the integration of performance media into it, is such that at regular intervals the overriding sense of the demonic momentarily gives way to the sense of the deity and the pure, and the patient is brought into cosmological or objective time, and brought from the existential immediacy of demonic experience in music. When this occurs, some aspects of the attitudes of others, contrary to the subjective reality of the patient, can come briefly to the surface. A general point here is that the relation of the "I" and the "me" to the demonic is not completely stable and is subject to some modification.

It is in the midnight watch that the organization of ritual action, as it is regularly performed, provides the conditions for the total collapse of the "me" into the "I," and the individual can experience the demonic directly and as being in complete communion with his or her body. This is because alternative contexts at the periphery of the patient's reality are subverted or suspended. Also, it is because, given that the demonic receives its most elaborate development in the music and dance of this period, the patient's "I" and "me" are brought into a stable and identical relation with the dominating world of the demonic. As the motion of the dance builds, alternative possibilities in a cosmic unity are suppressed, only one, the demonic, is elaborated, and demonic trance is potential.

The demonic trance of exorcisms is distinct from many other trance processes both in Sri Lanka and elsewhere. In accordance with the analytical schema I have adapted from Mead, demonic trance is a process of the negation of self through reduction. The multiple selves of a "normal" and healthy individual become suspended and the process of self-construction in the mundane world is reversed. The self of the patient is reduced to a single demonic mode of being, which is dangerously outside cultural constraint. Demonic possession is the emergence to dominance of nature over culture, nature in its disorderly aspect, as the display of aggression, passion, and violence, often appearing in the behavioral display of demon trance.

Other trance processes, for instance, those in which the individual is brought into communion with the divine (I refer to trances at such major shrines as that of Kataragama, where individuals are infused with the sense or spirit of the god Kataragama; see Kapferer 1977b), might be understood, as distinct from demonic trance, as the negation of self through adduction.

Rather than a reversal of the process of the construction of a self occurring, there is a drawing together of the multiple selves of the subject. This is achieved through the heightening of the Attitude of the Other and the Generalized Other in terms of fundamental culturally valued and shared cosmic principles and their summation in the deity. Through this process, which is entirely counter to the process in demonic trance, the individual enters into direct experience with the other and ceases to objectify through a "me" the subjective "I." The "I" collapses into the "me" which is totally subsumed in the other as deity. The individual rises above himself or herself and negates any consciousness of self through engaging in a process by which he or she becomes one with a transcendent other. There is some support for my argument here in the terms used by Sinhalese to distinguish deity entrancement **(arude)** from demonic possession **(yak avesa)**. **Arude** is from the Sanskrit **(arudha)** which means to mount upon or to ascend. This is not connoted in the term **avesa** which carries the sense of intrusion and subordination.

Attention to the above different processes which might occur in apparently the same phenomenon could account for the way in which demonic trance is manifested as distinct from other trance forms. Self-negation through reduction is an individual phenomenon induced by, and inducing, separation from others. This is the typical form which demonic trance assumes. Self-negation through adduction might be expected to be a group phenomenon, which establishes its transcendental aspects by developing a subjective unity with others and above the level of the self. Indeed, trance forms in Sri Lanka which have the deity as their major reference often are occasions when groups of individuals enter the trance process.

I have argued that when the "me" moves into the "I," when what was an object at a distance ceases to maintain distance and becomes directly experienced, this can also involve a loss of consciousness or awareness of self. This, of course, must also mean that the individual will have no consciousness of other. Individuals who become subject to the kind of process I have outlined can potentially lose any sense of identity in a world of action and reflection. Indeed, the loss of a "me," and, therefore, the capacity to reflect, should also involve the loss of an "I." An "I," a minimal sense of a personal identity, whether demonic or otherwise, is critically dependent on a "me." Without the objectification of the subjective there can be no "I."

The direct experience of the object, of the demonic, as this is apparent in the trance of patients in Sinhalese exorcisms, exemplifies what Sartre terms "magicality" (1948:87). This occurs when objects of the horrible come face to face with the individual and then enter directly into the individual's experience. The entering of the frightening and the terrible into the self involves a loss of self, and the action of the body becomes the expression or signification of terror and fear. The subjective experience of the demonic created in the virtual forms of music and dance becomes actualized through trance in the vital movement or natural gesture of the patient, who is not aware or conscious of engaging in this action. Sartre expresses the process, in some ways reminiscent of the scenes of the ghostly portrayed by Henry James in **The Turn of the Screw,** in the following manner:

> In horror, for example, we suddenly perceive the upsetting of the deterministic barriers. That face which appears at the pane — we do not first take it as belonging to a man who might open the door and with a few steps come right up to us. On the contrary, he is given, passive as he is, as acting at a distance. He is in immediate

connection, on the other side of the window, with our body; we live and undergo his signification, and it is with our own flesh that we establish it. But at the same time it obtrudes itself, it denies the distance and enters into us. **Consciousness, played into this magical world, draws the body along with it, insofar as the body is belief.** It believes in it. The behaviour . . . is no longer ours; it is the expression of the face, the movements of the body of the other person which come to form a synthetic whole with the disturbance of our organism (Sartre 1948:86; emphasis mine).

The "magical world" or magicality to which Sartre refers is applicable to the trance behavior of patients and provides a deeper analytical understanding of the patient's move towards the demon palace. It is a crossing of all physical space which separates the house of human beings from the house of demons and iconically models the closing of the physical and mental distance between the object of the patient's horror and the patient. What was object, in one way a "me" distanced from an "I," has now moved through all physical deterministic barriers and has entered into the total and unconscious subjective experience of the patient. The patient can no longer stand apart from his or her own context. As Maurice Natanson observes for the Western psychiatric context (an observation which seems equally applicable to the Sinhalese contexts), the patient "is his situation." What is strange about the patient is that "he is 'not himself,' he is another, a demonic possibility of his being" (Natanson 1974:250). Exorcists often address the patient in trance by the name of the demon in possession, demanding that he release his hold. The power of the demon was demonstrated in one trance I witnessed; the patient bit the head off a cock: the demon claimed its sacrificial victim.

The movement to the demon palace culturally symbolizes the transformation of the self of the patient. It is a move from the patient's house (culture ordered) to the house of demons (nature disordered) and indicates the dominance of the consuming and potentially passionate and violent nature of the demonic in the patient. The exorcists sprinkle pure turmeric water on the patient, "cool" the patient, and touch the patient's head with the **igaha.** They subordinate the demonic to the order of the divine and simultaneously remove the demon from the patient's body. The patient typically collapses (all music and dance has stopped prior to this) and appears to be 'lifeless'. In terms of the Meadian analysis I have adopted, the patient is now not even in possession of a demonic self. The demon removed is now placed in the demon palace, externalized once more, but this time placed in structure, there to await the emergence of the deity which lies hidden within and which will destroy and fragment the unity which the demonic has momentarily achieved.

As the processes leading to the **avatara balima** and patient trance are those constitutive of a demonic self, the episodes which follow establish the conditions for the reconstruction of a self in the normal world. This reconstruction begins in the dances which follow the trance.[9]

The Dance of the Gods and the Reconstruction of the Everyday

The torch **(vilakku pade)** and the arrow dance **(igaha pade)** manifest the dominating presence of the deity. In the **vilakku pade** the dancers place torches at the demon palace, lighting it up and opening it to view. The demon palace is revealed in its full completed objective meaning as not just the place of demonic disorder, but also as the place in which the deity resides. The demon palace is, in a sense, a modeling of the cosmic hierarchy and the demons now located within it are subject to its crushing and fragmenting force. What was implicit in the structure of the demon palace is now made explicit. Its meaning changes, therefore, from a place of demonic disorder to one in which this disorder is subsumed in the higher order of the divine.

During the **vilakku** and **igaha pade**, the exorcists begin to play on the dance form. This is mainly oriented to the audience, the exorcists reducing this aspect when they confront the patient. They hold the patient, therefore, in the power of the dance as they are beginning to alter its form. Metaphorically, the play on the dance is a play of the gods, and through this play the exorcists begin to decompose the aesthetic unity of dance and music in which the demonic was created. The exorcists commence a transformation of the ritual context, which develops throughout the remainder of the midnight watch, ending with the reobjectification of the demonic, stripped of its illusion and revealed in its absurdity.

I described the dance and music preceding the **vilakku** and **igaha pade** as creative of cosmic forces and unifying them in the one totality of dynamic movement and flow of gesture. The dances include the divine within the demonic, but it is the overwhelming sense of the latter which develops. Within the structure of the music and dance the demonic is linked with the divine in dynamic tension. They exchange symbolic significance, the fire of the deity is also the fire of the demonic and creates a general sense of supernatural force. The deity and the demonic, although constituted in different combinations and modulations of sound and gesture, are conjoined. In the overall rhythm, movement, and reversible time structure of the music and dance, each is emergent in the context of the other. The demonic and the divine merge in the total flow of the dance, in which a sense of the demonic is overriding, and their objective relation in the cosmic order, of deities as superior to demons, is obscured and made continually uncertain. While the conjunction of the deity and the demonic in dance and music can be seen as a means for exposing the demonic to the transformational power of the divine, the full meaning of this as evident in objective reflection can be obscured in its experiencing. Indeed, even during the **vilakku** and **igaha pade**, when the divine is understood to be fully apparent, patients will sometimes appear to slip back into trance. What was past in the patient's experience may be reconstituted in the present, for the dance of the deity is composed out of the same basic elements in which the demonic was formed.

The exorcist-dancers, in contrast to the earlier episodes of dance, now in their play on dance commit errors, stumble, and fumble. They destroy the motional flow of the dance and, thereby, its generative and regenerative force. The dancers "accidentally" drop a lighted torch, so overcomplicate a dance movement that their limbs become hopelessly entangled, and, in the middle of a swirling dance, trip and fall. The dancers fail to match their steps to the rhythm of the drums. The gestures of the dance are no more in fluid unity, and the dance-gesture begins to break down into its compositional units. Occasionally the dancers stop in mid-movement to converse with a drummer or audience member. The dancers are not one with the dance and begin to separate themselves from the reality they constructed. Dance is made to shatter its own illusion.

In the play on dance, the moving totality of the music and dance is broken, and the gestures and rhythms of the demonic and the divine are "disambiguated." The gestures of the divine are separated from their embodiment within the turbulence of the demonic. The play on dance so disrupts the musical and dance structure — makes it disjoint and discontinuous within itself — that it ends its reversibility and the capacity of the demonic to take form in the context of the divine, to subvert that which is objectively dominant over it. By breaking the flow, the play on dance stops the process of musical time, which I described as approximating the originary time of the phenomenological reduction. This is significant, for a world in the making is effectively halted at the moment of its completion, at a moment when the deity is ascendant over the demonic and when the demon has been effectively drawn from the patient's body. The divine is "frozen" in its relation of dominance to the demonic. The play on dance prepares the way for a movement back into the irreversible time structure of the objective or cosmological time ordering of the rite, which becomes part of its realizable inner structure and not, as before, restricted to its outer form.

Further, the fragmentation of the unitary structure of music and dance in the play on its form destroys the particular systemic basis of the musical and dance aesthetic whereby they can establish a unity with the subject. The play on dance makes pieces of music and pieces of the dance into objects of reflection more at a distance and less objects formed in the direct and immediate experience of them. The play on dance creates dance movement as an object freed from its subjectivity in experience and prepares the way for the explication of the objective structure of the supernatural world, which has been immediately disclosed in experience, but whose objective order has yet to be explored. Explicitly, the play on dance refuses the complicity which binds the subject to the object in its experiencing, and makes the object independent of its subject. It urges the subject to adopt an objectifying attitude to that which has been formed in the immediacy of sound and the visualization of its movement.

Indeed, the play on dance actively reconstitutes an everyday world and prepares for the reintroduction of its rationalities, through which an objectifying attitude is brought within the ritual context of the patient. This is so in the **vilakku** and **igaha pade** when the dancers begin to converse with one another and members of the audience. It is most evident in the final dances of the midnight watch, the **adavv,** which are also a play on the dance form. In the **adavv** dances, as I have described, the exorcists select members of the audience, the household head, and other individuals of status in the community, for whom they enact very short dance movements in return for cash payment. The receipt of this payment is usually the occasion for jocular comment, depending on the amount given. The **adavv** dances restore an everyday social order in the midst of the ritual action.

This everyday world is not held apart from the patient, as it was in the evening watch. Now included within the patient's context it can, in effect, be harnessed to the transformational aims of the rite. Its introduction establishes a condition for a reformation of the normal attitude, both towards the world of the supernatural and towards the mundane realities which are incorporated within it.

That the order of an everyday world should be reconstituted within a context where the deity is ascendant is metacommunicative of the power of the divine, which both transcends the everyday world and includes its order within it. This contrasts with the demonic, whose reality, elaborated in the episodes of music and dance leading to the hour of midnight, destroys the social order and isolates human beings from their social relationships of daily life. The mundane can generate and maintain its order in the presence of, and through, the deity and be encompassed by it; this is the metamessage of the play on dance.

In the music and dance of the midnight watch the audience was placed in a subjective world largely constituted in the terms of the culturally understood subjective attitude of the patient. Nonetheless, this was a world engaged in the process of its own transformation through the conjunction of the demonic with the divine. The generative structure of music and dance, the combination and recombination of the elements of its form, gave rise to the demonic and then the power of the divine, which ultimately overpowers the demonic. This is made the direct subject of experience through the musical and dance forms, an experience which is the most intense for the patient, who is at the focus of the ritual action, but also part of the potential experience of the audience, which is positioned in the same process. With the play on dance, the audience, and to some extent the patient, is removed from the process, and the foundation is prepared for objective reflection on the nature of the world which has been directly revealed. An everyday reality which begins its reconstitution in the context of the play on the dance form also establishes a context in which the patient can potentially reobjectify a self. This is one of the main significances of the exorcism drama which follows and in which the objective attitude of the other is elaborated in a medium which gives full play to reflection and intellection.   In   the   drama,   the   patient   is   confronted   with   the objectifications, constructs, and typifications of the paramount reality of the everyday world. In the music and dance, a world in its experiencing and in the process of its transformation is directly revealed, but the full objective meaning of this experience is potentially withheld from those who are given up to their aesthetic, and awaits exploration.   The objective structure of experience, how experience should be conceived in a normal and rational world, is a key theme of exorcism drama.

9. The Comedy of Gods and Demons

Wherever there is life, there is contradiction, and wherever there is contradiction, the comical is present.

Soren Kierkegaard, **Concluding Unscientific Postscripts**, 1846

The analysis of comedy can no more be funny than the analysis of water can be wet.

James Feibleman, **In Praise of Comedy**, 1939

The comic drama of exorcism carries forward and completes the transformational process established in the preceding ritual events.[1] The comedy has many features of an "anti-rite" within the ritual as a whole and finally destroys the demonic and unmasks its illusion. Exorcism comedy is an attack on form, and specifically an attack on limiting form; in this it probably shares a great deal with the comic medium in other parts of the world. The comic, the excitement and enjoyment of it, is critically dependent on the recognition of an objective and rational world which is all around it, but which may not be explicit in the comic discourse. An objective world and its taken-for-granted assumptions are bared before the comic. While comedy often appears to defy a rational order, and to break it up and disorganize it, comedy implicitly restores order. But it does so in a way which overthrows any limiting, "over-determined," or restricted perspective possible in the cultural and social world of meaning and experience. The demonic is just such a limiting perspective and, as "irrational" in the normal Sinhalese cultural view, is an ideal target for comedy.

The dramatic form of exorcism comedy is important to an understanding of the transformational role of the comic in major demon ceremonies. I isolate three aspects of dramatic form as these relate to exorcism: (a) drama as quintessentially internally reflexive, (b) drama as subjective distancing, and (c) drama as a discursive symbolic form.

The internally reflexive character of the dramatic form is connected with its typical dialogical mode, whereby two or more exorcists (and sometimes members of the audience) engage in a verbal discourse (and associated gestural action). As the actors develop this discourse, they open up what they do and what they present to conscious cultural interpretation. In the drama the exorcists "reason" the world and elaborate on its meaningful possibilities. Drama comments, through its actors, upon its own process and structures interpretation in its unfolding.

Drama is also subjectively distanced both in itself and from its audience. That is, the actors who perform objectify the world and themselves in drama. They interact with other actors **indirectly** through the objectifications, constructs, and typifications of the reality in which they participate and as they appear to view it. Theirs is an intersubjective world which achieves its process in the different and changing standpoints of the actors upon their own action and the actions of others. The shifts in standpoint or perspective between the actors maintains the action at objective distance from the audience. A drama is **before** an audience and, internally distanced in its own action, creates itself as an object of intellection and reflection for its audience.

The reflexive and distanced properties of exorcism are further facilitated by its discursive symbolic mode of everyday speech. Constrained within the rules of language, ordinary speech is **par excellence** the instrument of objectivity and the organ of common-sense truth. Words, in the speech of everyday life, do not have necessarily precise meaning in themselves, but achieve their meaning through their stringing out in utterances and in the context of use. The context words describe and its meaning as comprehended in thought (which is presupposed by the very engagement in speech) are emergent in what words sign and signify in their relation. Through the discourse of speech, meaning becomes fixed, is made relatively precise, and the connotative potential of words becomes narrowed. Words in discourse constitute statements to the effect that those denoted objects, persons, things, etc. also connote the quality described in the sentence or utterance. Speech, in this sense, is inherently propositional, and through it the truth or falsity of experience and knowledge in the everyday world is discovered. Truth or falsity is revealed in the interrelation within the utterance of what is signified with what does the signifying in accordance with the cultural conventions of language use. For example, to name the Buddha in the context of an utterance which generally connotes filth and pollution and to give the Buddha such a connotation is, in the terms of ordinary common-sense objective knowledge, to establish a relation which is untrue. In speech, a whole range of social contexts within experience can be constituted in a conscious field of awareness without these contexts actually being physically present. It follows that in speech a great variety of ideas and understandings can be "contextualized," subjected to conscious reflection, and so organized that their truth and falsity can be submitted to examination with reference to objective knowledge.

Prior to the drama the connotative quality of the meaning of ritual action is carried to participants, and specifically to the patient, in a presentational symbolic form.[2] The demonic and the divine, composed in the combination and recombination of the elements of sound and gesture of the prevailing media, are made immediately present, as the direct subjective experience of their formation in music and dance. Music and dance **are** their context, and they do not formulate or describe context as something which is outside them. Their context is **in** them. This is their power as well as their limitation. Insofar as experience is constituted within them, they can reveal qualities which otherwise might be hidden in the world as objectively conceived, interpreted, and established at a distance from the direct experience of it. This is an aspect of what Heidegger

(1977:180) refers to as the "unconcealedness" of art (see also Gadamer 1977:213-28). But music and dance as presentational forms only establish context by the immediate presencing of it and, therefore, are restricted in the variety of contexts they can bring and hold together within their performance. While a variety of contexts might be present in the reflective imagination of the listener or spectator, these lie with the subject and are not necessarily a firm and immediately evident dimension of the musical and dance object as they present themselves to perception. Furthermore, within musical and dance forms different contexts or experientially meaningful possibilities of the contexts included within them tend to crowd each other out, or else are fused within their rhythmic movement and gestural flow. Thus a shift to demonic rhythm excludes an immediate sense of the divinity, and **vice versa,** or includes them both so that they become inseparable or indistinguishable within the whole form of dance and music.

The ritual action of the evening watch, and much of the midnight watch, couched in presentational symbolic media, organizes a process within the objective structure of the rite (a sequentially ordered series of events in discursive form) of assertion and counterassertion. The demonic is presented as controlling, polluting, and potentially terrifying; the divine is presented as dominant over demons, purifying, and negating of demonic power. These are propositions underlying the logic of exorcism and determining of its outer structure, the sequencing of its event and action. They are created and made valid through the presentational aesthetic of the rite, which constitutes the process of its inner structure. Throughout the rite the exorcists monitor and "test" the degree to which the exorcism is achieving its efficacy in terms of the predictions reached in the exorcism's objective outer structure (e.g., the **kukulu pade** and the lime-throwing divination, p. 152). But the fundamental objective truth of the propositions and basic assumptions underlying the rite are not submitted to test, and the nature of demons and their relations to deities are not exposed to question. For major exorcisms to achieve their curative purpose, the nature of the cosmic order and the position of gods, human beings, and demons within it must be revealed both in the truth of their experiencing **and** as objective truth. In the view of exorcists, the mind must be brought to a conscious realization of the fundamental validity of the objective order of the cultural and social world of human action.

The transposition from the presentational media of the rite to the drama enables the basic assumptions which are taken for granted in the rite's objective structure to be examined in the structure of its inner process. In the discourse of speech organized within the internal reflexive and distanced dramatic action, the ideas and understandings which are at the core of the rite can be objectified, disengaged from their imbeddedness in presentational symbolic forms, and brought into a variety of new combinations. Moreover, their meaning and validity can be tested by being passed through a number of contexts relevant to human action and experience and made present and brought to consciousness in the dramatic dialogue.

Comedy extends the properties already instrinsic to drama. In exorcism, the comedy establishes the central ritual events and actions in what other scholars have termed a "play frame." Bateson (1973:157) has drawn attention to one of the principal features of the play frame. He argues that its organizing metamessage is that all statements which appear within it are untrue. I would modify this for the comedy of exorcism. Thus, rather than all statements being untrue, the metamessage of drama in a comic frame tells participants to question the truth of all statements appearing within it, that what appears within it has no strict necessity (see

Douglas 1975). Handelman (1979), in a way similar to Douglas' (1975:101-07) analysis of jokes as anti-rites, extends Bateson's argument and contrasts what he terms the "ritual frame" to the "play frame." The former, he states, transforms cognition through the metamessage "let us believe," while the play frame transforms cognition through the metamessage "make-believe" (Handelman 1979:220). Put another way, and in relation to exorcism, until the comedy the process within the ritual context of the patient is the assertion of belief, whereas the process within comic drama is the suspension of belief.

Further, comedy (also jokes and much generally that is recognized as humor and fun) thrives on inconsistency. The organizing principle of comedy is **inconsistency**, as Handelman (1979) also notes for the play frame. This contrasts with the **consistency** which is the organizing principle of the prior ritual events. Thus, in the evening and midnight watches, deities and demons are constituted in the one totality which is internally logically coherent. This is made all the more so through the aesthetic of music and dance, whose own internal coherence further binds the demonic and the divine in the one context.

Exorcism comedy, therefore, in its suspension of belief and internal inconsistency, stands in a relation of overall contrast to the preceding ritual events which affirm belief and which are internally consistent in their logic and organization. In such a relation of contrast, exorcism comedy is also potentially a transformer of the meaning and action developed in the preceding ritual events, insofar as these are introduced into its comic frame. Symbolic articles, ideas, and understandings brought into relation within the comedy are open to radical rearrangement as a function of their becoming exposed to the organizing principles of the comedy. In this, new meanings previously not apparent within the ritual context are likely to emerge. More particularly, comedy thriving on inconsistency also **discovers inconsistency**, and thus contradictions, incompatibilities, and fissures in a world of meaning and experience which previously may have been hidden from consciousness are opened up and thrown into relief.

Perhaps more than any other medium, comedy builds meaning. It goes back to first base, not even taking for granted the fundamental assumptions in terms of which human beings understand their existence, and creates a world anew. As comedy builds meaning, it also destroys it, and this is congruent with its organizing principle of inconsistency. Comedy discovers the inconsistencies in the meanings it constructs. This building and destroying which is the dynamic movement of comedy (which, incidentally, parallels the earlier ritual events in which deities and demons in dynamic tension build and destroy the sense of the other) also gives it the power to form an ever-expanding universe of meaning. It is entirely appropriate to a reaggregational phase in a transition rite of healing, a phase which is concerned both to effect a cure through the broadening of perspective on the world and to replace a patient into the movement and dynamic of daily life.

Comedy lives in the discovery of alternative possibilities, bounces one possibility of meaning off another, realizes them as contradictory and opposed, and attempts to falsify that which we take to be objectively true in the world. Many scholars have noted that comedy reduces. Exorcism comedy reduces **and** augments, and through it the objective hierarchical order of the Sinhalese cosmos is sustained. As the comedy bursts from one meaning context to another, so it forms progressively more inclusive domains of meaning. In this the divine is able to maintain its composure even while comedy puts it to the test. The demonic, however, fails to maintain its unity and is discredited and reduced.

The Comedy of Life and the Drama of Death

The comic acts of the **Mangara pelapaliya** immediately follow the **adavv** dances. I begin by focusing on some of the general aspects of this comedy and conclude with a discussion of the episode of Mahasona's death (**Mahasona dapavilla**) which ends the period of the midnight watch.

In the comedy, the audience is both an attentive observer of the action and occasionally takes an active part in it (see Figure 7). The audience is not apart from the ritual action as in the evening watch, but is centrally engaged. The patient, however, tends to be maintained more at the margin of the comic acts. The exorcist-actors direct most of the comedy towards the audience, and when they turn to the patient at the end of each comic act, return to a mode of ritual presentation similar to that of the earlier ritual events. The comic discourse is stopped, often a short drum rhythm played, and the actor approaches the patient with a symbolic article and revolves it three times over the patient's head.

The **Mangara pelapaliya** begins with songs in praise of god Mangara. His identity as a deity capable of controlling the demon Mahasona is specifically elaborated, as is his dominant position, relative to demons, in the cosmic hierarchy, and, by extension, the dominant position of deities generally. The songs and salutations to Mangara are performed before the demon palace, into which Mahasona is now understood to have entered, and are addressed to the offering platform which is situated above and hidden behind the painting of Mahasona. The songs and actions make explicit what is already implicit in the design of the demon palace. That is, the divine is present within the context of the demonic, but is in a relation of dominance to the demonic. While the action set in the medium of song asserts the power of Mangara, the comic drama which immediately follows questions this assertion and subjects it to test.

The two actors who develop the comic discourse stand in an opposed relationship. The relationship is itself comic, for one is consistently out of tune with the other, as Laurel is to Hardy. The drummer as "straight man" represents "Everyman," a human being in possession of normal rational faculties and not subject to illusion. The exorcist-dancer, who presents the various symbolic articles, represents the opposite pole of irrationality, acting in terms of what is false and clearly not true. This is exemplified in the reading of the document of authority of the **Mangara pelapaliya**. The exorcist-dancer does not recognize the letters of the alphabet, but responds to them as they appear visually to perception — as in his response to the letter **ayanna** as representing a monkey resting on a walking stick (p. 156). This opening comic act might be interpreted as symbolizing the formation of speech and the beginning of reflective consciousness and thought. It marks the transition from action in a perceived world of direct experience to one in which the objects of experience become subject to objective interpretation. This is also the way the comedy begins in the other major exorcisms.[3] It contains the important metamessage of the exorcism as a whole, which is that perception can play tricks and that appearances may hide the objective truth.

The relationship between the drummer "straight man" and the exorcist-dancer is one which heightens the reflexive nature of the discourse, for its regular feature is that the two exorcists engage in mutually inconsistent interpretations of what they have before them. One misconstrues the utterance of the other (e.g., the confusion of **sesat** with **satek**, p. 158). The patterned interchange of misinterpretation creates, I suggest, a consciousness, among the members of the ritual gathering, of what it is that has been misinterpreted, and affirms the proper and legitimate interpretation, even though this might not be overtly expressed in the discourse.

In the **Mangara pelapaliya,** symbolic articles, ideas, and concepts, are brought into impossible combinations of meaning. Such impossibility of combination and juxtaposition is a potential element of comedy anywhere and is consistent with the comic form. Indeed, one aspect of the realization of the comic resides in situations (as in the punchline of a joke) when apparent contradictions, opposites, or inconsistencies are made to exist together in the one context **as inconsistencies** (for example, see p. 156, the confusion of Sri, an honorific, sacred title with Riri, the polluting Blood Demon).

The reading of the document of authority which gives license to perform the **Mangara pelapaliya** names the various acts and objects which should be performed and presented, and immediately makes relevant the objective order of the everyday cultural world. Those which are denoted verbally, then, physically appear as material objects, but they are denoted contrary to what they are in common-sense knowledge and presented as they might immediately appear to perception. They receive connotations appropriate to their new denotations elaborated in the comedy. But these themselves are subject to authentication, and the absurdity of calling them what they are not is exploded in the comedy itself. What I term the comic moment, a point when openly apparent contradictions and inconsistencies are conjoined in the one context of action and meaning, is destructive of the comic tension (see also Koestler 1964). The development of the comic has, as a property of its internal dynamic, the destruction of itself. The "life" of comedy is in its vital and creative tension as it builds inconsistencies into context, and the fullness of its life is manifested when it conjoins and resolves these inconsistencies in the final absurd summary of the process. For example, in the comic reading of the document of authority I recorded in Chapter 7, the tension built as the exorcist stumbled out the letters. The members of the ritual gathering laughed and otherwise expressed amusement at the various jokes and comic allusions. They laughed uproariously, however, when the exorcist drummer summed up the process with, "Don't read it letter by letter, you fool. You must make words of those letters and then read the words." (p. 157).

But in the fullness of the life of the comic moment is also its "death." The comic is reborn in the emergence of new comic tension and in the birth of new inconsistencies moving towards resolution. I will discuss the life, death, and rebirth dimensions of the comic process later. What I stress here is that this internal dynamic of comedy, its rapid movement from one comic moment to another, not only maintains comic tension, but also gives to comedy the capacity continually to expand and elaborate meaning. The movement of comedy through comic moments in quick succession is its creative force.

I have stated that the comic moment is a resolution in inconsistency. Those ideas and concepts which are brought together as inconsistent must be seen to be inconsistent or contradictory. It is here that the blasphemy, ribaldry, and obscenity which fill the comedy of exorcism drama achieve much of their significance. Obeyesekere (1969:204-07) isolates a number of functions of obscenity in the drama of the **Sanni Yakuma** exorcism. He states that obscenity assists members of the ritual gathering to overcome their fear of demons; that obscenity and crude horseplay at the expense of the Buddha and the gods enable Sinhalese cathartically to release tensions arising from their interaction with these "authority figures" in normal daily life; that through this release, inner terrors can be laughed away; and that obscenity is appropriate to the demonic character. All these functions of obscenity fail to delineate sufficiently the role of obscenity in the developing form of the comic drama or to isolate sufficiently its importance within the total process of the exorcism itself (see Kapferer 1975).

Douglas (1975:106), who takes a more general perspective, comes closer to the point. She argues that jokes and obscenity are to be distinguished from each other. In her view, obscenities are intrusive upon social situations, whereas jokes are emergent within social situations and disclose hitherto hidden meanings and structures underlying their ordering. Douglas states that the joke "exists by virtue of its congruence with the social structure. But the obscenity is identified by its opposition to the social structure . . . " (1975:106).

I am in broad agreement with Douglas' argument regarding jokes and consider it to be applicable to the comedy of Sinhalese exorcism as a whole. There is also point to her position on obscenity (for example, the demons who appear in the dramatic episodes of the morning watch — who are considered as illegitimate intruders into the world of human beings, and who oppose its order — employ such obscenity). But it would be a mistake in the context of Sinhalese exorcism, to treat obscenity as distinct from jokes. The various dimensions of the comedy and humor of Sinhalese exorcism drama which might be separately described as obscenity, ribaldry, blasphemy, puns, malapropisms, spoonerisms, etc., all exist together as part of one piece with the "joke form" of the comedy. They create the comic and take their particular form through their organization within the comic frame.

The "joke" of Sinhalese comic drama is that it reveals the hidden structure and order which underlie the creation of the polluting and dangerous demonic world of dominating disorder in the previous episodes of the exorcism. The comedy springs the elaborate trap which an exorcism sets for demons. The obscenity, ribaldry, and blasphemy of exorcism are the means for bringing the "joke" in the structure to conscious realization. Obscenity underlines the joke and gives it force.

Obscenity is likely to be a major element of the joke or comic form when essentially opposing and contradictory ideas, principles, and ways of ordering the world exist together within the one context. Obscenity emphasizes the incongruity of apparent congruity. It accentuates and makes inconsistency apparent, and this can be integral to the achievement of the vital comic moment. Prior to the comedy, the demonic and the divine are conjoined in the ritual process. They work in opposition, are in dialectical tension, and yet can appear to be in harmony. During the music and the dance both are emergent in the other. They appear to spring from the same plane of phenomenal existence. The obscene and ribald humor of the comic drama draws attention to the fundamental contradiction of the demonic and the divine and, by extension, to their constitution at different levels in the cosmic hierarchy.

In the **Mangara pelapaliya**, the objects, the **sacra** of the divine, are passed through the comic drama. They are subjected to obscene and ribald connotations, but they maintain their sanctity, their worth as objects of honor, authority, and power. At the end of each act they are reauthenticated for what objectively they are in such utterances as, "That is the tusker which god Mangara tamed" (p. 160). Shorn of ambiguity by the comedy (which lives on building ambiguity only to explode it) and, by extension, the ambiguity which the divine may have achieved through association with the demonic in the previous ritual episodes, the symbolic articles are reasserted as objects of divine power. Each is then brought into direct relation to the patient and revolved to reequilibrate the humors. Finally, they are replaced on the roof of the demon palace, further emphasizing the dominance of the divine over the demonic.

A common observation concerning fun, humor, jokes, and the comic generally, is that they disorder and disorganize, level and reduce. Douglas stresses the disorganizing aspect of jokes. She also states that they "do not affirm dominant values, but denigrate and devalue" (1975:102). This is critical to her important conceptualization of the joke as an anti-rite, whereby the hierarchy and order established in ritual are destroyed. The comedy of exorcism certainly has the character of an anti-rite, as I have already suggested. But to accept Douglas' position unreservedly, at least in relation to the comic drama of exorcism, would be to overlook some important features of it. The comic drama, as I am sure Douglas would admit, is more than a joke. It is an organization of jokes, of comic events and situations ordered into a process, and it is more accurate to view this process as having a double aspect. It is **disorganizing** and **organizing** at the same time.

Thus the process of the comedy is one of continual arrangement and rearrangement of ideas and meanings, always with reference to normal everyday Sinhalese cultural and social typifications. The sense of the comic is emergent from the appropriateness or inappropriateness of the combination of ideas and meanings, as these are occasioned within the frame of the comic drama. The direction of the comic process is towards the affirmation of dominant values in the Sinhalese world order, and it achieves this precisely through what appears counter to it, denigration and devaluation.

I mentioned at the beginning that the patient for much of the **Mangara pelapaliya** is marginal to the comic action. The exorcist-actors do not direct their comic action to the patient or strive, as they do in the comic acts of the morning watch, to elicit laughter or other signs of amusement from the patient. Nonetheless, the comedy by its rapid movement from context to context elaborates ideas and attitudes of "normal" unafflicted Sinhalese both to previous events in the exorcism and to common occurrences in everyday life. The laughter of the audience at the comic antics of the exorcists not only indicates its enjoyment of the "joke," but also communicates that the members of the ritual gathering share a common and objective attitude towards the world whereby they can recognize the comic.

Many of the jokes and comic allusions of the drama are standard and regular fare in the nonritual everyday world, as is the obscenity and blasphemy. Expressions like **puka** (anus) and "Buddha's Mother," or "Seven Deaths" (a blasphemous reference to the seven reincarnations of the Buddha leading to Nirvana) are capable of quick recognition as humorous and as onslaughts on form. They immediately introduce a sense of contradiction and inconsistency — basic ingredients of the comic — into the drama. Obscenity and blasphemy, as well as standard jokes, are thus key devices in further establishing the comic frame of the drama, the comedy of which is already part of the general expectation of those who attend the rite. Indeed, they can be conceived of as being in the same relation to comedy as is the beat to music; they maintain the rhythm of the comic.

Obscenity and standard jokes are taken for granted objects of humor, and can quickly evoke laughter which outwardly attests and communicates the Attitude of the Other. Individuals in the discourse of the comedy can respond to the comic in different ways and are alive to different facets of its humor. Obscenity and standard jokes, however, have already preestablished, and built into them as form, what is funny or comic about them. Thus they have the capacity to evoke the same response, i.e. laughter, from the audience at the same time; they can unify an audience in an agreed comic situation perhaps more readily than can, for example, a joke or comic dialogue developed originally and spontaneously.

Laughter, or other indications of amusement, at the discourse and action of the exorcists is more than a sign of the recognition of the comic. It is symbolic of what I have previously referred to as a "We-relationship." (p. 191) Organized in terms of the jokes, comic allusions, and antics of the exorcists, members of the ritual gathering **laugh together.** Essentially this unity communicates that what they might individually and subjectively realize as comic is part of the subjective understanding of others. The source of their laughter and the nature of their understanding in the laughter is externally open to view and objectified in the contexts as they are presented to them in the comedy. To laugh or be amused with others is to be one in a community of laughter and amusement. It is symbolic of community, of oneness with others, and is close to what I understand Turner to mean by "communitas" (1969, 1974; similarly on laughter specifically, Douglas 1975:104; Kapferer 1977b, 1979a).[4]

The We-relationship, that strong sense of mutuality produced in the general laughter and amusement at the comedy, is distinct from the unity which is a potential of the elaborate episodes of music and dance. This is obviously so in one way, for the members of the ritual gathering are not united in the demonic. But in another way, exorcism comedy with its emphasis upon reflection in terms of other perspectives simultaneously with the one being presented can potentially maintain individual awareness of self and other. Members of the ritual gathering might enter directly, through the comedy, into the subjective understandings of their fellows assembled at the occasions, but they do not form a unity with the comic contexts or comic characters (e.g., the exorcist-dancer). It is the very fact that they can stand apart and objectify aspects of what is presented as distinct from and independent of themselves which enables them to participate in and to recognize the comic. Comedy, and the awareness of the comic, is a celebration of the Attitude of the Other as this is formed in the rationalities of the everyday world, and it depends on the fullness of an attention to life, what Schutz terms **attention à la vie,** in all its varied and frequently inconsistent and contradictory dimensions.

I have discussed some of the general features of the comedy of the **Mangara pelapaliya,** which also applies to the later comic acts. More specifically, the comic acts of the **Mangara pelapaliya** structurally mediate one mode of appearance of the demonic (the form manifested in the **avatara balima,** p. 153) with another (the form apparent in the **Mahasona dapavilla,** p. 162). In the former manifestation, the demonic appears as an integrated and internally consistent whole, but in the latter the demonic is presented as internally disjoint and inconsistent. Further, it should be recalled that the **avatara balima** marked the highest point in the "life," dominance, and unity of the demonic. The demon in the **Mahasona dapavilla** is shown to be disunited and enacts his own "death." Broadly, the two appearances of the demon mark a transformation of the demonic, and the **Mangara pelapaliya** both symbolically reflects the transition between the two objectifications of the demonic and effects the transformation. Overall, the **Mangara pelapaliya** is a process of transformation within the broader transformation occurring within the period of the midnight watch.

The transition which is occurring is simultaneously in two directions, each the reverse of the other. Thus, the demonic is moving from life to death, while the patient and also the audience are moving from a condition of death to life. This double movement is set in process by the emergence of the divine to dominance and the corresponding control and subordination of the demonic. In terms of the objective structure of the rite, and in the views of exorcists, the physical hold and possession of the patient's body by the demonic has now largely been broken by the withdrawal of Mahasona. The exorcists say that by the end of the **avatara balima** the main curative mantra severing the demon connection have been uttered. Freed from the physical grip of the demon, therefore, the patient is progressing to life, and this is also the case with the audience. In the major episodes of music and dance, for example, the audience was individuated and isolated in the midst of a ritual context dominated by the demonic. They were brought experientially into contact with it and, indeed, brushed with death.

The comedy mirrors in its form and content the reverse bidirectional transition which is occurring. Many scholars have commented on the life-giving and regenerative aspects of comedy (e.g., Bergson 1921; Feibleman 1939; Langer 1953). Douglas (1975:105, 109) notes the death, rebirth, and regenerative quality of jokes in funeral and initiation rites. She also states that "death" and "regeneration" are the properties of the joke form. Insofar as comedy as a form is disorganizing and organizing, decomposing and composing, as I explained earlier, the ideas of death and regeneration are consistent with the comic process.

The comedy of the **Mangara pelapaliya** is filled with reference to death and pollution (decomposition) and to life and purity (composition or recomposition). These are placed in relations of contradiction and in oscillation within the structure of the comic process. In accordance with this, death and pollution on the one hand, and life and purity on the other hand, have their essential contradiction thrown into relief as part of the general enjoyment of the comic. This enjoyment is also constituted in the oscillating dynamic of the comedy, which, for example, converts objects and ideas which in the objective cultural world are normally associated with life, purity, and the divine into their contradiction of death, pollution, and the demonic. To repeat an earlier example, "Sri," indicative of the sacred, becomes "Riri," indicative of the polluting and demonic; an elephant, a vehicle of the gods, the carrier of the divine in religious procession, a symbol of power, becomes reduced to a polluting and powerless state (p. 160).

Death and life joined in the comedy, each becoming the other, underlines a general theme of exorcism, that death and life are constituted in the one totality of existence, are in contradiction, and are in dialectical relation. Their dialectical relation is given particular emphasis in the movement of comedy, and perhaps comedy is a medium well-suited for the conscious realization of this. The continual oscillation, conversion, and reconversion in meaningful interpretation can also be conceived as iconic with a transitional ritual phase, one in the process of transforming the objects and identities which are included within it.

In my usage a transition in status, identity, or object meaning is also a transformation when this involves a rearrangement of the relations in which they were initially constituted so as to form a different status, identity, or object meaning. One aspect of such a transformational transition is the disengagement of a status, identity, or object from one relational set and its replacement in an alternative relational set composed within the same overall relational matrix. The oscillating movement of comedy, founded in its principle of inconsistency, **destabilizes** a status or object in its prior established relational set. For example, the overall movement of comedy, and the general instability of meaning or identity which it produces, is consistent with a transition in process. Furthermore, this is brought to consciousness by the discourse of speech. Comedy, in addition, can focus attention on the fact that one relational definition of status, identity, or object meaning is in contrast to and inappropriate with its alternative. The recognition of inappropriateness is integral to the comic and is dependent on the awareness of the objective rational world to which the comic continually points and, indeed, builds in its movement.

The oscillating, destabilizing character of the comedy of the **Mangara pelapaliya** extends an understanding of its import. Not only does the comedy symbolically reflect the transitional, it effects the transition. It disengages, destabilizes, the relation of the divine with the demonic and from its association with death and pollution, such a relation having been vital to the curative and general transformation of the rite. At the same time, the comedy begins the process of reforming the deity in its appropriate relational set and at a higher level of ordering in the matrix of the cosmic totality. However, while the divine or its objects are in the comedy, their relations and meanings are always unstable and uncertain. This gives added reason as to why the comic discourse is stopped at the end of each act, for this halts the oscillating and destabilizing comic process and fixes the respective symbolic articles, and by extension the deity, in its true objective position of dominance in the cosmic totality. At the same time, life, a force of the deity, dominates over death. This objectivated assertion, tested and authenticated in the comedy, prepares the way for the destruction of the demonic. Demons are disordered, decomposed, and fragmented by the higher ordering of the divine, in accordance with the hierarchical principle of the Sinhalese cosmos. This, as we shall see, is objectified in the second appearance of Mahasona. The objectification of the divine in terms of a rational cultural order brings forth a reobjectification of the demonic, which finds its constitution in the same rationality.

The comedy of the **Mangara pelapaliya** also moves the patient and the audience towards life and away from death. I have already discussed the point that the audience is no longer individuated and isolated. The comedy reestablishes the everyday typifications and constructs which are the basis of intersubjectivity and concerted social action. The audience shares in this mutually agreed upon world and indicates its unity with it by enjoyment and laughter.

The awareness of a living reality of everyday life, which is vital in the recreation of normal rational perspectives, is also produced by the comedy as a nonlimiting form. The comic discourse of the **Mangara pelapaliya** erects restricted frameworks of meaningful interpretation, and then explodes them in the comic moment which is a realization of the restriction. By this the comedy expands meaning, and as it does so the diverse realities of everday life become apparent in it. Thus a sacred document of authority becomes the basis for reference to tourism, ablution habits, the lack of leisure of the working class, funerals, astrology, gambling, and so on (see p. 156). As if to underline further a return to life, the comedy makes death and pollution the butt of its jokes, effecting a further subjective distancing from the sense of death present in the earlier ritual episodes. The exorcists make absurd commentary on the awesome events of the **avamangale**, during which the demonic as devourer was summoned, and they make absurd reference to the elephant as an object of sacrifice (p. 160).

The full effect of the comedy and of the objectified world formed within it is realized in the events which follow the **Mangara pelapaliya**. These (the **Kalu Vadi paliya** and the **Mahasona dapavilla**) are performed without dialogue. The sense of the comic extends to them, but it is devoid of its oscillation produced by comic discourse.

Mangara, authenticated in the comedy, is a hunter and killer of demons. Metaphorically, Mahasona and Mangara cannot live together in the one "house," and this is symbolized by Mahasona's leaving the demon palace. But before he does so he is sought out by Kalu Vadi, the servant of Mangara and a demon searcher. The **Kalu Vadi paliya** models the power of the divine and what will shortly happen to Mahasona. An exorcist-actor in the guise of Kalu Vadi "discovers" the demon in the cock lying before the patient and eventually succeeds in striking it with an arrow, the **igaha**, the powerful and demon-destroying weapon of Isvara, and the symbol of the controlling authority of the demon lord, Vessamuni (p. 162).

Mahasona appears immediately at the end of the **Kalu Vadi paliya**. This appearance of Mahasona reveals what was previously hidden from perception in the manifestation of Mahasona in the **avatara balima**. The mask of the **avatara balima** is a highly abstract symbolic representation of the demonic which obscures in its abstraction the demonic as concretely and objectively described in the ordinary world. It is the objectification of the demonic illusion in the powerful form of its culturally understood manifestation to a patient.

In the second appearance of Mahasona, however, the demon is presented in his fully revealed, true and objective form — as he should be seen by the normal and nonafflicted. Mahasona is a filling out of the form represented in the painting of Mahasona placed at the front of the demon palace. He comes from the palace in the fullness of his ambiguity, mirroring in form his essential absurdity and his terrible potential. His head, as the relevant myth concerning his origin relates, appears to be set on his shoulders back to front. His body is misshapen. The parts seem to be out of tune with the whole, quite unlike the earlier manifestation of the demonic, in which the relation of mask to body and to movement appear to be in harmony each with the other. Mahasona revealed in his actual and completed form is like the liminal, monstrous, but internally inconsistent figures described by Turner (1967).

In effect, Mahasona, appearing as he actually is, is unmasked. As exorcists and healthy others understand it, the demonic is frightening in the illusion of its terrible and fearful aspect. To break the illusion is to end much of the control and power which the demonic can apparently achieve over human beings through its mastery of the illusory. The appearance of Mahasona in his true form, then, ends much of his power, and the loss of the mastery of the illusory is one of the symbolic aspects of the enactment of his death.

Revealed in his proper aspect, Mahasona is objectified before the patient. He is no longer the objectification of the patient's subjective understandings, as these are culturally understood. Mahasona is now objectified largely in accordance with the Attitude of the Other, with his typification in everyday life. He is presented in terms of how healthy others see him and not in terms of the patient's own restricted and limited subjective view. Mahasona, disjoint and out of proportion, combines in inconsistent relation absurd and terrifying qualities, and in this sense reflects upon himself. Mahasona's internal reflexivity of form, essentially a form in unstable relation within itself, is a factor, I suggest, which makes him into an object at subjective distance and inhibits the degree to which he can enter into direct and immediate unity with those he confronts. As he reflects upon himself, he creates the condition for those to whom he is fully revealed also to reflect upon him, and at a distance from themselves.

While Mahasona is revealed as he should be objectively conceived, this is initially so only before the members of the ritual gathering. The entry of the demon into the arena is obscured from the patient's view by the holding of the white cloth in front of the patient (see p. 162). By and large the patient can perceive the demon only through the sense of sound, in the loud drumming which announces his entry, and in the cries and howls of the demon as he emerges from the palace. The patient somewhat dimly perceives the demon through sight in the gusts of burning **dummala** which billow above the performance arena. The patient is presented with a limited perspective on the demonic, and therefore is potentially thrust back into his or her own subjective world. Often the patient begins to shake and tremble — indications of a movement into trance.

The reaction of the patient contrasts with the attitude of the members of the audience. The mood of the comedy of the **Mangara pelapaliya** continues to prevail among them, and this is assisted by the full appearance of Mahasona in his inconsistent, fully concretized form before them. Some will stroke his hair and caress his body as he moves towards the patient. The stealthy creeping of Mahasona towards the patient has most of the ingredients of a joke, with the patient as its butt. The audience is made aware of the inconsistency in Mahasona's presentation and is not subject to the illusion. The patient, however, is set in the illusory reality of Mahasona's terrifying aspect. The members of the gathering often laugh when the patient cries out in apparent alarm, or otherwise recoils in apparent terror, when Mahasona finally bursts through the cloth and nuzzles up to the patient. Relatives of the patient, and others in the audience, will urge the patient to see the demon as they see him, for Mahasona is now revealed in his concreteness. In other words, the patient's relatives and others urge the patient to see the joke and to adopt their attitude towards the demon. The essential joke of the event is further underlined when the demon falls "dead" on the mat before the patient; male relatives of the patient who carry the demon away howl in clearly accentuated cries of mock mourning.

The comedy of the **Mangara pelapaliya** authenticates the divine by its questioning. In so doing, it reintroduces the rationalities of the culturally objective everyday world, and thus establishes a condition for the breaking of the demonic illusion. It broadens perspective and expands beyond a limited reality of the supernatural constrained within the solipsistic subjective attitude of the patient. The attitudes of others towards the divine, the world of daily experience which the deity can transcend, and the demonic are all exposed to conscious reflection. The patient is drawn to a reality as others see it, and in the **Mahasona dapavilla** is impelled to adopt their objective attitude. The killing of Mahasona signs the death of the relevance of the patient's own subjective attitude towards the demonic. The comedy, insofar as the patient can become subjectively distanced from himself or herself, and can reconstitute self as an object and through the attitudes of others, has a potential curative power. This is a possibility of comedy itself as it opens the actions, ideas, and objects which it organizes to a fullness of conscious reflection. I discuss this more fully in relation to the comedy of the morning watch.

I stressed the comedy of the **Mangara pelapaliya** as reflecting a transition in process and as integral in effecting that process. The comedy of the **Mangara pelapaliya** is related structurally and directly to Mahasona's reobjectification, and the **Mahasona dapavilla** symbolizes both the general import of the comedy in which the deity was confirmed and the death and regeneration quality of the comic form itself. Mahasona's shape in appearance is homologous with the form of the comedy which preceded his entry. He represents in himself the inconsistency of the comic and its revelation of contradiction. Moreover, his disjointedness is metacommunicative of the fragmentation of the demonic when confronted with the deity. Mahasona is in the process of dissolution even before he completes it by taking his own life. Emergent from the life of comedy, and finding himself in an objective world brought to life by the comedy, Mahasona begins his decomposition and moves towards death.

The Comedy of Demons: The Morning Watch

While the deity has been restored to its proper position of dominance, the demonic has yet to be tested and shorn of the ambiguity it still retains. The main demon is dead, but the reason for this death has not been fully revealed to consciousness. The morning watch completes as one of its themes the reobjectification of the demonic, confirms the demonic absurdity, and destroys the demonic as powerful and relevant to normal experience in daily life.

My analysis of the comic acts of the morning watch assumes much of what I have already argued in relation to the **Mangara pelapaliya** and extends upon it. I focus explicitly on the transformation of the demonic: in particular, on the way the comedy of this period establishes demons as not only inferior to deities, but also as inferior to human beings. It is in the comedy of the morning watch that the joke which previously lay hidden within the structure of the exorcism, in the organization and media of performance, is thoroughy revealed. Demons are shown to be out of place in the everyday world of human beings. Moreover, they are demonstrated as victims of their own illusion of dominance and control, tricked by their own artifice. The demons as tricksters are revealed as subject to the trick and, therefore, subordinate to those whom they sought to delude.

The death of Mahasona is followed by a long break **(Maha te)** which, depending on the amount of time available (exorcists are concerned to finish the ritual by sunrise or shortly after) is between half an hour to an hour. Refreshments are served to the exorcists and to members of the ritual gathering. The break is highly significant, for while the comedy of the previous episodes created the everday in the comic, the break actualizes the contexts of the everyday. Gossip groups, broken up during the midnight watch, re-form. Individuals move around the performance arena, share daily news, and perhaps go inside the house. The ordering of everyday life reemerges firmly in the actions and movements of members of the audience.

The beginning of the morning watch is heralded by a loud drumming, followed by the entry of Pandam Paliya (the torch bearing apparition), the first act of the **Ata paliya** (see p. 168). In these actions he demonstrates his terrifying character as a being of disorder. But he also betrays his absurdity. He walks around the arena half bent over with his behind exaggeratedly protruding. (I have witnessed occasions when a member of the audience has laughingly given it a resounding slap.) He occasionally stumbles. Pandam Paliya is ridiculous in his very grossness. The Pandam Paliya act concludes with the patient presenting the demon with an offering, in return for which the demon is expected to remove any illness due to his agency. This is repeated for all the demons to follow; unlike the other demons, however, Pandam Paliya, leaves the arena as he entered it, without undergoing any change.

The most important feature of Pandam Paliya as with the appearance of Mahasona before him, is that the demon does not engage in any dialogue with the exorcist "straight man." Pandam Paliya merely postures, and thus the demonic retains some of its ambiguity and terrifying potential. For the demonic to be totally destroyed, all ambiguity concerning its relation to human beings and its position within the cosmic order must be removed and the demonic fixed firmly in its objectively known inferior position and placed unquestioningly outside the community of human beings.   The demonic must be destroyed as a "symbolic type" of domination and reordered as a symbolic type of subordination and pollution.

The concept of symbolic type is important for understanding the transformational process of the morning watch. But I also contend that it is of potential value in the analysis of ritual transformation in general (see also Handelman 1978, 1979; Handelman and Kapferer 1980; Ernst 1978; Kapferer 1977b, 1979a, 1979b). Grathoff (1970), following Klapp (1949), defines a symbolic type as being constituted below the level of social roles as they are usually described. Thus, unlike social roles, symbolic types are characterized by highly stereotyped action patterns, they do not have their role correlates (e.g., father/son, student/teacher) which are emergent in reciprocal face-to-face interaction, and most importantly, because they are not roles, they cannot be modified in a process of mutual interaction. Symbolic types, of course, have their counterparts, as in demon/deity, but these are abstractions, reifications, constituted outside the reciprocal typificatory schema of ongoing social action in the everyday world. Symbolic types, like demons for much of an exorcism ritual, do not engage in mutual interaction with human beings. The patient, exorcists, and others might engage in interaction with the demonic (they give offerings to the demons in exchange for which the demon is expected to relinquish his hold), but in this interaction with the demonic as symbolic type, the demonic is not modified. The demonic might be withdrawn from the patient's body and/or repelled, but the demon as type remains basically unchanged. Rather, as I have described, it is the patient, exorcists, and others who come into relationship with the demonic who become modified, and modified in demonic terms, not **vice versa.** In everday social interaction between role partners each becomes progressively modified in terms of the other through, for instance, the mutual awareness that each possesses multiple identities which are potentially relevant in their interactions.

The fact that symbolic types are restricted in the degree to which they can be modified in a process of mutual tending means that they place limits on interaction in the contexts in which they appear. They reduce the field of relevant understandings whereby individuals come to comprehend the context in which they act. Symbolic types define contextual relevances and link them together, subsume them, within their own form. The symbolic type of FOOL makes the context of action a foolish one. Similarly the symbolic type of GOD makes the context a sacred one, as does the symbolic type of DEMON make the context demonic, and so on.

Grathoff (1970:122) argues that symbolic types are likely to emerge in contexts of social inconsistency, or where some typificatory scheme fails to maintain a unity of context. Rituals, often performed at times of cultural and social inconsistency (at times of seasonal and life transition) or occurring in situations of disjunction in the cultural, social, and personal fabric, are occasions when symbolic types can be expected to emerge. Symbolic types determine contexts and force a unity upon them in the terms of their type. Emergent in ritual, they extend to it a further capacity to unite individuals within the one context of meaning and action.

The diagnosis and definition of demonic illness unites the experience of the patient and others in the meaning context of a demonic symbolic type which is a unity of disorder. A disorder in personal experience and in a wider social world is rendered coherent and meaningful by the demonic. By attacking the symbolic type of demon as a controlling agent of illness and transforming it as type into another possibility of being (one which is incapable of achieving a unity of context in which human beings are engaged and as weak and subordinate to human beings) exorcism can potentially end the basis upon which a patient can maintain a "sensible" demonic understanding of experience. Demons reobjectified as absurd and grossly inferior to human beings have their legitimacy as agents of illness removed. Insofar as the demonic and its construction as a dominant symbolic type uniting all in its presence **in itself** constitutes the illness, the destruction of the demonic in this mode and its reordering as type can be conceived as in itself a cure.

The symbolic type of demon (and any symbolic type) becomes subject to transformation when the conditions for its constitution are subverted. In exorcisms the symbolic types of demons are constituted under three conditions. First, they are formed in an already delimited context which is separated from the everyday world and are not made to unite in their form its multiple and changing realities. This is further effected by the internally consistent performance media of music and dance in which the demons "appear." These give to the demonic its own particular consistency and enable it to unite context as well as to unite with it. Second, a condition of demonic formation is abstraction. Demons are not constituted as concretely graspable figures (the painting of Mahasona being the exception), but, formed in the music and dance, "appear" directly and immediately in experience. Furthermore, they are fluid and moving, continually changing in context but in overall consistency with it. The elements from which the demonic is formed in music and dance are capable of achieving different combinations as a function of alterations in the organization of rhythm and gesture. But these combinations and recombinations do not transform the type of demon **per se**, and certainly not as a graspable object exposed to reflection at a distance. In addition, the demonic is enabled to fuse with the deity, for both are constituted in the whole form of music and dance, which, like an abstract painting, creates the combination and recombination of elements as consistent within and given to the whole form. The more graspable figure of the demonic in the **avatara balima** is an abstract, fluid, and moving form. The relation of mask to body and to gesture is harmonic, and any shifts in the mode of presentation are maintained as consistent within the whole form. The final condition of the formation of the demonic symbolic type is that it does not take on any role whereby it can be modified in a process of mutual interaction. Demons are mediated through the intermediary role of exorcists or directly in the music and dance, where they are not held apart as objects exposed to the logic of discourse.

Demons become vulnerable to a transformation of type when these foregoing conditions of their existence in ritual are subverted. Thus the introduction of contexts of meaning and action hitherto external to the rite during their formation must force them, if they are to subsume and unify contextual relevance to their type, to include these contexts in their type or to transcend context and thereby assert dominance by such transcendence. The latter in terms of my argument should enable a maintenance of type, whereas the former may threaten a transformation. The second appearance of Mahasona demonstrates this, for he incorporates the changed principle of inconsistency elaborated in the comic into his type, and thus transforms into an internally inconsistent symbolic type and not a consistent type as before.

Similarly, the presentation of the demonic in a nonabstract form exposes it to transformation. Thus Mahasona, Pandam Paliya, and all the demons which subsequently appear in the drama are introduced as concretized, graspable figures. Most important, their masks are relatively fixed forms and do not have the unity and elasticity of the mask in the demonic presentation in the **avatara balima**. In Bergson's (1921:37) sense they are "something mechanical encrusted on the living," and are inherently comic. This quality of the demon masks communicates the normal cultural view of the demon as essentially a limited and limiting form. The fixity of the mask creates not only a sense of the disjointedness of the demon body, but inhibits the degree to which the demon can change "face" in accordance with changes in context and, therefore, unify with context.[5]

We are now in a position for understanding the transformational reobjectification of the demonic during the morning watch and the important role of comedy. The comedy elaborates ideas, understandings, and contexts of meaning and action around the demons who are concretized, nonabstract, and fixed in form. The demons become determined rather than determining, for they enter into interaction and discourse with human beings and become subject to modification in this interaction. In the comedy, the demons are shown to be incapable of unifying context or unifying with it. The contexts of meaning and action constituted in the comedy spiral out of their control. The demons are reduced in the world of human beings and unlike the deity cannot transcend it or even reconstitute themselves within it. They are returned to a level below the cultural world of human beings and are reestablished as the filthy, polluting, and stupid creatures they objectively are.

The exorcist-actor in the guise of the various demons which follow Pandam Paliya makes his demons assume social roles or role types drawn from daily life and combines these with the presentation of the demons as symbolic types indicated by their masks and dress. The role each demon assumes in discourse is made to reflect on the demon's outer appearance. In this the terrifying possibility contained in the outer form of the demonic, which may be perceived as consuming, dominating, and fierce, is made absurd in the context of demonic talk. The exorcist "straight man" shows demons as, indeed, they declare themselves to be, irrational and totally incapable of behavior appropriate to the cultural and social typifications of the ordinary everyday roles they assume. The comedy which brings the demonic inconsistency to realization paradoxically, however, reorders the demons as totally consistent with an alternative symbolic typification which is implicit, if not already explicit, in their outer appearance. Demons in their grotesquerie, with their huge gleaming teeth and curving tusks, matted hair, "faces" contorted and fixed, and general disheveled appearance, are absurd, distorted, and out of balance in themselves. They are objects of disorder, and this fits with the irrationality, filth, and obscenity of their talk. In other words, through the medium of comedy the demons are changed from dominant, if disordered, symbolic types to the symbolic type of the ridiculous and subordinate.

The social roles or role types which the demons assume are many. Kalas Paliya (Cloth-bearing Apparition) is presented as a pure and virginal young girl looking for her lover, but has this modified in discourse by the drummer "straight man," who calls her a whore and a slattern. Gulma Sanniya (Stomach Worm Demon) assumes the role of a pregnant woman (p. 174). Maru Sanniya (Death Demon) is a bus traveler. (I observed one performance in which Maru Sanniya actually boarded a bus, which had conveniently stopped nearby the exorcism house, to the great astonishment of the passengers!) In their roles, demons try to be the dominant partner. For example, Salu Paliya addresses the drummer "straight man" by the familiar and endearing term for child, or, in this context, son (**puta**), implying a father (demon)/son (drummer) role relationship. This becomes progressively modified in the course of the brief interchange so that the nature of the relationship becomes reversed, with the drummer in the superior role of "father." Gulma Sanniya, after being addressed as "son" by the drummer, tries to assert his superiority by assuming the role of "elder brother" to his "younger brother," as he calls the drummer. The absurdity of this is exploded in the fun and humor generated by the thought of such a relationship.

In these interchanges, and others similar to them, human beings are placed in a relationship of superiority to demons. Demons give the drummer offerings. The joke here is that it is clearly the opposite of the practice through the entire rite, when human beings give offerings to the demons. The comic discourse involves the drummer's ensnaring the demons in clever wit and repartee and making them the butt of the comedy. The drummer plays tricks on the demons (see Gulma Sanniya episode, p. 173), and caught on a rise, the demons reveal themselves as pathetic figures, and they howl and cry at the insults and obscenities hurled at them.

The demons break all manner of cultural and social convention. The straight man reveals Maru Sanniya as someone who steals ration books, who defecates and urinates on temple grounds, who shaves his head to impersonate a Buddhist monk. Kendi Paliya farts as he stumbles around the arena and drinks the pure water from the sacred pond. The demons confuse words and find difficulty in talking everyday Sinhala.

Demons are shown to be without the cultural knowledge to act in the society of human beings. Kendi Paliya says that he knows that the water he carries purifies and cures. But he bungles the mantra and botches the appropriate ritual procedure. Like other demons he fails his cultural test (p. 169).

The demons are made to be inferior to human beings and also to deities. In the **Ata paliya**, the demons "play" with the symbolic articles of divine and human power. Salu Paliya converts the protecting and purifying cloth curtain, the **kadaturava**, into a shawl and a cinema screen. He doesn't know that it symbolizes the power of the Buddha and also that of Pattini. A demon carries the **igaha** disrespectfully under his armpit and pointing to the ground, instead of over his shoulder and pointing up, the ritual mode of its carriage in the prior events. Kendi Paliya befouls the purity of the water he carries. The actions of the demons are symbolic of their inversion of the unifying principles of the cosmic hierarchy, but such inversion is not powerful and threatening as before. The demon "play" destroys any sense of awe which may have surrounded the demonic in the earlier ritual episodes and which the symbolic articles they carry were instrumental in forming. In a way the demons, by divesting the symbolic articles of their power, also divest themselves of power. At the end of each act the demons sign their subordination to the symbolic articles and recognize that they are objects for their own control. They shuffle absurdly away.

Demons are weakened in the comedy. The become almost benign. Each of the **sanni** demons, for example, agrees to remove any illness he may have caused, and some demons even deny that they had any malevolence towards the patient at all. In the comedy they are presented as a succession of symbolic types of the demonic, each failing to unify context, and each becoming fixed in its alternative mode of absurdity and weakness. They are made thoroughly unambiguous figures of fun.

While the concluding acts of the **Dahaata paliya** are for the **sanni** disease-spreading demons who are not conjured at the start of the **Mahasona** (though in the **Sanni Yakuma** they are summoned in the period of the evening watch), these acts stand in an interesting structural relation to the earlier ritual events of the evening watch leading to the **avatara balima** of the midnight watch. In these prior ritual events the major illness-causing demons were summoned separately. Their illness was withdrawn from the patient, but the demonic remained in the ritual context. The overpowering sense of an unfragmented demonic unity was built in the music and dance, reaching its final realization in the **avatara balima**. The comedy of the

Dahaata paliya is a total reversal of this. In the comedy, a demonic unity is decomposed into its independent units and, furthermore, these parts are made inconsistent within themselves, in effect, fragmented. This is iconic with the project of exorcism as a whole, which is to fragment the demonic and to break the powerful unity which demons can achieve. The comedy destroys each of the demons in turn, and it attacks the elements upon which a powerful unity of the demonic can build.

The final act of the **Dahaata paliya**, the appearance of Deva Sanniya, is a symbolic statement of the demonic as a fragmented unity. This is represented in the mask of Deva Sanniya, which is presented in most performances. Modeled upon it are miniaturized representations of the eighteen **sanni** demons, indeed a unity in fragmentation. The act is very brief and accompanied by no dialogue. The symbolic type of the demonic is restored, without a role and moving towards abstraction, but in its proper objective mode as an internally differentiated inconsistency, or a consistency of inconsistency. An additional aspect of the Deva Sanniya act is the symbolic metacommunication of the disordering of the demonic as a function of its replacement within the cosmic hierarchy. Deva Sanniya is understood by exorcists to be high in the ordering of the demon world and close to being a deity. Some say he is associated with Pattini. It is reasonable to interpret his appearance as the restoration of hierarchy surmounted by the divine and as indicative of the control of demons and their subservience within the hierarchy. When Deva Sanniya and all the other demons presented in the comedy leave the arena, they give homage to the patient and place offerings at the top of the **kapala kuduva**, they sign the cosmic order implicit in its structure (see p. 114). The Deva Sanniya act fixes the demonic in a mode shorn of ambiguity and clearly subordinate. In this sense it contrasts with the opening act of the Dahaata Paliya comedy, the act of Pandam Paliya, in which the ambiguity of the demonic, its terrible potential, was retained.

Following the Deva Sanniya act, the demonic once more appears in its abstraction in the enactment of the **dekone vilakkuva** (double torch). The episode is performed with none of the power of the **avatara balima**, and is the final dispersal of the demonic (see p. 175). It is enacted perfunctorily. One exorcist group, who extended to me the great pleasure of observing their performances, usually gave this act to a young boy of twelve who was in training to become an exorcist.

With the final demonic dispersals, the domination of the Buddha and the gods in the cosmic hierarchy is then given absolute assertion, with the exorcists and the patient giving homage to the Buddha and the Guardian Deities — female patients walking in procession to the **mal yahanava** (Chapter 7).[6]

Overall, the exorcism models a process of the rebuilding of the cosmic order. Starting in the evening watch, the exorcism progressively elaborates the demonic, until in the midnight watch it reaches its highest unity. But at this point the demonic is brought into contact with the higher ordering of the divine. The power of the divine disrupts and disorders the demonic, and thus begins the demonic retransformation and reobjectification. This disruption of the demonic, concomitant with its reordering within the cosmic hierarchy, continues and receives overt expression in the comic dialogues of the comic acts of the **Mangara pelapaliya** and the **Dahaata paliya**, which also test and assert the truth of cosmic relations. The divine is shown to be above the cultural order of the human world and to transcend comic disruption, and so is legitimated as a superior ordering to that of the everyday world of human beings. The demonic, however, is **disordered by culture** (a logical inverse of the illusion of demonic control whereby demons disorder culture) and is reduced beneath the social contexts formed within it, and so the hierarchical relation of the divine to human beings and to demons is restored.

The Patient in the Comedy of Demons

Comedy and the various modes of the comic have been widely observed as having a health-giving and curative value. Most anthropologists have seen its function in the release of tensions, whereby the comic or joke form embodies the tensions located in the structure of society, or in individuals and their interpersonal relations, and functions to give them culturally acceptable expression and release in the course of social action. I too have argued somewhat similarly when I state that the comic form incorporates contradictions and places them in dynamic tension. But this is where the argument I have developed parts company with so-called functionalist positions in anthropology. No doubt comedy in exorcism, as Obeyesekere says, allows fear and terror to be laughed away (Obeyesekere 1969), but such tensions can be released and overcome in a great many other ways. The tension release "theory," whether applied to jokes or to comedy, seems to me to be impoverished and denies to jokes and comedy their other important qualities (see Handelman and Kapferer 1972).

The comedy of exorcism is potentially health-giving and curative for two reasons. First, as I have already discussed, it destroys the objective grounds upon which a patient and others can sensibly interpret experience as the consequence of demonic control. But what may be objectively destroyed may nonetheless persist subjectively. Here is the second potential aspect of the efficacy of comedy. A patient drawn within a context organized in comedy can be exposed to a process whereby subjective awareness is reconstituted in terms of attitudes external to himself or herself. Both the objective curative dimension of comedy and the subjective dimension are, I consider, properties of the structural form of comedy itself. This structural form (comedy's internal reflexivity, its oscillation and shifting standpoints whereby it expands perspective, its subjective distancing — all of which are interrelated), while not exclusive to comedy, is perhaps most extremely developed within comedy. A context organized in comedy establishes the conditions for individuals to stand outside their own subjectivity and to constitute themselves as objects, to have an awareness of self in relation to others, and to organize their self-understanding in an objective world which is intersubjectively affirmed, which extends around them and is itself pointed to and constituted in comedy: the patient's self is reconstituted in the comedy.

The above capacity of comedy receives impetus as a function of three additional factors. First, the comedy occurs after extended ritual events when the patient has been submerged in an existential subjectivity dominated by the demonic and in which the ordinary social world has been suspended. A potential of this condition is that the patient can lose an awareness of a social self, as in trance. Second, the comedy organizes its content in terms of the Attitude of the Other and the Generalized Other. The exorcist straight man and the demons adopt "ordinary" social roles and place them in process within the dramatic action, giving rise to understandings of appropriateness and inappropriateness according to common-sense everyday knowledge. Third, the exorcists and the audience enjoin the patient to participate actively in the comic action. This last is highly important, for it places pressure on the patient to enter into a reflective awareness on his or her surrounding context. This increases further the power of comedy to engage in the structuring of the patient's self-awareness, to form the way the patient conceives himself or herself (as well as others) in the rational world which comedy, implicitly at least, is reconstructing.

In the **Dahaata paliya,** more than in the **Mangara pelapaliya,** the patient is firmly entrenched in the midst of the comic action and in a world as others see it. The demons come right up to the patient and avow they had nothing to do with the illness. Maru Sanniya tries to talk with the patient and Gulma Sanniya does a mock diagnosis of illness and makes frequent reference to the patient (see p. 174). During the morning watch the exorcists and the audience exhort the patient to laugh, or show other signs of amusement in other words, symbolically to express that he or she shares in their attitude towards the world. The laughter of human beings, particularly laughter as shared enjoyment in a community of others, is culturally viewed by Sinhalese, in the context of exorcisms, as the laughter of order and of a full attention to and awareness of life in the everyday world. It indicates a stability of mind and body. Patient laughter is indicative of the reequilibrating of the patient's mind and body.

In the morning watch, kin and others who may have earlier assisted the patient in giving offerings to the demons usually desist from such action. The patient is completely alone in a world in which the terrible nature of demons is not sustained, and, as long as he or she withholds laughter and amusement at the comic scene, or fails to see the joke, becomes in the view of many in the audience almost as absurd as the comic figures presented before the patient.[7] The patient is expected to laugh even at that which appears frightening and terrifying. Here is one significance of the Maru Sanniya act (p. 172).

I stated earlier that at intervals in the ritual process exorcists engage in action to monitor the progress of the patient; to test whether the exorcism is effecting its objective of achieving a cure. The appearance of Maru Sanniya is one such episode. He is the most terrifying of the **sanni** demons. Maru Sanniya is the epitome of disorder, and particularly of mental disorientation. He is the demon of madness, and the wild and uncontrolled manner of his behavior when he appears in the drama is symbolic of this. Maru Sanniya also brings death. He is a manifestation of Mara, Buddha's main adversary (see p. 112), as is Riri Yaka of the **avamangalle** period. When Maru Sanniya first appears he is potentially highly terrifying. He singles out members of the ritual gathering, isolates them from their fellows, and fixes them in his glare. Fear and terror momentarily reassert themselves in the midst of the comic. Maru Sanniya, in the performance of the act I most frequently witnessed, shows himself as the master of illusion, of the trick. He sprouts teeth, as if from nowhere. But the comic is also asserted. The demon's movements are stiff and mechanical, they do not have the flow and movement of something living. He is laughed at by members of the audience, and they grin and push him away when he tumbles through their midst.

As in the episode of Mahasona's death, a cloth is held before the patient — obscuring Maru Sanniya from view as he creeps stealthily towards the patient. When he leaps through the curtain, most patients whom I have observed cringe and cower. But the audience, including close kin, exhort the patient to laugh at what is as absurd as it may be terrifying. Maru Sanniya will take a hair from the patient and cook it on a flaming torch. He displays his devouring nature, but in some of the performances I have observed he burns his fingers and howls in pain.

In the acts of the **sanni** demons especially, exorcists direct considerable effort to making the patient laugh. Occasionally the comedy is extended beyond the scheduled ending of the **Dahaata paliya** (approximately 6:00 A.M.

until the patient indicates amusement, which symbolically affirms that the patient is released from an overriding fear of the demonic, has adopted the attitudes of others towards the demonic, and has returned to a consciousness of a world as others live it. The actors mark the inconsistencies in the comedy by their own action, and the agreement that these are absurd and out of place in a rational order is ratified and signed by the audience's own amusement and laughter. Exorcism comedy models a world to consciousness. Simultaneously, exorcism comedy in its internal structure and through the engagement of the patient in its action can draw the patient into the many realities it elaborates and to a proper perspective upon them, bringing a patient back to life and possibly to health in the flow of its movement.

Exorcism comedy is important in the practical work of reorienting the patient's own subjectivity in accordance with an objective social order. Its curative power is, however, further facilitated by its particular ordering within the rite as a whole. The patient, until the end of the major dances of the midnight watch, is brought into direct experiential contact with demonic and divine forces in dynamic tension. The patient is in process within the inner structure of the rite and contained within a reality of his or her own experience. He or she is made subject to the illusion of form within an existential reality where forms take shape directly in perception and in the unity they achieve with the subject. These "shapes" are within the field of the patient's consciousness but, at the same time, beyond the patient's objective grasp. In the comedy, however, the patient is cast into a reality which is objectified and consciously cognized in culture, a reality made graspable in its constructs and typifications. The objects of experience are made into the objects of reflection and opened to the logical discourse of speech. Perception becomes conception, and the truth or falsity of that which has been directly perceived and subjectively experienced is made subject to the test of objective cultural knowledge. In the comedy, the patient is made to stand outside subjective experience, and so is enabled to regain a consciousness of self in a rational order. Through the comedy, a balanced and broadened perspective on reality is made possible, a proper mental attitude is restored, and mind is reunited with body in their proper relation.

Comedy: Anti-rite and Anti-structure

The comic drama of exorcism lampoons the demons and subjects them to ridicule. It makes fun of prior events and practice relevant to the demon ceremony. The comedy also discovers the comic in the structure and contexts of everyday life outside the domain of ritual. The demonic is to be found not simply in the illness of a demonic victim, and potentially in those horrifying figures who crowd the Sinhalese universe; the demonic is also discovered in the passion, lust, greed, and anger of men and women in the everyday world. The demonic is in those political and social orders which appear to constrain and restrict the actions of men and women in their daily lives. It is in falsity and illusion. The demonic is present in the actions of those who appear to be other than they actually are.

Both Turner (1973b:174-78) and Douglas (1975) especially, have stressed that humor, fun, pranks, and jokes are an attack upon form. I have found Douglas' stimulating argument, that the joke is an anti-rite, of immense value in uncovering the transformational process of exorcism comedy. In the comedy, the joke of the rite is fully revealed. It is the punchline of an exorcism. Demons who control, delude, and trick through their powers of illusion, who appear to dominate and determine, are themselves deluded and tricked.   The apparently dominating are revealed to be the most subordinate. Those who determine are themselves determined.

The exorcism is held to honour the demons, and they are treated as if they are gods.   They are given offerings which seem appropriate to the gods — incense is burned, flowers and foods, such as rice and fruit, are given.   But the incense has the smell of death and pollution even while flamed as fire it "destroys" and repels the demons.   The flowers are shredded and dead. The foods are cooked and mixed with pollutants such as oil, flesh, and blood. What appears as suitable for the gods is suitable only for demons. The offerings carry the idea of the polluting and destructive quality of the demons. But the demons in their acceptance of them become vulnerable to their own destruction. Like the gods, the demons are presented with ceremony. Music is played, and the magnificent dance is in their honour. But as they are called and celebrated, so are the gods, whose authority and purity will destroy, control, and repel the demons.   In the dance and the dancer resides the divine.   In like manner, elaborate and beautiful offering baskets and edifices are built for the demons.   The edifices are the "temples" of the demons, and the images of the demons, like but unlike the gods, are displayed. But the baskets and edifices are traps. Their magical design is one which ensnares the demons and makes them subject to the control of human beings and the gods. The offerings in the baskets are the "bait" with which the traps are set. Hidden within the magnificent edifices constructed for the demons are the gods, who will subjugate the demonic. The entire rite, in one of its major dimensions, can be seen as the elaborate springing of a demonic trap, a means for refixing the demons in a cosmic order which they have momentarily escaped. What began as a celebration and as an honoring of the demons becomes the means for their dishonoring. In the comedy the demons are revealed as figures upon whom an enormous joke has been played.

The comedy attacks both the form of the rite in which the demonic rises to dominance, and the demons themselves. It levels and reduces the demons, and restores the hierarchy of the cosmos. Through the comedy, meaning is rearranged, and the context of the demonic is transformed. The comedy is destructive and regenerative. Within it an attention to life in all its consistency, inconsistency, motion, and fluidity is emergent. The demons as relatively fixed and mechanical figures, and as creatures of disorder, have no place in the life of the comedy and themselves are disordered by it.

So far I have examined the comedy in relation to its location within the rite and as integral in effecting its process. I conclude my discussion of it with reference to the wider social and political setting of exorcism practice, the total situation of the joke in Douglas' analysis. It is in terms of this wider social and political setting that the comedy receives much of its vital rhythm. Moreover, it is because of this that the comedy of exorcism has force as social and political commentary and, therefore, achieves broader import than simply the curing of a patient. I return to a theme at the beginning of this book (see Chapter 2). There I stated that the comedy of exorcism draws attention to the nature of a social and political order, the forces within it, and its constraining and oppressive quality.

Exorcists are well placed to draw attention to falsity, and the illusory, in the everyday social order — to point to the "demonic," destructive, false, and oppressive character of its controlling agents. Exorcists, like many comedians the world over, are in various ways socially marginal but, nonetheless, entirely subject to the order of the everyday world and to the power, authority, and constraint of those who dominate it. They mainly come from a low caste in the hierarchical order of Sinhalese society. To some extent, exorcists constitute the "joker in the pack." They are the bearers and repositories of a great deal of cultural knowledge in which much of this order finds its legitimation. In my view, exorcists are learned men. It is they who placate the demons and invoke the gods to relieve the suffering of men and women. Thus they exercise a degree of power and control, yet status and prestige is denied them in the normal working world. The members of the berava caste to which exorcists belong are often confronted by the discriminatory practices of those who place their own castes higher in the social order. The caste to which exorcists mainly belong has, in the recent past, felt the oppressive bite of the order of Sinhalese society (see Chapter 3). Exorcists, in general, belong to the urban working class and the rural peasantry. They must daily experience the officiousness and delays of government bureaucracy, the difficulties in finding employment, the problems of feeding and clothing their families on often meager earnings, and the illusion of false hopes contained in the promises of politicians.

The comic dialogues I have reported focus attention on the plight of the working class. Thus in the **Mangara pelapaliya** the sacred sun and moon symbol (**sesat**) is referred to as a lowly creature and through this the poverty of the working class becomes a theme for comic expansion. In the Maru Sanniya act of the morning watch the problems of dealing with government bureaucrats are revealed (p. 172). In one Maru Sanniya act I witnessed, the demon appeared accompanied by a complete public address system made from banana trunk. He assumed the role of a politican on the hustings and harangued the gathering. Sri Lanka was then moving towards its national elections. Maru Sanniya made all kinds of grandiose promises. Everyone was to have cars, all would eat meat, the problem of unemployment would be solved, and so on. He took the opportunity to criticize a local strike of the medical profession. A common demon role in the comedy is that of a local police chief, and in this role the demon threatens to beat and batter the drummer "straight man" in response to the latter's abuse.

The falseness, corruption, and immorality of the Buddhist clergy is regular fare in the comedy of exorcism. Their alleged illicit sexuality is often the subject of the biting wit and ribald humor of the comedy. In one performance of the **Vadiga patuna** comic drama of the **Suniyama** exorcism I observed, a drama which portrays the myth of origin of the rite, three exorcists dressed as the brahmins who, as the myth relates, initiated the **Suniyama** entered the performance arena. All wore dark glasses and carried rolled umbrellas, symbols of their status and standing in the everyday world. One brahmin was old and staggered on a stick around the arena, another was presented as middle-aged, and the third was a prepubescent youth. The whole comedy developed around the theme of the competition between the two older brahmins for the younger brahmin's sexual attention. The brahmins were associated with Buddhist monks. Comments were passed on the trials and tribulations of being an old monk, and how the more youthful monks have better sexual success with young initiates into the clergy.

Douglas has argued that comedy is an attack on form. But it is not necessarily, at least in exorcism ritual, an attack on all form. Feibleman is more accurate when he states that it is an attack on **limiting** form. Comedy "criticizes the finite for not being infinite" (1939:201). By this he means that comedy confronts and subverts those ideas and practices which place controls, constraints, and restrictions on life. Thus comedy is entirely to be expected in exorcisms, for it reveals the finite and restrictive nature of the demonic, and exposes as false the claims of the demonic to be infinite, to unite all in its being. Again, comedy is completely appropriate to the emergence of the divine, which is infinite and can contain and order all in its presence and in its idea.

The comic drama of exorcisms expands to criticize the limits and restrictions, the "demonic," in everyday life: the constraints placed on the working class, the barriers established by government bureaucracy, and so on. To this I add that the comedy of exorcism attacks falsity, illusion, and pretence, which in themselves, as in the case of a demonic victim, might impose limitation. Thus, politicians are lampooned and have the demonic discovered within them. So too are monks who lay false claim to a morality they should, but may not, practice.

10. Epilogue:
A Celebration of Demons

> Art constantly effects a pilgrimage to the
> source; it liberates the word in restoring its
> primordial power, the image as one of genuine
> origination, the gesture as spontaneous. As the
> origin of man's inspiration, art is celebration.
>
> Mikel Dufrenne, **"Structuralism and**
> **Humanism"** 1970

The demonic is the fatal twist of culture, the inversion and negation of
its order. Demons are the embodiments of the manifold dimensions of life's
suffering and are the ultimate contradiction of life: death. They symbolize
the destructive possibilities of a cultural and social order, the rending of its
fragile fabric in anger, desire, greed, hunger, passion, and violence. Demons
reach into and intrude upon the lives of human beings, gaining strength in
weakness and coming to life in individual and social disorder. The demonic
is the most powerful symbol of destruction, not only of human beings and
their world order, but also of an encompassing cosmic whole. For Sinhalese,
the demonic can be a terrifying commentary on life's condition and
individual experience within it. The Sinhalese encounter with the demonic
ties the disturbance in individual experience into its wider cultural and
social context, and is a metaphor for the personal struggle of Sinhalese
within an obdurate social world.

A perspective upon reality in terms of the demonic is an "underview,"
as too is an ethnography which reflects upon aspects of Sinhalese life and
culture through a description of the nature of demons and a discussion of the
rituals to overcome their attack. This view, however, has value for a
broader prespective upon the religious and ritual world of ordinary Sinhalese
Buddhists. It complements those studies, for example, which focus at the
apex of the religious system, upon the teachings of the Buddha and their
daily practice, upon the Buddhist monks, and upon the deities and their
worship. These studies, of course, are vital to any understanding of religious
life in modern Sri Lanka, but, perhaps more than any other single form of
ritual practice, demon ceremonies direct attention to the totality of the
Sinhalese Buddhist religious system, its foundation in an overarching

conception of a cosmic unity, the complexity of the internal structure of this unity, and the central principles which underlie its process. The demonic threatens a cosmological unity at its base, creates it as problematic and, therefore, attacks the religious and broader cultural ideas by which Sinhalese comprehend their lives in the world. Exorcisms are one commentary on the nature of the Sinhalese Buddhist world view. They start from the bottom, rebuilding a proper cultural perspective and, in doing so, constitute an exegesis on the religious and cultural order.

Demon ceremonies reflect the many influences (Hindu, Mahayanist, and, of course, Theravadin Buddhist) which have shaped Sinhalese Buddhist culture, a culture which is variously shared by Sinhalese at every social level. Exorcisms have an ancient lineage stretching deep into Sri Lanka's past, but they are no less a modern practice. However, the major exorcisms especially are largely a Sinhalese working-class and peasant practice. The class bias of exorcism is part of a general process of religious change in Sri Lanka and reflects ideological forces in a society in which religion plays a major social, economic, and political role. The class character of exorcism is one example of the role of ideas in structuring action, a central unifying theme of my analysis, and of the factors which underlie the change and development of ideas and practice.

Sinhalese Buddhism is a topic of often hot debate among ordinary Sinhalese, as it is among foreign and Sinhalese scholars and intellectuals. Sinhalese middle class especially regard exorcism to be inconsistent with "true" Buddhist practice and sometimes describe it as a "folk religion" and as the practice of the poor and ill-educated. Indeed, everyday Sinhalese distinctions between practices labeled as "folk religion" and Buddhism proper are reminiscent of the scholarly distinction of the Great Tradition of the texts and the Little Tradition. Regardless of the legitimacy of this distinction as a basis for scholarly argument, in the social historical context of modern Sri Lanka it is part of a class ideology. This ideology is formed in the conditions of a capitalist economy and both refracts the relations structured within it and is a vital force in the reproduction of these relations.

Religious ideas and practices comprise an element of the symbolic discourse of class and status, and variations and changes in religious ritual are produced in this dialectic of class and religion. Within urban centers at least, the central institutions of religious worship, the temples, are in the control of the middle class and its dominant fractions. Rituals performed outside the temple and independent of its monks are occasions when working class and peasants have greater control over their religious action; this may account for the continuity of traditional ritual practice among them. This aside, that traditional rites like exorcism are practiced mainly by the working class and peasantry gives them potentially added symbolic significance as expressive of the subordination of this class in the wider society. As I have described, exorcism comedy gives voice to everyday difficulties which Sinhalese peasants and working class confront. Metaphorically, the fragmentation and reduction of demonic victims to a powerless and determined condition mirrors the situation of Sinhalese working class and peasants who are subordinated and reduced before the demon State, and its agents of power. The demonic signs the condition of the Sinhalese working class, whose very humanity is threatened in the daily struggle and toil of life, and whose conditions of existence, as one comic episode related, can be equated with the lowest of creatures.

My main concern, however, was with demon ceremonies as healing rites and with their transformational process. I examined the diagnosis and social definition of demonic illness and the related question of why women are so often patients. This extended into a consideration of the cultural logic underlying major demon ceremonies, followed by an analysis of exorcism performance.

Demonic attack signs a disturbance of the cosmic order as this centers upon the person of the patient and, in effect, is potentially a total disordering of the person in all dimensions of his or her existence. Demonic disorder is at its extreme a disruption of the complete physical, mental, and social being of the patient. The diagnosis and definition of demonic illness can realize the full possibility of demonic malevolence and its understanding can incorporate, not only the individual person of the patient to the idea of the demonic, but also the more extended context of the household and an immediate circle of kin.

Demonic illness **is** the illness and cannot be reduced easily to terms independent of the cultural ideas, constructs, and typifications in accordance with which it is comprehended. It cannot be broken down into a set of labels applicable to another system of understanding and practice. Thus the terms of Western biomedical science or Western psychology or psychiatry at best only provide partial frameworks for comprehending any individual occurrence of demonic attack and at worst deconstitute the phenomenon at hand. This is not another version of a cultural relativist thesis, common in anthropology, which guards the cultures of its enquiry against the intrusion of ideas and theories drawn from outside, and which often specifies another method and another theory for every culture which becomes the subject of enquiry.   It is, however, an argument against methodologies and theoretical persuasions which, in the urgency of their protagonists to generalize, destroy the phenomena of enquiry and, perhaps, devalue the strength of their own theories to comprehend human action. The generality of a theory ultimately rests in the specificity of its application, and this is threatened if its generality contradicts its specificity, that is, if, in order to generalize, a theory must deny critical properties of that which it strives to inform and understand.

Demonic illness is an emergent phenomenon.   In the course of its diagnosis and definition aspects no less part of the illness are constructed into it.   What the illness is, is inextricably connected with its particular mode of cultural understanding.   Undoubtedly, a disturbance of individual well-being precedes its recognition as demonic attack, and the factors underlying this disturbance may be comprehensible in terms of other systems of explanation. But once the demonic is implicated in the illness, additional possibilities relating to its cause and comprehension by others are built into the situation and can come to constitute the nature of the patient's illness experience.   The illness assumes a particular demonic character relevant to the system of explanation within which it is set, and the regularities of physical, mental, and social disorder which comprise the etiology of demonic illness are directly connected with the cultural logic of explanation within which individual disturbance is diagnosed and defined.

Demonic illness is not necessarily a purely individual problem. The process of diagnosis is one which not only relates the patient to a wider context, and makes the illness "sensible" in that wider context, but also links the patient's experience with that of others. Others' problems can become symbolized in the patient's demonic condition, and the shadow of the demonic cast over a context inclusive of a patient and others may contribute to the illness' being viewed as serious and demanding of a major ceremony. The social "strategic" aspects of demonic attack which may be evident in any specific instance are integral to the logic of exorcist diagnosis, whereby the patient's distress is made meaningful by reference to an outer world of daily action. That a wide array of social problems may be addressed through demonic illness is consistent with its mode of explanation and is not independent of it. Demonic illness potentially links together multiple dimensions of disturbance witin the single overarching idea of demonic disorder, and major demon ceremonies achieve much of their efficacy by attacking this idea, and the principles relating to it, and by rendering it absurd.

Demon ceremonies are healing rites and household rituals, and the one is coterminous with the other. Demonic attack pollutes the victim and also the house and threatens the well-being of its members. Additionally, it makes the house potentially dangerous to others and can be disruptive of social relations centering on the house. Major public exorcisms present before the neighborhood the purification of the victim and the house and establish the basis for the reestablishment of normal interhousehold relations. A symbolic significance of the food distribution at major exorcisms is the rearticulation of the household's social relations. The reordering of the household into its wider social context at an exorcism is consistent with the overall logic of cure, which is to restore the structuring of relations at each level within the cosmic totality.

Illness is the irregularity which disrupts the regularity of daily life. It is the disorder of being in the very circumstances of life's existence, and strikes without warning. This is how Sinhalese understand the demonic, for demons attack suddenly, disordering the entire being of the person as they disorder life's conditions. Illness is not part of life's schedule, and, conceived demonically, it attacks the basis of a cultural and social order which human beings impose. The frequency by which experiential disturbance understood as illness can occur and the fact that the demonic is an ever-present possibility of its comprehension gives additional importance to exorcism as a major household rite, a rite which takes the person and the household in their wider context and strives in its logic of cure to restore an order to life's condition, within which the disturbance of the demonic has emerged.

Women are the most frequent victims of demon attack. When they are ill they see themselves and are seen by other women and men as likely to be caught in the demon gaze. The vulnerability of women to demonic affliction is a common-sense Sinhalese cultural understanding and in itself accounts for the frequency with which women are treated by exorcism. Such a common-sense view can be accounted for by the cultural principles which underlie the identity of Sinhalese women. I explored this as an alternative to functionalist and psychodynamic arguments which, although they may account for the specific instance, cannot account for the pattern (i.e., without systematically excluding the great range of situationally specific factors or variance from one case to the next) and are highly reductionist in explication. Moreover, these approaches to the question of the frequency of women in possession and healing rites do not incorporate satisfactory accounts of why men may be patients.

Men also are vulnerable to demonic attack and comprise a significant minority of exorcism patients. They are constituted in the same circumstances of cultural existence, are subject to similar processes of natural and cultural disturbance, and so on. However, their exposure to the possibility of demonic malevolence is a socially situated product of their engagement in the everyday world and is not an expectation of their identity as men **per se,** as it is for women. The cultural principles which underlie female identity place women at a central point of conjunction in the matrix of cultural and social relations. As a focus of major conjunction in themselves, women also occupy a position of structural weakness which brings them into a category relation to the demonic. Demons are conceived as attacking weak points in structural articulation generally. Further, the culturally constituted identity of women both makes them a major symbolic focus upon whom others can play their difficulties, and culturally sensitizes them to express in their bodies and selves the disorders emanating from a world around them. It is these factors and others integral to their identity as women which continually move them into the orbit of exorcist practice. The demonic strikes at the heart of a cultural and cosmic order. Women are the major symbols of the vulnerability of this order, and they are made enduringly conscious of this in their daily cultural social practices.

Major demon ceremonies themselves reveal the nature of demonic illness and the dimensions of a Sinhalese Buddhist world view in which the demonic is an ever-present possibility. Indeed, major exorcisms construct, as they simultaneously destroy, the reality of a patient, his or her submission to the mastery of the demonic illusion and to a terrifying demonic disorder. Demon ceremonies follow the same basic cultural logic, and their organization of event and action varies little from one enactment to the next. I concentrated my analysis upon one exorcism, the ceremony of the Great Cemetery Demon, in order to uncover the nature of its transformational process, a process which in its general features is shared by all the large-scale exorcisms.

Rituals are more than the organized symbolic reflection of central cultural ideas. They work with ideas and are directed to asserting as well as changing a world of experience and action which is comprehended through the ideas which rituals present. Rituals act practically upon the world; this is effected through their major defining quality: rituals place ideas in a dominant relation to action and constrain action and experience within them. For this reason, ritual can play a vital role in the reproduction of social relations insofar as these relations are mediated through ideas. Rituals can also transform action and experience; this they do by attacking and restructuring the ideas in terms of which action and experience are comprehended. The transformational capacity of ritual is highly evident in healing rites; indeed, their practical efficacy depends on this capacity, and for this reason such rituals are a rewarding context for the examination of the ritual process.

The governing ideas and principles of exorcism are contained in the objective structure of exorcism which composes ideas in systematic relation and in terms of the logic of hierarchy and of transformation in the cosmic order. The sequential arrangement of exorcism events and their internal organization is a rendering along a horizontal plane of the vertical dimension of the cosmic order. The process of exorcism is a rebuilding of the cosmic hierarchy, and the engagement of a patient in this is also the means whereby patient identity and experience is potentially transformed. A central analytic concern was to explore how transitions and transformations in the objective structure of exorcism ritual are communicated to and formed within the experience of the patient and other participants, for it is on these that the practical work of exorcism ultimately depends.

Exorcists are concerned to change the experiential condition of their patients and to bring patients back into a normal conception of the world. The capacity of music, song, dance, and comedy to effect a cure is explicitly recognized by exorcists. My analysis showed that the internal structural properties of these aesthetic forms, elaborated as they are at particular points in the ritual progress, variously model expected transitions and transformations, constitute the transitional and transformational process in their internal structural form, and can engender what is integral in their form in patients and others engaged in their realms. Music and dance have the capacity to unite the objective with the subjective as a function of the direct experience of them. In this, the ideas of a cosmic reality and its opposing possibilities are revealed in the immediacy of experience. Further, the body, which is the experiential seat of the illness, is set in motion and in flight with the temporalizing and spatializing qualities of the organization of the sound and gesture of music and dance, and the body is subjected to the experience of the combination and recombination of their formative elements. Through this the body is ordered and reordered in conjunction with the cosmic process included and set into dynamic motion within the musical and dance forms.

It is in the relation of music and dance to the comedy of exorcism that the self of a patient can be reconstituted in accordance with the normal and rational objectifications and typifications of the cultural order. The reconstitution of a patient, the restitution of the patient as a normal human being in possession of the rational faculties appropriate to action in the eveyday world, is a major aspect of the potential efficacy of exorcism. Music and dance deny reflective distance, the capacity to objectify a world at a distance from the experiencing of it. This and other aspects of the music and dance of exorcism in effect deconstitute the social self of the patient and, as exemplified in trance, may ultimately negate any objective or reflective consciousness of self in the world and reduce a self to its pure experiencing. Deprived of the capacity to reflect upon self at objective distance, to expose self to the rationality of thought, a possibility is created for the emergence of a demonic mode of being —— which is a self in restricted experience and beyond the objective control of reason.

The music and dance of exorcism can be seen as preparing the way for comedy. Comedy, unlike music and dance, is quintessentially a reflexive form which places the objects of experience at reflective distance and, furthermore, does not restrict perspective to that which is included within it. Comedy implies and points to a world outside itself. The world is not so much **perceived** but **conceived** in the comic medium. Individuals thrust into the context of comedy have the reality in which they were placed made available to the grasp of consciousness, have aspects of a reality objectified and counterposed before them and maintained at a distance from direct experience. The comedy of exorcism progressively displays a rational world in the very irrationality of the comic movement, and continually explodes towards a world as it should be conceived. As comedy reformulates the world to consciousness, so the patient can potentially reformulate a self, one in accordance with the multiple perspectives which comedy elaborates.

The aesthetic of exorcism is intregral to the analysis of exorcism as performance. The analysis of ritual without a systematic consideration of the media of performance and without an attention to the way participants are structured to the central action limits a general anthropological understanding of the nature of the ritual process. A reduction in analysis to the formal properties of a "text" which ignores key dimensions of the way a "text" becomes contextualized and "textured" in practice fails to recognize that important properties of the meaning of the "text" may only be realized in performance. Within the structure of any "text," given the cultural setting, are several possible meanings or interpretations. Exorcism is a major example of this, for in its unfolding it explores a variety of meanings and reveals them differentially to participants. Ritual, and certainly exorcism, decodes its meaning and structures interpretation in the progress of its performance. The engagment of participants in the decoding and structured interpretation of exorcism performance is integral to the achievement by exorcism of its tranformational and transitional project. I have taken the aesthetic of exorcism as critical for the analysis of performance, for it is in the aesthetic that ideas, symbolic objects, and actions are brought into relation constitutive of their meaning. I stress that their relational ordering is a property of the aesthetic of exorcism itself and should not be considered independently of it. The transposition of ideas, objects, and actions from one aesthetic medium to another progressively extends upon their meaning, elaborates upon it and effects transformations in meaning and interpretation. For example, the demonic assumes an overall consistency of form with the divine in the aesthetic of music and dance, but in the comedy the demonic is disarticulated from its symbolic mesh with the divine and rendered in its objective relation of clear and unambiguous subordination.

The aesthetic of exorcism informs an understanding of the process of exorcism. But also the marvelous demon ceremonies which exorcists perform contribute to a more general understanding of the nature of aesthetic forms themselves. Victor Turner writes that, "Song, dance, graphic and pictorial representation, these and more, broken loose from their ritual integument, become the seeds of concert music, ballet, literature, and painting. If ritual might be compared to a mirror of mankind, its conversion into a multiplicity of performative arts gives us a hall of mirrors, each reflecting the reflections of the others, and each representing not a simple inversion of mundane reality, but its systematic magnification and distortion, the ensemble composing a reflexive metacommentary on society and history as they concern the natural and constructed needs of humankind under given conditions of time and place" (1977:73). If artistic form as we have come to know it has indeed developed by breaking loose from its ritual integument, perhaps also we have lost some insight into how artistic form organizes human experience and reveals the hiddenness of human existence. Exorcists, by placing major aesthetic forms into complex relation within their rites and turning them to practical purpose, explore the very nature of the aesthetic and the kinds of human experience possible within them. The significance of the ritual work of exorcists passes in my view well beyond the immediate practical concerns of exorcists and their clients. I have tried to indicate some sense of this. Ultimately, the book is intended as a small tribute to the subtleties of Sinhalese exorcist knowledge, the marvels of their art, and the contribution which they make to an understanding of humankind.

Notes

1: Introduction

1. Rappaport's definition of, and general approach to ritual strikes me as altogether too formalist. He excludes an attention to symbolic content for which Tambiah (1981:138) rightly criticizes him. Rappaport, of course, by excluding what he defines as content makes the classic error of distinguishing form from content, and possibly mis-locating both. His discussion of ritual as "liturgical order" or "fixed sequences of words and acts" fails to realize that such a liturgical order is also a dimension of the symbolic content of ritual (see Rappaport 1979:175, 206).

2. All these characteristics of ritual (which appear to be taken-for-granted in much anthropological literature and continually reproduced as part of a "theory" of ritual) should, of course, be viewed problematically. Repetition or redundancy, for example, as a formal property of ritual, is a case in point. The repeated enactment of apparently the same acts and utterances in the course of a rite is not necessarily a mere repetition. What may appear as the same acts and utterances are likely to have changed significance in the altering contexts of the ritual process —— a point demonstrated in the detailed work of Victor Turner on Ndembu ritual. One, perhaps, never steps in the same ritual twice.

3. The work of Clifford Geertz is exemplary of the "blurring of genres." Geertz (1972:5) sees his approach to anthropology as "essentially a semiotic one" but also as an approach which invokes Max Weber, "Believing ... that man is an animal suspended in webs of significance he himself has spun ..." The anti-humanism and inattention to agency for which structuralist and semiotic approaches are often criticized is tempered in Geertz' appeal to the interpretavist perspective of Weber and the latter's stress on individual agency. These orientations, and add to them Geertz' free references to phenomenology and hermeneutics, are often opposed and their protagonists are engaged in a continuing mutual critique. Geertz' eclecticism is not in itself to be disparaged as he might disparage that of

others: "eclecticism is self-defeating not because there is only one
direction in which it is useful to move, but because there are so many: it is
necessary to choose" (Geertz 1973:5).   I find the eclecticism of Geertz,
throughout his **oeuvre,** difficult because he seems to cover up and escape the
clear differences which characterize the various orientations he weaves
together in his mellifluous style.

4. Lévi-Strauss (1981), in the final volume of his major work on myth,
makes his most explicit statement on ritual and directly opposes his position
to the approach developed by Victor Turner.   He denies the value of what he
views as Turner's central concern with emotion, and the stress which
analysts of ritual place upon the communicational and informational aspects
of ritual (Lévi-Strauss 1981:669-70).

Lévi-Strauss' argument is characteristically insightful and powerful. He
emphasises an orientation concerned with the internal structure of ritual
and in terms of the phenomenon itself, or at least as the phenomenon is
recognized by Lévi-Strauss.   He attempts to incorporate ritual into his
overall analytical scheme, locating it in the terms of his formal discussion
of myth and music in accordance with their relation to language. He states
that the analysis of ritual should concentrate on **how** the action, gesture,
words etc. "are saying," rather than focus upon **what** they are saying. "The
performance gestures and the manipulation of objects are the devices which
allow ritual to avoid speech" (Lévi-Strauss 1981:672).   The key features of
ritual for Lévi-Strauss are its fragmentation and attention to minute detail
(what he terms "parcelling out") and the multiplication of these details
through repetition.   Parcelling out and repetition are **the methods of ritual**
whereby it patches up holes and stops gaps, and attempts to work against
"any kind of break or interruption that might jeopardize the continuance of
lived experience" (Lévi-Strauss 1981:674). This last point strikes me as very
close to Victor Turner's general perspective on ritual.

The analysis I pursue in the later chapters of this book takes a feature
of exorcism ritual which Lévi-Strauss might describe as parcelling out, and
examines it as part of a process whereby ritual rebuilds a cosmic order. In
my analysis I regard the feature of repetition as being more than a
multiplication of detail in that it constitutes a series of definitions and
redefinitions of a progressive ordering and reordering of cosmic relations.

I find the approach to ritual outlined by Lévi-Strauss to be stimulating
and obviously worthy of extension.   However, his definition of ritual and
formalized understanding of the phenomenon is perhaps too limited and
reified and, in my view, ritual is not a form located at the same analytical
level as music or myth. Further, I am suspicious of a position which argues
from a "pure form" or essentialist conception of ritual (Lévi-Strauss
1981:671-75). I am also hesitant about accepting Lévi-Strauss' contention
that ritual is non-analytical and non-discursive in contrast to the
discursiveness and thought of myth. If the devices of ritual replace speech
they may also be conceived of as the way ritual "speaks," or discursively
"thinks" itself. Lévi Strauss fails to realize that ritual might be fruitfully
regarded as a cultural practice in which culture "demystifies" itself. Ritual,
for me, is the analytical method of culture, its hermeneutic.

Turner, in effect, recognizes the analytic of ritual in his descriptions
(especially in his discussion of the positional location of symbols in rites and
their movement to dominance), and seeks to uncover the "method" of ritual.
This is most apparent in his early accounts of Ndembu ritual (1967, 1975). In
some ways Turner could be seen as restoring to cultural members their
capacity to analyze themselves, a capacity which Lévi-Strauss ultimately
reserves for himself.

5. I would not like to include all those which may be taken as structuralist or semiotic approaches within my general characterization. Many semiologists on the Continent such as Derrida, Eco, and Kristeva do not seem to hold to a narrow "linguistic" perspective, are greatly influenced by phenomenology, and depart in many ways from the line espoused by Saussure. "One phase of semiology is now over: that which extends from Saussure and Peirce to the Prague School and structuralism ... a critique of this 'semiology of systems,' and of its phenomenological foundations, can only be made if it begins from a theory of meaning, which must necessarily be a theory of the speaking subject" (Kristeva 1969, cited in Giddens 1979:264). It should also be stressed that what is broadly termed "semiotics" has many influences which diverge from Saussure and which were formed independently of Saussure's work (see Giddens 1979, for a useful summary).

6. More specifically it is the existentialists for whom Lévi-Strauss reserves his most trenchant attacks. He states that the philosophy following on "Existentialism —— a self-admiring activity which allows contemporary man, rather gullibly, to commune with himself in ecstatic contemplation of his own being —— cuts itself off from scientific knowledge which it despises, as well as from human reality, whose historical perspectives and anthropological dimensions it disregards, in order to arrange a closed and private little world for itself, an ideological Cafe du Commerce, where within the four walls of a human condition cut down to fit a particular society, the habitues spend their days rehashing problems of local interest, beyond which they cannot see because of the fog created by their clouds of dialectical smoke" (Lévi-Strauss 1981:640). I find much to sympathize with in this statement of Lévi-Strauss, especially the subjectivist reductionism which characterizes some of the existentialist philosophies.

A brilliant defense of a phenomenological position, and one which does not disappear into the mists of subjectivism, is presented by Mikel Dufrenne (1967, 1970). Dufrenne confronts the anti-humanism and scientism of many of those who would espouse a structuralist method. He is also critical of some phenomenologist and existentialist approaches, as Lévi-Strauss (1981) is critical of certain would-be structuralist perspectives.

7. Without a concern for performance, a structuralist analysis may not be able to escape Ricoeur's (1963) telling critique that if structuralism proposes to study meaning it is "le sens du non-sens" or "a syntactical arrangement of a discourse that says nothing" (Shalvey 1979:110).

8. My view of performance here, at least in terms of the problem of efficacy, bears some similarity with Austin's (1962) concept of "performative" which has recently received some anthropological attention in relation to the analysis of ritual (Tambiah 1968, 1981; Rappaport 1979). Basically, a performative is that illocutionary speech act in which the saying is the doing. A performative is constitutive of that of which it speaks. This concept when applied to ritual does not sufficiently recognize that such acts are constituted in a context which imparts to the performative much of its apparent power. Rappaport (1979:190) argues some aspects of this point indicating that the performative dimensions of ritual acts are intensified in the liturgical order of the rite. If this is so, then the value of a concept like performative, added to an already weighty battery of analytical terms, is diminished —— it being more to the point to examine the ritual context as this is formed and reformed in the performance structure of the rite.

9. Tambiah (1981) has recently drawn attention to the importance of the performance and aesthetic modes of ritual, and uses as one example Sinhalese exorcism. His approach is very like a perspective I have adopted in earlier papers (Kapferer 1977a; 1977b; 1979c) which like that of Tambiah is heavily dependent on the work of Susanne Langer. The theoretical

orientation I develop towards the aesthetic in ritual in this book departs in major ways from my earlier reliance on Langer.

10. As Feyerabend (1978) argues so brilliantly in relation to the physical sciences, an emphasis on method can be its own "method of deception" —— its truth being the result of a methodological conformism. When Feyerabend says this, of course, he is not opposed to systematic and careful analysis and thought, as he has been accused by some critics. Rather he is opposed to the closed mindedness which an emphasis on method sometimes encourages, its blindness to possibility and its killing of imagination. Much of what Feyerabend says could be usefully attended to by anthropologists who often seem prone to trendy conformism. There is in some quarters of the social sciences a view that method somehow transcends ideology, ignoring the possibility that it may hide what is the most ideological, a point made time and again by Feyerabend. This possibility seems to have escaped even the powerful intellect of Levi-Strauss who declares for his method and denies any importance to his own philosophy (Levi-Strauss 1981:638).

11. Radcliffe-Brown (1933) in his study of the Andaman Islanders was among the first in anthropology to isolate the importance of aesthetic form (specifically music and dance) within the structure of ritual performance, and in relation to a general concern with the nature of experience and meaning. His is an expressivist approach and not too distant from many still pursued in anthropology. "Just in the sense that words have meanings, so do some other things in culture —— customary gestures, ritual actions and abstentions, symbolic objects, myths —— they are expressive signs" (Radcliffe-Brown 1933:x). Since Radcliffe-Brown there have been numerous other attempts in anthropology to take account of the significance of the aesthetic or the structure of performance modes in ritual (e.g., Needham 1967; Jackson 1968; Blacking 1974; Jules-Rosette 1975; Schiefflin 1976; Blacking and Kealiinokomoku 1979; Hanna 1979). I have focused on a phenomenological perspective because it is an approach which takes as a central problematic the nature of experience, consciousness, and reflexivity —— all of which are important to any study of the ritual process. The phenomenology which I apply is concerned with dissolving the subject/object contrast, and examines the production of subjectivity through participation in an "inter-objective" world; subjectivity, and its experience and the meaning of this experience in conscious awareness is emergent through a "being-in-the-world" and as a process of reflexivity.

12. I refer to the method developed out of "situational analysis" which is the detailed examination of an event of social action as it is constituted through the practice of cultural actors and as it achieves significance in relation to a wider field of practices (see Gluckman 1958; Mitchell 1956). The extended-case method (see van Velsen 1964, 1967; Garbett 1970) takes the one set of persons through a series of socially constituted events arranged in their historical unfolding and examines the structure of actions and interpretations produced. The object of this method is to introduce "history" and process into an otherwise static description and, more importantly, to reveal "social structure" as being continually formed, reformed, and transformed in the structure of its practices. The analyses which pursued this method were concerned with examining underlying cultural and social principles of practice but in a way which viewed such principles as themselves being transformed in their practices. Bourdieu (1977:36-37, 202 fn. 33) draws attention to the method in reference to the work of van Velsen and in relation to the similarity in their approach to kinship and marriage, which Bourdieu treats as a structure of practice to be examined in context.

The extended-case method is opposed to the treatment of ethnographic case material as "apt illustration" which gives limited attention to the "illustration" as a structure of practice embedded within a wider field of practices. Given the drift of current anthropological discourse, the method invites closer attention (especially since its authors were concerned to explore social practice in relation to underlying contradictions, the events of their analyses being the surface manifestations of these contradictions as conflict). In my view Turner's (1957) classic study, **Schism and Continuity in an African Society** (a model of the extended-case method), is still in advance of many current approaches which attend to practice as structuring or "structurating" of cultural and social orders.

2:    Exorcism, Class, and Change in Urban Sri Lanka

1. People I categorize as working class or as peasantry are generally landless, or have minimal rights to land, own little other property, and have limited control over economic production except through the sale of their own labor. Sinhalese middle class, in contrast, typically own some land and other property (usually houses) and control the labor of others through their property ownership and positions of authority in government or private organizations. Most of those whom I define as middle class are in white collar occupations or have controlling entrepreneurial roles in a market trading economy.

2. The following analysis is to be extended in a monograph currently in preparation and co-authored with Kingsley Garbett and Michael Roberts. The book is based on ethnography collected in Colombo and along the urbanized south western coast. The argument concentrates on historical processes leading to the formation of the class structure of modern Sri Lanka and the transformation of Sinhalese Buddhist cultural forms and practices within the process of class formation.

3. The Buddhist revival was also paralleled by similar reformist movements among the Tamil and Muslim communities (Pathmanathan 1979; Samaraweera 1979).

4. The proliferation of lay Buddhist associations controlled by locally powerful elements along the south western coast is well-documented by Roberts (1970). Some typical names of these associations at the turn of the last century were: The Buddhist Theosophical Society, The Society for the Aid of the Buddhist Doctrines, and The Society for the Illumination of the Buddhist. Roberts' description of the activities of some of these associations foreshadows much of my argument below. He records "The main object of the Society of the Illumination of the Buddhist of Panadura, for instance, was teaching the youth Buddhism and the secular sciences. There was one association with branches in Colombo, Ambalangoda and Galle which was intended to advance the knowledge of the Sinhalese people and to promote their languages so as to further the unity of the race, to enable decisions to be reached scientifically and to broaden the use of the (Sinhala) language." (Roberts 1970:16).

5. This is suggested by the fact that many Sinhalese middle class switched from Christianity to Buddhism following the Donoughmore Commission which introduced universal franchise. They were sometimes referred to as "Donoughmore Buddhists" (Ames 1963:48). Woodward (1969:44–45) notes that for the 1931 and 1936 elections (when there was virtually no political party organization) caste, religion, and personal wealth were critical factors in electoral success. According to Woodward, E. W. Perera, an outstanding member of the first State Council, was defeated primarily because he was a Christian. "The campaign literature of his

Buddhist opponent is said to have alluded to the virtues of Buddhism that are lacking in Christianity (1969:47)."

6.   While the Buddhist revival became a potent nationalist force this was not so from the beginning. In the early stages of the revival British colonial authorities patronized the movement and viewed it as a possible agency of their political control. De Silva (1979:146) writes that in the nineteenth century Governor Gregory "initiated a policy of active interest in and sympathy for the Buddhist movement. This he did by his patronage to the movement as well as by consciously seeking to emphasize the neutrality of the government in religious affairs." Gregory's successor, Arthur Gordon (1883-1890), continued the policy. It seems that these British Governors misinterpreted the Buddhist movement as a return to traditional ways. Gordon and later governors withdrew their support of the movement and in line with a general colonial policy of indirect rule backed more conservative forces in Sinhalese society, namely the Kandyan aristocracy.

There is some evidence that the Sinhalese leaders of the early lay associations of the Buddhist movement saw their activities to be in line with colonial government interests.   The Society for the Aid of Buddhist Doctrines in Panadura (just south of Colombo) saw a role in assisting in "the clearance and maintenance of roads, the prevention of false litigation, the prevention of gambling disturbances and the promotion of good behaviour and self-help. (A similar Buddhist association in Gintota, just north of Galle) . . . believed in assisting government to collect its taxes in time" (Roberts 1970:16).

The administrative and political functions of some of the early Buddhist associations is very possibly an extension of the relative autonomy which various caste communities may have achieved along the coast under the relatively "weak" colonial control of the Portuguese and, less so, of the Dutch. (There is much in the development of the social order of modern Sri Lanka in the early colonial periods which bears comparison with other similarly peripheralized societies. See Wallerstein, 1974 and, especially, Schneider and Schneider, 1976, on Sicily). Broadly the Buddhist associations can be interpreted as emerging in a context of greater State control under the British which threatened local autonomy. However, what I suggest is that these Buddhist associations, at least initially, should not be seen as nationalistically inspired or even as nascent elements of a later nationalist movement (see Jayawardena 1972). To argue this way is teleological and, moreover, is to locate a nationalism in a type of organization and not as emergent within the process of a wider structure. In my view, the Buddhist movement and its various associations **became** nationalistic as a function of the working out of fundamental contradictions in the colonial order itself. One such obvious contradiction was contained in the logic of British colonial rule whereby, based as it was in a political and economic capitalist structure, it sought to control through essentially non-capitalist and "traditional" institutions of the subordinated population. The fact that Buddhist reformism revealed itself as non-traditional and engaged the interests of a rising capitalist class in effect constituted a threat to the way the British maintained their colonial rule and ideologically justified it. The opposition of Buddhist reformism to British rule developed within the particular overarching structure of British colonial rule. The nationalism of the reformism, therefore, was not necessarily intrinsic to the organization of Buddhist reform.

7.   During this century a Young Men's (and Women's) Buddhist Association was formed, patterned after the Y.M.C.A., Buddhist Sunday School classes were conducted, devotional songs modelled along the lines of Christmas carols sung etc. (see Ames 1963:284; Obeyesekere 1970a:46,62).

8. Obeyesekere (1970a:52-53) discusses the highly charged symbolic meaning of the "**anagarika**" role and its production within the modern social and political context of Sri Lanka. He points out that it can best be understood in its relation of contrast with the role of the Buddhist monk. A person in the **anagarika** role wears a white robe (unlike the yellow robe of the monk), which is worn in a distinctive way. The **anagarika** does not shave his head (again unlike the monk) and this signifies greater involvement in the everyday world. A person in the **anagarika** role is an example of the purity and perfection of the Buddha's way, the ideal in the midst of the mundane. The entry on the meaning of **anagarika** in the **Encyclopaedia of Buddhism** (1966 Fascicle 4:513) published in Sri Lanka states that, "Among the most venerated disciples of the Buddha were people who had been scavengers and barbers before entering the Order, who won that veneration by practising virtue **(sila)** in the Order. The doors of the Order are wide open, and anybody could enter and work out his salvation. This attitude was based on the belief that the birth of a person does not matter much and what matters is his action or conduct. One becomes high or low by the various actions one performs."

9. The influence of the Anagarika Dharmapala was particularly noticeable among Sinhalese intellectuals. Amunugama (1979) discusses his influence on Sinhalese intellectuals and particularly on the Sinhala novelist, Piyadasa Sirisena.

10. Caste, the social relationships formed through it, and Sinhalese and ruling colonial ideas about caste, was and is of critical importance in an understanding of the social and political shaping of modern Sri Lanka. The way in which social relations ordered through the hierarchy of caste affected the fortunes of different communities sharing a common caste identity is beyond the scope of this book. The rich historical material presented by Michael Roberts (1982) details the importance of caste for coastal Sinhalese (especially the karava, but also for other castes) in the structuring of their relations in a developing capitalist economy. (See also my Chapter 3 on the berava community in this book.)

Broadly, I conceive of caste in modern Sri Lanka as chiefly significant in a context of underlying class processes and as a particular manifestation, in everyday social and political discourse, of the dynamics of class relations. Caste is one of the cultural forms which class assumes. It is an element in the reproduction of the structures of class domination and is one of the major factors in class fractionalization. Through shared caste identity (in itself motivated in the social, economic, and political circumstances of a dominant capitalist economy), middle-class Sinhalese are bound in common association with others over whom they dominate in a class system. This creates caste as a factor in the reproduction of class power even while it is an agency of the fractionalizing of the middle class, working class, and peasantry.

Cultural ideas relating to caste, and especially those ideas concerning the position of castes within a ranked hierarchy of caste, are part of a powerful ideology of class domination. The meaning of caste ideas and their significance when introduced into an everyday discourse is not to be discovered by an examination of such ideas in and of themselves but in their articulation within a structure of class relations. If caste sometimes appears as the contradiction or, perhaps, the negation of class, it is so as a function of the historical transformation of caste, of the relationships of caste and of the meaning of caste, within the process of the formation of a class structure.

11. Following a recent change in government, restrictions on overseas travel have been relaxed. A new wave of overseas migration has begun to

the oil-rich states of the Middle East. During a return visit to Galle in 1979, I discovered that many of the previously unemployed or marginally employed karava youth had joined in this migration, becoming a source of new-found wealth to the community.

12. The rise to entrepreneurial prominence of the karava traders was an element in a rise in rank of the caste community, and this in turn helped win the support of other karava who were economically and politically subordinate to them. The karava were traditionally a nonlanded caste who predominantly engaged in fishing. Caste rank in Sri Lanka was traditionally based on a feudal system of land control and ownership, which was determined by the nature of the service performed for a king or feudal lord (**rajakariya**). Those who had no land and performed polluting work, which the karava largely did as killers of fish, were placed low in the caste hierarchy. The farming caste (goyigama) is traditionally acknowledged as the highest caste. The movement of many karava out of fishing, their accumulation of landed property (often at the expense of peasants from other castes), and the achievement of prominence in the local and national political arena, have contributed to a rise in caste rank whereby many in urban areas view karava as almost on a par in caste rank with goyigama. Karava, of course, claim that they have always been equal to goyigama in rank. Middle-class karava, the descendants of the early traders, become rankled visibly when they or their children are referred to as fishermen. Some go as far as to say that they were never fishermen, but were descended instead from Indian trading castes or **chetties**. Most state that fishing was simply what they did to earn a living, and that in reality they held a high caste rank as soldiers to the ancient Sinhalese kings, who entrusted them with guarding the seaboard against foreign invasion. At the front of funeral and temple processions, when the community presents its public face, are carried the caste flag and a sword, symbols of their military past (Raghavan 1961). Generally, however, the success of the karava commercial ventures resulted in an increase among all karava of a new pride in their caste identity and welded them behind the entrepreneurs who were the standard-bearers of their new esteem.

13. Marx distinguished between religious fetishism and a variety of fetishes in the economy, two of the most important being commodity fetishism and the fetishism of capital (see Cohen 1978:115-113 for an excellent general discussion, and also Taussig 1980, for a specific anthropological application of the concept of commodity fetishism). For Marx a religious fetish simply lacks the power attributed to it. However, an economic fetish **does** have some of the power it **appears** to have but not for any inherent reason (e.g. the power which may be seen to inhere in capital and commodities is their illusion of appearance). An economic fetish has power in its articulation in a system of production which also is generative of its modes of appearance which become fetishized. My usage of fetishism to apply to Sinhalese religious practice is in accordance with Marx' perspective on economic fetishism. That is, religious ideas and practices do have power but not in themselves, rather through their articulation within a class structure.

Marx' concept of economic fetishism is closely related to his broader approach to ideology, an approach which informs the direction of the analysis in much of this chapter. "It is to be noted here, as in general with ideologists, that they inevitably put the thing upside-down and regard their ideology both as the creative force and the aim of all social relations, whereas it is only an expression and symptom of these relations" (Marx and Engels 1976:444).

14. While the distinction made here between **preta** and **kumbhanda** has its significance in the relations of class, there is a general cultural understanding among many exorcists and some lay Sinhalese which associates the **kumbhanda** with the temples and especially the Buddha relics. Marasinghe (1974:23-238) discusses the etymology of the term **kumbhanda**. He suggests that it might derive from the practice of urn burial. For example, a **kumbhanda**, in brahmanic and Sanskrit literature is referred to as a pot in which the bones of the deceased are collected **and**, has the further sense of a receptacle from which the spirit of the dead person rises. The Buddha **dagaba** (relic chamber) could be conceived as akin to a burial urn and the association of the **kumbhanda** with the temple area a possibility, therefore, of cultural thought.

15. Obeyesekere (1975a;1977a) argues that the ritual activities of middle-class Sinhalese, their increasing appeal to the deities and to sorcery rites, is largely a function of psychological anxieties associated with urbanized conditions. This may be so, but what I direct attention to is the production of such "anxieties" within the process of a social and political order. Moreover, I stress that the management of such anxieties takes the form and the direction it does because of the way control and power in the social and political order is culturally conceived in relation to the supernatural. My point is that middle-class worship of the deities is not simply a function of anxiety interpreted in psychological terms which reduces out of the fact that it is a **middle-class anxiety** formed in the relations of the society as a whole.

16. Obeyesekere (1981) presents a detailed analysis of seven individual cases of mystical experience which involve considerable ritual innovation. Most of the individuals concerned might be categorized as lower-status members of the middle class.

17. Members of the working class see exorcism as entirely appropriate to their identity as Sinhalese Buddhists. On one occasion I was present in a fisherman's house when the family was discussing a daughter's illness. She had been to the hospital for medicine but her fever had not yet abated. Her grandmother was then visiting the house and in an accusing manner blurted out to the girl's mother and father, "Why don't you get a **gurunanse** (an exorcist) and have a **tovile** performed? Now new fashions have come to Galle . . . you only go to doctors. We are not Christians. We want to do work according to Buddhism."

3: Exorcists

1. The navandanna are traditionally the artisan caste who provided the silversmiths, blacksmiths, and coppersmiths in the Kandyan provinces and also the Low Country. They also provide the carpenters, woodworkers, and lacquer workers (see Ryan 1953:111-13). There is a large community of navandanna in Galle; they live in areas adjacent to the main goyigama-dominated neighborhoods. Many of the navandanna are prominent in the gem business. Knox (1911) and Davy (1821) rank them as high in the hierarchy of caste and close to the goyigama. My general observations in Galle town indicate that this is still the case. In the text I have noted that some berava change their names to ones indicative of higher caste rank. Their choice of navandanna names may be facilitated by their engagement in occupations (e.g., as sculptors, carpenters, etc.) which are similar to those understood to be traditionally pursued by navandanna.

2. Weaving is an occupation traditionally associated with the berava (Ryan 1953:124), and, I suggest, is linked with the more modern role of tailor.

3. Sixty-five berava men in this area are in cash-earning employment. Twenty-nine of these are in occupations dependent on knowledge held traditionally in their caste community. These occupations include: **tovil** organizer (5), actor (3), dancer (4), drummer (6), mask-maker (4), puppeteer (1), temple painter (6). The non-traditional occupations filled by berava of the area are: building contractor (6), small shop owner (1), curio manufacturer (2), jeweller (1), electrician (2), mechanic (2), carpenter (2), tailor (4), hospital orderly (3), driver (1), housepainter (2), ticket collector (2), laborer (6), pavement hawker (1), pickpocket (1). Many of those engaged in the non-traditionally oriented occupations occasionally ply their traditional knowledge and participate in exorcisms.

4. The 1824 census, which included information on caste distribution, indicated that the greatest concentration of berava was in the Tangalle and Matara areas, where they constituted 3.5 percent of the Sinhalese population. Ryan (1953:291) states that from his information it is unlikely that the proportion of berava to the total population has increased.

5. Ryan (1953:124-28) points to sub-castes within the berava, particularly in the Kandyan areas, the major sub-caste being that principally connected to funeral drumming. I did not encounter distinct sub-castes among the berava where I worked. It is clear, particularly in rural areas, however, that the high- or low-status ranking of specific berava lineages reflected the particular ritual expertise or practice of lineage members.

6. The life histories I have collected from berava indicate that few of them gained an education, particularly in the early part of this century, in either formal government or private missionary-run educational institutions. What education they did receive was from charitable organizations who worked in berava communities.

7. These exorcism performers were individuals whom I had seen performing in berava groups, and who were learning the art. The main dancer and comic actor, however, was a man who had gained most of his experience working in tourist hotels. To my knowledge he had no regular contact with berava.

8. The salagama became in colonial times associated with the occupation of cinnamon peeling and are concentrated in areas where this was a major industry (Ryan 1953:108). Possibly because of the economic advantage they achieved in the colonial period, they have gained important positions socially, economically, and politically in modern Sri Lanka. They are generally regarded as relatively high in the island's caste hierarchy. Members of this caste are frequently aligned with the karava in the political and economic life of Galle and also in the wider national arena.

9. I have not discussed the importance of the expansion of the tourist industry in producing variation in exorcist practice and, in my view, leading to significant changes in the art. Tourist hotels, anxious to meet the tourist interest in the "exotic," give employment to exorcists to perform "devil-dancing." This employment is lucrative, relative to what an exorcist might otherwise earn. One disadvantage with the attraction of exorcists into tourist entertainment is that it is often the younger exorcists, those who are learning their art and who will comprise the next generation of exorcists, who are drawn into the tourist world. As a result, the passage of traditional knowledge concerning the exorcist art is threatened. Young exorcists are removed from a situation of routine practice and are detached from, and enabled to operate independently of, a learning context commanded by older exorcists more steeped in the esoteric domains of their tradition.

4:   Demonic Illness: Diagnosis and Social Context

1. The nine forms of Riri Yaka are:

	Principal Humor Affected	
Iramudun Riri	bile/blood	attacks at midday
Maru Riri	wind	causes death
Avamangalle Riri	phlegm	causes death
Tanipala Riri	wind	attacks near crossroads, intersections, etc.
Wanda Riri	bile/blood	causes barrenness
Gopalu Riri	bile/blood	attacks near cattle
Totupola Riri	phlegm	attacks at river crossings, near streams, or washing places
Dala Riri	bile/blood	causes general fright
Rata Yakkum ne Riri	bile/blood	afflicts women generally and attacks particularly when they are menstruating

2.   Exorcists adjust the cost of major exorcisms to suit the income of the household. This produces some variation in the amount which will be charged. Many clients cannot afford to pay immediately the cost of a performance and will pay the exorcist over an extended period.

3.   Relatives and neighbors of the exorcism household contribute food and other material items to be used for the ritual (e.g., banana tree trunks for the offering baskets and the decoration of the ritual structures, coconut leaves, coconuts,), as well as their assistance in the ritual preparations.

4.   Wirz (1954:89-94) gives a general description of this rite. It is performed between approximately 11:00 A.M. and 2:00 P.M. Basically it is similar to the evening and midnight watches of the other major demon ceremonies (see Chapter 7). It concludes with the burning of an effigy (pambaya) at the cremation place (purale), which is located at some distance from the patient's house. This act and the events preceding it are similar to those performed in the avamangalle period of a large-scale ceremony (see p. 146).

5.   There are other rites available for the treatment of illness in children. Those performed, though rarely, by exorcists are for the bala-giri female demons (see Wirz 1954:96-102).

6.   My family provides an example of great satisfaction with exorcist practice. Our seven year old son, Roland, developed an abscessed tooth and we were advised by a Colombo dentist that it should be surgically removed. This involved a general anaesthetic (our son was horrified) and the operation caused some pain and trauma. But we thought that the danger had been averted. Imagine our surprise a few days later when our son's face suddenly

ballooned. It seemed that the abscess had not been removed, the dentist had failed, and our son was suffering from malpractice. By odd chance our son experienced this sudden swelling while we were on the way to visit an exorcist friend in the countryside. Our friend immediately suspected demonic agency and performed a **tel mantirima.** A few moments passed, then the abscess burst and the swelling immediately subsided. Roland showed no further trace of illness.

7. Performance itself as integral to the effectiveness of ritual has been noted for other ethnographic contexts (e.g., Tambiah 1977, 1981; Kleinman 1980).

8. There is some tendency for instances of demonic attack to cluster together. Thus when one household in a neighborhood is afflicted by demons, other households often follow suit. I think this exemplifies one of the general theses of this chapter, the argument that once one instance of demonic attack is recognized, the demonic as part of the experience of others becomes an increasing possibility.

9. Of popular concern in daily life is the Buddhist thesis of rebirth. Often children are reported in the national press as being living evidence of the truth of this thesis. It is possibly because of the widespread attitude that children are not likely to delude their elders that considerable verity is attached to such instances.

10. Alexander (1982:59-60) describes **sittu** organization in a fishing village. As he records for the area in which he worked, in Galle all the **sittu** organizers I encountered were women. Some middle-class women in Galle join **sittu,** but they do so often in the face of opposition from their husbands.

11. Wahumpura are a middle-ranked caste. In accordance with typifications of the traditional caste order, members of the caste are associated with the occupation of jaggery **(hakkuru)** making.

12. I encountered one woman, considered by others in her neighborhood to be insane, who had twenty major exorcisms performed over a period of fifteen years.

13. Obeyesekere (1981) presents the most thorough attempt for the Sinhalese context to link the personal and psychological experiences of individuals with the sociocultural world in which they live. Obeyesekere's argument combines a psychoanalytic orientation with a Weberian perspective and is primarily directed to an examination of the deep, usually psychological, processes underlying individual agency in the construction of religious and cultural symbols and ritual practice. This analysis is a valuable antidote to the more structural and less individualistically centered approach I adopt. My orientation shares with that of Obeyesekere a concern for the nature of human individual experience and its importance for anthropological description. I differ from him, however, as to how this may be best approached, suspending as far as possible judgements concerning the inner psychological condition of an individual except as this is grasped through an external, intersubjective world of objectified experiences: objectifications which are formed out of the social and emerge through the contradictions and process of an historical and material reality upon which consciousness, and experience reflected in consciousness, is shaped.

14. My whole analysis in this chapter, and the work of others such as AmaraSingham (1980) in the Sri Lanka context, supports the methodological importance of Fabrega's (1971) criticism of the static nature of some medical anthropological analyses which ignore the process of illness construction.

5:    Exorcisms and the Symbolic Identity of Women

1. Ortner (with Whitehead 1981) has now extended beyond her 1974 position, but without any radical disclaimer. Her current work is directed more firmly to grounding the study of gender in the structure of practice and in the transformation of social and political relations. I received a copy of Ortner and Whitehead's **Sexual Meanings** too late in the preparation of this monograph to consider the general argument that it is the organization of "prestige systems" which are of key importance in influencing gender ideas (1981:25-26).

2. AmaraSingham (1978:103) suggests that Ortner's general formulation should be reworked to fit the Sinhalese Buddhist context. This is so given that Buddhism explicitly places "the ultimate goal of human life beyond or outside culture." My application of Ortner's argument is one which attempts to adapt it to the specific Sinhalese Buddhist situation in which gender ideas are constituted.

6:    The Demonic Illusion: Demons and the Cosmic Hierarchy

1. Boyd (1973) explores in some depth the position of Mara in Sinhalese Buddhism. He makes an interesting comparison between Mara and Satan. For extended discussions of the role of Mara in Sinhalese Buddhism, see Ling (1962) and Marasinghe (1974).

2. The three major deities of the Hindu pantheon, Shiva, Vishnu, and Brahma are represented in their benign and malevolent aspects at **bali** ceremonies. As presented in clay images and in the organization of the central ritual structure, which is marvelously decorated with flowers, they dominate the other supernaturals present, but at a lower level of structure in the cosmos. Neville (1954, vol. 1:342) gives a list of some of the planetary deities and demons which are given offerings at **bali** ceremonies. He records that Vishnu is depicted in the form of a **raksa** and also describes the image of Graha Bhairava. Bhairava is a demonic manifestation of Shiva.

3. The ability of the gods and demons to manifest themselves in different forms is contained in the concept of **avatara.** Among Sinhalese exorcists this term is used widely to refer to different forms of the same supernatural being. This is distinct from the Hindu textual tradition, where **avatara** is mainly restricted to the various manifestations of Vishnu.

4. Ames (1964a:44) reduces the vast host of supernatural beings into three broad classes: benevolent deities; benevolent/malevolent deities; and malevolent demons and ghosts. While my own information broadly agrees with such a classification, I stress the process of the Sinhalese cosmological system in which individual beings regardless of their rank order in the cosmos can assume a malevolent aspect. In a sense it is possible for even the lowest beings in the cosmic hierarchy to become benevolent. Thus demons, upon receiving offerings and upon being resubordinated in the hierarchical order, reverse their malevolence and agree to help restore patients to health. This is sometimes a feature of the dramatic discourse between demons and human beings at the close of major exorcisms.

5. According to Wirz (1954:128), **gara** "means sickness, ailment, poison, but also antidote . . ." The ceremonies within which they appear are directed to general misfortunes (poor harvests, failure in other economic and domestic endeavors, etc.). In the Galle area they are particularly associated with fishing and will be placated to overcome both the dangers of this occupation and to ensure improved catches. When presented in ritual

(in the **gam maduva** ceremony for Pattini and in the rite specifically performed for them, the **Gara Yakuma**), they are depicted as climbing out of the sea onto dry land.

There are twelve **gara** demons; these are different but equivalent manifestations of the twelve forms of Kalu Kumara. Thus Vata Kumara (Round Prince) is equivalent to Vata Gara, Tota Kumara (Ferry Crossing Prince, also connected to the humor of water) to Tota Gara, Riri Madana Kumara (Heat, Fire of Sexual Passion Prince) to Riri Madana Gara, Sohon Kumara to Sohon Gara, etc. This information adds support to my general contention that the myriad demonic forms in the Sinhalese cosmos constitute multiple refractions of each other.

6. Many of the mythical events recorded for one demon are completely interchangeable with other demons. Except for the name of the demon, I sometimes recorded almost word for word the same events in the lives of different demons.

7. Exorcists say that Riri has the face of a monkey. Some exorcists state that he is a demonic form of Hanuman of the **Ramayana.**

8. In the Wilhelm Geiger (1960) translation of the **Mahavamsa**, the great chronicle of Buddhism in Sri Lanka, one of the ten paladins of the Sinhalese hero Dutthagamani is referred to as "Mahasona" (another being Gothaimbara). Geiger (1960:159 fn. 1) cites another text in which Jayasena is named as a demon subdued by Gothaimbara. It seems to me that the "Mahasona" of the **Mahavamsa** and Jayasena of the other text are one and the same. This is certainly indicated in the myth cycle concerning Gothaimbara, the event of his killing Jayasena only being one in a sequence of other events. The Gothaimbara myth cycle is being prepared for publication.

9. In the version reported by Wirz (1954:34-35) Jivahatta is violently dismembered by the women. I also collected similar accounts.

10. My usage of the term "hierarchy" has much in common with that elaborated by Dumont (1970). I stress the principle of encompassment in hierarchy, and that the hierarchy of the Sinhalese cosmos is one which emphasises "status" over "power." The "political" is encompassed in the cosmic hierarchy, and is secondary, as well as mediating, of forces with greater ordering capacities in the cosmic scheme. A fundamental message of the various demon myths is that political authority and power, the authority and power of kings, for example, is unable to generate the overall order of the hierarchy of the cosmic whole. Although Dumont excludes Sri Lanka from his general argument, I think an examination of demon myths might support an extension of Dumont's theses to Sri Lanka. In particular, I consider that Dumont's discussion of kingship and power in the Indian system is applicable to the Sri Lankan case.

11. The boar, of course, has multivalent symbolic properties. In Hindu tradition, Vishnu as the Boar (Varaha) killed the demon Hiranyaksa, and raised the earth on his tusks to save it from being submerged in the depths of the cosmic ocean. (Hopkins 1971:102; see also, O'Flaherty 1976:35). There are similar Sinhalese myths, though one I recorded named Maha Brahma as the divinity who took the form of the boar. The link between Sinhalese Buddhist exorcist tradition and Indian traditions is obvious, and exorcists recognize the boar as one of the manifestations of Vishnu. It is possible to interpret Mahasona's riding the boar of Vishnu as not simply indicative of his inversion of the cosmic order, but as signifying the uncertainty of his dominance and the immanence of Mahasona's destruction by the deity. The boar is also a symbol of royal power, and thus of Mahasona's strength. Hopkins (1971:109) notes that the boar was adopted as a dynastic emblem of South Indian Calukya kings.

7:    The Exorcism of the Great Cemetery Demon: Event and Structure in
      Major Exorcisms

      1. The main distinguishing events of the **Iramudun samayama** occur at
midday, when Riri Yaka in his midday form (Iramudun Riri) is at his most
powerful.   The events, similar in their mode of presentation to the
avamangalle episode in the larger all-night demon ceremonies (see p. 146),
are marked by the exorcist entering a funeral bier (**mala darahava**) and
offering himself as a corpse to the demon. A straw dummy (**pambaya**) of a
human being is placed at his feet, and Riri is tricked into taking it rather
than the exorcist. The exorcist is then taken in the bier together with the
dummy to the **purale** (cremation place) at some distance from the ritual
house. The mood of this episode is comic, and the participants, particularly
the close male relatives of the patient who should carry the bier, take
delight in their fooling of Riri. The ritual ends at the cremation place with
the burning of the straw dummy, which contains the essence of Iramudun
Riri. This event, with certain variations, is sometimes enacted in the all-
night exorcisms, but this is rare.
      2.   Several descriptions are available of exorcism performances.   My
article "Entertaining Demons" (1975) gives a fairly comprehensive account
of one performance of the **Mahasona** (also Kapferer 1977a, 1979a, 1979c, for
less detailed descriptions).   Paul Wirz (1954) gives the most complete
descriptive coverage of exorcism practice in an area close to where I
worked. This is a major reference for anyone interested in exorcism and
provides valuable comparative data for the description I give here. The late
Michael Egan has described in the greatest detail the **Mahasona** based on
material collected in the Hambantota District some thirty miles to the
southeast of where I worked. There are some differences between what he
recorded and what I describe here. However, the basic overall form of the
rite seems to be much the same. Tambiah (1981:144-149) has summarized
the main events of the **Mahasona** as observed by Egan. While the listing of
these events differs from my own (see Table 5), it is interesting that in
many ways the broad analytical interpretation provided by Tambiah probably
fits my material even better than it does the observations recorded by Egan.
It should be stressed here that Michael Egan is mainly concerned with a
detailed computer analysis of the verses and songs included in the **Mahasona**.
Unfortunately his study, entitled **A Configurational Analysis of a Sinhalese
Healing Ritual** has not been published and this is a pity, for it would be
invaluable for our ethnographic knowledge of Sri Lanka.   The work of
Gananath Obeyesekere is vital to any student of ritual in Sri Lanka, and he
has published a number of excellent descriptions of exorcisms. His article
on the **Sanni Yakuma** is perhaps the most relevant to this description
(Obeyesekere 1969). Goonatilleka (1978) has published an important book on
Sinhalese masks which includes not only a description of the masks used in
exorcism but also an account of the **Sanni Yakuma** exorcism. I am not sure
where the material was collected, which is relevant since his data differ in
certain details from my own and also that of Obeyesekere.   The overall
structure of events in the rite described by Goonatilleka is, nonetheless,
broadly similar.
      Other accounts of exorcism performances which may be valuable to
those interested in comparing my material and in gaining a sense of their
occasion are those of Yalman (1964); Sarachchandra (1966); Halverson
(1971); and Ames (1978). Stirrat (1977) gives a description of an exorcism

among Sinhalese Catholics and, as would be expected, it is considerably different from those among Sinhalese Buddhists well south of his research area.

3. The failed exorcism to which I refer organized key ritual events out of appropriate sequence according to exorcist tradition. This break with appropriate sequencing involved the following rearrangement of ritual episodes: the **Mahasona dapavilla** (death of Mahasona), followed by the **avatara balima,** and then the comedy of the **Mangara pelapaliya.** That Mahasona should appear first and not at the end of this sequence was at the insistence of the patient's household and against the advice of the exorcist. The members of the patient's household were concerned that their exorcism be as dramatic as possible and had spread information that the patient would become entranced. Such information often adds to the size of an audience. In my view the change in the sequencing contributed to the complete disarray which occurred. The exorcists lost their command over the ritual action, fights broke out in the audience, and the exorcists themselves were subjected to considerable aggression by household members. The exorcist who performed the **avatara balima** was beaten and punched. This is a potential of the cultural ideas which relate to this episode, though on this occasion the reaction was extreme.

4. Masks, clothing, and drums are the personal property of individual exorcists. These are inherited from father to son, although occasionally an exorcist's teacher will give his ritual dress and masks to a student.

5. The **madu puraya** does not wear a cloth mask in the preparation of food offerings to be given to the demons. This contrasts with practice in major rites for the deities, where the ritual assistant who prepares food offerings wears a mask to prevent the offerings from becoming polluted by human breath.

6. Goonatilleka (1978:24) refers to the **sima midula** as the **yaga vedikave** or "demon forest." Such a term is entirely appropriate to the function of the performance arena as the gathering place of the demonic, but I did not encounter the term in the exorcist traditions in which I worked.

7. In a few exorcisms I have seen a special shelter for the patient (**atura pandala** or **atura maduva**) erected away from the house but at one side of the performance arena. It is common practice in the **Suniyama** exorcism for the major ritual structure (**atamagala**) to be constructed at one end of the porch of the patient's house, and occasionally inside the house. This is never done for the other demon exorcisms, the **vidiya** always being constructed on open ground in front of the house. On some occasions a special hut (**maduva**) is built for a **Suniyama** which includes the **atamagala,** the performance arena, and the place where the patient is seated. This hut will be decorated with a variety of fruits, leaves, etc. It is similar to the hut and enclosure built for the major deity ceremonies of the **devol** and the **gam maduva.**

8. A **riyana** is a traditional Sinhalese measure which is the length between the bone on the inside of the elbow to the tip of the fourth finger (Peiris 1956:89, after Knox 1911).

9. The four outer **torana** of the **Mahasona vidiya** are sometimes linked to the central **pancha massa** by four arches (**arukku**). This is relatively uncommon in the area of Galle town but is more frequent practice in rural areas. My evidence suggests that this is the traditional mode of construction of the **Mahasona vidiya.** The overall shape of the **Mahasona vidiya** is intended to model that structure traditionally erected at a funeral site. This is consistent with the underlying logic of the events which center on the **vidiya,** which associate the demonic with death and which are engaged with bringing about the "death" of the demonic.

10. On some occasions a clay image of Mahasona, instead of a painting, will be made and placed on the ground beside the **vidiya.**

11. The seven main leaves used to decorate the **vidiya** are from the following trees. I also indicate some of their major symbolic associations.

Bo	**(Ficus religiosa)** —— the sacred tree of Buddhism. The tree under which the Buddha achieved Enlightenment.
Na	**(Mesua ferrae)** —— after the Bo tree, perhaps the second most sacred tree in Sri Lanka. This tree, the ironwood, is the tree of Natha who is understood as being the next Buddha. It is a tree of symbolic significance in the deity ceremonies of the **gam maduva** and **devol maduva.**
Nuga	**(Ficus benghalensis)** —— the banyan tree is connected with Vishnu, the deity who protects Buddhism in Sri Lanka. Also linked with the planetary deity of Saturn (Senasuru).
Sal or hal	**(Rourea minus)** —— the tree under which Gautama Buddha was born. Leaves are prominently used in the **Rata Yakuma** exorcism, which is a ritual taking birth as a major symbolic theme. The resin from the tree is used to make **dummala,** the incense which attracts demons and which, when burned, repels pollution.
Weta-Keya	**(Pandanus zeylanicus)** —— associated with Kalu Kumara and Kalu Yaka. Also linked with the planet Mercury **(budu).**
Wara	**(Caloptris gigantea)** —— connected with the Moon. The leaves have a milky white sap and are viewed as having a high medicinal value.
Divul	**(Aegle marmelos)** —— the fruit of this tree is the woodapple **(beli)** which is understood by Sinhalese to have a high medicinal value. Linked with the Moon. Divul leaves traditionally are placed on the head before bathing on the Sinhalese New Year.

Many other leaves are used in the decoration of the structure and these, like the above, have symbolic associations with the supernatural, both deities and demons. I give a list of some of the more important leaves: **del** (**Scille hyacinthina**); **kos** (**Atocarpus integra,** or breadfruit tree leaves); **kebella** (**Aporosa lindlayana**); **burulla** (**Leea indica**). All the foregoing leaves are categorized as **kiri gas** (milk trees) and are associated with the phlegm humor, which is the humor principally affected by the **sanni** demons. In addition, coconut leaves, areca palm leaves, and mango leaves are major decorative elements of all ritual structures at exorcisms. A full description of the plants and trees used in ritual and their symbolic associations demands a separate article.

12. **Pillu** or **pilluva** is a powerful form of black magic.

13. **Trisula** is the weapon of Isvara and symbolic of his power and authority.

14. Some exorcists say that the terms **vidiya** and **purale** are interchangeable and synonymous. Indeed, in the **Iramudun Samayama** (for which no **yak vidiya** is built) the **purale** functions in a way similar to the **vidiya.**

15. My point in the text is that the structures or ritual buildings become progressively polluting as the demons enter them. However, the deities emerge within these structures as powerful and controlling over the demons, and by their power trap the demons within these structures. Overall, though, the structures are conceptualized as holding impurity within them and must be destroyed at the end of the rite.

16. One exorcist informant conceived of the streets of the **vidiya** as a series of concentric circles. At the center is Brahma. Radiating out from the center and in the following order are the streets of the gods, demons, human beings, and ghosts. This information, of course, is consistent with the view of the **vidiya** as modeling the order of the cosmic totality - a meaning which is disclosed in the course of exorcism.

17. A bamboo whistle approximately four inches long. One myth records that it was made by God Mangara from the windpipe of a wild buffalo (a manifestation of Yama, god of Death) which he tamed and rode (see Wirz 1954:51, fn. 4). It omits a high-pitched shrill sound.

18. The patient should be seated facing away from the direction from which Maruva (Death) comes. Each day Maruva is understood to come from a different one of the eight cardinal directions, and therefore, the seating position of the patient is determined accordingly. This is not always practical and exorcists say that the patient will be sufficiently protected if the right side of the body is not oriented in the direction of Maruva. This positioning of the patient is consistent with Sinhalese cultural ideas which equate the left side of the body with impurity, weakness, and death, and the right side with purity, strength, and life.

19. Neville (1954, vol 2:64) gives a slightly confusing account of the origin of these objects, but it lends support to the connection of the objects with the Vijaya-Kuveni myth. He gives evidence for the symbolic association of the **tolabo** lily with the leopard's tooth or tongue of Kuveni. Some of my own informants insisted that the plants, and especially the coconut, are symbolic of a leopard's skull. Neville, moreover, provides evidence for the origin of the **hiressa** vine in the Naga world and states that the coconut is symbolic of the head of Ganesh, and that Vishnu resides within it. The association of the coconut with Ganesh agrees with its symbolic meaning in other ritual contexts in exorcisms and elsewhere. Neville adds that the gods Isvara and Ganesh are associated with the pestle. This conflicts to some extent with the information given to me by exorcists who associate it with Maha Brahma. However, the association of the pestle with the power of the deity accords generally with the significance that my informants attached to the pestle as containing the power of the male principle. In this sense, and by extension, it could be interpreted as a Shiva (Isvara) lingam.

20. The songs in **bali** ceremonies explicitly associate the **kadaturava** with the Buddha's ending of the pestilence which afflicted the Lichchavis at Visalamahanuvara (see Kola Sanniya myth, Chapter 6). One song links the opening of the **kadaturava** with the return to health of the Lichchavis, and its words celebrate the return to sight of the blind, the dancing and walking of the crippled, the singing of the dumb, and the hearing of the deaf. Generally, the **kadaturava** is associated with the peacefulness and power of the Buddha.

21. In all the exorcisms, the order of the offerings varies according to the sex of the patient. Thus if the patient is female, the first offering, after the placement of the **Mal bulat tattuva** should be to Kalu Yaka. When the patient is a male, the first offering is usually to Suniyam Yaka. Kalu Yaka, because he is primarily associated with females, is often not given a major offering in major exorcisms performed for males. Should he be given an offering, however, it should follow that given to Suniyam Yaka. In some exorcisms the proper ordering as it was explained to me is not followed.

In the **Sanni Yakuma**, an offering basket should not be given to Mahasona during the evening watch. If Mahasona is an agent in the illness, then his basket should be presented during the midnight watch. It was stated that Mahasona and Sanni Yaka stand opposed, and that they ideally should not be given offerings at the same time. I am unclear as to why this should be so. The offerings during the evening watch of the **Sanni Yakuma** are typically to Kalu Yaka, Riri Yaka, and to Sanni Yaka. In the **Rata Yakuma,** Sanni Yaka is not given offerings in the evening watch, the offerings taking place in the morning watch.

22.   Neville (1954, vol. 2:71) cites a song in which the deity Sakra is responsible for the creation of **dummala.** This accords well with the ambiguous properties of the substance which is both attractive and repellent of demons.   Sakra is generally understood as a trickster god.   The association of **dummala** with the power of the Buddha might be representative of the general tendency of Sinhalese exorcists, as a developing historical process, to link more firmly the main symbolic articles of their work with Buddha and events in his former lives.

23.   The **rasas** are central concepts in the famous treatise on drama, the **Natyasastra,** written by Bharata Muni (**circa** second century A. D.). Bharata lists eight **rasas: srngara, hasya, karuna, raudra, vira, bhayanaka, bibhatsa,** and **adbhuta** (awesome). The meaning Bharata assigns to them is the same as that stated by exorcists; the latter, however, add a ninth **rasa, santi rasa.** This is also the case with the tenth century Hindu philosopher of aesthetics and commentator on the Bharata, Abhinavagupta, in his **Abhinavabharati** (see Masson and Patwardhan 1970). The work of the Bharata Muni was known throughout the great centers of learning in India and had great influence upon Sanskrit literature. Clearly, Bharata's work must have developed upon popular traditions, traditions with which exorcist practice is closely allied. It is possible that exorcists have some knowledge of the theory and philosophy of Sanskrit aesthetics and may in modern times have had certain aspects of it communicated to them by Indian, Sri Lankan, and Western scholars interested in their work. Relatives of some of the exorcists with whom I studied teach aspects of the exorcist art (specifically dance and drumming) at one university in Sri Lanka. However, it is my impression that knowledge of the **rasas,** and an emphasis on their importance in the work of exorcism, is deeply embedded in exorcist practice quite independently of the influence of scholarly traditions.

24.   The color of the cloth is not always red. Often it is any **colored** or multicolored cloth. The color of the cloth is understood by exorcists to produce disquiet, a mental disturbance, or the mental confusion of the demonic in the patient. Structurally, therefore, the cloth as colored and indicative of the demonic contrasts with the **kadaturava** which as white or colorless is also indicative of quietude and the Buddha.

25.   One seventy year-old and extremely reliable exorcist informant stated that ideally there should be three dancers and that together they represent the **tri murti** of the Hindu pantheon: Brahma, the creator; Vishnu, the developer and protector; and Shiva, the destroyer.

26.   Some of the older dancers stated that the dress and other ornamentation should be distributed at the twelve points of the body corresponding to the twelve points of the zodiac (see Wirz 1954:117). These twelve points are in turn linked with specific major deities in the Sinhalese pantheon and with the lesser planetary deities. My information suggests that the dress, and ornamentation of the dancers encode the hierarchy and order of the Sinhalese cosmological system. The details of this, as I recorded them, are highly imprecise, there being considerable disagreement among the exorcists whom I interviewed regarding which deities, planets, zodiacal signs, etc. are linked to which part of the body, its dress and ornamentation. Some of my data on the zodiacal signs and their relation to the body, as I collected this from exorcists, is at marked variance with the data recorded by Wirz, but this might be a consequence of variation across different exorcist traditions.

27. There are five basic dance steps (**pada,** positions of the feet), and it is in their combination that the various dances (**pade, natum)** are formed. Each of the basic steps corresponds with a particular vocalized sound; these correspond with the five basic elements (**pancha mahabhuta).** As I was given them they are: **tat** (apo, water); **dith** (vayo, wind); **ton** (tejo, fire); **nan** (**Pathavi,** earth); **jen** (akasa, ether). Given the information that I have presented here it follows that the combination of the five dance steps is also a combination of the basic elements of material form. It is in this combination that the powers of the supernatural are created and made manifest, which of course accords well with exorcist views concerning the creative energy of the dance.

Zimmer (1972:152) in his discussion of South Indian bronze representations of Shiva as the Lord of the Dance captures much of the sense of my description here, as well as aspects of my later argument in Chapter 8. Zimmer states, "The details of these figures are to be read, according to the Hindu tradition, in terms of a complex pictorial allegory. The upper hand . . . carries a little drum, shaped like an hour-glass, for the beating of the rhythm. This connotes Sound, the vehicle of speech, the conveyor of revelation, tradition, incantation, magic, and divine truth. Furthermore, sound is associated in India with Ether, the first of the five elements. Ether is the primary and most subtly pervasive manifestation of the divine Substance. Out of it unfold, in the evolution of the universe, all the other elements, Air, Fire, Water, and Earth. Together, therefore, Sound and Ether signify the first, truth-pregnant moment of creation, the productive energy of the Absolute, in its pristine, cosmogenetic strength." As Zimmer says, the dance of Shiva is "an act of creation," and "the forces gathered and projected in his frantic, ever-enduring gyration, are the powers of the evolution, maintenance, and dissolution of the world."

28. At temples the typical course of movement around the Bo tree and the **dagaba** is clockwise.

29. The fire of the torches is specifically associated with Gini (fire) Pattini. The action of holding the flaming torches against the chest is more elaborately performed in the dance episodes of the **Rata Yakuma,** where clearly the seven queens are manifestations of Pattini. Neville (1955, vol. 3: 96) denies this relation, but I think he is mistaken. The action I have described has mythical reference to the confrontation of Devol Deviyo and the goddess Pattini. Pattini threw up seven barriers of fire, which she plucked from her breast, to prevent the landing from India of Devol Deviyo on the southern shores of Sri Lanka. Devol, however, succeeded in extinguishing the fires and because of this power, and others that he demonstrated (e.g., he could transform sand into sugar) was admitted to the company of Sinhalese deities. The dancers, by holding the flaming torches to their chests, signify the powers of Pattini and Devol Deviyo.

30. Most of the exorcists with whom I discussed the **adavv** stressed that they were for fun and enjoyment. None suggested that they were for the gods. However, Chitrasena, who has created the traditional dances of the Sinhalese into a major nationally and internationally appreciated art form, tells me that the exorcist traditions of the Kandyan areas view the **adavv** as invocational of the gods. This is consistent with their structural location in the order of the low country exorcisms I describe.

31. Exorcists associate the symbolic articles presented in the **Mangara pelapaliya** with deities **and** with demons. That these articles are generally understood to mediate the divine and the demonic is significant for my analysis of the transformational role of the **Mangara pelapaliya** in the **Mahasona** exorcism as a whole (see Chapter 9). There is variation among exorcists as to the specific deities and demons mediated by the symbolic

objects, but general agreement that the demons involved are the **gara** demons. It is possible that the specified twelve acts are for the twelve gods (**dolos deviyo** who comprise the major deities of the Buddhist pantheon below Buddha and Sakra, see Obeysekere 1966; Gombrich 1971a:181-185). As Gombrich records, the membership of this category is highly variable from area to area. The list below of the symbolic articles and their divine and demonic associations was given to me by an eighty year old exorcist in Galle town, who is generally regarded as an expert among berava on the deeper knowledge of exorcism. His information reflects some inconsistencies, but in my view, is the most reliable which I collected. It checks out with much of the more incomplete data I received from other exorcists.

My informant stated that the **Kalu vadi** act, which follows the **Mangara pelapaliya** in my account of the **Mahasona**, can be included as part of the **Mangara pelapaliya**, but always at the end. The mediating object of Kalu Vadi (who was referred by my informant as a god - "Kalu Vadi devatava") is the **malsara** (flower-arrow), the weapon of Anangaya (god of love) and connected with Pushpa Gara.

Event in Mangara Pelapaliya	Deity	Article	Demon
1	Pattini Bumi Devi Polova mahi kantava	**watatira** (curtain)	Vata Gara
		payata pavada (cloth spread on ground at funerals)	Sohon Gara
2	Maha Brahma	**kude**	Gnana Gara
3	Vishnu	**kodiya**	?
4	Isvara	**sesat**	Kila Gara
5	Rama	**horana**	Okanda Gara
6	Gandharva	**davul/tammattam**	Molan Gara
7	Hevisi band is a combination of 5 and 6, sometimes, including 8.		
8	Saraswati	**vina**	?
9	Bhairava	**li-keliya**	Sellan Gara
10	Devol	**atmana-keliya**	Desa Gara
11	Saman	**at bandima**	Dala Raja Gara
12	Yama	**mi bandima**	Patti Gara

32. Wirz (1954:30) records that Kalu Vadi is a servant and companion of Mahasona. The myths and songs I collected definitely associate him

with Mangara. This is to some extent supported by Wirz' own evidence when he refers to Kalu Vadi devatava, indicating in this context an association with the deity, and that Kalu Vadi hunts in an area belonging to "the female deity Devi Mangra." It is possible that Wirz has confused Devi Mangra with Mangara Deviyo. Nonetheless, I should stress that Kalu Vadi is an ambiguous character, a demon, but linked with the divine.

33. Exorcists explicitly relate the **nanumura paliya** to the ritual bathing and placing of unguents on the head customarily practiced by Sinhalese at the Buddhist New Year in April. It also has explicit connection with the **nanumura mangalya** ("Festival of Anointing") described by Gombrich (1971a:134-139; also, Seneviratne 1978:56-60) performed for the Buddha image and as part of ancient Sinhalese royal ceremonial. The twelve acts which are ideally performed in the **nanumura paliya** are for the twelve major gods **(dolos deviyo)** of the Sinhalese pantheon.

34. Goonatilleka (1978:26) lists twelve **paliya** and says that they normally reduce to seven. Some exorcists in the area in which I worked said that there are more than the eight **paliya** I have listed. I did not encounter a statement to the effect that there are twelve **paliya**, although such a number would be consistent with earlier episodes in the rite, for example, the twelve **paliya** of the **Mangara pelapaliya** and the twelve **paliya** of the equivalent episode in the **Rata Yakuma**.

35. Indeed, a few exorcists insisted that formerly there were eighteen **paliya**, each connected to one of the **sanni** demons. One exorcist said that the **paliya** are the female counterparts of the male **sanni** demons.

36. Exorcists explicitly link the symbolic object carried by each **paliya** with a particular deity. One exception is the cock presented by Kukulu Paliya, which exorcists maintained was simply the sacrificial victim. No exorcist linked the cock with Kataragama, for example, which is a possibility as the cock is one of the emblems of this deity. The torches of Pandam Paliya are linked with Devol Deviyo and are said to burn with the destructive and purifying fire of Pattini and Devol Deviyo; the cloth or shroud of Salu Paliya is conceptualized as the golden shroud of the goddess Pattini; the pot of Kendi Paliya is understood to contain the purifying water from the sacred pond of Anotattavila in the Himalayas; and the pot of the Kalas Paliya is the golden pot of Polova Mahi Kantava, or Bumi devi, the goddess of the Earth and witness of the Buddhas' struggle against Mara.

37. It is conceivable that the **kapala kuduva** has some of its meaning rooted in the Hindu myths of Shiva the Brahmanicide. O'Flaherty (1976:160, 278-87) discusses various such myths concerning Shiva's beheading of Brahma. She states that "The skull-bearer is the epitome of Shiva's demonic side: Raksasas drink out of skulls and carry tridents. The beheading is sometimes regarded as bringing evil upon mankind . . . the head of Brahma that Shiva cut off united with the Naga gods to torment mankind and extort offerings" (1976:280). Some exorcists do explicitly link the **kapala kuduva** to similar Shiva myths. But Shiva (Isvara), as should now be clear, is a central deity in exorcism practice; the rice pounder, which is the axis of the **kapala kuduva**, is associated with the power of Maha Brahma and also with Isvara. The top level of the structure where the offerings to the **sanni** demons and to Deva Sanniya are placed is referred to as the head of the structure, and Deva Sanniya is linked by some exorcists to Maha Brahma (but also with Pattini). Metaphorically, the Deva Sanniya act is a reassertion of structure and the stability of hierarchy. The placing of the offerings at the top level of the structure might be a symbolic replacement of the head or skull **(kapala)** of Maha Brahma and, therefore, a return to an ordered unity.

The **kapala kuduva** can be interpreted as incorporating key messages of the exorcism rite as a whole. While it symbolizes the cosmic hierarchy it also symbolizes a return to an ordered unity of the body. In exorcist thought, the order of the cosmos is also the order of the body. Exorcists are quite explicit in this regard with reference to the **kapala kuduva.** Thus they refer to the top tier of the structure as not only the level of the gods, but also as the "head," the middle level as the "stomach," and the bottom tier as the "feet."

In an important sense the **kapala kuduva** may be seen as modeling and encoding in its vertical order the horizontal process of the exorcism. Exorcists say that the evening watch of exorcism is for the feet, that the midnight watch is for the stomach (indeed the main offering of the **avamangalle** is placed on the stomach), and that the morning watch is for the head (the exorcist in fact presenting the closing offerings to the **sanni** demons on his head).

8:   Music, Dance, and Trance

1.   I stress that the full nature of the text is only revealed in its performance and, therefore, except for analytical purposes, it is difficult to maintain a distinction. There are implicit "rules" whereby exorcisms of recognized types (e.g. **Rata Yakuma, Suniyama** etc.) are produced in practice. These "rules" govern the organization of ritual space employed at various points of the rite; the orientation of action between exorcists, a patient, members of the patient's household and the audience generally, the sequencing of named ritual episodes; the style of performance etc. Exorcists can state aspects of these rules but they are not made fully explicit except in the context of performance. They are taken-for-granted elements of exorcist knowledge and are revealed, in the course of performance itself.

2.   Rappaport (1979:177) is probably making a valid statement when he says that "ritual and drama, at least in their polar forms, are best distinguished." He is incorrect, however, in basing a distinction on his observation that ". . . dramas have audiences, rituals have congregations. An audience watches a drama, a congregation participates in a ritual." This is a conceit which completely escapes a critical dynamic of the ritual process. It begs the question of the role of the audience or, as I prefer to say it, the ritual gathering, in ritual. Members of a ritual gathering at exorcisms are continually changing in their relationship to each other and to the central ritual events. This process is part of the performance structure of exorcism and integral to its transformations.

3.   Arnold Schönberg (1950, cited in Hofstadter 1965:188) writes of Western music that "every tone which is added to a beginning tone makes the meaning of that tone doubtful. . . . there is produced a state of unrest, of imbalance which grows through most of the piece, and is enforced further by similar functions of the rhythm. The method by which balance is restored seems to me to be the real idea of the composition." This expresses very neatly a major aspect of the music in the evening and morning watches of the exorcism. The developmental instability of the drumming is brought into balance in the recombination of sounds and a shift in their tonal quality at the point the deity is understood to exert power over the demonic. This is the idea of the music, however, which is only externally and consciously realized in the later drama of the midnight and morning watches.

4.   Various scholars have noted that words in music become subordinated to the musical form and may lose some of the intelligible

capacity which they possess in ordinary speech (see Langer 1953; M. Bateson 1974:161; Tambiah 1981:163-4). I would consider that words in music constitute a particular conjunction of form in which "meaning" is reducible neither to one form nor the other but produced in the conjunction itself. That is to say, the meaning or intelligibility of words in song is carried fully in the moment of listening to song. What was heard cannot be separated from the musical context of its hearing, and hence the difficulty some may express in reporting what it was they heard.

5. When exorcists are determined to produce a trance in a patient, the drummers cluster around the patient and play the insistent and fast rhythm of the demonic. They might keep this up for five or ten minutes, until such time as the patient enters a full trance.

6. The relative grace of the patient trance in exorcism compares with that which Crapanzano (1973:196) observes among the Hamadsha. Unlike Crapanzano, I noted no distinct difference between male and female patient entrancement.

7. Exorcists do not use drugs (alcohol, marijuana, etc.) to induce trance in a patient. Exorcists, however, often consume considerable quantities of arrack during an exorcism, but to my knowledge this is not used as a technique to induce self entrancement. Some exorcists eschew the consumption of alcohol as inconsistent with their Buddhist principles.

8. Mead's formulation of a theory of a self is acknowledged as fundamental in the sociological approach of "symbolic interactionism" as developed by such scholars as Blumer (1969) and Goffman (1971, 1972). These scholars have diverged from certain key aspects of Mead's approach (see Lewis and Smith 1980, for an extended critical discussion of Blumer's development). Goffman's orientation appears to me to be highly individualistic, and one which constantly stresses the strategic aspects of self-construction and interpersonal self-presentation. This is not a dimension which I detect in Mead, whose approach is also more consistent with the social phenomenological orientation I develop in this and other chapters.

I should stress that exorcists in the Galle area conceptualize the entire process of an exorcism as a movement of the patient from a sick self **(rogi atmaya)** to a not sick self **(nirogi atmaya)**. I discuss this process more fully in Kapferer, 1979a.

9: The Comedy of Gods and Demons

1. Wirz (1954:59) states that exorcism comedy is simply entertainment, "it is only interposed for diversion and has no deeper meaning." This is clearly untrue, as Obeyesekere (1963a, 1969) demonstrates in his excellent analyses of the **Sanni Yakuma**. In his discussion of comedy, Obeyesekere combines a psychodynamic perspective with the well-known structural-functional orientation to joking developed in anthropology (e.g., Radcliffe-Brown 1940, 1949; Evans-Pritchard 1965). The analysis here is intended to provide an alternative approach to the role of comedy in exorcism and attempts to explore the nature of the comic form and its significance in the structuring of meaning in relation to the exorcism as a whole.

2. Langer (1953, 1976), following Cassirer (1947), draws a distinction between presentational and discursive symbolism. While aspects of her analysis apply quite obviously to this chapter and to Chapter 8, I have some disagreement with her contrasting of presentational and discursive symbolism (see also Hofstadter 1965; Weitz 1954) as it may be applied to exorcism (but see Kapferer 1975, 1979c, where I make explicit use of Langer). Langer underestimates the combinational and recombinational

properties of presentational symbolism, accentuating this as a function of the discursive symbolic form of words in speech. Music and dance in Langer's terms are presentational forms, and I have already shown their important qualities of combination and recombination for meaning in experience. Moreover, these presentational forms are set within the overall discursive form of the rite as a whole; thus music and dance in exorcism have some of the qualities which Langer recognizes for discursive forms. Langer stresses that the meanings or imports of presentational symbols are carried in their simultaneity of presentation, and that their meanings are a property of their whole presentational forms. In her terms, discursive forms, like comic drama, are not simultaneous, but linear and progressive. This may be so, but I draw attention to the possibility that it may not be the discursiveness of the form **per se** which is important, but other properties of the form which condition its significance and which may be obscured in a presentational/discursive contrast. This is my approach to comedy, which, of course, can have both discursive and presentational characteristics, but these characteristics do not account for its complete significance as a comedy.

3. For example, the entry of the Brahmins in the **vadiga patuna** comedy of the **Suniyama** exorcism (Wirz 1954:83) models the discovery of speech. The exorcist-actors, as this drama is typically presented, struggle to identify the various ritual objects around them, try a number of "languages," and then begin to formulate Sinhala words in their efforts to make sense of what they find before them.

4. The laughter of human beings may be contrasted with the laughter of demons. Demons laugh convulsively when they enter the performance arena. But their laughter is the laughter of disorder, manic and exaggerated. They laugh at the sorrow and tragedy of others and fail to see the comic in themselves. They laugh in isolation and not in a community of others. When the audience laughs at them, the demons often cry.

5. The masks are not all fixed. Some of the masks have hinged jaws, or are half-masks which allow some mobility to the face. However, relative to the fully mobile face, they are fixed. This is so too with the mask of the **avatara balima,** but, as explained in the text, it does not appear as fixed or out of place within the fluid whole.

6. I am not clear why a female patient walks in procession at the end of an exorcism while a male patient as a rule does not. It could be connected with a cultural recognition of the greater disturbance to the cultural and social fabric caused by demonic attack on women (see Chapter 5). The obeisance of the patient to the Buddha and the gods at the end of the rite not only reasserts what began an exorcism, but can also be seen as a contrasting structural analogue to the trance period of the midnight watch. Thus, in the obeisance to the Buddha and the gods the patient is reunited with the dominant powers and principles of the cosmos and in a condition of full reflective awareness. In trance, the patient is united with a being at the base of the cosmic hierarchy and in a condition of relative unconsciousness.

7. It must be stressed that patients do not always laugh or demonstrate amusement, but I witnessed few such occasions. If a patient fails to show amusement, this does not mean that the exorcism is viewed as a failure, and **vice versa.** All I emphasize is that exorcists and the audience see amusement and laughter as an important sign of the mental readjustment of the patient, and that the concern to make a patient laugh is part of the regular structure of performance.

Bibliography

Alexander, Paul
>   1982   **Sri Lankan Fishermen.**   Australian   National   University
>   Monographs of South Asia No. 7 Canberra ANU Press.

AmaraSingham, L. R.
>   1973   "Kuveni's Revenge: Images of women in a Sinhalese Myth."
>   **Modern Ceylon Studies** (University of Sri Lanka), vol. 4, no.
>   1/2, pp. 76-83.
>   1978   "The Misery of the Embodied." In **Women in Ritual and
>   Symbolic Roles,** edited by Judith Hoch-Smith and Anna Spring.
>   New York: Plenum Press.
>   1980   "Movement Among Healers in Sri Lanka: A Case Study of a
>   Sinhalese Patient." **Culture, Medicine and Psychiatry,** vol. 4,
>   no. 1, pp. 71-93.

Ames, M.
>   1963   "Ideological   and   Social   Change   in   Ceylon."   **Human
>   Organization** vol. 22, no. 1 (Spring), pp. 45-53.
>   1964a   "Magical-animism and Buddhism: A Structural Analysis of the
>   Sinhalese Religious System." In **Religion in South Asia,** edited
>   by E. B. Harper. Seattle: University of Washington Press.
>   1964b   "Buddha and the Dancing Goblins: A Theory of Magic and
>   Religion." **American Anthropologist** 66:76-82.
>   1966   "Ritual   Prestation   and   the   Structure   of   the   Sinhalese
>   Pantheon." In **Anthropological Studies in Theravada Buddhism,**
>   edited by M. Nash, pp. 27-50. Yale Univeristy, Southeast Asia
>   Studies 13.
>   1978   "Tovil, Exorcism by White Magic." **Natural History,** vol. 87
>   no. 1 (January), pp. 42-48.

Amunugama, Sarath
>   1979   "Ideology and Class Interest in One of Piyadasa Sirisena's
>   Novels: The New Image of the 'Sinhala-Buddhist' Nationalist."
>   In **Collective Identities, Nationalisms and Protest in Modern
>   Sri Lanka,** edited by Michael Roberts.   Colombo: Marga
>   Institute.

Anagarika Dharmapala
  1965   **Return to Righteousness.**   Edited by Ananda Guruge.
          Colombo: Government Press.
Ariyapala, M. B.
  1956   **Society in Medieval Ceylon.**   Colombo: Dept. of Cultural
          Affairs.
Austin, J. L.
  1962   **How to do Things with Words.**   Oxford: Oxford University
          Press.
Badcock, C. R.
  1975   **Levi-Strauss: Structuralism and Sociological Theory.**   London:
          Hutchinson.
Bateson, G.
  1973   "A Theory of Play and Fantasy."   In **Steps to an Ecology of
          Mind,** edited by G. Bateson.   St. Albans: Paladin.   First
          published 1955.
Bateson, M. C.
  1974   "Ritualization: A study in Texture and Texture Change."   In
          Irving I. Zaretsky and Mark Leone.   **Religious Movements in
          Contemporary America.**   Princeton: Princeton University
          Press.
Berger, P. O., and Luckman, T.
  1971   **The Social Construction of Reality.**   London: Allen Lane.
Bergson, H.
  1910   **Time and Free Will: An Essay on the Immediate Data of
          Consciousness.**   London: Allen and Unwin.
  1921   **Laughter: An Essay on the Meaning of the Comic.**   Translated
          by C. Brereton and F. Rothwell.   London: Macmillan.   First
          published 1911.
Blacking, John
  1974   **How Musical is Man**?   Seattle: University of Washington
          Press.
Blacking, John, and Kealiinokomoku, Joann W.
  1979   **The Performing Arts: Music and Dance.**   New York: Mouton.
Bloch, Maurice
  1974   "Symbols, Songs, Dance and Features of Articulation."
          European Journal of Sociology 15:55-81.
Bloch, Maurice, and Bloch, Jean H.
  1980   "Women and the Dialectics of Nature in Eighteenth Century
          France."   In **Nature, Culture and Gender,** edited by Carol P.
          MacCormack and Marilyn Strathern.   Cambridge: Cambridge
          University Press.
Blumer, Hubert
  1969   **Symbolic Interactionism: Perspective and Method.**   New
          Jersey: Prentice-Hall.
Bourdieu, Pierre
  1977   **Outline of a Theory of Practice.**   Translated by Richard Nice.
          Cambridge: Cambridge University Press.
Bourguignon, E.
  1965   "The Self, the Behavioural Environment, and the Theory of
          Spirit Possession."   In **Context and Meaning in Cultural
          Anthropology,** edited by M. Spiro.   New York: Free Press of
          Glencoe.
Boyd, J. W.
  1973   "Satan and Mara: Christian and Buddhist Symbols of Evil."
          Modern Ceylon Studies (University of Sri Lanka), vol. 4, nos. 1
          and 2, pp. 84-100.

Briggs, Jean L.
    1970   **Never in Anger: Portrait of an Eskimo Family.** Cambridge,
            Mass.: Harvard University Press.
Cassirer, Ernst
    1947   **The Philosophy of Symbolic Forms.** 3 vols. Translated by
            Ralph Mannheim. New Haven: Yale University Press.
Codrington, H. W., ed
    1917   "Diary of Mr. John D'Oyly, 1810-1815." **Journal of the Royal
            Asiatic Society,** Ceylon Branch, vol. 25, no. 69.
Cohen, Abner
    1974   **Two Dimensional Man.** Berkeley: University of California
            Press.
Cohen, G. A.
    1978   **Karl Marx's Theory of History:** **A Defence.** Oxford:
            Clarendon Press.
Crapanzano, V.
    1973   **The Hamadsha:** **A Study in Moroccan Ethnopsychiatry.**
            Berkeley: University of California Press.
Davy, J.
    1821   **An Account of the Interior of Ceylon and of its Inhabitants,
            with Travels in the Island.** Ceylon: Tisara Prakasakayo.
De Silva, K. M.
    1979   "Resistance Movements in Nineteenth Century Sri Lanka." In
            **Collective Identities, Nationalisms and Protest in Modern Sri
            Lanka,** edited by Michael Roberts. Colombo: Marga Institute.
Devanandam, P. D.
    1950   **The Concept of Maya.** London: Butterworth
Dhammapada
    1857   Translated by S. Radhakrishnan. London: Oxford University
            Press.
Douglas, M.
    1966   **Purity and Danger: An Analysis of Concepts of Danger and
            Taboo.** London: Routledge and Kegan Paul.
    1975   **Implicit Meanings:** **Essays in Anthropology.** London:
            Routledge and Kegan Paul.
Dufrenne, Mikel
    1967   **Pour L'homme.** Paris: Seuil
    1973   **The Phenomenology of Aesthetic Experience.** Translated by
            Edward S. Casey et al. Evanston: Northwestern University
            Press.
    1970   "Structuralism and Humanism" in **Patterns of the Life-World,**
            edited by J. M. Edie, F. H. Parker, and C.O. Schrag. Evanston:
            Northwestern University Press.
Dumont, L.
    1970   **Homo Hierarchicus: The Caste System and its Implications.**
            London: Weidenfeld and Nicolson.
Encyclopedia of Buddhism
    1965   Fascicle 4. Colombo: Government Press.
Ernst, T.
    1978   "Aspects of Meaning of Exchanges and Exchange Items among
            the Onabasulu of the Great Papuan Plateau." In **Trade and
            Exchange in Oceania and Australia,** edited by J. Spect and J.
            P. White. **Mankind,** vol. 11, no. 3, pp. 187-97
Evans-Pritchard, E. E.
    1965   **The Position of Women in Primitive Societies and Other Essays
            in Social Anthropology.** London: Faber and Faber.

Fabrega, H.
    1971   "Some Features of Zinacantecan Medical Knowlege."
            Ethnology 10:25-43.
    1972   "The Study of Disease in Relation to Culture." **Behavioural
            Science** 17:183-203.
Feibleman, J.
    1939   **In Praise of Comedy: A Study in its Theory and Practice.**
            London: George Allen and Unwin.
Feyerabend, Paul
    1978   **Against Method.** London: Verso.
Firth, Raymond
    1973   **Symbols: Public and Private.** New York: Cornell University
            Press.
Gadamer, Hans-Georg
    1977   **Philosophical Hermeneutics.**   Berkeley: University of
            California Press.
Garbett, G. K.
    1970   "The Analysis of Social Situations." **Man** n.s., 5, no. 2, pp.
            214-27.
Geertz, C.
    1965   "Religion as a Cultural System."   In **Anthropological
            Approaches to the Study of Religion,** edited by M. Banton.
            Association of Social Anthropologists of the Commonwealth
            Monograph 3. London: Tavistock Publications.
    1972   "Deep Play: Notes on the Balinese Cockfight." **Daedalus,** vol.
            101, no. 1, pp. 1-37.
    1973   **Interpretation of Cultures.** New York: Basic Books.
    1980   "Blurred Genres." **American Scholar** vol. 49, no. 2, pp. 165-79
Geiger, Wilhelm
    1960   **Culture of Ceylon in Medieval Times.** Edited by H. Bechert.
            Weisbaden: Otto Harrassowitz.
Giddens, Anthony
    1979   **Central Problems in Social Theory,** London: MacMillan.
Gluckman, Max
    1958   **Analysis of a Social Situation in Modern Zululand.** Rhodes-
            Livingstone Institute Paper 28.   Manchester: Manchester
            University Press.
Goffman, Erving
    1971   **Presentation of Self in Everyday Life.**   Harmondsworth,
            Middlesex: Penguin.
    1972   **Interaction Ritual: Essays on Face-to-Face Behaviour.**
            London, Allen Lane: The Penguin Press.
Gombrich, R.
    1971a   **Precept and Practice: Traditional Buddhism in the Rural
            Highlands of Ceylon.** Oxford: Clarendon Press.
    1971b   "Food for Seven Grandmothers: Stages in the Universalization
            of a Sinhalese Ritual." **Man** n.s. 6:5-17.
Goonatilleka, M. H.
    1978   **Masks and Mask Systems of Sri Lanka.** Colombo: Tamarind
            Books.
Gramsci, Antonio
    1971   **Prison Notebooks: Selections.** Translated by Q. Hoare and
            G. Smith, New York: International Publishers.
Grathoff, R.
    1970   **The Structure of Social Inconsistencies: A Contribution to a
            Unified Theory of Play, Game and Social Action.** The Hague:
            Martinus Nijhoff.

Guruge, Ananda
    1965   "Introduction" to **Return to Righteousness: A Collection of Speeches, Essays and Letters of the Anagarika Dharmapala.** Colombo: Government Press.

Halliday, F.
    1971   "The Ceylonese Insurrection." **New Left Review** 69 (September–October): 55–90.

Hallowell, A. I.
    1955   **Culture and Experience.** Philadelphia: University of Pennsylvania Press.

Halverson, J.
    1971   "Dynamics of Exorcism: The Sinhalese Sanniyakuma." **History of Religions,** vol. 10, no. 4, pp. 334–59

Handelman, D.
    1979   "Is Naven Ludic?" **Social Analysis** 1:177–92.
    1981   "The Ritual Clown: Attributes and Affinities." **Anthropos** 76:321–70

Handelman, D., and Kapferer, B.
    1972   "Forms of Joking Activity: A Comparative Approach." **American Anthropologist,** vol 74 no. 3, (June), pp. 184–517.
    1980   "Symbolic Types, Mediation and the Transformation of Ritual Context: Sinhalese Demons and Tewa Clowns." **Semiotica,** vol. 30, nos. 1 and 2, pp. 41–71.

Hanna, Judith Lynne
    1979   **To Dance is Human.** Austin: University of Texas Press.

Heidegger, Martin
    1977   "The Origin of the Work of Art." In **Basic Writings,** edited by D. F. Farrell. New York: Harper and Row.

Hofstadter, Albert
    1965   **Truth and Art.** New York: Columbia University Press.

Hopkins, Thomas J.
    1971   **The Hindu Religious Tradition.** Encino: Dickenson Publishing Company.

Horton, R.
    1960   "A Definition of Religion and its Uses." **Journal of the Royal Anthropological Institute** 90:201–26.

Houtart, F.
    1974   **Religion and Ideology in Sri Lanka.** Colombo: Hansa Publishers.

Husserl, Edmund
    1952   **Ideas.** Translated by W. R. Boyce Gibson. London: George Allen and Unwin Limited.

Jackson, A.
    "Sound and Ritual." **Man** n.s. 3:292–99.

Jaspers, Karl
    1971   **Philosophy.** Translated by E. Ashton. Chicago: Chicago University Press.

Jayawardena, V. K.
    1972   **The Rise of the Labor Movement in Ceylon.** Durham: Duke University Press

Jules-Rosette, Bennetta
    1975   "Songs and Spirit: The Use of Songs in the Management of Ritual Contracts." **Africa** vol. 45, no. 2, pp. 150–66.

Kapferer, B.
    1975   "Entertaining Demons: Comedy, Interaction and Meaning in a Sinhalese Healing Ritual." **Modern Ceylon Studies** 6:16–63 Republished in **Social Analysis** 1:108–52

1977a   "First Class to Maradana: Secular Drama in Sinhalese Healing
         Rites."   In **Secular Ritual,** edited by S. F. Moore and B.
         Myerhoff. Assen: Van Gorcum.
1977b   "Rituals, Audiences and the Problem of Reflexivity: Exorcism
         and Festival in Sri Lanka." Paper read to Burg Wartenstein
         Symposium 76 (Cultural Frames and Reflections).
1977c   "Marginality, Processes of Urban Integration, and the Urban
         Poor."   Wenner-Gren   Foundation   for   Anthropological
         Research. Symposium on Shanty Towns in Developing Nations,
         July 1977. Burg Wartenstein, Austria.
1979a   "Mind, Self and Other in Demonic Illness: The Negation and
         Reconstruction of Self." **American Ethnologist** 6:110-33.
1979b   "Ritual Process and the Transformation of Context." **Social
         Analysis** 1:3-19.
1979c   "Emotion and Feeling in Sinhalese Healing Rites." **Social
         Analysis** 1:153-76

Karunadasa, Y.
1964   "The Buddhist Conception of Mahabhutas as Primary Elements
         of Matter." **University of Ceylon Review** (April): 28-46
1967   **Buddhist Analysis of Matter.**   Colombo: Department of
         Cultural Affairs, Government Press.

Kemper, Steven
1980   "Time, Person and Gender in Sinhalese Astrology." **American
         Ethnologist,** vol. 7, no. 4, pp. 744-58.

Kierkegaard, S.
1941   **Concluding Unscientific Postscripts.** Translated by D. F.
         Swenson. London: Oxford University Press. First published
         1846.

Klapp, O.
1949   "The Fool as a Social Type." **American Journal of Sociology**
         55:157-62.

Kleinman, Arthur
1980   **Patients and Healers in the Context of Culture.** Berkeley:
         University of California Press.

Knox, R., ed.
1911   **An Historical Relation of Ceylon.** Glasgow: James Ryan.

Koestler, A.
1964   **The Act of Creation.** London: Hutchinson.

Kristeva, J.
1969   **Semiotike: Recherches pour une Semanalyse.** Paris: Seuil.

Kultgen, John
1975   "Phenomenology and Structuralism."   In **Annual Review of
         Anthropology,** edited by B. J. Siegal, vol. 4.   Palo Alto:
         Annual Reviews Inc.

Langer, S.
1953   **Feeling and Form.** London: Routledge and Kegan Paul.
1976   **Philosophy in a New Key: A Study in the Symbolism of
         Reason, Rite and Art.** Cambridge, Mass.: Harvard University
         Press. First published 1942.

Leach, E.
1961   **Rethinking Anthropology.** London: Athlone Press, University
         of London.
1962   "Pulleyar and the Lord Buddha: An Aspect of Religious
         Syncretism in Ceylon." **Psychoanalysis and the Psychoanalytic
         Review,** vol. 49, no. 21, pp. 80-102.

Leslie, Charles
    1976   **Asian Medical Systems: A Comparative Study.** Berkeley:
            University of California Press.
Le Vine, R.
    1973   **Culture, Behaviour and Personality.** London: Hutchinson.
Lévi-Strauss, C.
    1964   **Tristes Tropiques.** Translated by John Russell. New York:
            Hutchinson.
    1966   **The Savage Mind.** London: Weidenfeld and Nicolson.
    1969   **The Elementary Structures of Kinship.** Translated by J. H.
            Bell, J. R. von Sturmer, R. Needham. Revised edition.
            London: Eyre and Spottiswoode.
    1970   **The Raw and the Cooked.** Vol. I. New York: Harper and Row.
    1981   **The Naked Man.** New York: Harper and Row.
Lewis, David J., and Smith, Richard C.
    1980   **American Sociology and Pragmatism.** Chicago: University of
            Chicago Press.
Lewis, Gilbert
    1975   **Knowledge of Illness in a Sepik Society: A Study of the Gnau,
            New Guinea.** London: Athlone Press.
Lewis, I. M.
    1971   **Ecstatic Religion: An Anthropological Study of Spirit
            Possession and Shamanism.** Harmondsworth: Penguin.
Lieban, R.
    1967   **Cebuano Sorcery: Malign Magic in the Philippines.** London:
            Cambridge University Press.
    1977   "The Field of Medical Anthropology." In **Culture, Disease and
            Healing: Studies in Medical Anthropology,** edited by D.
            Landy. New York: Macmillan Publishing Company.
Ling, T. O.
    1962   **Buddhism and the Mythology of Evil: A Study in Theravada
            Buddhism.** London: Allen and Unwin
    1973   **The Buddha: Buddhist Civilization in India and Ceylon.** New
            York: Charles Scribner and Sons.
Loudon, J. B., ed.
    1976   **Social Anthropology and Medicine.** London: Academic Press.
MacCormack, Carol P.
    1980   "Nature, Culture and Gender: A Critique." In **Nature,
            Culture, and Gender,** edited by Carol P. MacCormack, and
            Marilyn Strathern. Cambridge: Cambridge University Press.
Malalgoda, K.
    1976   **Buddhism in Sinhalese Society 1750-1900.**   Berkeley:
            University of California Press.
Marasinghe, M. M. J.
    1974   **Gods in Early Buddhism: A Study in their Social and
            Mythological Milieu as Depicted in the Nikayas of the Pali
            Canon.** University of Sri Lanka. Vidyalankara Campus
            Publications Board, Kelaniya.
Marriott, McK.
    1955   "Little Communities in an Indigenous Civilization." In **Village
            India: Studies in the Little Community,** edited by McK.
            Marriott. Chicago: Chicago University Press.
    1968   "Caste Ranking and Food Transactions, a Matrix Analysis." In
            Structure and Change in Indian Society, edited by M. Singer
            and B. S. Cohn. Viking Fund Publications in Anthropology 47.
            Chicago: Aldine

Marx, Karl, and Engels, Frederick
1976   **The German Ideology.** Moscow: Progress Publishers.
Masson, J. L., and Patwardhan, M. W.
1970   **Aesthetic Rapture: The Rasadhaya of the Natyasastra.** vols. 1 and 2. Poona: Deccan College.
Mayer, A.
1960   **Caste and Kinship in Central India: A Village and its Religion.** London: Routledge.
McHugh, P.
1968   **Defining the Situation.** New York: Bobbs-Merrill.
Mead, G.
1934   **Mind, Self and Society.** Chicago: University of Chicago Press.
Merleau-Ponty, Maurice
1945   **Phenomenologie de la Perception.** Paris: Librairie Gallimard.
Mitchell, J. C.
1956   **The Kalela Dance.** Rhodes-Livingstone Paper 27. Manchester: Manchester University Press.
Moore, Sally F., and Myerhoff, Barbara G.
1977   **Secular Ritual.** Van Gorcum: Asen/Amsterdam.
Munn, Nancy
1973   "Symbolism in a Ritual Context." In **Handbook of Social and Cultural Anthropology,** edited by John S. Honigmann.
Natanson, M.
1970   **The Journeying Self: A Study in Philosophy and Social Role.** Reading: Addison-Wesley.
1974   **Phenomenology, Role and Reason: Essays on the Coherence and Deformation of Social Reality.** Illinois: Charles C. Thomas.
Needham, Rodney
1967   "Percussion and Transition." **Man** n.s. 2:606-14.
Neville, Hugh
1954   **Sinhala Verse.** Vols. 1 and 2. Edited by P. E. Deraniyagala. Colombo: Ceylon Government.
1955   **Sinhala Verse.** Vol. 3. Edited by P. E. Deraniyagala. Colombo: Ceylon Government.
Obeyesekere, G.
1963a   "The Great Tradition and the Little in the Perspective of Sinhalese Buddhism." **Journal of Asian Studies,** vol. 22, no. 2, pp. 139-53.
1963b   "Pregnancy Cravings (Dola Duka) in Relation to Social Structure and Personality in a Sinhalese Village." **American Anthropologist** 65:323-42.
1966   "The Buddhist Pantheon in Ceylon and its Extensions." In **Anthropological Studies in Theravada Buddhism,** edited by M. Nash, pp. 1-26. Yale University, Southeast Asia Studies 13.
1967   **Land Tenure in Village Ceylon.** Cambridge: Cambridge University Press.
1969   "The Ritual Drama of the **Sanni** Demons: Collective Representations of Disease in Ceylon." **Comparative Studies in Society and History,** vol. 11, no. 2, pp. 174-216.
1970a   "Religious Symbolism and Political Change in Ceylon." **Modern Ceylon Studies,** vol. 1, no. 1, pp. 43-63.
1970b   "The Idiom of Demonic Possession: A Case Study." **Social Science and Medicine** 4:97-111.
1970c   "Ayurveda and Mental Illness." **Comparative Studies in Society and History** 12:292-96.

1974   Some Comments on the Social Background of the April 1971 Insurgency in Sri Lanka (Ceylon)." **The Journal of Asian Studies** 33:367-84.

1975a   "Sorcery, Premeditated Murder and the Canalization of Aggression in Sri Lanka." **Ethnology**, vol. 14, no. 1, pp. 1-23.

1975b   "Psycho-cultural Exegesis of a Case of Spirit Possession from Sri Lanka." **Contributions to Asian Studies**, 8:41-89.

1976   "The Impact of Ayurvedic Ideas on the Culture and the Individual in Sri Lanka." In **Asian Medical Systems: A Comparative Study**, edited by Charles Leslie. Berkley: University of California Press.

1977a   "Social Change and the Deities: Rise of the Kataragama Cult in Modern Sri Lanka." **Man** 12:377-96.

1977b   "The Theory and Practice of Psychological Medicine in the Ayurvedic Tradition." **Culture, Medicine and Psychiatry** 1:155-81

1978   "The Fire-Walkers of Kataragama: The Rise of **Bhakti** Religiosity in Buddhist Sri Lanka." **Man**, vol. 37, no. 3, pp. 457-49.

1979   "The Vicissitudes of the Sinhala and Buddhist Identity through Time and Change." In **Collective Identities, Nationalisms and Protest in Modern Sri Lanka**, edited by Michael Roberts. Marga Institute, Colombo.

1981   **Medusa's Hair.** Chicago: Chicago University Press.

O'Flaherty, Wendy Doniger
1976   **The Origins of Evil in Hindu Mythology.** Berkeley: University of California Press.

Ortner, S. B.
1974   "Is Female to Male as Nature is to Culture." In **Woman, Culture and Society**, edited by M. Rosaldo and L. Lamphere. Stanford: University Press.

Ortner, S. B., and Whitehead, Harriett
1981   **Sexual Meanings: The Cultural Construction of Gender and Sexuality.** Cambridge: Cambridge University Press.

Pathmanathan, M.
1979   "The Hindu Society in Sri Lanka: Changed and Changing." In **Religiousness in Sri Lanka**, edited by John Ross Carter. Colombo: Marga Institute.

Peiris, R.
1956   **Sinhalese Social Organization.** Ceylon University Press Board, Peradeniya, Sri Lanka.

Pertold, O.
1973   **Ceremonial Dances of the Sinhalese.** Colombo: Tisara Prakasakayo.

Poulantzas, Nicos
1978   **Class in Contemporary Capitalism.** Schocken: New Left Books.

Prince, R., ed.
1968   **Trance and Possession States.** R. M. Bucke Memorial Society. Montreal (Proceedings of the Second Annual Conference).

Quinn, Naomi
1977   "Anthropological Studies on Women's Status." **Annual Review of Anthropology** 6:181-226. Palo Alto: Annual Reviews Inc.

Radcliffe-Brown, A.
1933   **The Andaman Islanders.** Cambridge: Cambridge University Press.

1940   "On Joking Relationships." **Africa,** vol. 13, no. 7, pp. 195-210.
1949   "A Further Note on Joking Relationships." **Africa** 19:133-40.

Raghavan, M.
1961   **The Karava of Ceylon: Society and Culture.** Colombo: K. V. G. de Silva and Sons.

Rahula, W.
1974   **What the Buddha Taught.** Revised edition. New York: Grove Press.

Rappaport, Roy A.
1979   **Ecology, Meaning and Religion.** Richmond, California: North Atlantic Books.

Redfield, R.
1956   **Peasant Society and Culture.** Chicago: University of Chicago Press.

Ricoeur, Paul
1963   "Symbole et temporalite." **Archivio di Filosofia** nos. 1 and 2.
1967   **The Symbolism of Evil.** Boston: Beacon Press.
1976   **Interpretation Theory: Discourse and the Surplus of Meaning.** Fort Worth: The Texas Christian University Press.

Roberts, M.
1969   "The Rise of the Karava." Ceylon Studies Seminar, 1969-70 series. Mimeographed.
1970   "The Political Antecedents of the Revivalist Elite within the MEP Coalition of 1956." Ceylon Studies Seminar 1969-70, series no. 11. Mimeographed.
1982   **Caste Conflict and Elite Formation: The Rise of the Karava Elite in Sri Lanka, 1500-1931.** Cambridge: Cambridge University Press.

Rosaldo, M.
1974   "Woman, Culture, and Society: A Theoretical Overview." In **Woman, Culture and Society,** edited by M. Rosaldo and L. Lamphere. Stanford: Univeristy Press.
1980   "The Uses and Abuses of Anthropology: Reflections on Feminism and Cross-Cultural Understanding." **Signs,** vol. 5, no. 3, pp. 389-417.

Ryan, B.
1953   **Caste in Modern Ceylon: The Sinhalese System in Transition.** New Brunswick, N. J.: Rutgers University Press.

Samaraweera, Vijaya
1979   "The Muslim Revivalist Movement, 1880-1915." In **Collective Identities, Nationalisms and Protest in Modern Sri Lanka,** edited by Michael Roberts. Colombo: Marga Institute.

Sarachchandra, E. R.
1966   **The Folk Drama of Ceylon.** 2d edition. Ceylon: Department of Cultural Affairs.

Sartre, Jean Paul
1948   **The Emotions: Outline of a Theory.** New York: Citadel Press.

Schieffelin, Edward R.
1976   **The Sorrow of the Lonely and the Burning of the Dancers.** New York: St. Martin Press.

Schneider, Jane, and Schneider, Peter
1976   **Culture and Political Economy in Western Sicily.** New York: Academic Press.

Schutz, A.
1963   **Collected Papers. Studies in Social Theory.** Vol. 1. Edited by A. Broderson. The Hague: Martinus Nijhoff.

1964   **Collected Papers. Studies in Social Theory.** Vol. 2. Edited by
       A. Broderson. The Hague: Martinus Nijhoff.
1967   **The Phenomenology of the Social World.** Translated by
       G. Walsh and F. Lehnert. Illinois: Northwestern University
       Press.

Seneviratne, H. L.
1978   **Rituals of the Kandyan State.** Cambridge: Cambridge
       University Press.

Shalvey, Thomas
1979   **Claude Levi-Strauss: Social Psychotherapy and the Collective
       Unconscious.** Amherst: University of Massachusets Press.

Shastri, P. O.
1911   **The Doctrine of Maya.** London.

Sheets-Johnstone, Maxine
1980   **The Phenomenology of Dance.** New York: Books for
       Libraries.

Sperber, Dan
1975   **Rethinking Symbolism.** Translated by Alice Morton.
       Cambridge: Cambridge University Press.

Spiro, M.
1967   **Burmese Supernaturalism: A Study in the Explanation and
       Reduction of Suffering.** New Jersey: Prentice-Hall Inc.

Srinivas, M. N.
1952   **Religion and Society among the Coorgs of South India.**
       Oxford: Oxford University Press.

Stirrat, R. J.
1977   "Demonic Possession in Roman Catholic Sri Lanka." **Journal
       of Anthropological Research,** vol. 33, no. 2, pp. 133-57.

Tagore, Rabindranath trans.
1915   **Songs of Kabir.** New York: Macmillan.

Tambiah, S. J.
1968   "The Magical Power of Words." **Man** n.s. 3:175-208.
1970   **Buddhism and the Spirit Cults in North-East Thailand.**
       Cambridge: Cambridge University Press.
1973a "Form and Meaning of Magical Acts: A Point of View." In
       **Modes of Thought: Essays on Thinking in Western and non-
       Western Societies,** edited by R. Horton and R. Finnegan.
       London: Faber and Faber.
1973b "The Persistence and Transformation of Tradition in Southeast
       Asia, with Special Reference to Thailand." **Daedalus,**
       (winter):55-84.
1977   "The Cosmological and Performative Significance of a Thai
       Cult of Healing Through Meditation." **Culture, Medicine and
       Psychiatry** 1:97-32.
1981   "A Performative Approach to Ritual" (Radcliffe-Brown
       Lecture 1979). **The Proceedings of the British Academy,** vol.
       65 (1979), pp. 113-69. London: Oxford University Press.

Taussig, Michael T.
1980   **The Devil and Commodity Fetishism in South America.**
       Chapel Hill: University of North Carolina Press.

Turner, Terence
1977   "Transformation, Hierarchy and Transcendence: A
       Reformulation of Van Gennep's Model of the Structure of
       Rites de Passage. In **Secular Ritual,** edited by S. F. Moore and
       B. Myerhoff. Assen: Van Gorcum.

Turner, V. W.
 1957   **Schism and Continuity in an African Society.**   Manchester:
        Manchester University Press.
 1967   **The Forest of Symbols: Aspects of Ndembu Ritual.**   Ithaca:
        Cornell University Press.
 1968   **The Drums of Affliction: A Study of Religious Processes
        among the Ndembu of Zambia.**   Oxford: Clarendon Press.
 1969   **The   Ritual   Process: Structure   and   Anti-Structure.**
        Harmondsworth: Penguin.
 1974   **Dramas, Fields and Metaphors: Symbolic Action in Human
        Society.**   Ithaca: Cornell University Press.
 1975   **Revelation and Divination in Ndembu Ritual.**   Symbol, Myth
        and Ritual Series.   Ithaca.   New   York: Cornell   University
        Press.
 1977   "Process,   System   and   Symbol: A   New   Anthropological
        Synthesis."   **Daedalus,** in Summer issue, Discoveries and
        Interpretations: Studies in Contemporary Scholarhship, vol. 1,
        pp. 61-80.
Van Gennep, Arnold
 1961   **Rites of Passage.**   Translated by Monika B. Vizedom and
        Gabrielle L. Caffee, Chicago: University of Chicago Press.
Velsen, J. van
 1964   **The Politics of Kinship.**   Manchester: Manchester University
        Press.
 1967   "The Extended-Case Method and Situational Analysis."   In **The
        Craft of Anthropology,** edited by A. L. Epstein.   London:
        Tavistock Publications.
Walker, B.
 1968   **The Hindu World: An Encyclopedic Survey of Hinduism.**   Vol. 2
        New York: Frederick A. Praeger.
Wallerstein, I.S.
 1974   **The Modern World System.**   Vol. 1.   (Capitalist Agriculture and
        the Origins of the European World Economy in the Sixteenth
        Century.) New York: Academic Press.
Waxler, N. E.
 1972   "Social   Change   and   Psychiatric   Illness   in   Ceylon: An
        Investigation   of   Traditional   and   Modern   Conceptions   of
        Disease and Treatment."   In **Mental Health in Asia and the
        Pacific,** edited by W. Lebra.   Hawaii: University of Hawaii
        Press.
Weitz, M.
 1954   "Symbolism and Art."   **Review of Metaphysics,** vol. 7, no. 3 pp.
        466-81.
Williams, Drid
 1978   "Deep Structures of the Dance."   In **Yearbook of Symbolic
        Anthropology,** edited by E. Schwimmer, pp. 211-30.   London:
        Hurst.
Wilson, P. J.
 1967   "Status Ambiguity and Spirit Possession."   **Man** n.s. 2: 366-78.
Winius, George Davison
 1971   **The Fatal History of Portuguese Ceylon.**   Cambridge, Mass.:
        Harvard University Press.
Winslow, Deborah
 1980   "Rituals of First Menstruation in Sri Lanka."   **Man** n.s. 15:603-
        25.

Wirz, P.
  1954   **Exorcism and the Art of Healing in Ceylon.** Leyden: E. J.
          Brill.
Wittkower, E. D.
  1970   "Trance and Possession States." **International Journal of
          Psychiatry** 16:153-60.
Wittkower, E. D., and Prince, R.
  1974   "A Review of Transcultural Psychiatry." **In Child and
          Adolescent Psychiatry, Sociocultural and Community
          Psychiatry,** American Handbook of Psychiatry, vol. 2. 2nd. ed.
          Pp. 535-50. New York: Basic Books.
Woodward, Calvin A.
  1969   **The Growth of a Party System in Ceylon.** Providence: Brown
          University Press.
Yalman, N.
  1962   "On Some Binary Categories in Sinhalese Religious Thought."
          Transactions of the New York Academy of Sciences, series 2,
          vol 24 no. 4, pp. 408-20.
  1963   "On the Purity of Women in the Castes of Ceylon and
          Malabar." **Journal of the Royal Anthropological Institute** 93
          (part 1): 25-58
  1964   "The Structure of Sinhalese Healing Rituals." **In Religion in
          South Asia,** edited by E. B. Harper. Seattle: University of
          Washington Press.
  1967   **Under the Bo Tree.** Berkeley: University of California Press.
  1973   "On the Meaning of Food Offering in Ceylon." **Social
          Compass,** 20:287-302.
Zimmer, Heinrich
  1972   **Myths and Symbols in Indian Art and Civilization,** edited by
          Joseph Campbell. Princeton: Princeton University Press.

Glossary

Most of the terms I have included are those commonly used by exorcists in their ritual practices. Some of the words are Sanskrit or relatively archaic Sinhala. The system of transliteration used is that conventionally employed by scholars of Pali and Sanskrit, and follows that recommended by Richard Gombrich in **Precept and Practice.** I have attempted to keep as closely as possible to the pronunciation and usage of exorcists. This glossary is intended as a guide to the reader, and, of course, is not an exhaustive list.

aḍavv—short dances, performed as offerings to the gods
adbhūta—awesome, marvelous
adukku—offerings to the gods
ädurā, yakädurā—an exorcist
aile—offering plate
ākāsa (Skt.)—ether, sky; one of the five elemental substances
aluyama—morning watch
ämbun kavi—songs which describe the origin and making of the ritual "buildings," offering baskets, and other ritual objects, and the association of these with figures of Sinhalese legend, deities and demons.
anagārika—"homeless"; an individual who assumes the Buddhist ascetic ideal but does not, unlike the Buddhist monk, remove himself from the midst of the everyday world.
añgika—gesture, finger positions of the exorcist dances.
añ keliya—horn ritual
apalē—bad planetary period
äpa nūl—magical thread tied around wrist or neck to halt the effects of demonic attack. Efficacy is ultimately dependent on a larger, more elaborate exorcism.
ārambha padē—beginning or opening, dance
ārūḍe (Skt. **āruḍha**)—possession by a deity
ārukku—arches, connecting the **torana** of the demon palace

āsirivāda kavi—praise songs for demons and deities; songs of benediction
äs vaha—evil eye
aṭakona kavi—song for the demons that come from the eight cardinal
    directions
atamagala—the major ritual building at the Suniyama exorcism
aṭa pāliya—eight presentations, comic acts which precede the entrance of
    the masked sanni demons
aṭa sil—observance of the eight Buddhist precepts
äṭ bändima—elephant tying, taming; event in the Mangara pelapāliya
atmana-keliya—stick game; event in the Mangara pelapāliya
ātura(yā)—exorcism patient
ātura maḍuva (pandala)—patient hut, "building" in which the patient is
    seated
avamangalle—death time (funeral); event in exorcism at point of transition
    from evening to midnight watch
avatāra—manifestation, form; specific form of appearance of deity or
    demon
avatāra bälima—gaze or sight of demon form; major period of entrancement
    during an exorcism during which a vision of a particular mode of
    appearance of the demonic might confront the exorcist; the illusory and
    powerful form of the demonic
āvēsa (yak āvēsa)—demon trance
āvuda—weapons of a god or demon

bädun—fried foods
bali, bali tovil—a rite for exorcising evil planetary influences
bandinava—to tie, bind; colloquially used to refer to marriage
bāra—a vow to a god
baraṭa—heavy steps in dance
berava—main caste from which exorcists are drawn
bhayānaka—terrible, terrifying
bhikku—Buddhist priest
bibhatsa—loathsome, disgusting; bibhatsa rasa, sense, feeling, mood of
    disgust and loathing
billa, pl. bili—sacrificial victim
bō—sacred tree (ficus religiosa) of Buddhism
bōsat—being who will become a Buddha
buduge—a shrine in which objects of Buddhist devotion are kept
burulla—leaves which form the skirt, or dress, of the sanni demons

chāmara—sacred yak's tail

dāgäba—Buddhist relic chamber, stūpa
dahaata pāliya—"eighteen presentations"; usual term for the comic acts
    concluding an exorcism, incorporating the events of the aṭa pāliya and
    the dahaata sanniya
dahaata sanniya—"eighteen disease-spreading demons"; collective term for
    the comic acts involving the pāli and sanni apparitions and demons; used
    synonymously with dahaata pāliya
dala—demon tusks
dāna—alms giving
dapanavā—stretch out
dehi käpima—lime-cutting ritual to ward off effects of evil eye and sorcery
dekone vilakkuva—double-torch appearance of demonic
dēvālē (-ya), pl. dēvāla—shrine to the deities

dēva, deviyō—a god

dēva lōka—world of deities

dēvatā kotuva—"fortress of the gods," points around the demon palace guarded by the gods; also used to refer to the superstructure of a **dāgäba**

dēvatāvā—godling; a being transitional between gods and demons; an honorific used towards demons in the early events of an exorcism

devol maḍuva—ritual for the god Devol Deviyo

doḷaha (doḷos) pelapāliya—twelve presentations; acts connected to the twelve gods of the Sinhalse pantheon

dōsa, pl. dos; tri or tun dōsa—illness, three illnesses caused by humoral imbalance

duka—pain, suffering

dummala—resin of the **sal** tree, under which the Buddha was born and died

gäbe—division within offering basket, sometimes of larger ritual structure

gam maḍuva—village ceremonial for the gods, mainly Pattini. The rite includes major events relating to god Mangara and the **garā** demons

gāndharva—celestial musicians

garā yakku—a category of relatively benign demons, twelve in number. Their female counterparts are the **giri** demons. The demons figure prominently in some of the major rites to the deities.

Garā Yakuma—ritual for the **garā** demons, now rarely performed

gejji—small bells tied to the shins of exorcist dancers and masked actors

gevala prēta(yā)—ghosts haunting the house and causing its inhabitants illness

gini sisila—event in dance where exorcists "burn" their chests with the fire of torches

giniam āhara—foods in the "heating" category

gñati prēta(yā)—ancestor ghost

goḍadiyamas—roasted meat from land and water creatures

gokkola—young coconut palm fronds

goṭu(va)—small offering package, given to **sanni** demons

Goṭhaimbara, Godembara—the slayer of Jayasena which gave rise to the latters' rebirth as Mahasona

goyigama—farmer caste; most numerous caste in Sri Lanka

graha dēva—planetary deities

gurunānsē—teacher, respectful term of address to an exorcist

hāl—husked rice

hāsya—laughter, comedy; **hāsya rasa**, laughter, comic mood

hataravaram deviyō—four guardian deities; the dominant, over-lording deities of Sri Lanka

hīn tāla—light drum rhythm

hōranä(va)—horn

hō vaha—thought evil

īgaha—arrow of Īsvara

indul—leavings, left overs

Iramudun Samayama—exorcism for Rīri Yakā, specifically in his **avamangalle** form

Īsvara—Shiva; as the Lord of the Dance, in the view of some exorcists, considered to be the originator of exorcism

Īsvaradähäna—"Isvara lie down," the spell which Bashman Asura stole from Isvara

iyalle—exorcist group

kaḍaturāva—white cloth screen held between patient and offerings, and which is suddenly removed to reveal demon objects or demons
kaḍinama—quickening drum rhythm
kahadiyara—refers to pot containing turmeric water in exorcism
kalpa—a major Buddhist age or span of time, an eon
Kaḷu Kumāra—Black Prince whose main victims are women
Kaḷu Vädi pāliya—appearance of the "Black Hunter" demon
Kaḷu Yakā—Black Demon, a lower form of the Black Prince
kannalavva—invocation to Buddha and the deities
kapāla kūduva—"skull offering nest"; rectangular structure erected at front of demon palace throughout comic episodes of an exorcism
kapurāla—priest of deity shrine
karāva—caste whose occupation is often associated with fishing
karma (col. **karuma**)—law of cause and effect
karuṇā—compassion, kindness
kasapän—clean water, strained of impurities
kata vaha—mouth evil
kattarikka(ya), pl. **kattarikki**—offering stands
kavi—song
killa, pl. **kili**—pollution
kiri gas—trees of milk (sap) category
kodivina—sorcery
koḍiya—flag
Kōla Sanniya—chief of the sanni demons
kotale—an earthen pot
kudē—umbrella
kumbhāṇḍa—spirits

lē—blood
li-keḷiya—stick game

maḍu purayā—exorcist assitant, priest of the ritual hut
mäḍuyama—midnight watch
magul berē—ceremonial drumming
mahabhūta—elemental substances of matter
mahagedara—ancestral house of a kindred group
Mahasōnā—the Great Cemetery Demon, also the name given to the exorcism
Mahasōnā dāpavilla—event depicting "death" of Mahasona
Mahasōnā Samayama—the exorcism ritual of Mahasona
Mahasohon samayam padē—gathering time dance of Mahasona exorcism
maha tē—major exorcism refreshment interval before the start of the morning watch of exorcism
Mahāvamsa—the major chronicle of Buddhism in Sri Lanka
mala dārahäva—an episode where the exorcist is carried as a corpse in a funeral bier. Commonly performed in the **Iramudun Samayama**, and occasionally in the **avamangalle** of a **Mahasōnā**
mala prēta—ghosts of dead human beings
mal bulat dīma muhuna atha pisa dāmima—"flower betel face wiping" offering
mal bulat tattuva—flower/betel offering basket, used to protect and purify patient
mal yahanāva—"flower fence," main offering place to Buddha and Guardian Deities at an exorcism
Mangara pelapāliya—"procession" for Mangara, major comedy of the midnight watch of a **Mahasōnā**

mantra kārayō—specialist in the utterance of magical verses
Māra, Maruvā—the Harbinger of Death, the main adversary of Buddha
Maru Rīri—Rīri Yakā in his form as the demon of death
mātrā—body posture in dance
māyā—illusion
māyama—trick
mī bändīma—wild buffalo tying, taming; event in **Mangara pelapaliya**
mini—corpse
minis lōka—human world
mithyā dṛṣṭi—heretical views, antagonistic to Buddha's teaching
mōl gaha—rice pounder, axis of **kapāla kūduva**, protective of patient
mudun male—central offering place in **vīdiya** of **Raṭa Yakuma**
muddara—document seal, stamp
muttara—urine

nānumura pāliya—the annointing presentation; mimed comic event in **Raṭa Yakuma**
nāṭuma, pl. nāṭum—dance
navandanna—artisan caste
nīcha kula—"low caste offering," given to Mahasona at **avamangalle**
nirvāna (col. Sinhala **nivan**)—Buddhist state of non-existence
nūla—thread
nūl bändīma—short rite in which a thread is tied to alliviate illness caused by malign spirits

olī—astrologer caste
Ōm Namō—salutation to Buddha and/or Isvara. It often begins a **mantra**

pāda(ya)—step, used to refer to a dance step
padē—dance
pädura upata—song about the "history of the mat"
pambayā—straw effigy burnt in closing events of **Iramudun Sumayama**
pancha māssa—offering table for god Mangara; the central fifth platform of the **Mahasōnā vīdiya** and is a term sometimes applied to the **Mahasōnā vīdiya** as a whole
pandama—large cloth torch
paṅduru—coin offering
panikki—barber caste
pathāvi (Skt)—the elemental substance of earth
payata pāvāda—cloth spread on ground at funerals; also at festivals under the feet of elephants carrying sacred objects
pēna—oracle
perahära—temple processions
pidēni(ya)—small propitiatory offerings to specific ghosts and demons
pillu vidiya—sorcery palace; alternative term for **Sūniyam vīdiya**
pin—merit
pinkama—a public performance of merit-making
pirit—purificatory and curative rites usually involving Buddhist monks as officiants
pita varala—hair tresses (of the exorcist-dancers)
pitta—humor of blood/bile
Polova Mahī Kāntāva—Bumi Devi, goddess of the earth
pol mal—coconut flowers
pōya—full moon day, usually an important day of Buddhist observance
prēta(yā)—ghost

puhul kapanāva—ash pumpkin cutting; an episode often performed in major
   exorcisms to cut malign demonic connection through sorcery, usually
   enacted at close of **avamangalle**
puka—anus
puluṭu—roasted grains
purāle—burial platform, place where the demonic essence is dissipated
putā—son, child, "little one"; term of endearment from adult to child
puvak mal—areca palm flowers

radā—washer caste
rājakāriya—system of "feudal" services
rāksa—planetary demon
rasa—mood, sentiment, taste
Raṭa Yakuma—main exorcism for female patients attacked by Kalu Kumara
raudra—anger, rage; **raudra rasa** —— a mood of angry rage
Rīri Yakā—Blood Demon, close associate of Mahasona
riyana—traditional Sinhala unit of measurement
rōgi ātmaya/nirōgi ātmaya—"sick self/not sick self," used by exorcists in
   reference to the curative process of their exorcisms

sal—the tree under which Buddha was born and died. In theory, the tree
   from which **dummala** is made
samayam padē—gathering time dance
samayam toppiya—headcap of dancer
saṃsāra—rebirth, transmigration
samyak dṛsti—orthodox teaching, oriented along the correct path -
   indicated by the Buddha's preaching
sāndayāma—evening watch
sannas patraya—document of authority
Sanni Yakuma—exorcism for Kola Sanniya, and eighteen disease spreading
   demons
santi rasa—sentiment of calmness, quietude, tranquility
sastra kārayō—astrologers
satek—lowly creature
saumya—peaceful, untroubled
sema—phlegm humor
sembuva—bronze pot
sēsat—sun/moon symbol
srngāra—erotic, lustful; **srngara rasa,** mood or erotic feeling or verse
Sūniyam—demon of sorcery
Sūniyama—rite specifically designed to alleviate the effects of sorcery

tāla—drum rhythm
tel mantirima—short curative rite which makes use of oil empowered by the
   chanting of **mantra**
tammaṭṭam—double drum
tanikama—mental and physical "aloneness"; a symptom and pre-condition of
   demonic attack
taṭṭuva—offering basket
tējō (Skt)—the elemental substance of fire, heat
tel kāma—food prepared by an admixture of oil
tōḍu—earings
torana—major panel in exorcism **vidiya** and place in the **vidiya** where
   offerings to demons and deities will be put
tovilē—exorcism

tovil gedara—exorcism household
trisūla—trident of Īsvara

silambu—silver foot bracelets
sīmā(va)—limitation to a defined period of an illness: the period during
    which the symptoms of an illness should abate; also, a sacred boundary
sīmā midula—performance area of an exorcism, the space which is bounded
    by the main ritual structures of an exorcism
siraṣapāda kavi—"head to foot" song
sītala āhara—cooling foods
sittu(va)—rotating credit association

tun yama—the three dangerous periods of a major exorcism; the evening,
    midnight and morning watches

usṇa ginijal—fever

vadiga paṭuna—major comic episode of **Sūniyama** exorcism
Vaisravaṇa, Vessamuni—lord of the demons
valalu—arm bangles
varama—authority
vas—evil influence, poison; often used in conjunction, or
    synonymously with **dos** as in "May all the **vas dos** be removed"
vasdaṇḍa—demon pipe
vāta (Sinh.)—humor of wind
vaṭa—round, as in Vaṭa Kumāra (Round Prince) or, whirling as in **vaṭa pade**
    (whirling dance)
vāyō (Skt.)—elemental substance of wind
vedarāla—traditional medical practioner, herbalist
Vesak—Buddhist festival (celebrating the birth, enlightenment, and death of
    the Buddha)
vīdiya—demon palace
vī—unhusked rice
vihāra—Buddhist temple
vilakku—thin torches
vīṇā—stringed instrument
vīra—heroic dynamic energy; **vīra rasa** —— mood of heroic dynamism

watatira—curtain surrounding sacred objects

yādini kavi—songs of the origin and exploits of the demons
yakā, yakṣa, pl. yakku—demon
yak āvēsa—demon possession, trance
yakṣa diṣṭi—demon eyesight, gaze; **yakṣa diṣṭi kirima** —— offering to the
    demon eyesight, the intensifying of the demonic gaze
yakṣa lōka—demon world
yakṣabhūta vidyāva—"science of spirits"; the specialism of exorcists and a
    branch of **ayurvedic** medicine
yantra—magical design, worn as amulet or necklet

Subject Index

abstract form
    destruction of, 223; and demonic
    in mime, dance, **avatara balima**,
    222
aesthetic form
    as the systemic unity of
    subject/object 181; as
    constitutive of experience,
    disclosure, 7, 8
ata paliya, 116
    analysis of, 220-1, 223-4;
    description, 168-71;
    intermediaries of
    divine/demonic, 166-7, 260n;
    and transformation of symbolic
    types of, 223-6
audience
    appearance of Mahasona and,
    218-19; changing position of, and
    ritual transformation, 181, 261n;
    dance and, 193, 194; efficacy of
    exorcism and, 60; and evening
    watch, 183-5; individuation in
    dance, 7, 191; and midnight
    watch and, 190-1, 211, 214, 218-
    9; and morning watch, 220, 226-8
avamangalle
    audience focus and, 190;
    description, 146-9
avatara
    concept of, 251n

avatara balima, 192,
    and demonic as abstract,
    consistent, determinant
    symbolic type, 222; contrasted
    with **dekone vilakkuva**, 225;
    demonic illusion in, 194;
    description, 153-4; trance of,
    196, 198; violence in, 153, 254n

berava caste, 9, 37-48
    contradiction in ritual role, 40-
    41; discrimination against, 39-
    40
body
    and music, 188, 189; in dance
    and cosmic order, 62, 192, 193,
    257n
Buddhist revival
    and class structure of caste
    communities, 25-30; and
    colonial rule, 20-25; as class
    ideology, 22, 24-25
Buddhist temple
    and class relations, 25, 26, 28,
    29, 31-34

caste
    and class 26, 38-39, 69; as
    "culture of class," 245n
class
    and caste, 26, 38-39, 69;
    defined, 18; religion as

language of, 31; and religion as practice 31-36

cock
in **kukulu pade**, 152; symbolic significance, 142

color
coding of cosmic relations, 116

comedy
of **ata paliya**, 168-71 220-1, 223-4; as anti-rite, 207, 228-31; as attack on limiting form, 207, 230; and attitude of other, 215; comic moment, 212; of **dahaata sanniya**, 166, 167, 171-5, 176, 223, 224-5, 227; deity authenticated in, 217, 219; and disordering, fragmentation of demonic, 224-25; life/death dynamic of, 212; of **Mangara pelapaliya**, 155-61, 211-20; properties of, 209-10, 214, 216, 217, 226; and reconstitution of "normal" attitude, 226-28; and **Sanni Yakuma**, 212-13; and transformation, 215-17, 219

cosmos
demonic and cosmological time, 189; formed in music, 188-89; hierarchy of, 113-14; supernaturals as multiple refractions of underlying principles of, 116; transformational logic of, 124-27

culture
not opposed to, in unity with, nature, 105; women as closer to, 108

dahaata sanniya (see also comedy)
distinct from **ata paliya**, 166; demons of, 167; comedy of, 171-5; 224-6, 227, 230

dance
and cosmic creation, 192, 194-5; 257-58n; description of dress, 149-50, 192; and **mahabhutas**, 258n; of **Mahasona**, 151-54, 192-95, 203-6; "play" of, 154, 203-6; in **Rata Yakuma**, 164; and reconstitution of paramount reality, 205; and reflexivity, 205-6; relation to music, 42, 192-93; in **Sanni Yakuma**, 163-64; and temporality, 193; and trance 196-7; and virtual gesture, 194-5

death (see also Mara, Yama)
in comic movement, 212, 216; comic theme in **dahaata paliya**, 170; comic theme in **Mangara pelapaliya**, 157, 159, 161, 104; as ultimate project of demon attack, 61; of Mahasona, 162-63, 218; as Mara, 112; Mara Sanniya as, 167; as decomposed form, polluting, 104-5

dekone vilakkuva (double torch) 153

demons, demonic, 115
articulation with deities, 116; and cosmological time, 189; formation in dance, 193-94; fragmentation in comedy, 205, 219, 225; and transformational logic of hierarchy, 124-125; as incorporative forms, 125; as metaphoric of class relations, 35-36, 230, 233; in musical rhythm, 188; as not merely idioms of illness, 87-89, 234; origin myths of major demons 118-24; **sanni** demons and relation to **pali** apparitions, 166-67; symbolic type of, 222

demon attack
as constitutive of context, 49, 63, 89, 90; and female patients, 105-110, 235-36; and male patients, 106, 107, 110, 235; as not reducible to individual patient, 89-90,234; patient symptoms, 50-53, 57, 58, 61; severity of, 61, 62; as transformation of identity, 81, 89

demon palace (see **vidiya**)

Deva Sanniya, 117-18, 166, 167, 175;
as fragmented demon unity, 225

devatava
as transitional supernatural being, 117

Devol Deviyo
in dance, 152; myth, 258n

devol maduva, 30

diagnosis
and social definition of illness, 63-64, 88-90, 98-99, 101; elaborative logic of, 61, 62; diagnostic indicators, 50-52; and mockery by Gulma Sanniya, 173-75; and principle of reciprocal validation, 90

Dipamkara Buddha
    and Riddi Bisava myth, 112
discursive symbolic form, 208, 209,
    262-63n
drama
    constitutive properties of, 207-
    10; reflexivity in comic, 209
drumming, 145, 187,
    demon rhythms, 188; for trance,
    196; verbal "notation" of, 42, 151
duka (suffering), 16-17
    comic references to, 174
dummala
    symbolic conversion in use, 185
    symbolic significance, 142, 257n

evil eye, mouth, and thought, 52
experience
    of audience in dance, 191;
    common experience through
    aesthetic object, 191-2; of
    demonic, 50, 51, 60; and
    modeling in dance, 195; musical,
    186, 188-89; and self, 198-203;
    objective constituted in
    subjective, 195; symbolic
    mediation of, 180
exorcism (see also **Iramudun
Samayama, Mahasona, Rata
Yakuma, Sanni Yakuma, Suniyama**)
    audience in, 181, 184-85, 191;
    and Buddhist revival, 29; and
    chronic illness, 86; distinguished
    from other practices, 13-14;
    encompassing form of major
    exorcisms, 129; as "folk
    religion," 31; and gender, 56, 57;
    as household ritual, 91; learning
    of, 42-47; and middle class, 18-
    19, 20, 23, 34; transformational
    logic of, 179-80; treatment of
    children, 55, 57, 68, 249n;
    treatment efficacy, failure, 59-
    60, 90, 130, 249n 254n;
    treatment hierarchy, 53-55
exorcists (see also berava)
    and caste discrimination, 39; and
    control of knowledge, 41;
    disjunction between ritual
    authority and status, 40-41;
    learning histories of, 43-47;
    status and 41-42; traditions of,
    48; trance and, 197
extended-case method, 9, 242n

female identity
    as centre of nature/culture
    dialectic, 105-6, 107, 107, 235-
    6; contrasted with male
    identity, 106-7, 109, 235;
    female relation to demonic,
    101, 150; typifications of, 93-
    94, 100
fetishism
    defined, 246n; of middle-class
    religious practice, 29, 33
food
    distribution of and inner logic
    of exorcism, 72-75, 235

gam maduva ceremony, 118, 130,
    161
gara demons,
    118, 251n, 252n; and Mangara,
    161, 259n; and deity relations,
    259n
ghosts (see **preta**)
Gothaimbara, 121, 144, 252n
great tradition/little tradition
    as class construct, 30, 31, 233
guardian deities, 113, 114, 175
    and **namaskaraya**, 139, 143,
    most complete form at apex of
    cosmic hierarchy, 124
Gulma Sanniya
    comic dialogues, 173-75, 223,
    224, 227

hierarchy
    body and cosmic, 257n;
    as central principle of cosmic
    relations, 114; and dance, 150,
    192, 205; fragmenting force of,
    126-27, 205; marked in
    offerings, 117; and music, 188-
    89; principle of
    encompassment, successive
    subsummation, 124, 252n; as
    ordering of multiple refractions
    of supernatural, 117-18
humors, 14, 51-52,145 color code
    of, 116; and dance dress, 150;
    gesture and, 152, 155; and Kola
    Sanniya origin myth, 123,
    relation to **mahabhutas**, 116,
    257n
Huniyam (see Suniyam, sorcery)

ideas
  as determinant of action in
  ritual, 3-4, 236; objectified in
  supernatural, 3
ideology
  and "culture" 19-20
igaha, 115, 144, 175
  description, 143; use in dance,
  152, 153; use in Kalu Vadi
  episode, 162
illusion
  Buddha as immune to, 112, 113;
  concept of maya, 111-12;
  demonic, 125-26, 226-81;
  destroyed in dance, 204-6; of
  kukulu pade, 152; of Mahasona
  destroyed by comedy, 218; as
  metaphor of cosmic process,
  113; and trickery of Maru
  Sanniya, 227
Iramudun Samayama, 55, 27, 129,
  137, 249n; main distinguishing
  ritual events, 130, 134-35, 253n
Isvara (Shiva)
  in bali ceremonies, 251; the
  Brahmanicide, 260n; in dance,
  149, 151, 192, 194, 258n; lingam
  and pestle, 256n; and Mahasona
  myth, 121; tri murti and, 257n;
  weapons of, 115, 255n

kadaturava, 140, 162
  in ata paliya, 168; emotion and
  colour of, 257n; in evening
  watch, 185; Kola Sanniya myth
  and, 256n
Kalas Paliya
  comic dialogues, 170-71
Kalu Kumara (see also Kalu Yaka),
  117; origin myth, 121-122
Kalu Yaka, 117, 120, 125
  offering basket, 140, 141, 142;
  origin myth, 121-122
Kalu Vadi
  servant of Mangara, 162, 218;
  mediating function of, 162, 259n
kannelavva, 143
  Mangara, 154
kapala kuduva
  in dahaata paliya, 168, 171, 225;
  as encoding exorcism
  transformational process 260-
  61n; as symbolic of cosmic
  hierarchy, 114, 260n

karava caste, 25-30
  overseas migration 27-28
karma, 15-17
Kataragama, 113, 114, 118
  articulation within cosmic
  whole, 116 in dance, 192
kavi, 143
  atakona kavi, 149; avamangalle
  samayam kavi, 147; Mahasona
  asirivada kavi, 144; padura
  upata kavi, 146; and rasa, 143-
  4; sirasapada kavi, 144-5
Kendi Paliya
  comic dialogues, 169-70, 224
Kola Sanniya, 118, 125
  origin myth, 106, 123-24, 128,
  166-67
kumbhanda, 33, 115, 247n
Kuveni, 120, 122, 140

laughter
  demonic, 263n as signifying
  mutuality, 215; of patient, 227-
  8, 263n

Madana Yaka, 85, 122, 252n
mahabhutas, 116, 177
  in dance, 192, 257-58n; and
  logic of offerings, 137; in
  music, 188
magicality, 202-3
Maha Brahma, 136, 140, 259n
  in dance, 192 and kapala
  kuduva, 260n
Mahasona demon
  in avamangalle, 147;
  cosmic connections of, 116;
  death of, 162-63, 218;
  inversion, 126; manifestations
  of, 125; masked appearance as
  homologous with comedy, 218,
  219; non-abstract form of, 218,
  222-23; origin myth, 106, 120-
  21; relation to Mangara, 218;
  song of, 144; and symptoms of
  illness, 51, 52, 63, 78
Mahasona exorcism, 55, 59, 62, 67,
  107, 137, et seq.; ata paliya,
  166, 167, 168-71, 220-28;
  avamangalle episode, 146-49,
  190; avatara balima, 153-54,
  194, 196; dahaata paliya, 165-
  66; dahaata sanniya, 167, 171-
  75; dances, 151-54, 192-97;
  demon offering and baskets,

140-42; encompassing ritual
form of, 129; evening watch,
137-49, 183-90; ghost offerings,
137, 139; **Kalu vadi paliya**, 162,
217-18; listing of events, 138;
Mahasona's death, 162-63, 217-
19; **Mangara pelapaliya**, 154-63,
211-20; midnight watch, 149-63,
190-219; morning watch, 165-75,
220ff; **vidiya**, 131, 133-34
male identity
typifications of, 101; contrasted
with female identity, 108-7, 109,
235
mal yahanava, 139, 140
Mangara
connection with Kalu Vadi, 162,
259-60n; as contradiction of
Mahasona, 218; **kannelavva**, 154;
symbolic articulation of gods and
demons, 259n; transitional
character of, 161, 215ff
Mangara pelapaliya, 154-63, 211-20
deity/demon symbolic
articulation, 259n; as
transitional between contrasting
objectifications of demonic, 215,
219
mantra, 14, 53, 54, 142, 143
Mara, 120, 125, 133, 147
mask
in **avatara balima**, 153, 222; in
dekone vilakkuva, 175; as non-
abstract form, 218, 222-23; as
"unmasking," 218
Maru Sanniya
comic dialogues, 171-73,
terrifying nature of, 176, 227
maya (see also illusion), 111-12
mime
in **Rata Yakuma**, 164-65; in
Sanni Yakuma, 164
moha (delusion), 124
motivation
"in-order-to" and "because"
motives, 96-98, 109-10
music
body and, 188; creative force,
188; dance and, 192, 193; divine
and demonic rhythm, 188; time,
temporality, 186-88; verbal
"notation," 42, 151

Natha, 113, 114
articulation within cosmic
whole, 116

objective structure
of ritual, 180
obscenity
in comic dialogues, 157-60,
168-70, 173-74; and
standardized humor, 214; as
underlining "joke" of comedy,
213
oli caste, 69, 70

Pandam Paliya, 166, 168
as symbolic type, 220, 222
panikki caste
rank of, 69
patient (**aturaya**)
in **dahaata paliya**, 227; in
dance, 191, 204; and
deconstruction of self, 198-203;
in evening watch, 183, 185-86;
in **Mangara pelapaliya**, 214; and
reconstruction of self, comic
drama, and cure of, 226-28; and
restricted perception in
Mahasona dapavilla, 219; ritual
seating, 139; and trance, 196-
97, 202, 203
Pattini, 116, 150
birth and relation to Riddi
Bisava, 118; in dance, 152, 192
performance
definition, as structure of
practice, 6, 7, 180; curative
efficacy of, 59-60; as
progressive disclosure, 176-77,
180, 181; and "text," 180, 261n;
and transformation, 179-80
performative, 214n
Polova Mahi Kantava (Bumi Devi),
133, 150, 171, 259n
pollution
cause in illness, 50, 52; comic
theme in **dahaata paliya**, 168-
71, 176, 216-17; of demons,
117-18, 136, 256n; as effect of
demonic attack, 61-2, 88; as
form in decomposition, 104-5
possession (see trance)
presentational symbolic form,
208-9, 262n
preta, 16, 66, 78, 115
offering basket, 137; offering
to, 139
purale, 134-35, 153

raksa, 115-18

rasa, 143–44, 195
in **avatara balima**, 153, 154; and
relation to Sanskritic tradition,
257n; in **vilakku** and **igaha pade**,
154
Rata Yakuma, 55, 112, 118, 130, 137
dance, mime drama, 164–65;
vidiya, 133–34
reciprocal validation
as principle of diagnosis of
demon attack, 90
reflexivity
comedy and the production of
patient consciousness and, 226–
28; and dance, 194, 205–6; in
drama and comedy, 207–10;
internal to Mahasona's form in
appearance, 219; in music, 189
repetition
in ritual, 3, 239–40n
Riddi Bisava, 133
and dance and mime of **Rata
Yakuma**, 164–65; myth, 112;
relation to Pattini, 118
Riri Yaka, 118, 125
and **avamangalle**, 146–49; forms
of, 249n; myth, 120; offering
basket, 142; origin song of, 147–
48; and symbolic inversion, 126
ritual
as cultural hermeneutic and
exegesis, 175, 177, 240n; idea
and, 3–4, 236; as interrelation of
aesthetic, 7, 237–8; limitation of
definitions of, 2–3, 339n, 340n;
and performance, 4–8; as
progressive disclosure, 176–7,
180–81

Sakra, 115, 125
salagama, 46, 248n
Salu Paliya
comic dialogues, 168–69; as
mediate between deity/demon,
166, 260n
Saman, 113–14, 120
Sanni Yakuma, 55, 86, 130, 137
dance and drama of, 163–64;
vidiya, 33–34
Sanni Yaka (see also Kola Sanniya)
origin myth, 123–24
self
comedy and reformation of self,
226–28; deity trance as self

transcendance, adduction, 201–
2; demon trance as self
negation through reduction,
202; Mead approach to, 198–201
sima midula, 131
song (see also **kavi**)
form of, 261–2n
sorcery, 34, 57, 68, 78, 83, 85–6
space
spatializing property of dance,
192–93
Suniyam, 34–5, 55, 57
as demon/deity, 117; offering
basket, 142
Suniyama, 34–5, 55
atamagala, 131, 134, 135;
contrast with other exorcisms,
130; male patients in, 57;
vadiga patuna comedy of, 230
symbolic type
constitution of demonic as, 222;
defined, 221; transformation
and reobjectification of demon
types, 222ff

text
as emergent through
performance, 7, 61, 180, 237;
structuralist perspective upon,
5, 6
time
dance and spatialization of,
193; demons and, 189;
inner/outer ritual time, 189–90;
musical, 186–88; "originary" and
measured, 186–87
tourism
and exorcism, 248n
trance, 59, 67, 84
in **avatara balima**, 196–198;
contrast between exorcist and
patient, 196–7; as conversion of
virtual gesture into natural
gesture, 197; and dance, 195,
197; as deconstitution of self,
198–203; lack of consciousness
in, 198; and magicality, 202–3;
theories for female possession,
92–96
transformation
of being in cosmic hierarchy,
124–6; in transition rites, 179–
80

Vaisravana (see Vessamuni)
Vata Kumara, 121
    origin myth, 122
Vessamuni, 112, 115, 120, 127, 144,
    218
vidiya, 131–34
    of Kalu Kumara, 134, 148, 175;
    for **Mahasona** 133, 136, 141; for
    Rata Yakuma, 133; relation of
    patient to, 135, 203; for **Sanni**
    Yakuma, 133–4; for **Suniyama,**
    133, 134, 148; symbolic

    significance of, 134–6, 203, 254,
    255n
Vijaya, 120, 122, 140, 256n
Vishnu, 113, 114, 121, 126, 128;
    as **raksa,** 118, 251n; relation
    within cosmic whole, 116

We–relationship, 191, 215
world guardians, 115

Yama
    as wild buffalo in comedy, 161

Author Index

Alexander, P. 250n
AmaraSingham, L.R. 106, 107, 120, 250n, 251n
Ames, M. 21, 22, 24, 30, 31, 111, 112, 113,116, 117, 243n, 244n
Amunugama, S. 245n
Anagarika Dharmapala 24-25
Ariyapala, M.B. 18, 85, 112

Badcock, C.R. 102
Barthes, R. 5
Bateson, M. 261n
Bateson, G. 11, 209
Berger, P. O. 63
Bergson, H. 187, 216, 222
Blacking, J. 242n
Bloch, J. H. 102
Bloch, M. 102, 242n
Blumer, H. 262n
Bourdieu, P. 6, 29, 242n
Bourguignon, E. 197, 198
Boyd, J.W. 251n
Briggs, J. L. 102

Cassirer, E. 262n
Codrington, H. W. 21
Cohen, A. 5
Cohen, G. A. 246n
Crapanzano, V. 262n

Davy, J. 247n
Derrida, J. 7, 241n
De Silva, K. M. 24, 244n

Devanandam, P. D. 111
Douglas, M. 210, 213, 214, 215, 216, 228, 230
Dufrenne, M. 5, 7, 8, 181, 187, 193, 195, 232, 241n
Dumont, L. 73, 252n

Eco, U. 241n
Egan, M. 253n
Eliot, T. S. 178
Engels, F. 246n
Ernst, T. 221
Evans-Pritchard, E. E. 262n

Fabrega, H. 87, 250n
Feibleman, J. 216
Feyerabend, P. 242n
Firth, R. 5

Gadamer, H-G. 209
Garbett, G. K. 242n, 243n
Geertz, C. 5, 3, 19, 181, 239n, 240n
Geiger, W. 18, 252n
Giddens, A. 241n
Gluckman, M. 242n
Goffman, E. 262n
Gombrich, R. 14, 15, 16, 17, 30, 33, 113, 114, 115, 117, 118, 258n, 260n
Goonatilleka, M. H. 253n, 254n, 260n
Gramsci, A. 19

Grathoff, R. 221
Guruge, A. 24

Halliday, F. 35
Hallowell, A. I. 198
Halverson, J. 253n
Handelman, D. 210, 221, 226
Hanna, J. L. 192, 242n
Heidegger, M. 208
Hofstadter, A. 186, 261n, 262n
Hopkins, T. J. 252n
Husserl, E. 6, 187

Jackson, A. 242n
James, W. 202
Jaspers, K. 51
Jules-Rosette, B. 242n

Kapferer, B. 50, 69, 112, 156, 165,
    201, 215, 221, 226, 241n, 253n,
    262n
Kealiinokomoku, J. W. 242n
Kemper, S. 16
Kierkegaard, S. 207
Klapp, O. 221
Kleinman, A. 87, 250n
Knox, R. 247n, 254n
Koestler, A. 212
Kristeva, J. 241n
Kultgen, J. 6

Langer, S. 186, 187, 193, 194, 216,
    241n, 261n, 262n
Leach, E. 111, 117, 189
Leslie, C. 17
Le Vine, R. 92
Levi-Strauss, C. 5, 6, 186, 240n,
    241n, 242n
Lewis, D. J. 262n
Lewis, G. 87
Lewis, I. M. 93-100
Lieban, R. 87
Ling T. O. 177, 251n
Loudon, J. B. 87
Luckman, T. 63

Malalgoda, K. 21, 22
Marasinghe, M. M. J. 30, 247n, 251n
Marriott, McK, 30, 73
Marx, K. 246n
Masson, J. L. 257n
Mayer, A. 73
McHugh, P. 64
Mead, G. H. 198-201, 262n
Merleau-Ponty, M. 197

Mitchell, J. C. 242n
Moore, S. F. 3, 5
Munn, N. 180
Myerhoff, B. G. 3, 5

Natanson, M. 6, 191. 203
Needham, R. 242n
Neville, H. 251n, 265n, 257n, 258n

Obeyesekere, G. 10, 22, 24, 25,
    30, 31, 33, 35, 50, 93, 97, 102,
    106, 113, 120, 123, 128, 166,
    167,
    198, 212, 226, 244n 245n 247n
    250n, 253n, 258n, 262n
O'Flaherty, W. D. 118, 252n, 260n
Ortner, S. B. 102, 103, 251n

Pathmanathan, M. 243n
Patwardhan, M. W. 257n
Peirce, C. 241n
Peiris, R. 254n
Pertold, O. 161
Poulantzas, N. 19
Prince, R. 197

Quinn, N. 103

Radcliffe-Brown, A. 242n 262n
Raghavan, M. 246n
Rahula, W. 15, 16
Rappaport, R. A. 3, 239n, 241n,
    261n
Redfield, R. 30
Ricoeur, P. 1, 5, 241n
Roberts, M. 21, 22, 69, 243n, 244n,
    245n
Rosaldo, M. 102
Ryan, B. 37, 38, 39, 247n, 248n

Samaraweera, V. 243n
Sarachchandra, E. R. 43, 253n
Sartre, J-P. 202, 203
Saussure, de F. 241n
Schieffelin, E. R. 242n
Schneider, J. 244n
Schneider, P. 244n
Schönberg, A. 261n
Schutz, A. 6, 96, 98, 187
Seneviratne, H. L. 140, 260n
Shalvey, T. 241n
Shastri, P. O. 111
Sheets-Johnstone, M. 192, 193, 195
Sperber, D. 5
Spiro, M. 10, 198
Stirrat, R. J. 98, 253n

Tambiah, S. J. 3, 30, 142, 239n,
    241n, 253n, 250n, 261n
Taussig, M. T. 246n
Turner, T. 179, 180
Turner, V. W. 5, 6, 7, 135, 179, 218,
    228, 238, 240n, 243n

Van Gennep, A. 7, 179
Velson, J. van 242n

Walker, B. 111
Wallerstein, I. S. 244n
Waxler, N. E. 52
Weitz, M. 262n
Whitehead, H. 102, 103, 251n

Williams, D. 193
Wilson, P. J. 95
Winius, G. D. 20
Winslow, D. 14, 91
Wirz, P. 14, 31, 42, 43, 53, 85, 112,
    118, 120, 122, 123, 130, 136,
    139, 165, 249n, 251n, 252n,
    253n, 256n, 257n, 259n, 262n
    263n
Wittkower, E. D. 197
Woodward, C. A. 243n

Yalman, N. 16, 73, 102, 253n

Zimmer, H. 258n